Genesis

Genesis

AN EXPOSITIONAL COMMENTARY
VOLUME 1   GENESIS 1:1 – 11:32

JAMES MONTGOMERY BOICE

ZONDERVAN
PUBLISHING HOUSE
OF THE ZONDERVAN CORPORATION   GRAND RAPIDS MICHIGAN 49506

GENESIS, VOLUME 1
Copyright © 1982 by The Zondervan Corporation
Grand Rapids, Michigan

First printing July 1982

Library of Congress Cataloging in Publication Data

Boice, James Montgomery, 1938--
  Genesis, an expositional commentary.

  Includes bibliographical references and index.
  Contents: v. 1. Genesis 1:1--11:32, Creation and fall—
  1. Bible. O.T. Genesis—Commentaries. I. Title.
BS1235.3.B63   222'.1107   82-7031
ISBN 0-310-21540-4 (v. 1)   AACR2

Except where otherwise indicated Scripture references are from *The Holy Bible, New International Version* (North American edition). Copyright © 1978 by New York International Bible Society.

Printed in the United States of America

82 83 84 85 86 87 88 — 10 9 8 7 6 5 4 3 2

To Him
who is the Alpha and the Omega
the First and the Last
the Beginning and the End

Contents

Preface

In February, 1979, several weeks after I had begun my exposition of Genesis for the congregation of Tenth Presbyterian Church in Philadelphia, which I serve as pastor, a member of the congregation approached me and asked, "Why in the world are you beginning a verse-by-verse exposition of a book like Genesis? After all, it's not like John [on which I had spent eight years] or Romans. What theological meat can you hope to find in Genesis?"

I replied, as I have many times to similar questions since, that on the contrary Genesis is full of theology—and that of the best kind. It is *basic*, occurring as it does at the beginning of God's inscripturated revelation. And it is *mingled with life*. The theology of Genesis is found in the life stories of the numerous great and sinful men and women who fill its pages.

As I have worked through Genesis in the years since that early conversation my opinion of the depth and importance of Genesis has been strengthened. The doctrines of God, man, sin, judgment, justification by faith, salvation, the covenant, prayer, discipleship—all are found in these pages. Besides, there are the beginnings of such basic human institutions as the family and human government, with suggestions for the proper place and management of each one.

I am reminded of a paragraph by Martin Luther, written as part of his well-known introduction to the Old Testament but particularly applicable to Genesis: "I beg and faithfully warn every pious Christian not to stumble at the simplicity of the language and stories that will often meet him there. He should not doubt that, however simple they may seem, these are the very words, works, judgments, and deeds of the high majesty, power, and wisdom of God."

It has been my plan in verse-by-verse exposition to stop occasionally for a more extended treatment of key themes, as these are suggested by or come up in the course of the narration. I have done that here. The first example (which occurs at the beginning) is a four-chapter treatment of Genesis 1:1, surely a most important verse in any Christian theology. Genesis 3:15, the so-called protoevangelium, is also treated at comparable length. On three occasions I have dealt with intriguing and sometimes problematic themes: five competing theories of creation, the fall of Adam, and whether the flood of Noah's day was of local or universal extent. I hope these slight digressions balance the strict textual expositions in an interesting way.

The studies in this volume have occupied almost two full years of regular Sunday morning preaching at Tenth Church. As I write this preface, those expositions are continuing and I anticipate an eventual completion of the entire book. Obviously, the time required for the writing of these studies (in addition to their preparation) and for the necessary stages in the production of the book detracts from time I might have spent in other areas of need at Tenth Church and in Philadelphia. Some congregations would resent that. But not the congregation at Tenth Church! On the contrary, these people have encouraged me in this work and have made many valuable suggestions that I have incorporated into the manuscript. I wish to express special appreciation to them.

I am greatly indebted to Miss Caecilie M. Foelster, my secretary, who types all this material—some of it more than once—and who then carefully checks details, such as Scripture references, proofreads and then helps me in the preparation of the indices. She has helped me with the manuscripts of nearly all my books, beginning with *The Sermon on the Mount,* which appeared in 1972.

I anticipate great blessing from this volume, not because I have done it but because God has promised to bless all serious study and proclamation of His inerrant and everlasting Word. May it be as He says: "As the rain and the snow come down from heaven, and do not return to it without watering the earth and making it bud and flourish, so that it yields seed for the sower and bread for the eater, so is my word that goes out from my mouth: It will not return to me empty, but will accomplish what I desire and achieve the purpose for which I sent it" (Isa. 55:10, 11). No author can have a greater or more holy ambition than to be part of that great purpose. So be it, Lord Jesus Christ. Amen and amen.

JAMES MONTGOMERY BOICE

Philadelphia, Pa.

Genesis

1

In the Beginning

(Genesis 1:1)

In the beginning God created the heavens and the earth.

These are exciting days in which to be studying Genesis. They are especially exciting for theologians and other students of the Bible, for much has recently been written on Genesis and there is new openness to looking at the book in the light of scientific data and theories as well as at science in the light of the Bible. They are also exciting from the viewpoint of recent developments in science, particularly those bearing on the origins of the universe.

Science has undergone what can almost be described as a revolution. For generations the prevailing view of the universe had been what is known as the Steady State theory. That is, the universe has always been and will always be. It is ungenerated and indestructible. Such a view was materialistic and atheistic. It contained no place for God. In recent years this view has given way to the theory that the universe actually had an instant of creation. It came into being fifteen to twenty billion years ago in a gigantic fireball explosion that sent suns and planets tumbling outward from this center into the form we observe them now. Moreover, they are still moving outward. In contrast to the Steady State idea, this is called the Big Bang theory in reference to the instant of creation.

The change in scientific thinking goes back to 1913, when an astronomer at the Lowell Observatory in Flagstaff, Arizona, Vesto Melvin Slipher, discovered through his study of the shifting light spectrum of very distant stars that the galaxies in which these stars were found appeared to be receding from the earth at tremendous speeds—up to two million miles per hour. Six years later, in 1919, another American astronomer, Edwin Hubble, used Slipher's findings to formulate a law for an expanding universe, which pointed to a moment of creation. Meanwhile, Albert Einstein's theories of relativity were shaking Newtonian physics. And two Bell Telephone Laboratory scientists, Arno Penzias and Robert Wilson, were using new and sophisticated electronic equipment to pick up background radiation from all parts of the universe, which they now identified as the leftover "noise" of that first great explosion.

To be sure, there are still many problems. Current scientific theory puts the origin of the universe at a point approaching twenty billion years ago, which some Christians find unacceptable. Again, the Big Bang theory, even if true, tells us nothing about the thing or One who caused it. Nor does it throw light on why the universe has such astonishing complexity and order or how life originated or many other things. Yet this is still exciting if for no other reason than that "the Big Bang theory sounds very much like the story that the Old Testament has been telling all along," as *Time* magazine wrote recently.[1]

Robert Jastrow, Director of the National Aeronautics and Space Administration's Goddard Institute, puts it even more strongly. He is known for two very popular books, *Red Giants and White Dwarfs* and *Until the Sun Dies*. Now, in *God and the Astronomers,* he writes of the dismay of scientists who are brought by their own method back to a point beyond which they cannot go. "There is a kind of religion in science; it is the religion of a person who believes there is order and harmony in the Universe. Every event can be explained in a rational way as the product of some previous event. . . . This religious faith of the scientist is violated by the discovery that the world had a beginning under conditions in which the known laws of physics are not valid, and as a product of forces or circumstances we cannot discover. . . . At this moment it seems as though science will never be able to raise the curtain on the mystery of creation. For the scientist who has lived by his faith in the power of reason, the story ends like a bad dream. He has scaled the mountains of ignorance; he is about to conquer the highest peak; as he pulls himself over the final rock, he is greeted by a band of theologians who have been sitting there for centuries."[2]

None of this should make the theologians smug, however. They should remember that they have not been without difficulties in their attempts to understand Genesis and that the ancient Hebrews were not without wisdom when they forbade anyone under thirty to expound the first chapter to others.[3]

ROOTS

The significance of Genesis is not in its proof or disproof of scientific theories, however, any more than the significance of science is in its proof or disproof of the Bible. It is important for its teaching about the origin of all things, which is what the word "Genesis" means. Genesis takes us back to the beginnings, and this is very important because our sense of worth as human beings depends in part on our origins.

In a smaller but very dramatic way, we have recently witnessed something like this in American pop culture. In early 1977 a serialized presentation of Alex Haley's *Roots*, a book in which this distinguished black author traced the historical origins of his family back through their days of slavery in the old South to his African progenitors, was first aired on American television. This series was a success of such proportions that it astonished planners and producers alike. By the end of its seven-night run, *Roots* commanded 66 percent of the television audience—about 130 million people— and had become the most watched television program ever. It has been rebroadcast, both here and abroad, and has caused hundreds of colleges to provide *Roots* courses. In the aftermath of that historical week in January, thousands of Americans scrambled into libraries to search out their own family origins. The National Archives in Washington found itself flooded with requests for ancestral information. What caused this astonishing phenomenon? Some have suggested that it was Haley's frank and wise handling of the racial issue. But Haley does not think this is the explanation, nor do many others.

---

[1]"In the Beginning: God and Science," a Time Essay by Lance Morrow, *Time,* February 5, 1979, p. 149.

[2]Robert Jastrow, *God and the Astronomers* (New York and London: W. W. Norton & Company, 1978), pp. 113, 114, 116.

[3]Jerome, "Letter to Paulinus," Epistle 53. Cited by Martin Luther, *Luther's Works*, Vol. 1, *Lectures on Genesis Chapters 1–5,* edited by Jaroslav Pelikan (St. Louis: Concordia, 1958), p. 3.

The reason for the popularity of *Roots* is that it discovered a sense of present dignity and meaning for one black family by tracing its link to the past and thus also providing a direction for the future. In this it gave a sense of meaning to us all.

In an earlier age this would not have been so important, because many people at least still had a sense of history. They knew where they had come from and hence had an optimistic outlook on what the future would hold. But that has evaporated in current culture so that, as a number of writers have correctly pointed out, this has become the "now" generation in which any firm anchor to the past has been lost. We have been told that the past is meaningless. Everything is focused on the present. We are told by the advertisers that "we only go around once." We should forget about the past and not worry about the future. It sounds like good philosophy. But the loneliness and anxiety of a philosophy like that is almost intolerable. Consequently, when *Roots* came along many identified with Haley's search for the past and for dignity.

R. C. Sproul, founder of the Ligonier Valley Study Center in western Pennsylvania, has analyzed this in terms of secularism, which means "living within the bounds of this age" (from the Latin *saeculum,* meaning age). It is to live with our outlook confined to this period alone—without the past, without a future, above all without God, who is in both past and future and controls them. He writes of the secular man, "Man in the twentieth century has been busily engaged in a quest for dignity. It is a very earnest quest. The civil rights movement developed the cry, 'We are human beings; we are creatures of dignity; we want to be treated as beings of dignity.' So also have others. But the existentialist tells us that our roots are in nothingness, that our future is in noth-

ingness, and he asks, 'Think, man, if your origins are in nothing and your destiny is in nothing, how can you possibly have any dignity now?' . . .

"If our past history tells us that we have emerged from the slime, that we are only grown-up germs, what difference can it possibly make whether we are black germs or white germs, whether we are free germs or enslaved germs? Who cares? We can sing of the dignity of man, but unless that dignity is rooted substantially in that which has intrinsic value, all our songs of human rights and dignity are so much whistling in the dark. They are naïve, simplistic and credulous. And the existentialist understands that. He says, 'You're playing games when you call yourselves creatures of dignity. If all you have is the present, there is no dignity, only nothingness.'"[4]

This is what Alex Haley saw and what those many thousands of Americans saw who took their clue from Haley and began to search through libraries for their history. It is what makes Genesis important. Genesis is important because it gives us our origins—not merely the origins of one particular family but the origins of matter, life, values, evil, grace, the family, nations and other things—in a way that unites us all.

Without the teachings of this book life itself is meaningless. There are even parts of the Bible that are meaningless. Without this book, the Bible would be like the last acts of a play without the first act, or a meeting of a corporation's trustees with no agenda. Henry M. Morris has written, "The books of the Old Testament, narrating God's dealings with the people of Israel, would be provincial and bigoted, were they not set in the context of God's developing purposes for all mankind, as laid down in the early chapters of Genesis. The New Testament, describing the execution and implementation of God's plan for man's

---

[4]R. C. Sproul, "What Is Man's Chief End?" *Tenth: An Evangelical Quarterly,* July, 1977, p. 67.

redemption, is redundant and anachronistic, except in the light of man's desperate need for salvation, as established in the record of man's primeval history, recorded only in Genesis. . . . A believing understanding of the Book of Genesis is therefore prerequisite to an understanding of God and his meaning to man."[5]

ALL THINGS WISE AND WONDERFUL

In our study of Genesis we are going to look at each of these matters in detail, but as we start we can cast our eyes ahead over a few of them. They are a part of those many things both "wise and wonderful" that confront us in the Word of God.

1. The first great matter of the Bible, the one related most directly to our origins, is *God*, who has no beginnings at all. He is the first subject mentioned: "In the beginning God created the heavens and the earth."

This sentence is among the most profound statements ever written, which we shall see when we come to study it in greater detail. But even here we must see that these words already take us beyond the farthest point that can be viewed by science. Science can take us back to the Big Bang, to the moment of creation. But if that original, colossal explosion obliterated anything that came before it, as science suggests, then nothing before that point can be known scientifically, including the cause of the explosion. The Bible comes forward at this point to tell us simply, "In the beginning God. . . ." We may want to bring God down into our little microscope where we can examine Him and subject Him to the laws of matter, of cause and effect, which we can understand. But fret as we might, God does not conform to our desires. He confronts us as the One who was in existence *before* anything we can even imagine and who will be there *after*

anything we can imagine. Ultimately it is He alone with whom we have to do.

2. The opening chapters of Genesis also tell us the origin of *man*, the matter we have been looking at most closely in this chapter. Without this revelation we may look to ourselves in this present moment and conclude, as did the French philosopher Renè Descartes, "I think; therefore, I am." But beyond that even the simplest philosophical question confounds us. Our son or daughter asks, "Daddy, where did I come from?" and we answer with an explanation of human reproduction. "Yes, but where did you and Mommy come from? . . . Where did Grandma come from?" The questions baffle us apart from the divine revelation.

John H. Gerstner, Professor of Church History at Pittsburgh Theological Seminary, tells this story concerning Arthur Schopenhauer, the famous nineteenth-century philosophical pessimist. Schopenhauer, did not always dress like a product of Bond Street—he often dressed more like a bum—and he was sitting in a park in Berlin one day when his appearance aroused the suspicions of a policeman. The policeman asked him who he thought he was. Schopenhauer replied, "I would to God I knew." As Gerstner points out, the only way he could have learned who he was would have been to find out from God, who has revealed this to us in Genesis.

3. Genesis gives the origin of the *human family* which is—moderns especially must take note—not something that has been dreamed up by fallen men and women but something established by God even before the Fall for our good. People have added to God's provision, but not by way of improvement. They have added polygamy, prostitution, promiscuity, divorce, and homosexuality. But these are corruptions of God's original order and bring frustration,

---

[5]Henry M. Morris, *The Genesis Record: A Scientific and Devotional Commentary on the Book of Beginnings* (Grand Rapids: Baker, 1976), pp. 17, 18.

misery, and eventual judgment on those who practice them. They are blessed only as they return to God's original plan for the home, the ordering of the sexes, and the responsibilities within marriage of both husband and wife.

4. Genesis tells us of the origins of *evil,* at least so far as man is concerned. I give this qualification for two reasons. First, because the account of the Fall involves temptation by the serpent and we are not told by Genesis where the serpent came from. (There are hints of it elsewhere.) Second, because there are philosophical questions about how evil could even come into a world created by a good and holy God.

This much *is* told us in Genesis: the evil that involves mankind is the product of our own choice, expressed as a rebellion against God, and it has affected us so totally that there is now nothing we can do to restore ourselves or regain that position of privilege and responsibility that we lost by rebellion. It is as if we had jumped into a pit. Before the jump we had a capacity for self-determination. We could use that capacity to remain on the edge of the pit or to jump in. But once we had exercised our freedom of choice in the matter by jumping, our choice was gone in that area and thereafter there was nothing we could do to restore our former state of blessedness. Moreover, because it was our choice and not that of another, we are guilty for what we have done and now quite rightly stand under the inevitable judgment of God.

5. We can do nothing. But God can—God can do anything—and the wonder of the gospel appears in the promise of One who would come to undo the results of Adam's transgression. The origins of *salvation* are therefore also to be found in this book.

This is true in two senses. First, there are promises of a Savior to come, as I have indicated. When Adam and Eve sinned and God came to them in the garden, He first rebuked the sin. But then He spoke of hope in the person of One who should crush the head of Satan. Speaking to the serpent He said, "He will crush your head, and you will strike his heel" (Gen. 3:15). As the book goes on, this cryptic statement is elaborated and explained. God spoke to Abraham of a descendant who would be the source of divine blessing to all nations: "Your descendants will take possession of the cities of their enemies, and through your offspring [singular] all nations on earth will be blessed" (Gen. 22:18; cf. Gal. 3:8). Still later, Jacob spoke of Him as a descendant of the tribe of Judah: "The scepter will not depart from Judah, nor the ruler's staff from between his feet, until he comes to whom it belongs and the obedience of the nations is his" (Gen. 49:10).

The second way Genesis foreshadows the coming of Christ is by its record of the institution and performance of the sacrifices, which He alone fulfilled.

6. A fifth and very important origin in Genesis is the doctrine of *justification by faith,* clearly seen first in the experience of Abraham. We are told: "Abram believed the LORD, and he credited it to him as righteousness" (Gen. 15:6). If righteousness was "credited" to Abraham, then Abraham had none of his own. It was the gift of God. Moreover, it was credited to him not on the basis of his works, love, service, or obedience, but on the basis of his faith, that is, on the basis of his taking God's word in the matter of salvation. In reference to this statement Paul later wrote, "The words 'it was credited to him' were written not for him alone, but also for us, to whom God will credit righteousness—for us who believe in him who raised Jesus our Lord from the dead. He was delivered over to death for our sins and was raised to life for our justification" (Rom. 4:23–25).

7. Genesis also contains the first teaching in the Bible of the *sovereign*

election of God in salvation. When Adam and Eve sinned, they did not come to God. They hid from Him. He took the initiative in seeking them out and in beginning to teach the means of salvation through the death of the Mediator. It was the same with Abraham. Abraham did not seek God. He did not even know who the true God was. But God called Abraham and made him the father of a favored nation through whom the Redeemer should come. God chose Isaac and not Ishmael. He chose Jacob and not Esau. In the New Testament Paul uses these examples to show that salvation does not "depend on man's desire or effort, but on God's mercy. . . . God has mercy on whom he wants to have mercy, and he hardens whom he wants to harden" (Rom. 9:16, 18).

8. Finally, there are the origins of *divine judgment*. In the story of God's encounter with fallen Eve and Adam we see accountability and a certain degree of judgment, but for the most part judgment is set aside or postponed. This is not so in the judgment of the flood under Noah, through which all but Noah and his immediate family perished. This is brought forward in the New Testament as a reminder of the reality and inescapability of the final judgment (2 Peter 3:3–10).

BACK AND FORWARD

When the secularists came along in the middle of the last century and cut the society of their day off from any sense of history, the deed was greeted with cries of joyous appreciation and great glee. To be freed from the past, particularly from the biblical past with its God of moral standards and threats of judgment, seemed to be true liberation. Man was free! And if he was free, he could do as he pleased—which is what he had wanted to do all along—without fear of God or judgment! Unfortunately, secular man did not see at what price this ghost of liberty had been won. Free of the past? Yes! And of the future too! But now man was adrift on a great sea of nothingness, a bubble on the deep, having come from nothing and drifting to a meaningless shore. No wonder that contemporary man is empty, miserable, frustrated. He is on the verge of a monumental breakdown. He gained freedom (so-called) but at the loss of value, meaning, and true dignity. No wonder he is searching for his roots, as Haley's video phenomenon reminds us.

Fortunately, men and women can go back . . . and forward too. But the past and future are not in Haley. They are in the Bible where we find ourselves as we truly are—made in the image of almighty God, hence, creatures of value; fallen tragically, yet redeemable by God through the power and grace displayed in Jesus Christ.

2

Fact or Fiction?

(Genesis 1:1)

In the beginning God created the heavens and the earth.

Genesis raises many questions. One is whether it is to be understood as fact or fiction. This is a question we must settle early, for our views about the nature of the book will determine how we interpret it.

If the story of the fall of Adam and Eve into sin is fiction, perhaps "theological fiction," as some would call it, it may be intended to give insight into what is basically wrong with us as individuals. It may show our frailty, sin, even our attitude of rebellion against God. But if it is not historical, if there was no literal fall, then there was no previous state of innocence and no guilt for having fallen from it. In other words, we are not sinful because of our own willful rebellion against God. We are simply sinful. We need a helper, perhaps a Savior. But we do not need to confess our sin and repudiate it. Similarly, if the flood is not history but only a myth created to teach certain eternal truths, the story may teach that God does not like sin. But it loses the fearful truth that God intervenes in history to judge sin and will judge it totally and perfectly at the end of time.

Is Genesis fact or fiction? Is it to be understood as a recounting of literal events? Or is it something like inspired poetry in which "spiritual" but not "historical" truths are taught? There are many who opt for fiction. Liberals have done this for years, calling Genesis "myth" or "fable." Recently even some prominent evangelicals have been willing to take this position.

ALL SCRIPTURE FROM GOD

The starting point for answering whether Genesis is fact or fiction—though it does not settle everything—is that Genesis is a part of Holy Scripture and has therefore been given to us by God and speaks with His authority. We think here of 2 Timothy 3:16: "All Scripture is God-breathed and is useful for teaching, rebuking, correcting and training in righteousness." When Paul wrote those words he had Genesis in mind as much as any other portion of Scripture. So if we accept his teaching, as all Christians should and must, this will have bearing on how we view Genesis.

The inspiration of Genesis does not settle everything concerning whether it is fact or fiction, for God can inspire fiction (for His own holy purposes) as well as He can inspire historical narration. Poetry is not always factually true, yet God inspired the poetry of the psalms. Our Lord told parables, which are stories told to make a clear spiritual point. Still, the inspiration of Genesis is not without bearing on the matter at hand in that it at least tells us that the book is the revelation of God to men (through the agency of the human writer) and not the gropings of any single man or men after the meaning of God or creation. When liberals talk of myth, fable, or fiction it is the latter conception they have in mind. They are putting Genesis on a level with any other document that may have come

19

down to us from ancient times. But it is not like any other document if it is truly given to us by revelation.

E. J. Young, former Professor of Old Testament at Westminster Theological Seminary (until his death in 1968), stated the matter succinctly: "The Bible is either a revelation of God, or it is simply the gropings of the Hebrew nation and the presentation of the best that they could find." If it is a revelation from God, then "God has told us about the creation, and we [should] believe that it is historical, that is, that it actually took place, because God has so spoken."[1]

THE ASSUMPTION OF SCRIPTURE

The second point bearing on our question is the teaching—or, perhaps more accurately, the assumption (since the issue is not handled in a formal way)—of the rest of Scripture that Genesis is historical. Put as a question the issue is: Does the rest of the Bible view the Book of Genesis as fiction, or does it view it as fact?

This is the point with which Francis Schaeffer begins his short study of *Genesis in Space and Time*. His position is that the mentality of the whole Scripture is that "creation is as historically real as the history of the Jews and our own present moment of time. Both the Old and the New Testaments deliberately root themselves back into the early chapters of Genesis, insisting that they are a record of historical events."[2] As a case in point, Schaeffer cites the 136th psalm, which praises God for His enduring love. The psalm begins with a doxology but then passes on to the reasons why we should praise Him. The first of these reasons is His work of creation:

who by his understanding made the heavens,
> *His love endures forever.*

who spread out the earth upon the waters,
> *His love endures forever.*
who made the great lights—
> *His love endures forever.*
the sun to govern the day,
> *His love endures forever.*
the moon and stars to govern the night;
> *His love endures forever.*
> (vv. 5–9)

Without any apparent break and certainly without any indication that he is now beginning to write in a historical rather than in a poetical or less than literal vein, the poet then goes on to list a second reason why God should be praised: His work of delivering Israel from Egypt:

to him who struck down the firstborn of Egypt
> *His love endures forever.*
and brought Israel out from among them
> *His love endures forever.*
with a mighty hand and outstretched arm;
> *His love endures forever.*
> (vv. 10–12)

The psalm continues to speak of the dividing of the Red Sea, God's leading of the people through the wilderness, the defeat of the kings who had been occupying the land into which they came (Sihon king of the Amorites and Og king of Bashan—it cites them by name), the gift of the land, and then finally, the blessings of God to Israel in what was then the present time:

to the One who remembered us in our low estate
> *His love endures forever.*
and freed us from our enemies,
> *His love endures forever.*
and who gives food to every creature.
> *His love endures forever.*
> (vv. 23–25)

---

[1]E. J. Young, *In the Beginning: Genesis Chapters 1 to 3 and the Authority of Scripture* (Edinburgh: The Banner of Truth Trust, 1976), p. 35.

[2]Francis A. Schaeffer, *Genesis in Space and Time: The Flow of Biblical History* (Downers Grove, Ill.: InterVarsity Press, 1972), p. 15.

What is involved here? Obviously a view of history and of God's specific acts in history according to which there is natural continuity between the acts of God in creation and the events of the present day. This means that the Genesis account is to be taken as history.

A person may still say, "I believe that Genesis is put forth in the Bible as if it were history, but I do not believe its account." This would be an honest person holding to convictions. But what we cannot say is, "I believe that the Genesis account is profoundly and spiritually true and that the Bible teaches this; it is poetry." The one who says that is either dishonest or else is a faulty interpreter of the Bible's teaching.

The Teaching of Jesus

A special aspect of the attitude of Scripture to Genesis is the teaching of Jesus Christ. This obviously carries special weight. We do not suggest that if Jesus did not specifically teach that the events and personages of Genesis were real events and real personages that the teaching of the rest of the Bible could therefore be abandoned. But it is surely of interest to those who profess to follow Jesus as their Lord to know what He said. His teaching has special weight if only because we revere the Lord highly.

Did Jesus consider the accounts of Genesis historical? Indeed He did! He quoted them as fact to prove other points in contention. When the Pharisees came to Jesus to ask a question about divorce—"Is it lawful for a man to divorce his wife for any and every reason?"—Jesus replied by a specific reference to Genesis 1:27 and 2:24. He said, "Haven't you read . . . that at the beginning the Creator 'made them male and female,' and said, 'For this reason a man will leave his father and mother and be united to his wife, and the two will become one flesh'? So they are no longer two, but one. Therefore what God has joined together, let man not separate" (Matt. 19:3–6). Jesus' reply assumes God to be the Creator of the first man and woman, Adam and Eve, as well as being the One who instituted marriage. In fact, it shows Christ's belief in the compatibility of the two parallel accounts of creation (in Gen. 1 and 2), since His reply contains a mutually supportive reference from each chapter.

In Mark 13:19, Jesus spoke of "the beginning, when God created the world."

The Ancient Cosmologies

None of this will have much weight with those who consider the Genesis accounts to be mere versions of those clearly mythical accounts of creation that circulated in the ancient east both before and after the time Genesis was written. There are the Babylonian Epic of Creation and the cosmologies of Egypt and Phoenicia. These have similarities to the accounts in Genesis. If Genesis is merely one of them, must we not think that Jesus was mistaken in His view of creation or at least (some have suggested this) merely adapted His teaching to the viewpoints of His day, though He Himself knew better, being God?

The opinion of the recognized dean of archeologists, William F. Albright, is helpful at this point. Albright was not an evangelical—though he became increasingly conservative as his studies progressed—yet he spoke openly about the lack of similarity between Genesis and the other ancient accounts. His own view was that Israel was a "rarely endowed people" who selected "the most vital elements in their religious literatures," combined them into "a new and richer synthesis," purified them by "the monotheism of Moses, and spiritualized [them] by the inspired insight of the Prophets." In other words, it was an almost purely human process. Yet in spite of this basic humanistic orientation, Albright argued that it is difficult to see how this early "mythological structure can be connected in any direct way whatsoever with the biblical story."[3]

Albright argued that the Babylonian Epic does have certain superficial resemblances to the Genesis account. It has seven tables, while the Jewish account represents creation as having taken place over a period of seven days. At some points the language is similar. But beyond that, hardly anything is the same. The Hebrew account is monotheistic. Its language is terse. The Babylonian account is polytheistic, verbose and crassly mythological.

At the beginning there are two monsters, represented as dragons: Apsu, the fresh-water subterranean ocean, and his consort Tiamat, the salt-water ocean that surrounds the earth. From these two spring a generation of deities, the last of which become so powerful that Apsu and Tiamat plot to destroy them. The result is a titanic struggle in which Tiamat is slain. Her body is split in two. The upper half is formed into the heavens. The lower half is formed into the earth. Men and women are made from the blood of Qingu, Tiamat's chief minister. The text says, "Punishment they imposed on him, his blood-vessels they cut open, with his blood they created mankind." Albright maintains, and I agree with him, that nearly anyone can see the vast gulf separating this obviously mythological account from the serious, historical account in Genesis.

Don't scholars still argue that the Genesis account is myth? Yes, some do. But I am reminded of a remark made by C. S. Lewis. He said that when some learned scholar tells him that portions of the biblical narrative are myth, he does not want to know what his credentials are in the area of his biblical scholarship but rather how many myths he has read. Myths were Lewis' business, and it was

his testimony that the biblical accounts were not among them.

Some will still argue that we are missing the point. For whether the language of Genesis 1 is mythical or not, these will still think it inadequate for giving a truly factual (by which they mean "scientific") account of creation. Let us think this through. The account of creation might have been written in one of three ways: 1) in scientific language, 2) in straightforward historical prose, or 3) in poetry. Poetry is out, for the reason that it does not go far enough. It does not tell us what we most want to know. This leaves scientific language and historical prose.

What would it take for the account of creation to be written in scientific language? My opinion is not worth much at this point, but I quote from Frederick A. Filby who has been a professor of chemistry in England for many years. He has registered his convictions in *Creation Revealed.* "The sciences which probe most deeply into the ultimate facts of matter and life are probably astro- and nuclear physics and biochemistry. But these sciences are written, not so much in language as in symbols. It takes many pages of symbols to discuss the nature of a single atom of hydrogen. It has been estimated that to give a complete account of the position of the groups and bonds in a single virus of 'molecular weight 300 million' would take a 200 page book.

"If the scientific description of a single hydrogen atom, or of a virus too small to be seen without a microscope, takes a book, what hope is there of ever giving a scientific account of the creation of man and the universe? Yet Genesis 1 in its original form uses only 76 different root words. If Genesis 1 were written in absolute scientific language to give an account of creation, there is no man alive,

[3]William F. Albright, "Recent Discoveries in Bible Lands" in *Young's Analytical Concordance to the Bible* (New York: Funk & Wagnalls Company, 1936, 1955), supplement, pp. 27, 28.

nor ever has there been, who could understand it. If it were written in any kind of scientific language, only the favored few could comprehend it. It would have to be rewritten every generation to conform to the new views and terms of science. It could not be written in our mid-twentieth century scientific language, for no earlier generation could have grasped its meaning, and to our children it would be out-of-date. The scientific description of the 'how' of the universe is beyond the understanding of any human brain, but Genesis 1 was written for *all* readers, not for *none*. . . .

"What then would be the best method for the Creator to use for (1) making a beginning to his book and (2) establishing that the God of the Bible is also the God of creation—in language simple enough for all men in all time?

"The answer is . . . Genesis 1 . . . the most amazing composition in all the world's literature, using only 76 different word-forms fundamental to all mankind, arranged in a wonderful poetical pattern yet free from any highly colored figures of speech. It provides the perfect opening to God's book and establishes all that men really need to know of the *facts* of creation. No man could have invented it: it is as great a marvel as a plant or a bird. It is God's handiwork, sufficient for Hebrew children or Greek thinkers or Latin Christians; for medieval knights or modern scientists or little children; for cottage dwellers or cattle ranchers or deep sea fishermen; for Laplanders or Ethiopians, East or West, rich or poor, old or young, simple or learned . . . sufficient for all! Only God could write such a chapter . . . and he did."[4]

I find that statement of conviction by a well-trained scientist compelling. Moreover, it is to the point, for the most fundamental of all issues is whether or not God has spoken in Scripture as the Bible claims He has. In the last chapter, I spoke of origins and beginnings, many of which are dealt with in Genesis. But Genesis serves another purpose, and that is to force us back to origins in the matter of our own thought values. It forces us to this: Has God spoken? Has He spoken here? Answer that in the negative, and all is chaos. Answer yes, and all that follows will become increasingly clear.

---

[4]Frederick A. Filby, *Creation Revealed: A Study of Genesis Chapter One in the Light of Modern Science* (Westwood, N.J.: Fleming H. Revell, 1963), pp. 15, 16.

3

In the Beginning God

(Genesis 1:1)

In the beginning God created the heavens and the earth.

When we say that Genesis is to be understood historically—as fact rather than fiction—we do not mean that we can understand it fully just because we are historical creatures. Genesis is history, but some of it is beyond us. This is nowhere more apparent than in its first four words.

I say "four words." But in the Hebrew the words corresponding to our phrase "In the beginning God" are just two: *Berasheth . . . Elohim.* Yet, as the late distinguished physicist Arthur Compton once said, these words are "the most tremendous ever penned."[1] Another scholar, John Gerstner, of Pittsburgh Theological Seminary, has written that even if all other evidences for the doctrine were lacking, "the first four words of the Book of Genesis are sufficient proof of the Bible's inspiration."[2] Why? It is because of the statement's profundity. The ancient Jewish people were not scientists. They were not even profound theologians or philosophers. So the fact that a relatively primitive people have bequeathed us a book embodying the most profound wisdom—the case with these opening words, as well as other passages—should convince us at the beginning that the book has been given to us by God.

In his study of this verse, Gerstner reflects on a statement made one day in his high school physics class. The professor said, "The greatest question which has ever been asked is why there is something rather than nothing." At the time the young student was impressed. But he gradually came to see that this is not a profound question at all. In fact, it is not even a true question. Because if nothing really is nothing, then nothing defies conception and the choice vanishes. What is "nothing"? If you think you can answer that question, you are the person least qualified to answer it. As soon as you say, "Nothing is . . . ," nothing ceases to be nothing and becomes something. "Nothing is what the sleeping rocks dream of," said Jonathan Edwards. Therefore, as Gerstner observes, "Anyone who thinks he knows what nothing is must have those rocks in his head."[3]

What was "in the beginning"? If the alternative is between God and nothing, there is really no choice. For nothing is nothing, and we are left with the statement "In the beginning God."

AN OBJECTION

We must deal with an objection. Some modern translations of Genesis begin differently from the NIV or KJV, and the casual reader as well as the technical scholar might therefore ask whether everything we have said so far is

[1]Quoted by Herschel H. Hobbs, *The Origin of All Things: Studies in Genesis* (Waco, Tex.: Word Books, 1975), p. 9.

[2]John H. Gerstner, "Man As God Made Him," in James M. Boice, editor, *Our Savior God: Man, Christ and the Atonement* (Grand Rapids: Baker, 1980), p. 20.

[3]Ibid.

wrong-headed. In some modern translations the opening words of Genesis are treated as a dependent or temporal clause rather than an independent clause, which changes the statement from an affirmation that God was in the beginning before all things to a statement that at some indefinite point in the past both God and matter existed and that God then began to form matter into the universe we know today. We see this translation in a footnote to the Revised Standard Version, which reads, "When God began to create. . . ." We see it in the New English Bible: "In the beginning of creation, when God made heaven and earth. . . ." Even the Living Bible says, "When God began creating the heavens and the earth, the earth was at first a shapeless, chaotic mass. . . ."

The implications of these translations are clear. Whether or not they are accurate—we will come to that question in a moment—they clearly deny (or at least overlook) an absolute creation. They make matter pre-existent and therefore do not give us an absolute beginning at all.

What shall we say about this interpretation? It is a possible translation, otherwise we would not have it in even some of our Bibles. The word *berasheth* can be taken as a construct. But the fact that this is a possible translation does not mean that it is correct. In fact, when we begin to look into the matter deeply there are several reasons why the older translation should be preferred.

First, there is the normal simplicity of the Hebrew sentence. If the opening clause of Genesis 1 is dependent, then the sentence actually concludes in verse 3 where God speaks and light comes into existence. This means that the sentence is quite long, possessing not one but two subordinate parts (the second being a multiple subordinate clause), and the real flow of the sentence would be: "When God began to create the heavens and the earth—the earth being at that time formless and empty, darkness being over the surface of the deep, and the spirit of God hovering over the waters—God said, 'Let there be light,' and there was light." This is unlike a true Hebrew sentence, especially an introductory sentence. It is often the case in German that a series of dependent clauses will begin a sentence and the verb will come twenty or thirty words later at the end, a feature of the language which Mark Twain once described as "falling down stairs." But this is not the case with Hebrew. Certainly there are dependent clauses. But these are not complex, and one is hard pressed to believe that, in this case especially, a complicated initial sentence is intended to begin the simple and classically straightforward account of creation that occurs in this chapter. Julius Welhausen was no conservative—he was, in fact, one of the key figures in the development of the documentary theory of the Pentateuch—but he called the translation we are objecting to "desperate."[4]

Second, as has often been shown, the word "create" (the second word of the sentence in Hebrew) is used of God alone and characteristically refers to His bringing into being something that is entirely new. Of course, God also forms things from existing material, but when that happens another word (usually "make" or "made") is used. "Create" refers to the production of new things from nothing. It is an inappropriate word if the creation referred to in these verses is merely the formation of the earth from preexistent matter.

Third, Genesis is a book of beginnings. But in telling us of these beginnings it has clearly failed at the most crucial point if, in fact, the best it can say

[4]Young, *In the Beginning*, p. 22. Young discusses the translation on pp. 20–25. He offers a more technical treatment in *Studies in Genesis One*, "An International Library of Philosophy and Theology" (Philadelphia: Presbyterian and Reformed Publishing Co., 1976), pp. 1–14.

is that at the very start matter just happened to be around.

Why is it that so many modern scholars and even some translators prefer to subordinate the first clause? E. J. Young suggests that the real reason is that the Babylonian Epic of Creation, which I referred to in the last chapter, begins this way and that these scholars have a prejudicial desire to have the Genesis account conform to it. The Babylonian account begins: "When on high the heavens were not named, and below the earth had not a name. . . ." It goes on in that vein for seven lines, introduces another temporal clause, and then gets to the main clause. By subordinating the opening clauses of Genesis 1, the scholars succeed in making Genesis somewhat parallel to the Babylonian account. But, as I have argued, Genesis does not begin that way. It begins by speaking of that absolute beginning of all things, which is God, and then provides us with the most profound insight into the question of origins. It overwhelms us with the profoundly simple statement: "In the beginning God."

A SET OF DENIALS

The phrase also instructs us concerning the nature of God who alone is the origin of all things. It suggests some negative statements and some positive statements.

The clearest negative statement is the denial of *atheism*. If God was in the beginning, then there was and is a God. How can it be otherwise? To say less would be to say that God is dependent on creation, being subject to the same laws, and therefore could not be at the beginning of creation as Genesis says He was. A second denial is *materialism*. When the text says that God was in the beginning, before creation, it sets Him apart from creation and therefore apart from the matter of which all else is made. Ours is not an entirely materialistic universe. Moreover, since God created

matter, matter did not always exist, which is what a true philosophy of materialism teaches. Finally, the opening statements of Genesis deny *pantheism*. Pantheism is the philosophy that God is in matter or is matter. It underlies most pagan or animistic religions. But if God created matter, then He is separate from it and is superior to it. Any religion that worships matter is idolatrous.

These and many other false philosophies err because they begin with man or matter and work up to God, if indeed they get so far. But Genesis stands against them all when it begins with God and sets Him forth as the originator of all things.

THE BIBLE'S GOD

It is not only through the suggestion of these negatives about God that Genesis 1:1 instructs us. It also suggests some important positive characteristics.

First, when Genesis begins with the words "In the beginning God," it is telling us that God is *self-existent*. This is not true of anything else. Everything else depends on some other thing or person and ultimately on God. Without these prior causes, the thing would not exist. We recognize this truth when we speak of the laws of "cause and effect." Every effect must have an adequate cause. But God is the ultimate cause and is Himself uncaused. God has no origins, and this means: first, that as He is in Himself He is unknowable, and second, that He is answerable to no one.

Why should God's self-existence mean He is unknowable? It is because everything we see, smell, hear, taste, or touch has origins, and consequently we can hardly think of anything except in these categories. We argue that anything we observe must have a cause adequate to explain it, and we look for such causes. But if God is the cause beyond everything, then He cannot be explained or known as other objects can. Like Robert Jastrow, whom we quoted in chapter 1, A. W. Tozer has pointed out that this is one reason why philosophy and science have not always been friendly toward the idea of God. These disciplines are dedicated to the task of accounting for things and are impatient with anything that refuses to give an account of itself. The scientist will admit that there is much he or she does not know. But it is quite another thing to admit that there is something that we can never know and which, in fact, we do not even have a technique for discovering. To avoid this the scientist may attempt to bring God down to his level, defining him as "natural law," "evolution," or some such principle. But God eludes him.

Perhaps, too, this is why even Bible-believing people seem to spend so little time thinking about God's person and character. Tozer writes, "Few of us have let our hearts gaze in wonder at the I AM, the self-existent Self back of which no creature can think. Such thoughts are too painful for us. We prefer to think where it will do more good—about how to build a better mousetrap, for instance, or how to make two blades of grass grow where one grew before. And for this we are now paying a too heavy price in the secularization of our religion and the decay of our inner lives."[5]

God's self-existence also means that He is not answerable to us, and we do not like that. We want God to give an account of Himself, to defend His actions. But while He sometimes explains things to us, He does not have to and often does not. God does not have to explain Himself to anyone.

Second, that God existed "in the beginning" means that He is *self-sufficient*. Self-existence means that God has no origins. Self-sufficiency means that God has no needs and therefore depends on no one. This is not true of us. We depend on countless other things—oxygen, for example. If our supply of oxygen is cut off, even for a few moments, we die. We are also dependent on light and heat and gravity and the laws of nature. If even one of these laws should cease to operate, we would all die immediately. But this is not true of God. These things could go—in fact, everything could go—yet God would still exist.

Here we run counter to a widespread and popular idea of God that says God cooperates with man and man with God, each thereby supplying something lacking in the other. It is imagined, for example, that God lacked glory and created us to supply it. Or again, that God needed love and therefore created us to love Him. Some talk about creation as if God were lonely and created us to keep Him company. But God does not need us.

God does not need worshipers. Arthur W. Pink, who writes on this theme in *The Attributes of God*, says, "God was under no constraint, no obligation, no necessity to create. That he chose to do so was purely a sovereign act on his part, caused by nothing outside himself, determined by nothing but his own mere good pleasure; for he 'worketh all things after the counsel of his own good will' (Eph. 1:11). That he did create was simply for his manifestative glory. . . . God is no gainer even from our worship. He was in no need of that external glory of his grace which arises from his redeemed, for he is glorious enough in himself without that. What was it moved him to predestinate his elect to the praise of the glory of his grace? It was, as Ephesians 1:5 tells us, 'according to the good pleasure of his will.' . . . The force of this is [that] it is impossible to bring the Almighty under obligations to the creature; God gains nothing from us."[6]

---

[5]A. W. Tozer, *The Knowledge of the Holy* (New York: Harper & Row, 1961), p. 34.
[6]Arthur W. Pink, *The Attributes of God* (Grand Rapids: Baker, n.d.), pp. 2, 3.

Some will conclude that the value of men and women is thereby lessened, but this is not the case. It is merely located where alone it is possible to sustain our value. According to our way of thinking, we have value because of what we imagine we can do for God. This is prideful, foolish, and vain. According to the biblical perspective, we have value because God grants it to us. Our worth is according to the grace of God in creation and to His election of us to salvation.

God does not need helpers. This truth is probably harder for us to accept than almost any other, for we imagine God as a friendly, but almost pathetic grandfather figure, bustling about to see whom He can find to help Him in managing the world and saving the world's race. This is a travesty. To be sure, God has entrusted a work of management to us. He said to the original pair in Eden, "Be fruitful and increase in number; fill the earth and subdue it. Rule over the fish of the sea and the birds of the air and over every living creature that moves on the ground" (Gen. 1:28). He has given those who believe on Him a commission to "go and make disciples of all nations, baptizing them in the name of the Father and of the Son and of the Holy Spirit, and teaching them to obey everything I have commanded you" (Matt. 28:19, 20). But none of these aspects of God's ordering of His creation has a necessary grounding in Himself. He has chosen to do things in this way, but He did not have to. Indeed, He could have done them in any one of a million other ways. That He did choose to do things thus is solely dependent on His own free will and does not give us any inherent value to Him.

God does not need defenders. We have opportunities to speak for God before those who would dishonor His name and malign His character. We ought to do so. But even if we do not, we must not think that God is deprived by it. God does not need to be defended, for He is as He is and will remain so regardless of the sinful and arrogant attacks of evil men. A God who needs to be defended is a God who can defend us only when someone is defending Him. He is of no use at all. The God of the Bible is the self-existent One who is the true defender of His people.

All this is of great importance, for when we notice that God is the only truly self-sufficient one, we may begin to understand why the Bible has so much to say about the need for faith in God alone and why unbelief in God is such sin. Tozer writes: "Among all created beings, not one dare trust in itself. God alone trusts in himself; all other beings must trust in him. Unbelief is actually perverted faith, for it puts its trust not in the living God but in dying men."[7] If we refuse to trust God, what we are actually saying is that either we or some other person or thing is more trustworthy. This is a slander against the character of God, and it is folly, for nothing else is all-sufficient. On the other hand, if we begin by trusting God (by believing on Him), then we have a solid foundation for all of life.

Because God is sufficient, we may begin by resting in that sufficiency and so work effectively for Him. God does not need us. But the joy of coming to know Him is in learning that He nevertheless stoops to work in and through His children.

Third, the truth that God was "in the beginning" means that He is *eternal*. It means that God is, has always been and will always be, and that He is ever the same in His eternal being. We discover this attribute of God everywhere in the Bible. Abraham knew God as "the Eternal God" (Gen. 21:33). Moses wrote, "Lord, you have been our dwelling place throughout all generations. Before the

---

[7]*Knowledge*, p. 42.

mountains were born or you brought forth the earth and the world, from everlasting to everlasting you are God" (Ps. 90:1, 2). The Book of Revelation describes him as "the Alpha and the Omega, the Beginning and the End" (Rev. 21:6; cf. 1:8; 22:13). The same book tells us that the four living creatures that surround the throne of God call out day and night, "Holy, holy, holy is the Lord God Almighty, who was, and is, and is to come" (Rev. 4:8).

That God is eternal has two major consequences for us. First, He can be trusted to remain as He has revealed Himself to be. God is unchangeable in His attributes. So we need not fear, for example, that although He has shown His love toward us once in Christ He may nevertheless somehow change His mind and cease to love us in the future. God is always love. Similarly, we must not think that although He has shown Himself to be holy He may nevertheless somehow cease to be holy and therefore change His attitude toward our transgressions. Sin will always be sin, because it is "any want of conformity unto, or transgression of, the law of God" (Westminster Shorter Catechism, A. 14), who is unchangeable. We may extend this by saying that God will always be holy, wise, gracious, just, and everything else that He reveals Himself to be. Nothing that we do will ever change Him. Again, God is unchangeable in His eternal counsel or will. He does what He has determined beforehand to do, and His will never varies. This is a source of great comfort to God's people. If God were like us, He could not be relied on. He would change, and as a result of that His will and promises would change. We could not depend on Him. But God is not like us. He does not change. Consequently, His purposes remain fixed from generation to generation.

The second major consequence for us of God's unchangeableness is that He is *inescapable*. If He were a mere man and if we did not like either Him or what He was doing, we might ignore Him, knowing that He might change His mind, move away from us or die. But God does not change His mind. He does not move away. He will not die. Consequently, we cannot escape Him. If we ignore Him now, we must reckon with Him in the life to come. If we reject Him now, we must eventually face the One we have rejected and come to know His own eternal rejection of us.[8]

THE GOD WHO IS THERE

In this lies the profundity of the first verse in the Bible. Indeed, we can go further and say that in some sense this verse may even be the most important verse in the Bible, for at the outset it brings us face to face with the God with whom we have to do. This God is not an imaginary god. He is not a god of our own inventions. He is the God who is—the one who is "infinite, eternal, and *unchangeable*, in his being, wisdom, power, holiness, justice, goodness, and truth" (Westminster Shorter Catechism, A. 4).

Sometimes we wish we could change Him. We are like the man who was climbing up a steep mountain on his way to the summit when he began to slip. Unable to stop himself he slid back down the treacherous incline toward a cliff which plunged a thousand feet to the canyon floor. He was sure he would be killed. But just as he was about to go over the edge he threw his hands out and managed to catch a small branch. There he hung. He had saved himself. But he could not get back onto the incline, and he knew it was just a matter of time until his grip loosened and he fell. He was not a very religious man. But this was obviously the time to become one, if

---

[8]I have borrowed portions of this section from a similar discussion in *The Sovereign God* (Downers Grove, Ill.: InterVarsity Press, 1978), pp. 126–32.

ever. So he looked up to heaven and called out, "Is there anyone up there who can help me?"

He did not expect an answer. So he was greatly surprised when a deep voice came back saying, "Yes, I am here, and I can help you. But first you are going to have to let go of that branch."

A long pause! Then the man looked up and called out again, "Is there *anybody else* up there who can help me?"

There is no one else. There is only God, the One who was in the beginning and who ever shall be. But He *is* able to help. More than that, He is willing to help and even urges His help on us. How wonderful it is that we meet Him at the beginning. Genesis 1 gives us a chance to come to terms with Him and receive the help He offers, knowing that we will certainly meet Him at the end.

4

God the Creator

(Genesis 1:1)

In the beginning God created the heavens and the earth.

In an earlier study I referred to a question that has been thought to be profound but actually is not: Why is there something rather than nothing? This is not profound for the reason that it is not even a true question. The question seems to offer us a choice between something and nothing. But what is nothing? As soon as we answer that, saying, "Nothing is . . . ," nothing ceases to be nothing and becomes something. If nothing really is nothing, nothing defies description. In fact, it defies mental conception of any kind. So the question boils down to: Why is there something?

In this form the question is not meaningless. On the contrary, it is one of the truly big philosophical questions. It can be stated in different forms— Where did the universe come from? Who made the atom? How did everything get to be as it is?—but in essence these are the same basic question. Something is there—an immense, intricate, and orderly something. It was there before we were, for we cannot even imagine our existence without it. But how did it get there? And how did it get to be as we detect it?

Genesis 1:1 is the answer to these questions. It tells us that "in the beginning *God created* the heavens and the earth."

THE CHRISTIAN ANSWER

There are other answers to the question of the origins of the universe, how-

ever, and it is these plus the Christian answer that we now want to consider. How many answers are there? Like all truly big questions, the possibilities are not numerous. In this case, there are just four.

First, there is the view that the universe had no origin. That is, there was no origin because in some form the universe always existed. Matter existed. This has been the dominant view of both ancient and modern science until relatively recent times, and it is still held by some. Second, there is the view that everything had a beginning and that this beginning was the work of a good personal being. This is the Christian view. Third, everything came into existence through the work of a personal being who is evil. Fourth, there is now and there always has been a dualism. This last view takes several forms depending on whether one is thinking of a personal or impersonal, moral or immoral dualism, but the views are related. This was the outlook of the ancient cosmologies referred to earlier, of which the Babylonian Epic is an example. It is still the characteristic view of the eastern religions and mysticism.

What are we to say concerning these four possibilities? The easiest to dismiss is number three, which gives a personal but evil origin to the universe. It says, in effect, that Satan is the creator. This is easiest to dismiss because it does not give an adequate explanation of the origin of the good. Evil can be conceived as

31

a corruption of the good—Satan can rebel against the Christian God—but it is not really possible to think of good as having emerged out of evil. In the former case, evil can be a misuse of otherwise good traits or abilities. But in the second case, there is no place for the good to come from.

We may state the problem in a slightly different way. For a power to be evil it (or he) must possess the attributes of intelligence and will. But since these attributes are in themselves good, he must be getting them from a good power. And this means that the good power must have existed previously and that the evil power is therefore not the origin of all things.

The fourth possibility, a dualism, is unsatisfying too, although this is not as quickly apparent as in number three. The reason is that, although belief in a dualism has often been quite popular and has endured for long periods of history, it does not stand up under close analysis. For having stated the dualism, we immediately want to pass behind it to some type of unity that includes the dualism. Or else we choose one part of the dualism and make it prominent over the other, in which case we are really easing into one of the other possibilities.

C. S. Lewis has written about this problem, pointing to what he calls the "catch" in the system. According to dualism, two powers (spirits or gods), one good and one evil, are supposed to be quite independent and eternal. Neither is responsible for the other, and each has an equal right to call itself God. Each presumably thinks that it is good and the other bad. But Lewis asks, What do we mean when we say, as we do in stating this dualism, that the one power is good and the other bad? Do we mean merely that we prefer the one to the other? If that is all we mean, then we must give up any real talk about good or

evil, and if we do that, then the moral dimension of the universe vanishes entirely and we are left with nothing more than matter operating in certain ways. We cannot mean that and still hold to the dualism. We have fallen back to possibility number one.

But if, on the contrary, we mean that one power really is good and the other really is bad, then we are actually introducing some third thing into the universe, "some law or standard or rule of good which one of the powers conforms to and the other fails to conform to." And this standard, rather than the others, will turn out to be the true God. Lewis concludes, "Since the two powers are judged by this standard, then this standard, or the Being who made this standard, is farther back and higher up than either of them, and he will be the real God. In fact, what we meant by calling them good and bad turns out to be that one of them is in a right relation to the real, ultimate God and the other in a wrong relation to him."[1]

So neither an evil origin for the universe, from which good arose, nor a dualism adequately accounts for reality as we know it. The real alternative is between the view that holds to an eternity of matter and the view that sees everything as having come into existence through the personal will of an eternal and moral God.

Let us look at Christianity's chief competitor, materialism. The origins of this view are lost in the past, but the view is clearly very ancient. It is found in the scientism of the Greek philosopher Epicurus, who taught that everything is composed of small building blocks of matter, conceived of as hard, indestructible particles. Epicurus called them atoms, which is where our word "atom" comes from. He probably derived his ideas from Democritus of Abdera who in turn was indebted to the little-known

---

[1]C. S. Lewis, *Mere Christianity* (New York: Macmillan, 1958), p. 34.

philosopher Leucippus. Leucippus may have gotten his ideas from a Phoenician philosopher named Moschus, who lived prior to 1000 B.C.[2]

Today this view is the dominant philosophy of western civilization, although not in the form Epicurus gave to it. For one thing, we know that the atom can be divided. We have done it. Again, we have been taught by Einstein that energy and mass are interchangeable, which is mind-boggling. Knowledge of this should in itself shake the presuppositions of materialism, but for the most part it has not seriously shaken them, and the western world continues to be philosophically materialistic.

Today's materialism usually does not deny that there is personality in the universe, but it conceives this as having arisen out of impersonal substance. It does not deny the complexity of the universe—even including such things as the intricacy of the atom—but it supposes that complexity came from that which was less complex and that in turn from something still less complex until eventually we arrive back at that which is ultimately simple, that is, to mere matter. Matter, it is supposed, always existed—because there is no further explanation. This view lies beneath most thought concerning evolution.

But this description of the origin of the universe has already introduced problems that the theory itself apparently has no means of solving. First, we have spoken of a form to matter and then of more complex forms. But where does form come from? Form means organization and perhaps purpose, too. But how can organization and purpose come from *mere* matter? Some would insist that organization and purpose were in the matter inherently, like genes in an egg or spermatazoa. But in addition to making

nonsense of the theory—this is no longer mere matter—the basic question still remains unanswered, for the problem is how the organization and purpose got even there. At some level, either early or late, we have to account for the form; and, if this is the case, we soon find ourselves looking for the Former, Organizer or Purposer.

Moreover, we have introduced the idea of the personal, and if we begin with an impersonal universe, there is no explanation for the emergence of personality. Francis Schaeffer writes: "The assumption of an impersonal beginning can never adequately explain the personal beings we see around us, and when men try to explain man on the basis of an original impersonal, man soon disappears."[3]

Genesis begins with the opposite answer. It maintains that the universe exists with form and personality because it has been brought into existence by an orderly and personal God. God was there before the universe came into existence, and He was and is personal. He created all we know, including ourselves. Consequently, the universe naturally bears the marks of His personality.[4]

GOD'S CREATION

But we may be missing something at this point. We are arguing for the Christian view of origins, which is not at all unimportant. But in the very act of arguing we are likely to miss (or postpone) a true wonder at God's creation, which is what a proper contemplation of these themes should cause. Biblical writers never fall into this pit. Consequently, when they look at creation they inevitably end up praising God, and when they praise God, one of the things they praise Him for is creation.

[2]Filby, *Creation Revealed*, pp. 43, 44.
[3]Schaeffer, *Genesis in Space and Time*, p. 21.
[4]Parts of the preceding section have already appeared in *The Sovereign God*, pp. 206–209.

You are worthy, our Lord and God,
   to receive glory and honor and power,
for you created all things,
   and by your will they were created
   and have their being (Rev. 4:11).

Can we not do that too? Our text tells us that God created "the heavens and the earth." As we contemplate these great canvases of God's work, are we not led to praise Him?

How vast the heavens are! When we look up into the sky on a clear night we see perhaps 10,000 points of light. A few of these are the planets of our solar system that shine by reflected light. Thousands belong to the special grouping of stars known as the Milky Way, to which our sun belongs. Other thousands are entire galaxies, which shine as one point because they are so distant. We say 10,000 points because that is what we can see with unaided eyes. But these 10,000 are only the tiniest fraction of the existing stars. A typical galaxy contains billions of individual stars— our galaxy alone contains 200 billion stars. Its form is of a giant spiral rotating majestically in space, its glowing arms trailing behind it like the distended points of a pinwheel. Our sun is in one arm of this spiral. It makes a complete rotation in 250 million years. These figures are staggering. But this is only our galaxy. There are thousands of others visible to the naked eye and billions more within range of the 200-inch telescope on California's Palomar Mountain.

As revealed to us by time exposure photography, these distant galaxies of stars display a seemingly unending array of beauty. Some are spirals like ours. Others are nearly spherical clusters. Others are flattened out like pancakes. Still others are irregular. All the stars in the heavens are clustered together in these intricate and beautiful groupings.

Again, the galaxies are scattered about in an irregular pattern. Between them there are vast amounts of space. The distance from one edge of an average galaxy to the other edge is approximately 600 thousand trillion miles. The average distance from one galaxy to another is 20 million trillion miles. If these numbers were to be written out in zeros, they would fill up several lines of type. So to avoid such large numbers astronomers generally use a unit of distance called the light year, that is, the distance light travels in one year at the speed of 186,000 miles per second. A light year is approximately six trillion miles. Translated into these terms, the size of an average galaxy is 100 thousand light years, and the distance between them is three million light years approximately.

The Andromeda Galaxy is the galaxy closest to our own Milky Way. It is separated from us by two million light years. This means that the light coming to us now from Andromeda has taken two million years to get here. Put in other terms, it means that when we look at Andromeda what we see is the galaxy as it existed, not a moment ago, but two million years in the past.

Moreover, the galaxies are not fixed in space but rather are moving away from each other at tremendous speeds. Vesto Melvin Slipher, the first to discover this fact, found that the galaxies he could observe were moving away from the earth at several million miles per hour. His scientific followers, Milton Humason and Edwin Hubble, showed that the most distant galaxies were retreating from us at the rate of 100 million miles per hour. Moreover, everything is retreating from everything. Nothing is coming toward us, nor is anything coming toward any other galaxy. This means that the universe is expanding. By working backward from the present position of the galaxies and their known speed, astronomers have placed the origins of the universe approximately 15 to 20 billion years in the past.

We turn to the stars themselves and find equal evidence of variety, design, beauty, and mystery. Not all stars are alike, though they seem to follow a similar pattern as they are born, burn, grow old, and eventually die.

At any given moment millions of stars are being born in space. They are born as clouds of interstellar gas contract under the force of gravity acting between the atoms that compose them. As they contract the temperature rises. Finally, at the critical temperature of twenty million degrees Fahrenheit, the hydrogen within the ball of condensed gas ignites in reactions similar to those that occur in the explosion of a hydrogen bomb. The release of this energy halts any further condensing of the gas, and the star continues to burn in that fashion for many billions of years. Our sun is at this stage.

Eventually the hydrogen in the star begins to be used up. It starts to swell and redden. Such stars are called red giants. As the last of its fuel is burned off, the star begins its final collapse under the force of gravity. If it is relatively small, it condenses to a tightly compressed sphere called a white dwarf. In one of these dead stars a few cubic centimeters of matter weigh a ton. If the star is large, a different fate envelops it. Instead of compressing quietly, it blows itself up, thereby scattering its elements—now containing carbon, oxygen, iron, gold and others—throughout the universe where they are eventually picked up by other suns or planets.[5]

> The heavens declare the glory of God;
>   the skies proclaim the work of his
>   hands.
> Day after day they pour forth speech;
>   night after night they display knowl-
>   edge.
> There is no speech or language
>   where their voice is not heard.
> Their voice goes out into all the earth,
>   their words to the ends of the world
>   (Ps. 19:1–4)

And what of the earth? We need not consider the earth and its marvels fully at this point. We have looked at the heavens carefully since this is the last point in Genesis at which the heavens are mentioned for themselves. From this point the chapter passes on to consider God's acts of creation on earth. (The sun, moon, and stars are mentioned only in regard to their giving light to the earth.) In a sense everything that occurs from this point on is about the earth. But we can note in passing that the marvels of the macrocosm (the world of large things) are repeated in the microcosm (the world of small things). Here we are confronted with electrons, protons, neutrons, nutrinos, and a seemingly endless variety of particles barely understood. The distances between these particles, proportionate to their size, are comparable to some of the distances involved in the solar system. If we were to take the simplest of atoms, the hydrogen atom, and blow it up billions upon billions of times to where the proton at its center would now be the size of a ten-inch soccer ball, the electron that circles this nucleus would now be the size of a golf ball and would be circling the proton at a distance of five miles. There would be nothing else within the circle!

To God Be Glory

On the basis of the first verse of Genesis we can define God as *the One who creates*. We cannot create. We often use the word of human endeavors, and human beings are creative in the sense we give to that word. But if we are to be precise, we will say that at the best we only form or fashion things in imaginative ways, and even then, it is the case that we get our imagination as well as all other physical, mental, and spiritual gifts from God. Strictly speaking, we are craftsmen. We use preexisting material. But God does create, and He does so on

---

[5]The technical astronomical data is taken from Robert Jastrow, *Until the Sun Dies* (New York: W. W. Norton & Company, 1977), pp. 22–25, 52, 53.

what is to us a vast and incomprehensible scale. We do not know how God has done it. But He has willed creation, and as a result all we know, see, and are have come into being.

If God were not the Creator, He would be only a part of the world process, coming and going, waxing and waning. He could not help us. E. J. Young has written, "If he is only a little bigger than we are, if he is only a big brother and nothing more, if he is only a part of the whole, then we are all in it together, God, you and I, and then there are no standards. There is no absolute. It is every man for himself, and all modern philosophies and ideas that are being spread in our days—new morality, new theology, and so on—are all perfectly admissible if God is only a part of the world process. If it is so, it does not matter whether he is dead or alive. . . . Let us live for the moment, let us live for our enjoyment; there is no absolute; there is no standard of morality, for all changes. What may be right today may be wrong tomorrow; so let us get through life as best we can."

But this is not the God of Genesis. "The Bible does not so speak. It tells us that God has created all things. That is why there is meaning in life, and why there are absolute standards that do not change. God tells us what is right and what is wrong, and that is why there is meaning in life. That is why you and I who believe in this God can very well say that our chief reason for existence is to glorify him and enjoy him forever."[6]

---

[6]Young, *In the Beginning*, pp. 26, 27.

5

Views of Creation: Evolution

(Genesis 1:1, 2)

In the beginning God created the heavens and the earth. Now the earth was formless and empty, darkness was over the surface of the deep, and the Spirit of God was hovering over the waters.

When Charles Darwin published *The Origin of the Species* in 1859, he received more abuse than perhaps any modern scientist. To be sure, even Einstein originally objected to Slipher's discovery of an expanding universe. He wrote, "This circumstance irritates me."[1] Others also objected. But none of these heaped personal abuse on Slipher. Darwin, by contrast, was greeted with: "Rotten fabric of speculation. . . . Utterly false. . . . Deep in the mire of folly [and] . . . I laughed till my sides were sore."[2] The remarkable thing, however, is that the theory that became the laughing stock and then eventually the battleground of the second half of the nineteenth century has now become widely accepted, not only by scientists, but also by a wide variety of people from most walks of life.

This is not to say that evolution is the only theory going. It is merely the dominant view today and is therefore the one with which any discussion of the theory of origins should start. Actually, our discussion in this and the following chapters is going to take us over five competing theories: 1) atheistic evolution, 2) theistic evolution, 3) the so-called "gap theory" popularized by C. I. Scofield, 4) six-day creationism, and finally 5) progressive creationism. We

are going to see what each of these theories has to commend it and then also explore its weaknesses.

Let us say at the beginning that a final answer as to how the universe came into being may not be attainable now. We may exclude some possibilities, both as Christians and as scientists. As Christians we may exclude even more. But this still falls short of a full answer to the "how." Indeed, even taking the explanations of origins in the order proposed above does not necessarily imply that the latter positions are better than the earlier ones. They are taken in this order simply because they have appeared in this order historically.

THE EVOLUTIONARY THEORY

We begin by noting that in spite of the association of evolution with the name of Charles Darwin, evolution itself is nothing new. It existed among the ancient Greeks, for example. Thales, Anaximander, Anaximenes, Epicurus, and Lucretius were all evolutionists. So also was Aristotle (384–322 B.C.), who believed in a complete gradation in nature accompanied by a perfecting principle. This was imagined to have caused gradation from the imperfect to the perfect. Man, of course, stood at the highest point of the ascent.

[1]Jastrow, *God and the Astronomers*, p. 28.
[2]Jastrow, *Until the Sun Dies*, p. 19.

Again, there were evolutionists in more modern times before Darwin. Some early precursors were Francis Bacon (1561–1626), René Descartes (1596–1650) and Immanuel Kant (1724–1804). The first biologist to make a contribution to evolutionary thought was Georges Louis Leclerc de Buffon (1707–1788), the French naturalist. Another was Erasmus Darwin (1731–1802), the grandfather of Charles Darwin. The first fairly complete theory of evolution was by the Chevalier de Lamarch (1744–1829), who became a professor in zoology at the Museum of Natural History in Paris and later popularized his views in *Philosophie Zoologique*.

It was Charles Darwin, however, who rightly captured the world's attention. His theory was developed to a degree that none of the others were and, perhaps even more importantly, it was supported by an impressive array of observations collected initially on the world-encircling tour of the *HMS Beagle* from 1831–1836. Darwin's theory may be arranged in the following postulates and conclusions:

Postulate number one: *variation*. There are variations within individuals of the same species.

Postulate number two: *overproduction*. In most cases, more individuals are born to a species than can possibly survive to maturity.

Conclusion number one: *struggle for existence*. In order to survive individuals must compete with other members of the same species.

Postulate number three: *survival of the fittest*. In a competitive environment only those individuals best fitted to survive will survive.

Postulate number four: *inheritance of favorable characteristics*. Fit individuals pass their "good" characteristics on to their descendants.

Final conclusion: *New species arise by the continued survival and reproduction of the individuals best suited to their particular environment.*[3]

What has happened to this theory in the one hundred or so years since the publication of Darwin's *Origin*? For the most part it is still held, though much work has been done in the one area that presents a flaw in the argument. As anyone can see, the chief mechanism of evolution according to Darwin's theory is "natural selection," the impersonal preference given to a certain variation in a species permitting one individual rather than another to survive. This is supposed to explain how the variety of forms we know came about. But this is precisely what it does not do. Natural selection may explain how certain individuals have more offspring than others and therefore survive, or survive and have offspring while other less favored individuals do not. But it does not tell us how there came to be the various organisms or "good" characteristics of organisms in the first place.

Thomas Bethell, editor of *The Washington Monthly*, has written of this problem in an article for *Harper's Magazine*. He observes, "There is, then, no 'selection' by nature at all. Nor does nature 'act' as it so often is said to do in biology books. One organism may indeed be 'fitter' than another from an evolutionary point of view, but the only event that determines this fitness is death (or infertility). This, of course, is not something which helps *create* the organism, but is something that terminates it."[4]

To deal with this problem evolutionists have come to speak of mutations as the primary source of variations. This was proposed first by a Dutch botanist, Hugo de Vries, in a work entitled *Species and Varieties: Their Origin by Mutation*

[3]This summary of Darwin's theory is taken from John W. Klotz, *Genes, Genesis and Evolution* (St. Louis: Concordia, 1970), pp. 34, 35.

[4]*Harper's Magazine*, Feb., 1976, pp. 70–75.

(1905). It has since been suggested that mutations are caused by cosmic radiations, the latter being perhaps far more intense than in modern times.

THE FOSSIL RECORD

What are we to say of Darwin's theory? We must begin by noting that there is no question on the part of any informed thinker or writer that there are varieties within a given species. This is simply to say that all individuals are not alike. Some are tall, some short. Some are strong, others weak, and so on. The question is whether these acknowledged variations are sufficient to account for the development of entirely different species and, second, whether such development has in fact occurred. (The possibility of the development of species in this manner does not prove that this is the way it happened.)

At this point we have to turn to the evidence for evolution, and when we do we must acknowledge that the only true *historical* evidence is the evidence of fossils. There are other things that might be seen as supporting evolution: the possibility of classifying organisms from the simple to the more complex, similarities of structure in "related" species, the existence of vestigial organs (that is, organs like the human appendix for which no present function is known), similar blood types between some species. But these are all circumstantial arguments, and in some cases they are also ambiguous.[5] The only truly *historical* evidence—evidence that evolution has actually occurred—are fossils.

The fossil remains *may* be evidence of evolution, but what is not adequately said today is that they do not prove evolution and are in fact highly questionable when applied to evolutionary theory. Let us begin with positive statements. First, although very fragmentary, the fossils do lend themselves to a historical sequence in which the more simple forms of life may be dated earlier (because found in older rock) and more complex forms of life may be dated later. Thus, although the very ancient dates given may be wrong, it does seem that algae, protozoa and sponges came first. After that are fish, reptiles, and amphibians, then the land animals, including the dinosaurs. Finally, there are the animals we know today, and then man. Another positive statement is that some species have become extinct, the dinosaurs being the most notable example. The combination of these two sets of observations suggests that new forms of life develop and that others become extinct—according to Darwin.

But it is not that simple. There are problems in fitting the fossil record into an evolutionary system. Moreover, these are so great as to bring the entire theory into question.

For example, if evolution is true, what we should expect to find in the fossil record is finely graded and generally continuous development from the simplest forms to the higher forms. Although this is often claimed for the fossil record, it is not what is in fact found when we study it closely. Certainly there are simpler forms in (presumably) earlier rocks. Higher forms (like man) come relatively late. But there are no gradual developments. On the contrary, the major groups appear suddenly, and there is little or no evidence of transition. Everett C. Olson, a well-known evolutionist, mentions this difficulty: "More important, however, are the data revealed by the fossil record. There are great spatial and temporal gaps, sudden appearances of new major groups, equally sudden appearances of old, including very rapid extinctions of groups that had flourished for long periods of time. There were mass extinctions marked by equally simultaneous death of several apparently little associated

[5]See Klotz, *Genes, Genesis and Evolution,* pp. 120–73.

groups of organisms. At the time the record first is seen with any real clarity [in Cambrian rock strata], the differentiation of phyla is virtually complete. As far as major groups are concerned, we see little clear evidence of time succession in differentiation with the simpler first and the more complex later."[6]

It may be argued at this point—indeed, it is argued by evolutionists—that the fossil record is simply incomplete, that if fossils for every prior form of life existed, such gaps would be filled. But in a hundred years of study the tendency has not been this way, and it is hard to convince oneself today that this will yet happen. It is not just a question of several missing links. There are hundreds of missing links. Moreover, the grouping of major species in certain past periods of earth's history works strongly against this argument. Christians can argue, even if they cannot fully prove, that special creation is a far better explanation.

A second major problem with the use of fossils to support evolution is the subjective nature of arranging fossil histories. It might be argued by one who has seen the difficulty just mentioned that there is nevertheless evidence for development *within* one of the ancient time periods, even if not from one to the other. The supposed development of the horse from the Eocene period to modern times is an oft-cited example. During 60 million or so years the horse is supposed to have increased in size, lengthened its limbs, reduced and then eventually discarded toes, and become a grazer. Many museums have skeletons or pictures that are supposed to represent this development. But the fossils do not prove this development. They may suggest it, and the development they suggest may in fact be right. But there is still no evidence that one supposed form of the horse gave place to another. In actuality the skeletons may have come from similar but otherwise unrelated animals. Moreover, even if the fossils of these horse-like animals prove a development, it is still not an example of the development of new species but only of a change within a species.

MUTATIONS

Another area of difficulty for evolution is the mechanism used to explain the emergence of significant variations in the species, chiefly mutations (sudden unexpected changes brought about by otherwise unexplained alterations in the organism's genes). This was the solution to the problem of "newness" proposed by Hugo de Vries. De Vries did his work with the evening primrose, a weed that he found in a potato field. He bred this plant over a period of several generations in the course of which he noticed a number of abrupt changes that he called mutations. He concluded that these were developments of such magnitude that the process itself could explain the emergence of new species.

Unfortunately, the new "species" of de Vries were not new species but simply varieties within the same species. Moreover, they were not produced by mutations in the sense of that word today but rather by breeding out recessive characteristics. In other words, de Vries produced nothing that was not in the plant originally.

De Vries' failure does not entirely discredit the theory, however, for mutations do occur and can be passed down from generation to generation. The question is whether these mutations are sufficient to account for new species.

[6]Everett C. Olson, "The Role of Paleontology in the Formation of Evolutionary Thought," *Bioscience*, 16 (1966), p. 39. Quoted by L. Duane Thurman, *How to Think About Evolution & Other Bible-Science Controversies* (Downers Grove, Ill.: InterVarsity Press, 1978), p. 103. Thurman discusses the problems raised by the fossil record at some length, as do also J. Kerby Anderson and Harold G. Coffin, *Fossils in Focus* (Grand Rapids: Zondervan, 1977).

Are they? Many evolutionists would say yes at this point. But it is important to note that no one has as yet demonstrated this to be so. In fact, there is important evidence to the contrary. Walter Lammerts is a rose breeder from southern California and the author of the books *Why Not Creation?* and *Scientific Studies in Creation.* He tells of attempts to breed roses with more petals or less petals, using every imaginable technique including radiation. He acknowledges that it is possible to use radiation to create roses with a significant increase in petals. But here is the point: there is a limit beyond which the increase in petals apparently will not go. If a rose has forty-four petals, for example, it may be reduced to thirty-two or increased to fifty-six. But that is all. Moreover, if the hybrid rose is left to mix with others from that point on, it does not retain its new characteristics but soon loses them. In fact, all the hybrid roses we have would soon turn to wild roses if left to themselves—because they are bred from the wild roses originally. And if that in itself is not enough to cast doubt on the theory, there is the fact that the "improved" roses did not attain their improved form naturally but rather through the concentrated and prolonged efforts of Lammerts and other breeders. In other words, even in so limited a matter as this there is need for a design and a designer, a planner and a plan.[7]

THE CRUCIAL AREAS

An essay such as this can only begin to suggest a few of the problems the theory of evolution poses. But even in such a short study, concentrating on the basic scientific evidence for and against evolution, we can hardly pass over the far greater and (from the point of view of the Christian) unsolvable problems that exist where the crucial points of evolution are concerned. There are four of them.

First, even were we to grant the truthfulness of the evolutionary system as currently put forth, we still have the problem of the origin of the matter from which the later forms sprang. Evolution implies matter by the very meaning of the word, for in order for something to evolve there must be something there in the first place to evolve, and that first something cannot evolve but rather must be either eternally present or created. Since the eternity of matter is today increasingly untenable, as we saw in a previous study, we must have God as Creator. And this obviously nudges us toward the Christian position, whatever our opinions of a greater or lesser degree of evolutionary development may be.

Second, there is the form of matter. We may speak of "mere" matter as if it were a simple irreducible entity, but we do not actually know of any such "simple" matter and cannot in fact even conceive of it. Everything we know, however simple, already has a form—generally a highly complex form. Even hydrogen, the basic building block of everything according to astrophysics, is not simple. It has a proton, neutron, and electron, all operating according to fixed laws. Where did this fixed form and laws come from? They did not evolve. They are in matter to start with.

Third, there is the emergence of life. This is a complex problem, and much has been done to develop laboratory models according to which life could have arisen on earth during the early ages of the planet. The most acceptable model is a three-stage process involving: 1) the origin of bio-organics (amino acids, sugars) from inorganic compounds (hydrogen, water, ammonia, carbon dioxide, methane); 2) the origin of bio-polymers (large molecules such as

---

[7]For a fuller discussion of mutations as a possible mechanism for evolution see Klotz, *Genes, Genesis and Evolution,* pp. 256–91.

proteins) from the bio-organics; and finally 3) the origin of primordial life (simple plant or algae-like cells) from the bio-polymers. But this is an extremely complex process, even assuming that this is how life came about, and therefore has an extremely low level of probability. True, scientists have achieved the first two of these stages in carefully controlled laboratory experiments. But the crucial third stage is elusive. And even in the second stage, the polymers seem to deteriorate faster than they would normally be created in anything approaching a natural environment. Again, it is not a matter of a single event of low probability. It is a matter of a long series of events, each with a very small probability, so that, as one writer says, "for all practical purposes the probability of this series of events may safely be regarded as zero."[8]

Two scientists, who nevertheless believe in the spontaneous generation of life, write, "The macromolecule-to-cell transition is a jump of fantastic dimensions, which lies beyond the range of testable hypothesis. In this area, all is conjecture. The available facts do not provide a basis for postulating that cells arose on this planet."[9]

The fourth of the truly great problems for an atheistic theory of evolution is the emergence of personality in man, or to be more specific, the emergence of the soul, spirit or God-consciousness. What caused non-man to become man? One writer asks, "Where did the soul of man come from? Why is it that the highest and best animals are unable to pray? They are unable to communicate in a rational way. They are unable to do the things that man is able to do. The lowest type of man upon the face of the earth is far higher than the highest of the animals, because he has the capacity to worship God and can be brought to be a child of God, able to live to the glory of God through Jesus Christ, and that is true of none of the animals." This writer concludes, "I am not ashamed to say that I believe in the first chapter of Genesis, but I should be ashamed to say that I held to any form of evolution."[10]

WHY EVOLUTION?

I conclude with this question. Why is it, if the theory of evolution is as weak as it seems to be, that it has the popular appeal acknowledged at the beginning of this chapter? Why is it that evolution is today's dominant view and not one of the other views mentioned? I think there are four answers, three of which I want to put in the form of statements and one of which I want to put in the form of a question.

The statements are these. First, according to evolution, everything— absolutely everything—is knowable, and this has obvious appeal. Everything comes from something else, and we can trace the developments back. It is a closed system. There is no need for anything from outside. Above all, there is no need for God who by the very definition of that word is one who is unknowable and who does not need to give an account of Himself. Second, according to evolution, there is one explanation for everything. Everything evolves: matter, life, ideas, even religion. We can project this framework from our own small world throughout the universe. Third, and this is perhaps the chief reason, if creation of the world by God is eliminated (as many clearly wish to do), evolution is the only other option.

[8]Donald England, *A Christian View of Origins* (Grand Rapids: Baker, 1972), p. 97.

[9]D. E. Green and R. F. Goldberger, *Molecular Insights into the Living Process* (New York: Academic Press, 1967), p. 407. Quoted by England, *Christian View*, p. 94. England discusses the problems with a theory of the spontaneous generation of life on pp. 33–100.

[10]Young, *In the Beginning*, pp. 56, 57.

On the basis of those three statements I now ask my question: Is it not possible, then, that in the last analysis the appeal of evolution is in its elimination of God and its exultation of man? In this system man does not merely become the highest point of creation, which Christians would themselves willingly affirm. He becomes the god of creation. Consequently, to challenge evolution is to blaspheme against man, and blasphemy against man is the sin from which there is now no pardon. Algernon Charles Swinburne gives expression to this spirit in his *Hymn of Man.*

But God, if a God there be, is the
  Substance of men which is Man.
Thou art smitten, thou God, thou art
  smitten;
Thy death is upon thee, O Lord.
And the love-song of earth as thou diest
  Resounds through the wind of her
    wings—
Glory to Man in the highest!
For Man is the master of things.[11]

Is man the master? If he is, then he can go his way and devise any theory of origins he chooses. But if he is not—if there is a God—then he is the creation of this God and owes this God allegiance.

---

[11]See Philip Edgcumbe Hughes, *Christianity and the Problem of Origins* (Philadelphia: Presbyterian and Reformed Publishing Company, 1974), p. 11.

6

Views of Creation: Theistic Evolution

(Genesis 1:1, 2)

In the beginning God created the heavens and the earth. Now the earth was formless and empty, darkness was over the surface of the deep, and the Spirit of God was hovering over the waters.

Atheistic evolution is no possible view of creation for Christians. It is ruled out simply because it is atheistic. But this does not mean that an evolutionary model must in itself be ruled out. Some who would retain belief in evolution while nevertheless identifying themselves as Christians are the theistic evolutionists.

Theistic evolution is the view of those who are committed to the theory of evolution and who retain it in full except at those few points where, as it seems to them, it is not entirely compatible with Christianity. They are theists because they believe in the Christian God. They believe that He has revealed Himself in Scripture. But they are also evolutionists because they think that evolution is right. That is, they believe that everything has evolved through long periods of time from primitive to more complex forms. They believe that life has evolved from non-life. They believe that man has evolved from the lower animals. Generally they accept the scientific data urged in support of evolution. The main difference between the theistic evolutionists and the atheistic evolutionists is that the former believe that God, specifically the God of the Bible, is providentially guiding the evolutionary process, while the latter attribute the identical developments to chance.

Another way of putting it would be to say that the God of theistic evolution is the God of the gaps. In the last chapter we pointed out four major problems with atheistic evolution: it cannot explain the origin of matter, the form of matter, the emergence of life, or the appearance of personality or God-consciousness in man. The theistic evolutionist would bring in God at these points. God creates matter and life. But aside from that the theistic evolutionist would view things as having happened precisely as his nonbelieving counterpart views them.

A Possibility

What are we to say to this view? The first thing we must say is that it is at least a possibility. We may put it like this. There is no reason for the Christian to deny that one form of fish may have evolved from another form or even that one form of land animal may have evolved from a sea creature. We may not believe that this has actually happened, for the reasons set forth in our last chapter. But in itself this view of creation is not biblically impossible.

The Hebrew word translated by our word "let," which occurs throughout the creation account, allows for this. It does not specify a method by which God caused most things to come into being. However, there are three points at which even the Genesis narrative seems to require something different. These are the points at which the powerful He-

44

brew word *bara*, rendered "created," rather than the word "let" occurs. *Bara* means to create out of nothing. It is used in verse 1, which speaks of the creation of the original substance of the universe out of nothing; verse 21, which speaks of the creation of conscious life (that is, of animals as opposed to plants); and verse 27, which speaks of the creation of man in God's image. At these points there is an obvious introduction into creation of something strikingly new, something that did not and could not have evolved from things in existence previously. So long as the evolutionist speaks of the Christian God as the One who has introduced these new elements and has guided the evolutionary development at other points also (so that the result is not the mere product of chance but rather the unfolding of God's own wise and perfect will), most Christians would say that, thus far at least, the approach of the theistic evolutionist is possible.

Some important Christian thinkers have said exactly this. No less weighty a scholar than B. B. Warfield, in an essay, "On the Antiquity and the Unity of the Human Race," said that although evolution "cannot act as a substitute for creation," it can supply "a theory of the method of the divine providence."[1]

Another example is the great Scottish divine of the last century, James Orr. In the years 1890–91, Orr gave the well-known Kerr lectures on the subject "The Christian View of God and the World," in the course of which he defended evolution. "In reality, the facts of evolution do not weaken the proof from design, but rather immensely enlarge it by showing all things to be bound together in a vaster, grander plan than had been formerly conceived. . . . On the general hypothesis of evolution, as applied to the organic world, I have nothing to say, except that, within certain limits, it seems to me extremely probable, and supported by a large body of evidence."[2] Even more significant is the essay published by Orr in that collection of conservative writings that appeared at the beginning of this century, *The Fundamentals,* from which the term "fundamentalist" came. In it Orr defends theistic evolution as propounded by R. Otto in *Naturalism and Religion.* He says at one point, "'Evolution,' in short, is coming to be recognized as but a new name for 'creation,' only that the creative power now works from within, instead of, as in the old conception, in an external, plastic fashion."[3]

Neither of these men was himself a theistic evolutionist, though Orr comes very close to endorsing the position. The point is simply that in the judgment of these cautious and eminently biblical spokesmen theistic evolution is a possible theory and therefore should not be rejected out of hand by Christian people.

Points In Favor

Possibility is not certainty, however, and it is only fair to say that for what they consider to be very good reasons other Christians reject this approach entirely. One of them is Davis A. Young, whose own position is progressive creationism. (We will discuss this position in chapter 9.) He writes against theistic evolution saying that it "leads logically and ultimately to the death of *genuinely biblical* religion." In the heading of his chapter in which theistic evo-

---

[1]B. B. Warfield, *Biblical and Theological Studies* (Philadelphia: Presbyterian and Reformed Publishing Company, 1968), p. 238. The original essay was published in *The Princeton Theological Review* (ix, 1911).

[2]James Orr, *The Christian View of God and the World as Centering in the Incarnation* (Grand Rapids: Eerdmans, 1960), p. 99.

[3]James Orr, "Science and Christian Faith," *The Fundamentals,* Vol. 1, edited by R. A. Torrey, A. C. Dixon and others (Grand Rapids: Baker, 1972), p. 346. Original edition 1917.

lution is specifically studied he calls this view "a house built upon sand."[4]

What are we to think of theistic evolution? Positively, we may say that it has two important points in its favor. First, truth is truth wherever it is found. So if evolution is true, as evolutionists certainly believe, and if the Bible is also true, then something like the view of the theistic evolutionists must be reality. Again, this does not mean that evolution *is* true. But it does mean that we must at least ask whether it is true or not, and if it is true, we must learn from it. We must remember at this point that many theories of science were once declared to be antichristian but are now held by Christians and non-Christians alike with no apparent ill effects to Christianity.

One example is Copernican astronomy. Copernicus discovered that the earth was not the physical center of the universe. This was immediately assailed by those who felt that the Bible taught differently. Today we recognize that biblical language that was thought to imply a central earth is merely phenomenal. That is, it describes things as they appear to an earthbound observer (for whom indeed the Bible is written) and not as things actually are from a scientific standpoint. But in Copernicus' day this was not seen, and Galileo, who held to the Copernican astronomy, was eventually compelled by irate churchmen to recant. Similarly, in the past there have been Christians who have opposed most advances in medicine— pain killers, anesthetics, operations— feeling that these wrongly oppose God's decrees. Others have opposed such scientific devices as lightning rods, arguing that lightning was from God and that if God chose to strike a building it was sinful on our part to oppose it. In all these cases the terrible warnings made

in support of the "Christian" position did not materialize and truth prevailed.

The second argument in favor of theistic evolution is that God seems to work according to this pattern in other areas. Theistic evolution posits a universe that operates according to fixed, universal laws into which, however, God sometimes intrudes, as in the creation of life from non-life or the implanting of God-consciousness in man. "Isn't this exactly what we see in life generally or, for that matter, in the history recorded for us in the Bible?" the theistic evolutionist might say. "For the most part the history of Israel and the church flows along naturally. Leaders arise, do their thing, and then die giving place to other rulers. It is only occasionally that God intervenes miraculously. To see this pattern at work in evolution is biblical. It is what we should expect on the basis of what we know of Christian history."

A HOUSE ON SAND

Then Christians should all be theistic evolutionists? Not necessarily! There are also important weaknesses in this view to which none should be blind.

First, there is a problem with the supposed truthfulness of evolution itself. The theistic evolutionist believes in evolution, as we have seen. But evolution is not necessarily true, as we have also seen. Indeed, there are important reasons for discounting it. One main reason for rejecting evolution is the lack of fossil evidence. To be sure, the evolutionist reads the fossil record differently, seeing in it a sketchy but adequate history of the development of higher forms of life from lower forms. But the record is at best incomplete and may, as creationists hold, actually provide better evidence for the creationist's view than for the evolutionist's. As we said in the

---

[4]Davis A. Young, *Creation and the Flood: An Alternative to Flood Geology and Theistic Evolution* (Grand Rapids: Baker, 1977), pp. 18, 23ff.

last chapter, it is not merely a question of a few missing links. There are hundreds of missing links. It is questionable whether there is any evidence for the development of one species from a lower species. What the fossil evidence actually shows—even granting the alleged antiquity of the earth and the accepted sequence of fossils and rock strata—is the sudden appearance of major groups of species. If evolution is true, we should expect to find a finely graded and continuous development. Since we do not, we can honestly object to the theistic evolutionist's first argument in support of his theory, namely, that evolution is true and that the Christian should not be afraid to acknowledge it.

Again, we must emphasize the fact that certain forms of evolutionary development may be true. But the creationist may well ask the theistic evolutionist whether he does not hold his position, not so much because of the scientific evidence for it, but only because it is the accepted (and only acceptable) theory in his field of work.

The second objection corresponds to the theist's second argument, just as the creationist's first objection corresponds to his first. The theistic evolutionist might appeal to the Bible as suggesting a pattern of God's dealings with the human race, which he also sees in evolution—general development according to fixed laws with only an occasional supernatural intervention. But we must ask whether this is really the biblical picture. According to evolution, the development of life on earth has proceeded over a period of several billion years with at best two or three divine interventions. Is this the pattern we find in Scripture? It is true that in biblical history miracles are not everyday occurrences, but they are not all that infrequent either. Hundreds of supernatural interventions by God are recorded. And as for the development of the rest of history along the lines of natural law, would it not be more accurate to say that all history is in God's hand and that it is being directed by Him in intricate detail according to His own perfect plans?

The theistic evolutionist would say that in his view God has directed evolution just as He has directed the history of Israel. But if God has directed evolution according to that pattern, it is not quite the kind of evolution real evolutionists talk about. According to them, evolution is a long, slow, wasteful, crude, inefficient and mistake-ridden process. The God of the Bible hardly fits those categories. If evolution is made to conform to His nature—efficient, wise, good and error-free—it is hardly evolution, and the theistic evolutionist who is really a *biblical* theist has become a creationist though he does not actually describe himself by that word.

Third, we may ask whether the method of creation viewed by the theistic evolutionist does justice to the biblical record. Since the method of God's creating the animals, birds, and fish is not given in Genesis 1, it may be that God effected this segment of His creation according to an evolutionary model. But in the case of man there does seem to be something of a method, at least in Genesis 2: "And the LORD God formed man from the dust of the ground and breathed into his nostrils the breath of life, and man became a living being" (v. 7). This suggests that in the creation of man God began, as it were, *de novo*. That is, He started with inorganic matter into which He then breathed life. It does not suggest that man developed from the lesser animals.

We could always say that man is made of dust even though the actual steps of his creation involved a lengthy development through lesser species. But we run into further difficulties when we get to the case of Eve, for Eve is said to have been created from Adam. This does not correspond to any evolutionary theory.

Again, there is the problem of the singularity of Adam. In Romans 5:12–21 and 1 Corinthians 15:22, 23, and 45 comparisons are made between Adam and the Lord Jesus Christ. It is basic to this comparison that Adam was an individual whose acts affected his progeny. Does this fit in with evolutionary theory? In evolution the basic unit is population, not an individual. At what point did Adam appear? Or did he appear? If God chose one individual from a population of pre-human but manlike beings and made him man, what happened to the rest? Questions like these make questionable whether the theistic evolutionist can defend his position on biblical grounds.

Death of Biblical Religion

This leads us to our last criticism, the one Davis Young alludes to when he says that theistic evolution leads "logically and ultimately to the death of genuinely biblical religion." There is an unbiblical view of the Bible that Young feels to be characteristic of these men.

Pierre Teilhard de Chardin is perhaps the best known and best read of the theistic evolutionists. He is French and is a Roman Catholic priest, which should speak well for his Christian commitment. He has a concern for the immaterial or spiritual as well as the material. He can even chide science: "Has science ever troubled to look at the world other than from without?"[5] But he is also an evolutionist of the most convinced stripe, and this determines his theology in the final analysis.

For de Chardin there is no question that evolution on the grandest scale has taken place. Therefore, if our understanding of Scripture seems to be in conflict with evolutionary views, it is our views of Scripture or even Scripture itself that must give way before science. He writes: "It may be said that the problem of transformism no longer exists. The question is settled once and for all. To shake our belief now in the reality of biogenesis, it would be necessary to uproot the tree of life and undermine the entire structure of the world. . . . One might well become impatient or lose heart at the sight of so many minds (and not mediocre ones either) remaining today still closed to the idea of evolution, if the whole of history were not there to pledge to us that a truth once seen, even by a single mind, always ends up by imposing itself on the totality of human consciousness. . . . Is evolution a theory, a system or a hypothesis? It is much more: it is a general condition to which all theories, all hypotheses, all systems must bow and which they must satisfy henceforward if they are to be thinkable and true. Evolution is a light illuminating all facts, a curve that all lines must follow."[6]

His thought is his own, of course. We do not suggest that all theistic evolutionists share it. Yet it is evident from these quotations why Young calls this view ultimately destructive. Biblical religion must by its very definition start with the Bible and make all other theories subordinate to that. In de Chardin's case, everything has become subject to evolution, and an ability to hear the reforming, correcting Word of God in Scripture has been lost. We must ask whether such a tendency is not present in all theistic evolution.

What should the Christian's proper position be? An openness to all truth certainly, but not the kind of openness that allows scientific theory or any other theory to sit in judgment on the truthfulness of God's written Word. Actually, the Christian's task is the opposite: to bring every thought into subjection to

---

[5]Pierre Teilhard de Chardin, *The Phenomenon of Man* (New York: Harper and Row, 1959), p. 52. Cited by Young, *Creation and the Flood*, p. 36.

[6]*Phenomenon of Man*, pp. 140, 218, 219. Cited by Young, *Creation and the Flood*, pp. 36, 37.

the written Word. Paul knew this. He wrote to those of his day, "The weapons we fight with are not the weapons of the world. On the contrary, they have divine power to demolish strongholds. We demolish arguments and every pretension that sets itself up against the knowledge of God, and we take captive every thought to make it obedient to Christ" (2 Cor. 10:4, 5). We may not know the whole truth in any given area. But we must know that our ultimate standard for truth—whatever it is—is the written Word of God.

7

Views of Creation: The Gap Theory

(Genesis 1:1, 2)

In the beginning God created the heavens and the earth. Now the earth was formless and empty, darkness was over the surface of the deep, and the Spirit of God was hovering over the waters.

In *The Invisible War* Donald Grey Barnhouse gives an illustration of what has come to be known widely as the gap theory of creation. A motorist was driving through America's great southwest and had planned to arrive at the Grand Canyon of Colorado from the south and then proceed on across it northward into Utah. He shared his plans with a friend who knew the area, but his friend immediately pointed out that what he wanted to do was impossible. On the map it looked as if he could drive north across the canyon, but that tiny fifteen-mile gap, which barely shows on the map, is actually a gigantic and impassable chasm. One can get north only by taking a detour over hundreds of miles of hot desert roads.

According to the gap theory, the first two verses of Genesis are like that. They appear to be continuous, but in between there is actually a long but indeterminate period in which the destruction of an original world and the unfolding of the geological ages can be located.

A Popular Viewpoint

This theory is also called the restitution or recreation theory. Arthur C. Custance, who has written an excellent book in the theory's defense, traces it to certain early Jewish writers, some of the church fathers and even to some ancient Sumerian and Babylonian documents. It crops up in the Middle Ages as well. It

was in Scotland at the beginning of the last century, through the work of the capable pastor and writer Thomas Chalmers, that the idea gained real coherence and visibility.

Chalmers was anxious to show that the emerging data concerning the geological ages was not incompatible with sound biblical exposition. So according to him, Genesis 1:1 tells of God's creation of an *original* world in which all things were good, for God cannot create that which is bad. Lucifer ruled this world for God. Lucifer sinned. God judged the world along with Lucifer, as a result of which the earth became the formless, desolate mass we discover it to be in Genesis 1:2 ("Now the earth was formless and empty, darkness was over the surface of the deep"). The earth continued like this for indeterminate ages in which the various rock strata developed. It was only at the end of this period that God intervened to bring new order out of the prevailing chaos, which is what Genesis 1:3–31 describes. These verses actually describe a recreation.

Chalmers wrote in the early 1800s, but his views thrived around the turn of the century as they were picked up by the various writers of early Fundamentalism. The best known was G. H. Pember whose book on the theory, *Earth's Earliest Ages* (1876), went through many editions. My own copy is the fourteenth.

50

Pember wrote, "It is thus clear that the second verse of Genesis describes the earth as a ruin; but there is no hint of the time which elapsed between creation and this ruin. Age after age may have rolled away, and it was probably during their course that the strata of the earth's crust were gradually developed. Hence we see that geological attacks upon the Scriptures are altogether wide of the mark, are a mere beating of the air. There is room for any length of time between the first and second verses of the Bible. And again, since we have no inspired account of the geological formations, we are at liberty to believe that they were developed just in the order in which we find them. The whole process took place in preadamite times, in connection, perhaps, with another race of beings, and, consequently, does not at present concern us."[1] In subsequent pages Pember developed his theory of the fall of Satan, the influence of demons in the world prior to Noah, and the relevance of this for the resurgence of spiritism that he observed in his day.

Arthur W. Pink held Chalmer's view and doubtless also learned from Pember. He wrote, "The unknown interval between the first two verses of Genesis 1, is wide enough to embrace all the prehistoric ages which may have elapsed; but all that took place from Genesis 1:3 onwards transpired less than six thousand years ago."[2]

Harry Rimmer was another influential writer. In 1941 he authored a book entitled *Modern Science and the Genesis Record*. In it he said, "The original creation of the heaven and the earth, then, is covered in the first verse of Genesis. Only God knows how many ages rolled by before the ruin wrought by Lucifer fell upon the earth, but it may have been an incalculable span of time. Nor can any student say how long the period of chaos lasted; there is not even a hint given. But let us clearly recognize in these studies that Moses, in the record of the first week of creation, is telling the story of God's reconstruction; rather than the story of an original creation."[3]

The single most effective teacher of this view was C. I. Scofield, who included it in his notes on Genesis in the astonishingly popular Scofield Reference Bible. From there it became the almost unquestioned view of Fundamentalism, though, as I have already pointed out, *The Fundamentals* themselves contain an article by James Orr which almost embraces evolution. In more recent times various forms of this theory have been held by C. S. Lewis, M. R. DeHaan, Donald Grey Barnhouse and others. Francis Schaeffer acknowledges parts of it as a possibility.[4]

EXEGETICAL STRENGTH

There is widespread opposition to the gap theory today, even on the part of very conservative writers. But these often dismiss it too easily, without adequate attention to the biblical data on which the gap theorists built. This theory may be wrong, but it is not possible to dismiss it cavalierly.

What are the lines of evidence for this theory? The first and by far the most important is its exegetical or biblical base. Indeed, without this, Chalmers, Pember and the others would have had no case at all. The exegetical argument has a number of parts. First, in the Masoretic text of Genesis, in which ancient Jewish scholars attempted to incorporate a sufficient number of "indicators" to guide the reader in proper pronunciation and interpretation of the

[1]G. H. Pember, *Earth's Earliest Ages and Their Connection with Modern Spiritualism and Theosophy* (London and Glasgow: Pickering & Inglis, n.d.), p. 28.

[2]Arthur W. Pink, *Gleanings in Genesis* (Chicago: Moody Press, 1950), p. 11. Original edition 1922.

[3]Harry Rimmer, *Modern Science and the Genesis Record* (Grand Rapids: Eerdmans, 1941), p. 28.

[4]Schaeffer, *Genesis in Space and Time,* p. 62.

text, there is a small mark known as a *rebhia* following verse 1. The *rebhia* is a disjunctive accent. That is, it serves to inform the reader that there is a break in the narrative at this point and that he should pause before going on to the next verse. The *rebhia* might also indicate that the conjunction that begins verse 2, a *waw*, should be translated "but" rather than the more common "and." (This has bearing on how the second verse should be translated because, as we will see, it could be rendered "But the earth became a ruin.") To be sure, the *rebhia* was not in the original text of Genesis and therefore represents only the considered judgment of the Masoretes, but their opinion may guide us to a correct interpretation.

Second, there is the structure of the creation account itself. Each of the accounts of the activity of God on one of the creative days ends with the words "And there was evening, and there was morning—the first [second, third, fourth, fifth, or sixth] day." In other words, there is a very marked parallelism. Moreover, on the second, third, fourth, fifth, and sixth days, those same sections begin, "And God said. . . ." It is only natural, therefore, to assume that the account of the first day of creation begins, not with verse 1 but with verse 3 where the parallel phrase occurs ("And God said, 'Let there be light.'"). If this is so, then the first two verses stand apart from the rest of the account and describe a creation prior to the work of God on the first day.

Third, there is the possibility (some would say necessity) of translating the Hebrew verb "to be" (*hyh*), which occurs in verse 2, not "was" but "became." So the verse would read, "But the earth became formless [that is, a ruinous mass] and empty [that is, devoid of life]." It is also possible that the

verb is to be taken as pluperfect with the meaning, "But the earth had become. . . ."

The arguments concerning the meaning of this basic Hebrew verb are long and tortuous, not ones that most people would readily or cheerfully follow. But they boil down to the point that this is at least a possibility and perhaps even a strong possibility. Those who oppose this view—Bernard Ramm in *The Christian View of Science and Scripture* is one—argue that those adopting it make a novel and very questionable interpretation rest on an infrequent and secondary meaning of the verb. But it is not at all evident that it is that infrequent or secondary. Let us take the matter of whether "became" is a secondary meaning first. In Arthur Custance's defense of the gap theory's exegetical base, the point is made that the Hebrew verb *hyh*, while frequently translated "was" rather than "became," nevertheless primarily means "became" for the simple reason that the Hebrew language does not really need a verb for "be." That is, if a Hebrew-speaking person wanted to say "The man is good," he would not use a verb at all but would simply say, "The man good." The verb would be implied. This sentence differs from the descriptive phrase "The good man," because the Hebrew way of saying that is "The man the good."

In his critique Ramm declares that "the Hebrews did not have a word for *became*, but the verb *to be* did service for *to be* and *become*.[5] But as Custance points out, the reverse would be more nearly correct, namely, that "they did not need a word for 'to be' in the simple sense, so made their word for *become* serve for *to be* and *become*."[6] In Custance's judgment the word should be translated "became" unless there are reasons to the contrary.

[5]Bernard Ramm, *The Christian View of Science and Scripture* (Grand Rapids: Eerdmans, 1954), p. 202.
[6]Arthur C. Custance, *Without Form and Void: a Study of the Meaning of Genesis 1:2* (Brockville, Canada: Doorway Papers, 1970), p. 104.

The other matter is frequency. John Whitcomb has written that there are only six examples in the entire Pentateuch of the verb *hyh* being rendered "became." This seems to be an error. Custance claims that there are at least seventeen cases in Genesis alone, but that is in the King James Version. Other versions give the translation in other instances. The Latin Vulgate has the equivalent thirteen times in just the first chapter. Some sample verses:

Genesis 3:1—"Now the serpent *had become* more subtle than any beast of the field." Most versions say "was," but this verse probably indicates that the serpent became subtle or crafty as the result of Satan's use of him for the purpose of tempting Eve.

Genesis 3:20—"Eve *became* the mother of all living." The King James Version says "was," but this is strange since no children had been born to her at this time. The New International Version recognizes the problem and translates the verse accordingly: "Adam named his wife Eve, because she would become the mother of all the living."

Genesis 21:20—"And God was with the lad [Ishmael]; and he grew, and dwelt in the wilderness, and *became* an archer."

Genesis 37:20—"We shall see what will *become* of his [Joseph's] dreams."

These translations are not beyond challenge, of course. But they do show the frequency of this possible translation of this verb. Custance's own conclusion is "By and large, therefore, I suggest that the rendering, 'But the earth had become a ruin and a desolation,' is a rendering which does more justice to the original and deserves more serious consideration as an alternative than it has been customary to afford it in recent years."[7]

Fourth, the words "formless and empty" (*tohu waw bohu*) may be verbal clues to a preadamic judgment of God on our planet. True, the words have various shades of meaning and do not necessarily indicate the destruction of something that had formerly been beautiful. But they sometimes do. Besides, there is the important text in Isaiah 45:18 which says, using the words of Genesis 1:2, that God did not create the world a ruin. If this is a direct reference to Genesis, as it may be, it says that God did not create the world in the state portrayed in Genesis 1:2. (On the other hand, it may simply mean that God did not create the world to be desolate but rather created it to be inhabited, as in the NIV translation.)

WHEN DID SATAN FALL?

This chapter has dealt largely with the exegetical support for the gap theory, because it is the point from which its adherents argue. These arguments have not been taken seriously enough by those who oppose the theory. But this is not to suggest that there are no other lines of support for the reconstructionists' view. A second line of support is *theological.*

This has to do with the fall of Satan. From Genesis 3 we learn that evil was already in existence at the time of Adam and Eve's creation, for Satan was there to tempt Eve. Besides, there are texts that suggest, not always clearly, that there was an earlier fall of Satan, followed by a judgment on Satan and those angels (now demons) who sinned with him. Of course, the fall of Satan may have occurred without any relationship to earth. But he is called "the prince of this world" and seems to have a special relationship to it. Is it not possible, even reasonable, that he may have ruled the world for God in an earlier period of earth's history—if there was such a period? And if this is so, couldn't a fall and judgment fit between Genesis 1:1

---

[7]Ibid., p. 116.

and Genesis 1:2? If not there, where does this Fall come in? The only other option would be before creation itself, which would put the creation of Satan before anything else we know.

There is also the problem of the first appearances of death. If the fossils indicate anything, they indicate a period of struggle, disease, and death prior to man's appearance. But if death came through the sin of Adam, how can death be evidenced in the fossil record unless the death witnessed is the product of God's judgment on the sin of an earlier world and race? There is another explanation of this that the creationist school supplies, namely, that the fossils were created by the Flood and so came after Adam. But the argument at this point—while it will not speak to creationists—should speak to most other schools of thought.

SOME LINGERING DIFFICULTIES

What should we think of this theory? It has commended itself to many in recent generations. It is a serious attempt to be biblical. It seems to solve the problem of the long geological ages. Should we adopt it? We should consider it seriously for each of the reasons just given, but before we adopt it we should also consider the difficulties.

One serious criticism of the gap theory is that it gives one of the grandest and most important passages in the Bible an unnatural and perhaps even a peculiar interpretation. This is hardly a conclusive argument, but it is probably the point at which most other Bible students and scholars begin to hesitate. Ramm puts it like this: "From the earliest of Bible interpretation this passage has been interpreted by Jews, Catholics and Protestants as the *original creation of the universe*. In seven majestic days the

universe and all of life is brought into being. But according to Rimmer's view the great first chapter of Genesis, save for the first verse, is not about original creation at all, but about reconstruction. The primary origin of the universe is stated in but one verse. This is not the most telling blow against the theory, but it certainly indicates that something has been lost to make the six days of creation anticlimactic."[8]

This same argument may also be stated biblically, which Ramm does not do but which would presumably have more weight with the gap theory advocates. To give just one example, we read in Exodus 20:11, "For in six days the LORD made the heavens and the earth, the sea, and all that is in them, but he rested on the seventh day." A person might point out that the verb used here is "made," not the powerful Hebrew verb "created" *(bara)*, and that this allows for a recreation or reforming. But that aside, the verse does sound like a description of an original creation. "It neither states nor implies recreation to most people."[9]

Second, the exegetical data, while impressive, is nevertheless far from certain. And it must be certain if we are to be expected to embrace such an unusual theory. I have argued above that critics of the gap theory have been far too cavalier in dismissing its supporters' exegetical arguments, but those arguments are still not clearly right. The Hebrew verb *hyh* may mean "became," but there is no doubt that it is also correctly translated "was" and that far more frequently. Again, *waw* may mean "but," although it more commonly means "and." And as for *tohu waw bohu*, this may simply mean that the land in question was uninhabitable. Whether that condition was the result of God's

---

[8]Ramm, *Christian View*, p. 201.

[9]L. Duane Thuman, *How to Think About Evolution & Other Bible-Science Controversies* (Downers Grove, Ill.: InterVarsity Press, 1978), p. 121.

judgment on the earth or was due to some other factor is to be determined from the context and not from the words themselves (cf. Jer. 4:23–26; Isa. 24:1 and 45:18). It is significant in this regard that, although the NIV supports the possibility of translating the Hebrew *hyh* as "become" in a footnote to Genesis 1:2, it does not render Isaiah 45:18 in a way that would support the gap theory.

Third, the gap theory does not really settle the problem posed by geology. Geology shows us successive strata of the earth's crust containing fossils of earlier life forms. Advocates of the gap theory wish to account for these in the supposed break between Genesis 1:1 and 1:2. But at which point in this break did the judgment of God enter in? If it came after the laying down of the fossil evidence, then death was in the world before judgment. If the judgment came first, then the conditions arising from that judgment could not be as the second verse of Genesis describes them (a cha-otic world submerged in darkness), for in such a world no plant or animal life could survive. The only escape from this dilemma is to imagine a gradually descending or advancing judgment in which the various forms of life are progressively snuffed out, but this is the precise opposite of what the geological strata seem to indicate. They show a progressive development of life from simpler to more complex forms.

Some gap theorists have seen this problem and have appealed to the Flood for producing the geological evidence. Rimmer appeals to both the earlier ages and the Flood. But if this is the case, we do not need the gap. The impression left is that the theory has not been carried through sufficiently to provide us with a clearly workable model. It may be possible. But we will want to consider the other views of creation before we settle on this as the only truly Christian possibility.

8

Views of Creation: Six-day Creationism

(Genesis 1:1, 2)

In the beginning God created the heavens and the earth. Now the earth was formless and empty, darkness was over the surface of the deep, and the Spirit of God was hovering over the waters.

In recent years the gap theory of creation, so popular with the early Fundamentalists, has been replaced by a school of thought known as six-day creationism or flood geology. This theory views the Genesis account as involving six literal days, posits a relatively young earth (maximum age 12,000 years), and explains the fossil record as having been formed by the great flood in Genesis 6 conceived as having been universal and of immensely destructive proportions. This theory is biblical, but it does not base its interpretation of Genesis on unusual schemes of thought, as the gap theorists do. True, its *geology* may be unusual (perhaps even forced, as some would claim). But because it is biblical, as well as scientific, creationism deserves the most serious consideration by Christian people.

Two organizations have been effective in advancing the creationists' viewpoint: the Creation Research Society of Ann Arbor, Michigan, and the Institute for Creation Research of San Diego, California. The first of these was founded in 1963 with Dr. Walter E. Lammerts as its first president. It has a current membership of 500 scientists who have the right to vote, and 1,600 non-scientists, who do not have the right to vote. The Society issues a quarterly journal and in 1970 published a school textbook entitled *Biology: A Search for Order in Complexity*. It has produced several other volumes. As indicated by the name, the members of the Creation Research Society engage largely in research relating to creation matters.

The second organization has been more active and is therefore better known. It is a division of Christian Heritage College, also of San Diego, and has as its leaders Dr. Duane T. Gish, who serves on the board of directors of the Christian Research Society, and Dr. Henry M. Morris, the institute's director. This organization sponsors frequent debates on evolution. The results of these debates, sometimes attended by many thousands of people, are printed, along with other items and articles in support of scientific creationism, in a monthly newsletter known as *Acts & Facts*. In the last ten years the institute has published more than thirty books on creationism, most of them written by Gish and Morris, though the best-known work, *The Genesis Flood*, was co-authored by Morris and Dr. John C. Whitcomb, Professor of Old Testament at Grace Theological Seminary, Winona Lake, Indiana.

These organizations have offered a powerful challenge to prevailing evolutionary theory and have carried their challenge into the public sphere as evidenced by the California biology textbook controversy, which began in November, 1969, and other recent court cases.

THE CREATIONISTS' MESSAGE

The message of the creationists, whether in debate or in their publications, is that evolution is impossible and that the facts (as we know them) best fit the creationist model.

Here is a lengthy but valuable summation of the creationists' position from the Whitcomb and Morris volume: "Although there may be considerable latitude of opinion about details, the Biblical record does provide a basic outline of earth history, within which all the scientific data ought to be interpreted. It describes an initial Creation, accomplished by processes which no longer are in operation and which, therefore, cannot possibly be understood in terms of present physical or biological mechanisms. It describes the entrance into this initial Creation of the supervening principle of decay and deterioration: the 'curse' pronounced by God on the 'whole creation,' resulting from the sin and rebellion of man, the intended master of the terrestrial economy, against his Creator.

"The record of the great Flood plainly asserts that it was so universal and cataclysmic in its cause, scope and results that it also marked a profound hiatus in terrestrial history. Thus the Creation, the Fall, and the Flood constitute the truly basic facts, to which all the other details of early historical data must be referred. . . .

"It seems most reasonable to attribute the formations of the crystalline basement rocks, and perhaps some of the Pre-Cambrian non-fossiliferous sedimentaries, to the Creation period, though later substantially modified by the tectonic upheavals of the Deluge period. The fossil-bearing strata were apparently laid down in large measure during the Flood, with the apparent sequences attributed not to evolution but rather to hydrodynamic selectivity, ecologic habitats, and differential mobility and strength of the various creatures."

So far as evolution is concerned, Whitcomb and Morris write that "evolution is the great 'escape mechanism' of modern man. This is the pervasive philosophic principle by which man either consciously or sub-consciously seeks intellectual justification for escape from personal responsibility to his Creator and escape from the 'way of the Cross' as the necessary and sufficient means of his personal redemption. . . . The decision between alternative theories does not therefore depend only on the scientific data but is ultimately a moral and emotional decision. . . . We therefore urge the reader to face up to the fact that the actual data of geology *can* be interpreted in such a way as to harmonize quite effectively with a literal interpretation of the Biblical records and then also to recognize the spiritual implications and consequences of this fact."[1]

A DETAILED MESSAGE

There are several points in this summary that ought to guide us in an evaluation of the theory. First, there is a concern for *biblical teaching*. More than this, creationists want to make biblical teaching determinative. This is the point at which the summary begins, for it seeks to make an initial creation, the Fall, and the Flood the three great points around which everything else is to be interpreted.

We have to admit here that the exegetical basis of the creationists is strong. They take the creation account of Genesis as literally as possible, arguing

[1]John C. Whitcomb and Henry M. Morris, *The Genesis Flood: The Biblical Record and Its Scientific Implications* (Philadelphia: Presbyterian and Reformed Publishing Company, 1961), pp. 327–30.

that the Hebrew word for "day" (*yom*) must refer to an actual twenty-four-hour day unless the context clearly indicates otherwise. They do not deny that *yom* can refer to an indefinite period, in which case it might be more properly translated "age," but they consider this usage to be relatively rare. Moreover, even where it does mean an indefinite period, this can hardly be stretched to include the billions of years that uniformitarian geology would assign to periods represented by the "days" of Genesis. Besides, in Genesis 1 the days are each said to have an evening and a morning. Whitcomb and Morris say, "Since God's revealed Word describes this Creation as taking place in six 'days' and since there apparently is no contextual basis for understanding these days in any sort of symbolic sense, it is an act of both faith and reason to accept them, literally, as real days."[2]

The perspicuity of Scripture has bearing here. True, not all Scripture is equally clear, but the creationist would argue that it is very clear at this point. "Suppose the creation did take place in six twenty-four-hour days," he might say. "How could God possibly tell us that more clearly or directly than by the language we have in Genesis?"

Second, the summary shows the weaknesses and perhaps even the ultimate *failure of evolution*, the "great escape mechanism" of modern man. Where does evolution fail? In addition to its failure to provide adequate supporting data from the fossil record, which I have already alluded to, Whitcomb and Morris lay particular stress on the problem evolution has with the first and second laws of thermodynamics. The first law of thermodynamics is energy conservation. It says that energy is neither created nor lost. It is simply changed

from one form to another. The second law states that in spite of this conservation the energy available for useful work does decrease so that the universe can properly be said to be "running down." To give just one illustration, the energy of the sun is not being destroyed by the combustion going on on its surface—the energy latent in the sun's matter is being converted to heat—but the heat largely dissipates into space and becomes useless.

A consequence of this second law is that in any closed system order tends to move in the direction of disorder or disarrangement. Take the example that Robert Kofahl and Kelly Segraves give in their book, *The Creation Explanation.* They ask us to imagine an orderly pile of ping-pong balls resting at the head of a flight of stairs. For the sake of the illustration they also ask us to imagine that the balls are perfectly resilient so that they are capable of bouncing forever without losing their original energy. Imagine that someone jars the balls so that the pile collapses and the balls begin to roll down over the first step and then bounce on down to the bottom of the stairs and so on around the room. What will happen? The balls will continue bouncing but in increasing disorder. They will not bounce back up into their original position and assemble themselves on the upper step, even though they continue bouncing for billions of years. There is a mathematical possibility of that happening, but it is a practical impossibility, which is to say: *It does not happen.* Yet evolution would have us believe that the complex order of the universe has come about from just such random happenings.[3]

Whitcomb and Morris conclude, "The plain facts of the situation, therefore, are that evolution has been simply assumed

---

[2]Ibid., p. 228.

[3]Robert E. Kofahl and Kelly L. Segraves, *The Creation Explanation: A Scientific Alternative to Evolution* (Wheaton, Ill.: Harold Shaw Publishers, 1975), pp. 33–35.

as the universal principle of change in nature, despite the fact that there is no experimental evidence supporting it and despite the still more amazing fact that universal experience and experimentation have demonstrated this universal principle of change to be its very opposite: namely, that of deterioration."[4]

But if the earth is young (only 12,000 years or so) and if it is the result of God's special acts of creation taking place within the short period of only six literal twenty-four-hour days, where did the various strata of the earth's crust come from? Even more important, where did the various fossil-bearing strata come from? Didn't these require long periods of time, hundreds of thousands if not billions of years of time, for their formation? The creationists' answer is that although the strata may have been laid down in various epochs—at the time of the initial creation (by fiat), during the work of the six literal days, or in our own relatively modern period—the significant, fossil-bearing strata are largely the result of the Flood.

The idea here is that a flood of worldwide proportions would be immensely destructive. It would require huge amounts of water pushed up from beneath and precipitated from above, presumably by the condensation of a vapor or cloud cover, with cataclysmic effects on the earth's crust. The amount of water necessary to cover the earth would carry virtually all soil with it into the oceans by erosion, where it would pile up in strata. Various creatures would be buried in those strata, the simpler and smaller on the bottom, the larger and more vigorous on top— hence, the appearance of various ages in which life developed from simpler to more complex forms. After the Flood new land masses would have emerged,

and some of these newly formed strata would have been exposed.

Creationists believe that their views are reinforced by additional considerations:

1. Present-day conditions are forming very few potential fossil deposits, and most of these are unusual. Nothing comparable to the known fossil beds of ancient times is being formed today, which makes us think that some past catastrophe was necessary to produce them.

2. The facts of geology do not support the view of essentially harmonious strata with the older levels on the bottom and the most recent on the top. There is a tendency in this direction, but the facts reflect a far more unruly situation. A universal flood accounts for these facts more adequately than the theory of lengthy geological ages and slow evolutionary development.

3. The existence of huge fossil deposits containing thousands of large complex species, such as the mammoth deposits in Siberia, are best explained either by the Flood or by the abnormal weather conditions that must have followed it.

After presenting this and other evidence, Kofahl and Segraves conclude, "The foregoing features of the fossil and geological records all seem to be in agreement more with the catastrophic than with the uniformitation concept of geological processes of the past. Thus, in this respect, fossils corroborate the structural data given previously and lend themselves readily to the framework of biblical catastrophism."[5]

How Old Is the Earth?

In spite of the careful biblical and scientific research that has accumulated in support of the creationists' view, there

---

[4]*The Genesis Flood*, p. 227.

[5]*The Creation Explanation*, p. 52.

are problems that make the theory wrong to most (including many evangelical) scientists. We conclude by listing the most important.

Data from various disciplines point to a very old earth and an even older universe. Some of the conclusions from this data, as well as some of the data itself, were presented in earlier chapters. There is astronomical data. One line of astronomical data concerns the speed of light. Light travels in a vacuum at a speed of 186,000 miles per second. Therefore, 1) if the speed of light is constant, and 2) the light we observe coming from the stars actually comes from those stars, and 3) if our distance measurements for these stars are substantially accurate, then the universe is at least as old as the light-travel-time coming to us from the most distant objects. The most distant objects we are able to observe are quasars. The travel time for light coming from these objects is more than ten billion years. Therefore, the age of the universe by this mode of reckoning is at least more than that. A second line of data is based on the apparent expansion of the universe. All parts of the universe are retreating from us and from one another at enormous speeds, the most distant observable galaxies at speeds in excess of 100 million miles per hour. Working backward from their present position and speed to the initial "big bang," the origin of the universe can be set at between 15 and 20 billion years ago. A third line of astronomical data concerns the nature and normal life of stars. Stars are of various ages, having been formed over the whole history of the universe from 15 to 20 billion years ago until today. Our own Milky Way galaxy is about as old as the universe. Our sun is considerably younger, about 5 to 10 billion years old.

The point of combining this data is that, although it is related in some ways, it is based on different approaches to the problems of age and on different assumptions. Yet it gives a roughly consistent picture. According to these methods, the universe would be about 15 to 20 billion years old, the sun about 5 to 10 billion years old and our solar system about 5 billion years old.

Second, there is the evidence of radioactive methods of dating earth (or moon) rocks. This method is based on the observation that certain kinds of unstable or radioactive elements decay from an unstable to a stable form at measurable rates. By measuring the amount of the original element and the amount of the derivative or "daughter" element in any given sample, an approximate age of the sample may be given. This is an admittedly uncertain method. Many criticisms have been given.[6] But valid or not, the data it gives points to an earth that is about 4.55 billion years old, which is in line with the astrological evidence. Even allowing for large percentages of error, this is still a long way from an earth that is only a few thousand years old.

Third, there is the evidence of nonradiometric dating. Types of data available in this category are: carbonate deposits, sediments, deposits of evaporites, the development of coral reefs, sea-floor spreading and other matters. These all suggest an earth older than that allowed by the creationist model.

We must say, as we summarize this first problem with the creationist view, that the creationists have given answers to each of these lines of evidence for an old earth and an even older universe. They have spoken of a lack of uniformity

[6]See Harold S. Slusher, *Critique of Radiometric Dating* (San Diego: Creation-Life Publishers, 1973); George Howe, "Carbon-14 and Other Radioactive Dating Methods" (Caldwell, Idaho: Bible-Science Association, 1970); C. S. Noble and J. J. Naughton, "Deep-Ocean Basalts: Inert Gas Content and Uncertainties in Age Dating," *Science,* Vol. 162, Oct. 11, 1968, pp. 265–67; as well as the appropriate sections in the books already cited.

of scientific laws in past ages; of a universe created "in motion," as it were, with light already in progress from a distant point; of radioactive dating methods as unreliable, sometimes giving wildly conflicting data, and so on. But when everything is considered, it seems to many persons (myself included) that the creationists are running against too many lines of more or less independent evidence against their case on behalf of a young earth. Therefore, whatever else may be true about their viewpoint, it is hard to believe that the creation of the earth and universe was recent.

Remaining Problems

A second problem, which bothers most geologists and some other people as well, is the use of the Flood to explain the various strata of the earth's outer crust, particularly those that contain fossils. Let us assume that the Flood was universal and immensely destructive. Let us also assume that the Flood carried most of the earth's soil and millions of dead or soon-to-be drowned organisms before it. Let us even assume that the simpler and less mobile organisms were buried first (and are therefore found in the lower layers of sedimentary rocks) and that the larger and more mobile creatures survived longer but were eventually overcome and buried in higher layers of rock. Assuming all of that—and some of it is questionable— how is it that plants, which are not mobile, show the same general distribution from the less complex to the more complex forms, or that fish (which the Bible does not say were killed and need not have been) are nevertheless included in the same general fossil distribution?

L. Duane Thuman raises these questions and asks, "How did the plants survive such a destructive flood and be-

come re-established so quickly that the dove could bring back an olive leaf? A worldwide flood which buried both plants and animals under sediment sometimes thousands of feet deep makes this highly improbable."[7]

A third and final problem, which we have not discussed up to now but which is very important to the creationists' view of Genesis 1, is the appearance of age. Since the universe is extremely complex, it gives the impression of having gotten to its present form through changes taking place over a long period of time. For example, a tree possessing hundreds of rings in its trunk gives the impression of its having reached that form by growing taller and thicker bit by bit over a period of many years. But according to the creationists, everything we see (including the original tree) was brought into being within six literal days. Therefore, it was either brought to a mature state extremely quickly, within minutes or hours, or else was created to look as if it had gone through a long and complex history. To Adam, newly created, the Garden of Eden may have seemed to have been around for years, but in reality it had been created for him in a mature form or was quickly brought to a mature form only three days previously. In the same way, say the creationists, the universe does indeed appear to have had a beginning 15 to 20 million years ago, but it was created in motion and is actually only 10 or 15 thousand years old. The same approach can be applied to the age of rocks, coral reefs, and other apparent evidence for an older earth or universe.

At this point it is possible to ridicule the six-day creationism theory. Some have! But this should not be done too quickly, particularly not by those who believe in the createdness of Adam. How old was Adam when he was created? There is no need to think of him as a

[7]*How to Think About Evolution*, p. 122.

baby. From whom would he have come? Presumably he was created fully grown. But if that is so, then it is not impossible to think that God might have created the rest of the universe "fully grown" also, according to the same pattern.

"But that would mean that God is deceiving us," object some, "and God cannot do that and be good." Whitcomb and Morris hit this objection head on, claiming that God cannot be accused of deceit inasmuch as He has given a revelation in the Bible of how things have actually been created. "If God reveals how and when he created the universe and its inhabitants, then to charge God with falsehood in creating 'apparent age' is preposterous in the extreme—even blasphemous. It is not God who has lied, but rather man who has called him a liar, through rejection of his revelation of Creation as given in Genesis and verified by the Lord Jesus Christ!"[8]

It is a shrewd point—yet not entirely convincing. Although God may have had to create Adam as a mature individual, and presumably did so, there is no reason to think on that basis that He therefore also needed to do so in other areas. Why would God make the tree look old rather than merely giving it time to grow old? What was the hurry? Or again, even if God did create the magnificent universe we know just thousands of years ago, why make it look as if it is much older? Why make the quasars look 10 billion years old? We cannot even see them. What possible point would such a creation have?

None of this is to suggest that God could not have done things in this fashion if He chose to do so. Nor is it to say that the creationists have not made a very good case for their position. But there are problems and questions, and it is because of these that the quest for an explanation by believing scientists goes on.

WHAT ABOUT SCIENCE?

There is one last point. The possibility of doing science in our day or any other day is undergirded by the assumption of certain laws of nature, operating in the past and continuing to operate on into the future. But according to the creationists, those laws were not operating or else were entirely different during the period of creation itself, and therefore any scientific investigation of creation is both impossible and illegitimate. Is that what our knowledge of God's ways leads us to expect? Are we given minds that can reason only to be told that at the point of creation the data they perceive and the basis on which they would reason are an illusion? If so, it is the end of science, at least in this area, and it may be the end of other thinking also.

If the earth and the universe look old when they actually are not, why should any of our observations be trusted? True, the Bible tells us much, and it can be trusted. But the Bible does not tell us everything. It does not even tell me that I exist. Perhaps I do not. Perhaps appearances in this area too are deceiving. Taken to its extreme, the idea of "apparent age" (or "apparent" anything) leads to skepticism, and we are not to be skeptics. We are to know and know we know—by the Word of God and by that limited but nevertheless extensive and extremely wonderful revelation of God in nature, perceived and understood by reason.

---

[8]*The Genesis Flood*, p. 238.

9

Views of Creation: Progressive Creation

(Genesis 1:1, 2)

In the beginning God created the heavens and the earth. Now the earth was formless and empty, darkness was over the surface of the deep, and the Spirit of God was hovering over the waters.

In the last four chapters we looked at four competing views of creation: atheistic evolution, theistic evolution, the gap theory and six-day creationism. Each has been well presented and well defended by able advocates; but each has problems, as we have seen. As a result, in recent years a fifth approach to the creation process has appeared: progressive creationism. Briefly stated, it says that God created the world directly and deliberately, that is, without leaving anything to "chance," but that He did it over long periods of time that correspond roughly to the geological ages. Moreover, this creation is still going on. Progressive creationism attempts to show how current scientific theories of the origins of the universe and the formation of the earth match the revelation in Genesis.

This approach is not entirely new. For example, some elements of the progressive creationists' description of the early formation of the earth sound much like things the gap theorists were saying earlier in this century. Parts of the theory would be affirmed by evolutionists.

One book that takes this position is *Genesis One & the Origin of the Earth* by Robert C. Newman and Herman J. Eckelmann. Newman, who holds a doctorate in astrophysics from Cornell University, is Professor of New Testament at the Biblical Theological Seminary, Hatfield, Pennsylvania. Eckelmann has

been an associate with the Center for Radiophysics and Space Research at Cornell University but is now pastor of a church in Ithaca, New York. A second book that espouses progressive creationism is *Creation and the Flood: An Alternative to Flood Geology and Theistic Evolution* by Davis A. Young, son of the well-known Westminster Theological Seminary Professor of Old Testament, Edward J. Young. Davis Young is Associate Professor of Geology at the University of North Carolina at Wilmington. Important to each of their views is the idea that the creative days of Genesis launch creative periods in the sense that the work begun on the earlier days continues to unfold in some form during the later days. The progressive creationists want to make possible the appearance of some new forms of vegetation in late geological periods even though the Genesis account places the creation of plants and trees on day three—to give just one example.

This view is held by many Christians who are in scientific fields, even though they have not published books on their position. It is held by quite a few biblical scholars and theologians.

A POSSIBLE INTERPRETATION

Since even scientists are unsure precisely how the earth may have formed, it is an exercise in speculation to suggest an early history of the earth and universe. Nevertheless, since an outline of that history is given in the first chapter of Genesis, it is not out of place to look at it in terms of current geological theory, which is essentially what the progressive creationists have done. The result is something like the following (composite) picture of development.

Initial creation. The first verse of Genesis tells us that "God created the heavens and the earth." It does not tell us how God created the heavens or the earth, nor when. So it is permissible to view this statement in terms of the prevailing "Big Bang" theory. That is, the universe had a definite beginning on the order of 15 to 20 billion years ago. At that point all the matter in the universe was together, but it began moving outward by sudden rapid expansion. Scientists estimate that nearly all elements would have been formed by the end of the first half hour. As matter expanded, galaxies, solar systems, and satellite bodies were formed. In this early period the earth would have been quite hot. Most of the water would have been in the atmosphere. Consequently, there would have been a heavy cloud layer that would have shrouded the earth in impenetrable darkness. As the earth cooled some of the cloud cover would have condensed and would have fallen as rain, thus forming oceans. Progressive creationists feel that this state of things is well reflected in Genesis 1:2, which says, "Now the earth was formless and empty, darkness was over the surface of the deep, and the Spirit of God was hovering over the waters."

The first day. After the first verse of Genesis the focal point of the creation narrative is the earth. Therefore, the statement of God in verse 3 ("Let there be light") refers to the appearance of light on earth. This would mean that the clouds covering the earth had now thinned enough for the light of the sun, which had been shining all along, to penetrate to the earth's surface. As the earth rotated there would be periods of night and day, although the sun and other heavenly bodies would not themselves be visible. This is called the first day of creation because it was the first significant event in the preparation of the earth for habitation.

The second day. On this day the cooling process continued with a further thinning of the clouds and a separation between them and the waters that now lay on the earth. These verses (vv. 6–8) speak of the firmament (correctly translated "an expanse" in the NIV), the waters under the firmament, and the waters above the firmament. What is distinct about this day is neither the existence of the cloud cover nor the existence of the waters that covered the earth; these existed before. The new element is the appearance of the firmament or atmosphere, what we would call the sky. This separated the two waters that before were close together. Interestingly, current scientific thought also views the development of the atmosphere and oceans as a fairly recent event in earth's history.[1]

The third day. This day marks the separation of the great land masses from the oceans and the appearance of vegetation on the land. Presumably the land appeared as the result of volcanic eruptions and the buckling of the earth's crust. Psalm 104:6–9 describes this appearance: "You covered it [the earth] with the deep as with a garment; the waters stood above the mountains. But at your rebuke the waters fled, at the sound of your thunder they took to flight; they flowed over the mountains, they went down into the valleys, to the place you assigned for them. You set a boundary they cannot cross; never again will they

---

[1]See P. Brancazio and A. G. W. Cameron, *The Origin and Evolution of Atmospheres and Oceans* (New York: John Wiley and Sons, 1964). Cited by Young, *Creation and the Flood*, p. 124.

cover the earth." These verses suggest that the land appeared gradually as it was drained of its covering.

Mention of the plants, particularly "seed-bearing plants and trees," creates some problems with the science of paleobotany. So far as we know, only very simple plants existed early— namely, seaweed, algae and bacteria— and these are associated with the oceans rather than the land. More complex plants appeared later. The seed-bearing plants mentioned in Genesis are found first in the Devonian period (about 400 million years ago). The first trees appear in the Pennsylvania period (i.e., about 320 million years ago). Again, the Genesis account seems to say that plants appeared before animals, but the fossil record shows that these appeared simultaneously. What can be done with these difficulties? It may be impossible at this stage to give a definitive answer, but two things may be noted. First, the creative acts compressed into Genesis 1:11 did not necessarily take place all at one time. They could have taken place over a fairly long period in which grasses could have come first, followed by herbs, followed by fruit trees. Second, most of the geological record is derived from marine rocks. Therefore, it does not necessarily give an accurate picture of what may or may not have existed on land. One does not really expect to find fossils of large land plants in such beds. As time goes on there may well be additional light on this particular period of the earth's development.

The fourth day. Light had been reaching earth since the first day of creation; it was through its influence that the vegetation created on day three was enabled to appear and prosper. But now the skies cleared sufficiently for the heavenly bodies to become visible. It is not said that these were created on the fourth day; they were created in the initial creative work of God referred to in Genesis 1:1. But now they begin to function as regulators of the day and night, "as signs to mark seasons and days and years" (Gen. 1:14).

The fifth day. On the fifth day God began to create living creatures. The word "create" *(bara)* is used here for the first time since verse 1, probably indicating a *de novo* act of God, unrelated to what had been done previously. Earlier God is said to have "separated," "made," and "formed" various things. The land itself is said to have "produced" vegetation. Not so with the birds and sea creatures! These were created by God and now began to fill the earth that had been prepared to receive them.

On this day too we have problems with the fossil record, as Young and others recognize. But these are not overwhelming. Young writes, "The fact that many marine invertebrate animals such as corals and trilobites appear in the fossil record prior to land plants implies a contradiction between Genesis and geology. We must, however, keep in mind the incompleteness of the plant record and our lack of knowledge as to the exact limits of the categories described in verses 20–22. It is important to point out that the major groups in view here, that is, birds, most fish, swimming reptiles such as crocodiles or the extinct mosasaurs, flying reptiles like pterodactyls, seals and whales, do appear later in the fossil record than most land plants. As a generality such is the case. Birds first appear in the Jurassic period, fish are well-developed from Ordovician onwards but proliferate in the Tertiary, complex marine and aerial reptiles are Mesozoic, and large swimming mammals are Tertiary."[2]

Young, as most other progressive creationists, allows for some overlap of the creative days.

---

[2]*Creation and the Flood,* p. 130.

The sixth day. One of the best arguments for the days of Genesis 1 being periods of long duration is the amount of creative activity recorded as having taken place on day six. God created land animals, divided into three general categories: livestock (that is, animals capable of being domesticated), creatures that move along the ground (the reference is to animals such as squirrels, chipmunks and woodchucks, and may include reptiles) and wild animals (that is, those that could not be domesticated). Many categories of each are involved because each is said to reproduce according to "their kinds" (plural). On this day God also created man, last but at the peak of the created order. Since God is said to have created each of these three categories of animals and man independently and after certain specific kinds, the possibility of general evolution seems to be discounted. Still there is no reason to rule out some kinds of development within species (microevolution), such as the alleged development of the horse. The language of the verses suggests a pause between the making of animals and the creation of man, and there may have been other pauses also.

The progressive creationists' view of God's creation is tentative, for not all scientific evidence is in and even the narrative of Genesis may not be understood as well as we shall understand it some day. But in general terms this is what the progressive viewpoint holds. Its adherents regard it as a reasonable harmony between the Genesis record and the facts of geology and other scientific disciplines.

WHAT ARE THE PROBLEMS?

Some of the problems with this view have already been suggested. The most obvious are the apparent discrepancies between the fossil record and the order in which plants, fish, and land animals

are said to have been created in Genesis. This is serious. On the other hand, it is not of such weight as to immediately disqualify the theory. Science assumes that life first appeared in the oceans or other watery places, but it does not know this and it is possible that life may have appeared on land before it appeared in the water. Moreover, if one discounts the earliest forms of life, such as algae, bacteria, and seaweed, which mean a great deal to botanists but are probably not in view in Genesis at all, the order of the appearance of life in Genesis and in the fossil record is quite similar.

Second, there is the linguistic problem of taking the days of Genesis as long periods, which the six-day creationists regard as impossible. This has already been discussed in presenting the creationists' view. Here we may simply note that there are at least two sides to the argument. On the surface it would be natural to take the word "day" in Genesis 1 as referring to a literal twenty-four-hour day. But even this is not without question, for the account clearly indicates that God did not establish the sun and other heavenly bodies for the regulating of "seasons and days and years" until day four. Augustine noted this 1500 years ago, and so have others. James Orr wrote, "It is at least as difficult to suppose that only ordinary days of twenty-four hours are intended, in view of the writer's express statement that such days did not commence till the fourth stage of creation, as to believe that they are symbols."[3] There are other places even in Moses' writings where "day" clearly means "period" (cf. Gen. 2:4; Ps. 90:4).

The third and, in my judgment, most serious objection to the progressive creation theory is that it introduces death into the world before the fall (or even the creation) of Adam. If death was

---

[3]*Christian View*, p. 421.

the punishment for sin, as the Bible seems to indicate, and if this punishment was imposed upon the whole world (including the animals) as the result of Adam's sin, then there could not have been death in the world before Adam, and the fossil record must be post-Adamic, as the Flood geologists state. Morris puts it tersely: "The day-age theory . . . accepts as real the existence of death before sin, in direct contradiction to the Biblical teaching that death is a divine judgment on man's dominion because of man's sin (Rom. 5:12). Thus it assumes that suffering and death comprise an integral part of God's work of creating and preparing the world for man; and this in effect pictures God as a sadistic ogre, not as the Biblical God of grace and love."[4]

The objection is serious, but these points must be considered:

1. The actual curse of God as the result of man's sin, recorded in Genesis 3, says nothing about the animals. It is a curse on four things only: the man, the woman, the serpent, and the ground for the man's sake. Nowhere is it said that the earth or universe underwent a drastic transformation, nor even that the serpent, though an animal, was to die in punishment for its part in the temptation. Its curse was only to crawl on its belly and thus be cursed "above all the livestock and all the wild animals" (Gen. 3:14).

2. The curse on Adam and Eve did not involve physical death only, though that was horrible enough in that they were created for communion with God who is eternal; it involved spiritual death. But this does not really pertain to the animal realm in that animals do not have God-consciousness in the first place. It is conceivable that animals could be created to enjoy a normal life span and then to die without this having any of the judgmental qualities death has for man.

3. The texts often cited from the New Testament in support of the view that death came to the animal world as a result of man's sin do not prove the point. Romans 8:19–21 does not contrast the present imperfection of the world with a more glorious past state but with the future state when it shall be delivered from its "bondage to decay" along with the final redemption of God's children. Similarly, Romans 5:12, though it speaks of the introduction of death into the world through Adam's sin, does not necessarily speak of the infliction of this penalty on any creature other than man.

4. It is hard to imagine a world of living things in which death does not occur in some form, if only because living things live by eating other living things. Even assuming that the carnivores were herbivores before Adam's fall, these still had to eat plants which thereby died. Did birds not eat insects? Did fish not eat other fish? We can imagine that the birds all ate berries; but even if the fish ate plankton, the plankton died.

In view of these points, progressive creationists would argue that death did indeed exist in the world before Adam —otherwise, how would he know what the threat of death meant ("You must not eat from the tree of the knowledge of good and evil, for when you eat of it you will surely die"). But it did not have the horror for the animals that it had for Adam and has for us today. Young writes, "The most that can be said with certainty about the effect of the fall on geological phenomena is that it introduced death and suffering into the human race for the first time. . . . It cannot be proved from the Scripture that the curse resulted in anything other than pain, sorrow, agonizing labor, and death for man and degradation for the serpent. Ideas about structural changes in the animals, death among animals, and drastic transformations in the laws

---

[4]*The Genesis Record,* p. 54.

of nature such as the laws of thermodynamics must from a Scriptural perspective forever remain pure speculations."[5]

A FRAMEWORK

We have come to an end of our examination of the various main views of creation, and it may seem that nearly everything is yet undecided. For many it may be; nearly anyone—anyone who can see the difficulties, whatever view he or she holds—will face problems. Still it is not true that everything is undecided. We have not settled everything, but we have established a framework in which our thinking about creation may go forward.

First, we have dismissed atheistic evolution and have come close to dismissing theistic evolution as well. This means that the world of man and things did not come about by chance happenings over long periods of evolutionary history but as the result of God's direct creative activity.

Second, we have suggested that any view that makes the earth a relatively new thing (on the order of 12,000 to 20,000 years old) flies in the face of too much varied and independent evidence to be tenable. Some would dispute this, of course. But in my judgment the earth and universe are indeed billions of years old.

Third, we have shown the possibility of God's having formed the earth and its life in a series of creative days representing long periods. In view of the apparent age of the earth, this is not only possible—it is probable. Nothing is to be gained by insisting that God had to create all things in six literal twenty-four-hour days.

This does not mean, however, that everything said by evolutionists about the many millions of years in which the earth and its life are supposed to have formed is factual. The periods involved may be considerably shorter than current evolution and geologic theory, since the main reason for insisting on such interminable ages is to give the amount of time supposed to be necessary for life to emerge through chance occurrences. In particular, there is no need to argue for the great antiquity of man. Man may be relatively recent, though how recent is unclear. (The fossil evidence for man's antiquity will be considered when the creation of man himself is discussed in chapter 11.)

Finally, we can make these "spiritual" applications. We have discussed the theory of evolution in which everything we know is supposed to have evolved by mere chance. We have rejected evolution. But there is a sense in which those who know God are enabled to evolve increasingly into that image of what He would have us be, and we rejoice in that. Again, we have discussed the gap theory. We have seen that there may be gaps in what is told us in the historical sections of Genesis; there may be gaps in our knowledge. But there are no gaps in the wisdom, knowledge or love of God, and in this we rejoice. We have discussed the twenty-four-hour-day theory. We have seen evidence for and against that option. But whether the days of Genesis are twenty-four hours long or much longer, all time is God's time and is used by Him. Our days are also God's days. Last, we considered progressive creationism. It may be close to the true picture. But we need to remember that there is never any true or lasting progress that is not God's doing and that where God works there is always progress. Let us ask Him to make progress with us as we strive to grow in the knowledge of His will and ways.

---

[5]*Creation and the Flood*, p. 168.

10

The First Five Days

(Genesis 1:3–23)

And God said, "Let there be light," and there was light. God saw that the light was good, and he separated the light from the darkness. God called the light "day" and the darkness he called "night." And there was evening, and there was morning—the first day.

And God said, "Let there be an expanse between the waters to separate water from water." So God made the expanse and separated the water under the expanse from the water above it. And it was so. God called the expanse "sky." And there was evening, and there was morning—the second day.

And God said, "Let the water under the sky be gathered to one place, and let dry ground appear." And it was so. God called the dry ground "land," and the gathered waters he called "seas." And God saw that it was good.

Then God said, "Let the land produce vegetation: seed-bearing plants and trees on the land that bear fruit with seed in it, according to their various kinds." And it was so. The land produced vegetation: plants bearing seed according to their kinds and trees bearing fruit with seed in it according to their kinds. And God saw that it was good. And there was evening, and there was morning—the third day.

And God said, "Let there be lights in the expanse of the sky to separate the day from the night, and let them serve as signs to mark seasons and days and years, and let them be lights in the expanse of the sky to give light on the earth." And it was so. God made two great lights—the greater light to govern the day and the lesser light to govern the night. He also made the stars. God set them in the expanse of the sky to give light on the earth, to govern the day and the night, and to separate light from darkness. And God saw that it was good. And there was evening, and there was morning—the fourth day.

And God said, "Let the water teem with living creatures, and let birds fly above the earth across the expanse of the sky." So God created the great creatures of the sea and every living and moving thing with which the water teems, according to their kinds, and every winged bird according to its kind. And God saw that it was good. God blessed them and said, "Be fruitful and increase in number and fill the water in the seas, and let the birds increase on the earth." And there was evening, and there was morning—the fifth day.

Creation is one form of God's self-revelation and therefore a means by which we may come to know Him. But, as Calvin points out in the introduction to his commentary on Genesis, our eyes are not "sufficiently clear-sighted to discern what the fabric of heaven and earth represents," and therefore we need the Scriptures to view creation rightly. "If the mute instruction of the heaven and the earth were sufficient, the teaching of Moses would have been superfluous."[1]

---

[1]John Calvin, *Commentaries on the First Book of Moses Called Genesis*, trans. by John King (Grand Rapids: Eerdmans, 1948), p. 62.

Having looked at the creation account through the various modern systems of interpretation, we therefore now turn to the account for the emphasis God Himself puts on His creative activity.

There are three main teachings. First, God Himself—the true, sovereign, wise and personal God—stands behind creation. Second, the work of this true, sovereign, wise, and personal God was an orderly work. Third, the creation was and is good, because it is the work of the God who is not only true, sovereign, wise, and personal but also morally perfect. Each of these points has implications for the way we are to relate both to God and His creation.

In the Beginning

The most obvious point is that God stands at the beginning of all things and is the One through whom all came into existence. We have noticed this in studying the first sentence of the chapter. When the Bible begins by stating "In the beginning God created the heavens and the earth," it is evident that we are directed first and primarily to the God who stands behind everything.

We also have this emphasis in the account of the first five days. Grammatically speaking, there is only one subject in all these verses: God Himself. Everything else is object. Objects are acted upon. Light, air, water, dry land, vegetation, sun, moon, stars, fish, birds, land animals—all are objects in a creative process where God alone is subject. In these verses we are told that God "saw" (vv. 4, 10, 12, 18, 21, 25), "separated" (vv. 4, 7), "called" (vv. 5, 8, 10), "made" (vv. 7, 16, 25), "set" (v. 17), "created" (vv. 21, 27), and explained to the man and woman what He had done (vv. 28–30). Moreover, before that, God spoke (vv. 3, 6, 9, 14, 20), as a result of which everything else unfolded.

We should note a number of things. First, in the Hebrew of this chapter the name for God is *Elohim*. This is a plural word. It is used as if it were singular—that is, with singular verbs and (usually) with singular pronouns referring back to it—to indicate that there is but one God only. But the fact that it is plural also suggests that there are *plural dimensions to God's being*. We must acknowledge that this in itself does not teach the doctrine of the Trinity. There is such a thing as a plural of greatness in the Hebrew language. Nevertheless, on the basis of the later revelation, particularly in the New Testament, we are right in seeing a preparation for that fuller revelation here. In John 1 we have a reference to the start of Genesis which goes: "In the beginning was the Word, and the Word was with God, and the Word was God. He was with God in the beginning" (vv. 1, 2). The Word is Jesus, as verse 14 shows. So John is saying that Jesus was with the Father and was acting with Him in the original work of creation. Later John says specifically, "Through him all things were made; without him nothing was made that has been made" (John 1:3).

In Genesis 1:26 we find God saying, "Let us make man in *our* image, in *our* likeness"—one of the places where a singular pronoun does not occur. In Genesis 3:22 we find, "The man has now become like one of *us*, knowing good and evil."

This is all very significant, because, when we recognize that the members of the Trinity are here at the beginning of creation, having existed before anything else, then the elements that we associate with the Trinity—love, personality, and communication—are seen to be eternal and to have eternal value. This is the biblical answer to man's fear of being lost in an impersonal and loveless universe.

The second thing we note about these first biblical statements concerning God is that God brought the universe into existence by speaking ("And God said"). This shows the importance of verbal or propositional revelation. There has been a tendency in some contemporary theological circles to deny the importance of words on the basis that what is really important are acts, particularly the acts of God in history. This has implications for one's assessment of the Bible, for in such a scheme the very words of the Bible lose importance and the Bible becomes only a more or less accurate pointer to what God has done historically. It has implications for the Christian life, because the emphasis falls on what God is doing rather than on what God has commanded. It even has implications for an understanding of history, for God is seen to be present wherever things are happening regardless of whether this accords with His written record of His nature and ways.

The creation account is a warning against this unbiblical and ultimately destructive approach. It is true that there can be a type of preoccupation with words that keeps one from actually coming to grips with the God who spoke them. But this is a far less common error in our day than cutting one's self free from the written revelation. Which came first, the word or the deed? Many today say, "Deed." But this is a distortion, as Genesis shows. God's acts are of great importance. The creation account is full of them. But it is wrong to say that the deed comes first. Rather, the word comes first, followed by the deed, followed by a further revelation in words to interpret the deed spiritually. This means that a hearty emphasis on the word of God is both biblical and mandatory, if one is to appreciate the acts of God prophesied, recorded, and interpreted in the Scriptures.

The third thing about this emphasis on God's being behind creation is that when we are pleased with creation, as we should be, our *praise should be directed to God,* who made all things, and not to creation itself. This is the first great dividing point between the religion of the Bible and most pagan religions. Pagans worship the object, sometimes the "spirit" or "god" perceived to be in or identical with the object. But the Christian looks beyond the object to the God who made it and praises Him. This gives him an understanding of the object that the pagan, for all his devotion to things, does not have. The Christian understands why the object is there, why it has the form it has and (to some extent) what his responsibility toward it is. He is delivered from fear or excessive veneration of the object, on the one hand, and an unmerited scorn or disregard of it, on the other.

Can we not say also that God is to be praised as Creator even before He is praised as Redeemer? We see this in an interesting sequence of those hymns of praise recorded in the fourth and fifth chapters of Revelation. The fifth chapter contains three hymns of praise to Christ for His work of redemption. But there is also the great hymn of chapter 4:

> You are worthy, our Lord and God,
>> to receive glory and honor and power,
> for you created all things,
>> and by your will they were created
>> and have their being.

In this hymn God is praised as Creator. It is significant that even before that, in verse 8, He is praised simply for being:

> Holy, holy, holy,
>> is the Lord God Almighty,
> who was, and is, and is to come.

As Francis Schaeffer says, "Our praise to God is not first of all in the area of soteriology. If we are being fully scriptural, we do not praise him first because he saved us, but because he is there and has always been there. And we praise him because he willed all other things, including man, into existence."[2]

When Schaeffer says that "God willed all things, *including man,* into exist-

[2]Schaeffer, *Genesis in Space and Time,* p. 27.

ence," he introduces the fourth thing that should be especially noted about God's being behind all creation: we are part of that creation, have been made by God, and therefore owe Him our total and *unfeigned obedience and devotion*. As Calvin says, "After the world had been created, man was placed in it as in a theatre, that he, beholding above him and beneath the wonderful works of God, might reverently adore their Author." Moreover, "all things were ordained for the use of man, that he, being under deeper obligation, might devote and dedicate himself entirely to obedience towards God."[3] We have not done this, of course. We have rebelled against God and are therefore in need of a redeemer. But having been redeemed and having been given a new nature according to which we have now become "new creatures" in Christ, we are enabled to worship and serve God properly.

AN ORDERLY UNFOLDING

God's standing behind all things is not the only point of the creation account. These verses also teach that creation was according to an orderly unfolding of the mind and purposes of God. That is, it was a step-by-step progression marked by a sequence of six significant days.

We have already seen that the length of time covered by these days may be an open question. Creationists insist that the days cover a literal twenty-four hours, but this is not necessarily the case. Sometimes the word "day" is used with broader meaning, even by Moses. It can mean a period of indefinite duration. The evidence of geology suggests to most people that the periods corresponding to the days of Genesis were long. However, questions like these, while interesting and necessary, obscure the equally valid and even more

valuable point that creation, however long it took, was a deliberate and orderly unfolding of God's purposes. God is a God of order, not chaos. He is a God of purpose, not chance. It follows that we should also be creatures of order and purpose. Instead of attempting to tear down, as Satan does, we should attempt to build up according to the pattern God gives in Scripture.

A MORAL PRONOUNCEMENT

There is a third point to the Genesis account of creation: God's moral pronouncement on what He has done. It appears in the repeated phrase "and God saw that it was good" (vv. 10, 12, 18, 21, 25; cf. vv. 3, 31). This pronouncement is not made because we can point to an object and say pragmatically, "That thing is useful to me and is therefore good to me." God's pronouncement on the goodness of creation came even before we were made. The pronouncement is made because the object is good in itself. As Schaeffer says, this means that a tree is not good only because we can cut it down and make a house of it or because we can burn it in order to get heat. It is good because God made it and has pronounced it good. It is good because, like everything else in creation, it conforms to God's nature.

Schaeffer writes of this divine benediction: "This is not a relative judgment, but a judgment of the holy God who has a character and whose character is the law of the universe. His conclusion: Every step and every sphere of creation, and the whole thing put together—man himself and his total environment, the heavens and the earth—conforms to myself."[4]

It is not only in its pristine state, that is, before the fall of man, that the earth and its contents are pronounced good. The initial blessing of God recorded in

---

[3]Calvin, *Commentaries on the First Book of Moses Called Genesis*, pp. 64, 65.
[4]Schaeffer, *Genesis in Time and Space*, p. 55.

Genesis 1 is repeated later even after the Fall. For example, it is repeated in God's covenant with the human race given at the time of Noah. In that unilateral covenant God says, "I now establish my covenant with you and with your descendants after you and with every living creature that was with you—the birds, the livestock and all the wild animals, all those that came out of the ark with you—every living creature on earth. . . . I have set my rainbow in the clouds, and it will be the sign of the covenant between me and the earth" (Gen. 9:9, 10, 13). Here God's concern is expressed, not just for Noah and those of his family who were delivered with him, but for the birds and cattle and even the earth itself. Similarly, in Romans 8 there is an expression of the value of creation in that God includes it in His promise of that future deliverance for which it as well as the race of men and women wait: "The creation itself will be liberated from its bondage to decay and brought into the glorious freedom of the children of God" (v. 21).

The value of creation, declared good by God, brings us to a natural conclusion: If God finds the universe good in its parts and as a whole, then we must find it good also. This does not mean that we will refuse to see that nature has been marred by sin. Indeed, the verses from Genesis 9 and Romans 8 are inexplicable apart from the realization that nature has suffered in some way as a result of man's fall. It is marred by thorns, weeds, disease. But even in its marred state it has value, just as fallen man also has value.

First, we should be *thankful* for the world God has made and praise Him for it. In some expressions of Christian thought only the soul has value. But this is not right, nor is it truly Christian. Actually, the elevation of the value of the soul and the debasement of the body and other material things is a Greek and therefore pagan idea based on a false understanding of creation. If God had made the soul (or spirit) alone and if the material world had come from some lesser or even evil source, this would be right. But the Christian view is that God has made all that is and that it therefore has value and should be valued by us because of this origin.

Second, we should *delight* in creation. This is closely related to being thankful but is a step beyond it. It is a step that many Christians have never taken. Frequently Christians look on nature only as one of the classic proofs of God's existence. But instead of this, the Christian should really enjoy what he sees. He should appreciate its beauty. He should exult in creation even more than the non-Christian, because in the Christian's case there is a corresponding knowledge of the God who stands behind it.

Third, we should demonstrate a *responsibility* toward nature, meaning that we should not destroy it simply for the sake of destroying it but rather should seek to elevate it to its fullest potential. There is a parallel here between the responsibility of men and women toward the creation and the responsibility of a husband toward his wife in marriage. In each case the responsibility is based on a God-given dominion (though the two are not identical). Of marriage it is said, "Husbands, love your wives, just as Christ loved the church and gave himself up for her to make her holy, cleansing her by the washing with water through the word, and to present her to himself as a radiant church, without stain or wrinkle or any other blemish, but holy and blameless" (Eph. 5:25–27). In the same way, men and women together should seek to sanctify and cleanse the earth in order that it might be more as God created it, in anticipation of its ultimate redemption. This does not mean that the universe cannot be used by man in a proper way. A tree can still be cut down to make wood for a home.

But it will not be cut down simply for the pleasure of cutting it down or because it is the easiest way to increase the value of the ground. In such areas there must be a careful thinking through of the value and purpose of the object, and there must be a Christian rather than a purely utilitarian approach to it.

Finally, after he has contemplated nature and has come to value it, the Christian should turn once again to the God who made it and sustains it moment by moment and should learn to *trust* Him. God cares for nature, in spite of its abuse through man's sin. But if He cares for nature, then He also obviously cares for us and may be trusted to do so. This argument occurs in the midst of Christ's Sermon on the Mount in which He draws our attention to God's care of the birds (animal life) and lilies (plant life) and then asks, "Are you not much more valuable than they? . . . If . . . God clothes the grass of the field, which is here today and tomorrow is thrown into the fire, will he not much more clothe you, O you of little faith?" (Matt. 6:26, 30).[5]

---

[5]Parts of this chapter are drawn from a section of Boice, *The Sovereign God*, pp. 205–15.

11

The Sixth Day

(Genesis 1:24–27)

And God said, "Let the land produce living creatures according to their kinds: live-stock, creatures that move along the ground; and wild animals, each according to its kind." And it was so. God made the wild animals according to their kinds, the livestock according to their kinds, and all the creatures that move along the ground according to their kinds. And God saw that it was good.

Then God said, "Let us make man in our image, in our likeness, and let them rule over the fish of the sea and the birds of the air, over the livestock, over all the earth, and over all the creatures that move along the ground."

So God created man in his own image,
in the image of God he created him;
male and female he created them.

In our study of the days of creation I have set the sixth day off from the other five, because man is created on the sixth day and there is something special about his creation. He is the peak of creation. Moreover, from this point on the story of Genesis is the story of man—in rebellion against God but also as the object of His special love and redemption.

To say that man is the most important part of creation might be thought a chauvinistic statement, as though we might as easily say, if we were fish, that fish are most important. But this is not true. Men and women actually are higher than the forms of creation around them. They rule over creation, for one thing—not by mere force of strength, for many animals are stronger, but by the power of their minds and personalities. Men and women also have "God-consciousness," which the animals do not have. No animal is guilty of moral or spiritual sin. Nor do animals con-sciously "glorify God, and enjoy him forever." The Bible stresses man's high position when it says toward the end of the creation account: "Then God said,

'Let us make man in our image, in our likeness, and let them rule over the fish of the sea and the birds of the air, over the livestock, over all the earth, and over all the creatures that move along the ground.' So God created man in his own image, in the image of God he created him; male and female he created them" (vv. 26, 27).

In these verses the uniqueness of man and his superiority to the rest of creation are expressed in three ways. First, he is said to have been made "in God's image." This is not said of either objects or animals. Second, he is given domin-ion over the fish, birds, animals, and even the earth itself. Third, there is a repetition of the word "created." This word is used at only three points in the creation narrative: first, when God created matter from nothing (v. 1); sec-ond, when God created conscious life (v. 21); and third, when God created man (v. 27). This is a progression, from the body (matter) to soul (personality) to spirit (life with God-consciousness). Lest we should miss this, the word "create" is repeated three times over in reference to the man and woman. As Francis Schaeffer writes, "It is as though God put exclamation points here to indicate that there is something special about the creation of man."[1]

How Old Is Man?

How old is man? This is a troublesome question, because there seems to be a conflict between the account in Genesis and the apparent evidence of science on this point. The various biblical genealogies (Gen. 5 is the earliest example) suggest that man is on the order of thousands—perhaps ten or twenty thousands—of years old. But anthropologists speak of man or manlike creatures being on the order of three and a half to four million years old. The work of the Leakey family in Kenya and Tanzania provides the best-known examples.

What are we to say of this conflict? It may be impossible to resolve it finally at this stage of our knowledge, but the issues can be put in proportion. First, we must say that this seems to be a real conflict and not merely a case in which we are dealing with two different ways of looking at the same evidence. It has been pointed out by biblical scholars, among them no less a scholar than Princeton's B. B. Warfield,[2] that the biblical genealogies are not necessarily all-inclusive when they list a series of descendants. That is to say, they may (and in fact do) leave gaps, so that a person identified as a "son" of the person coming before him in the list need not necessarily be a literal son but may be a grandson or great-grandson. Moreover, the gaps may sometimes be quite large, as for example, the summation of the genealogy of Jesus Christ occurring in Matthew 1:1 ("the genealogy of Jesus Christ the son of David, the son of Abraham"). Because of this, it is pos-

sible, even probable, that the genealogies of Genesis, which suggest a creation of Adam in a time scale of approximately 4,000 years before Christ (Bishop Ussher's date was 4004 B.C.), are actually summations of much longer periods. Still, even if we multiply the figure of 4,000 years three, four, or even five times, we are far from what most anthropologists are claiming. An origin of the race on the order of 12,000 to 20,000 years ago is very different from an origin three and a half to four million years ago.

It helps to put the fossil evidence in perspective, however, for not all fossils claimed to be human are necessarily so. Skeletal materials found at sites from historical times are essentially the same as those of modern man, called *Homo sapiens* ("thinking" or "discerning man"). But as one goes back beyond historical times there are increasing differences. Cro-Magnon man, who is prehistoric and whose remains have been found scattered widely throughout western Europe, was similar to people who exist today. He used bone and stone tools and made cave paintings of animals and other features of his world. Slightly farther back (on the order of 100,000 years) is the so-called Neanderthal man. He also used tools and buried his dead. But he was less human in appearance, having a receding forehead and a pronounced jaw. He seems to have been more apelike. Remains of this "man" were found in Europe, Israel, Zambia, and Rhodesia. Still farther back are a number of other essentially "modern" types found in France, Germany, and England, dating from perhaps 250,000 years ago, according to the most accepted calculations.

The so-called Peking man and Java man date from between 500,000 to 1,000,000 years ago. Sometimes crude tools have been found with these skele-

---

[1]*Genesis in Space and Time,* p. 33.

[2]"On the Antiquity and the Unity of the Human Race," *Biblical and Theological Studies,* edited by Samuel G. Craig (Philadelphia: Presbyterian and Reformed Publishing Company, 1968), pp. 238–61.

tons, but the chief reason for their being regarded as humans is that they apparently walked upright, hence are designated *Homo erectus*. Most anthropologists would call *Homo erectus* the first truly modern man. The discoveries of Richard and Mary Leakey in Africa, while frequently referred to as evidences of ancient men in the secular press, are at best pre-human creatures, even by the Leakeys' own judgments. They apparently walked upright, but they were quite small—about four feet in height—and had a brain capacity of about one-third that of modern man. The general impression one has of the skulls is that they represent extinct apelike rather than manlike forms.[3]

One other perspective needs to be thrown on this problem: the uncertainty in dating these apparently ancient human ancestors. One case is particularly worth noting. In the Paluxy River basin in central Texas, near the town of Glen Rose, fossilized tracks of men and dinosaurs apparently appear together.[4] This does not mean that either men or dinosaurs are of relatively recent history. Both may be quite ancient. But it does mean that something is wrong with the currently accepted time framework proposed by evolutionists, for according to that framework there should be a sixty-million-year gap between the last of the dinosaurs and man. Clearly, there may yet be great revisions in what anthropologists and other scientists are proposing.

In the interim what may Christians, who hold to the truthfulness of Genesis and who still want to be honest where scientific data is concerned, conclude? One scientist, Robert A. Erb of Valley Forge, Pennsylvania, concludes that fossil "man" is not necessarily man and that Christians do themselves a disservice when they regard all such as Adam's descendants. He writes, "I believe in a historical Adam and would tend to date him near the beginning of the Neolithic (new stone) age in the Near East (about 8,000 B.C.). Indeed, this step in the creative work of God may be the cause of what is known as the Neolithic Revolution, with the domestication of plants and animals, the building of cities, the invention of pottery, the beginnings of writing and such things. That Adam does not belong to the Upper Paleolithic age of 30,000 years ago is suggested by: the domestication of plants and animals in the account of Cain and Abel (Gen. 4:2) and Cain building a city (Gen. 4:17). In about six generations (neglecting the probable gaps in genealogy), Tubal-cain was working with metals (Gen. 4:22) and Jubal was making music (Gen. 4:21)."[5]

The conclusion is that, while the earth and universe may indeed be quite old (on the order of billions of years), there is no need to insist that man is millions of years old. His creation by God may be as recent as the genealogies of Genesis seem to indicate.

IN GOD'S IMAGE

When Genesis 1 speaks of the creation of man, as it does several times over, it is not concerned with the time at which he was created. What concerns the author of Genesis is man's being created "in God's image." This is repeated several times: "Then God said, 'Let us make man *in our image, in our likeness. . . .*' So God created man *in his own image, in the image of God* he created him." What does this mean? What does it mean to be made in God's image?

One thing it means is that men and

---

[3]See Young, pp. 146–51, for a summation of the fossil evidence.

[4]John D. Morris, "The Paluxy River Tracks," *Impact Series*, No. 35, May, 1976. A Publication of the Institute for Creation Research.

[5]Robert A. Erb, unpublished paper on "Miscellaneous Thoughts on Science and the Early Chapters of Genesis," p. 3.

women possess the attributes of personality, as God Himself does, but as the animals, plants, and matter do not. To have personality one must possess knowledge, feelings (including religious feelings), and a will. This God has, and so do we. We can say that animals possess a certain kind of personality. But an animal does not reason as men do; it only reacts to certain problems or stimuli. It does not create; it only conforms to certain behavior patterns, even in as elaborate a pattern as constructing a nest, hive, or dam. It does not love; it only reproduces. It does not worship. Personality, in the sense we are speaking of it here, is something that links man to God but does not link either man or God to the rest of creation.

A second element that is involved in man's being created in the image of God is morality. This includes the two further elements of freedom and responsibility. To be sure, the freedom men and women possess is not absolute. Even in the beginning the first man, Adam, and the first woman, Eve, were not autonomous. They were creatures and were responsible for acknowledging this by their obedience in the matter of the tree of the knowledge of good and evil. Since the Fall that freedom has been further restricted so that, as Augustine said, the original *posse non peccare* ("able not to sin") has become a *non posse non peccare* ("not able not to sin"). Still there is a limited freedom for men and women even in their fallen state, and with that there is also moral responsibility. In brief, we do not need to sin as we do or as often as we do. And even when we sin under compulsion (as may sometimes be the case), we still know it is wrong and, thus, inadvertently confess our likeness to God in this as in other areas.

It is relevant to the matter of morality that, when the sanctification of the believer is spoken of as being "renewed in knowledge in the image of its creator"

(Col. 3:10) or "conformed to the likeness of his Son" (Rom. 8:29), it is the moral righteousness of the individual that is most in view, though of course this may also refer to the perfection of personality in ways we do not as yet understand fully.

The third element involved in man's being made in God's image is spirituality, meaning that man is made for communion with God, who is Spirit (John 4:24), and that this communion is intended to be eternal as God is eternal. Although man shares a body with such forms of life as plants or flowers and a soul with animals, only he possesses a spirit. It is on the level of the spirit that he is aware of God and communes with Him.

Here lies our true worth. We are made in God's image and are therefore valuable to God and others. God loves men and women, as He does not and cannot love the animals, plants, or inanimate matter. Moreover, He feels for them, identifies with them in Christ, grieves for them, and even intervenes in history to make individual men and women into all that He has determined they should be. We get some idea of the special nature of this relationship when we remember that in a similar way the woman, Eve, was made in the image of man. Therefore, though different, Adam saw himself in her and loved her as his companion and corresponding member in the universe. It is not wrong to say that men and women are to God somewhat as the woman is to the man. They are God's unique and valued companions. In support of this we need only think of the Bible's teaching concerning Christ as the bridegroom and the church as his bride.

A Shattered Image

In this chapter we have been looking at man as God made him and intends him to be, that is, before the Fall or as he will eventually become again in Christ.

Although man was made in the image of God, this image has been greatly marred by sin. There are vestiges of the image remaining, but man today is not what God intended. He is a fallen being, and the effects of the Fall are seen on each level of his being: in his body, soul, and spirit.

When God gave man the test of the forbidden tree, which was to be a measure of his obedience and responsibility toward the One who had created him, God said, "You are free to eat from any tree in the garden; but you must not eat from the tree of the knowledge of good and evil, for when you eat of it you will surely die" (Gen. 2:16, 17). The woman was beguiled by the serpent and ate. She came to Adam; and Adam, who was not beguiled, nevertheless ate of it too, thereby saying to God, "I do not care for all the trees that You have given me; so long as this tree stands here in the midst of the garden it reminds me of my dependence on You, and therefore I hate it; I will eat of it, regardless of the consequences, and die."

Man's spirit, that part of him that had communion with God, died instantly. This is clear from the fact that he ran from God when God came to him in the garden. Men and women have been running and hiding ever since. His soul, the seat of his intellect, feelings, and identity, began to die. So people began to lose a sense of who they are, gave vent to bad feelings and suffered the decay of their intellect. This is the type of decay described by Paul in Romans 1 where we are told that, having rejected God, men inevitably "became futile [in their thinking] and their foolish hearts were darkened. Although they claimed to be wise, they became fools and exchanged the glory of the immortal God for images made to look like mortal man and birds and animals and reptiles" (vv. 21–23). Eventually even the body died. So it is said of us, "Dust you are and to dust you will return" (Gen. 3:19).

Donald Grey Barnhouse has pictured what happened as a three-story house that was bombed in wartime. The bomb had destroyed the top floor entirely, the debri of which had fallen down into the second floor severely damaging it. The weight of the two ruined floors produced cracks in the walls of the first floor so that it was doomed to collapse eventually. Thus it was with Adam. His body was the dwelling of the soul, and his spirit was above that. When he fell the spirit was entirely destroyed, the soul ruined, and the body destined to a final collapse.[6]

However, the glory of the gospel is seen at precisely this point, for when God saves a person He saves the whole person, beginning with the spirit, continuing with the soul, and finishing with the body. The salvation of the spirit comes first; for God first establishes contact with the one who has rebelled against Him. This is regeneration, the new birth. Second, God works with the soul, renewing it after the image of the perfect man, the Lord Jesus Christ. This work is sanctification. Finally, there is the resurrection in which even the body is redeemed from destruction.

Moreover, God makes a new creation, for He does not merely patch up the old spirit, soul and body, as if the collapsing house were just being buttressed up and given a new coat of paint. God creates a new spirit which is His own Spirit within the individual. He creates a new soul, known as the new man. At last, He creates a new body. This body is like the resurrection body of the Lord Jesus Christ through whom alone we have this salvation.[7]

---

[6]Donald Grey Barnhouse, *Let Me Illustrate* (Westwood, N.J.: Fleming H. Revell, 1967), p. 32; *Teaching the Word of Truth* (Grand Rapids: Eerdmans, 1966), pp. 36, 37.

[7]Parts of this chapter are drawn from a section of Boice, *The Sovereign God*, pp. 193–204.

12

Man, God's Regent

(Genesis 1:28–31)

God blessed them and said to them, "Be fruitful and increase in number; fill the earth and subdue it. Rule over the fish of the sea and the birds of the air and over every living creature that moves on the ground."

Then God said, "I give you every seed-bearing plant on the face of the whole earth and every tree that has fruit with seed in it. They will be yours for food. And to all the beasts of the earth and all the birds of the air and all the creatures that move on the ground—everything that has the breath of life in it—I give every green plant for food." And it was so.

God saw all that he had made, and it was very good. And there was evening, and there was morning—the sixth day.

In looking at the account of the creation of man by God in Genesis 1, we have already seen two points that are emphasized. First, man is created. This is repeated three times in verse 27, obviously for emphasis. Second, man is created in God's image. This is repeated four times in verses 26 and 27. Following this clue to what are the most important ideas, we come next to the teaching that man was to rule over creation as God's regent. This is mentioned twice, in verses 26 and 28.

Who is this who is to rule God's creation? What is he like? What are his gifts? To whom is he responsible?

For the purpose of this study I want to follow the substance of an address given by Dr. John H. Gerstner, retired Professor of Church History at Pittsburgh Theological Seminary, to the Philadelphia Conference on Reformed Theology in 1977. His address considered five things about man as God made him. First, man was *created*, and he still is. Second, man was created *male and*

female, and he still is. Third, man was created *body and soul*, and he still is. Fourth, man was created *dominant over the animals*, and he still is. Fifth, man was created *holy*, and he still is—not.[1]

CREATED BY GOD

We have already seen that man's being created in the image of God involves his having a personality, a sense of morality and spirituality. But in relation to his rule over the animals, to which we have now come, man's creation involves responsibility as well. If man were his own creator, he would be responsible to no one. But he is not his own creator. He is created by God, and this means that he is responsible to God for what he does in every area of his life and particularly for how he carries out the mandate to rule over creation. These verses record God as saying, "Let us make man in our image, in our likeness, and let them rule over the fish of the sea and the birds of the air, over the livestock, over all the earth, and over all the

---

[1]John H. Gerstner, "Man as God Made Him" in *Our Savior God: Studies on Man, Christ and the Atonement,* edited by James M. Boice (Grand Rapids: Baker, 1980), pp. 19–26.

creatures that move along the ground" (v. 26). To man He says, "Be fruitful and increase in number; fill the earth and subdue it. Rule over the fish of the sea and the birds of the air and over every living creature that moves on the ground" (v. 28). Dominion of any kind, but particularly dominion of this scope, implies responsibility.

Today in the western world there is a tendency to deny man's moral responsibility on the basis of some kind of determinism. It usually takes one of two forms. It may be a physical, mechanical determinism ("man is the product of his genes and body chemistry") or it may be a psychological determinism ("man is the product of his environment and of the earlier things that have happened to him"). In either case the individual is excused from responsibility for what he or she does. Thus, we have gone through a period in which criminal behavior was termed a sickness and the criminal was regarded more as a victim of his environment than as the victimizer. (Recently there is a tendency at least to reconsider this matter.) Less blatant but nevertheless morally reprehensible acts are excused with, "I suppose he just couldn't help it."

The biblical view of man could hardly be more different. As Francis Schaeffer correctly notes, "Since God has made man in his own image, man is not caught in the wheels of determinism. Rather man is so great that he can influence history for himself and for others, for this life and the life to come."[2] Man is fallen. But even in his fallen state he is responsible. He can do great things, or he can do things that are terrible.

God created the man and woman and gave them dominion over the created order. Consequently, they were responsible to Him for what they did. When man sins, as the Genesis account goes on to show that he does, it is God who re-

quires a reckoning: "Where are you? . . . Who told you that you were naked? . . . What is this you have done?" (Gen. 3:9, 11, 13). In the thousands of years since Eden many have convinced themselves that they are not responsible. But the testimony of Scripture is that this area of responsibility still stands and that all will one day answer to God at the judgment. "The dead were judged according to what they had done as recorded in the books" (Rev. 20:12).

People are also responsible for their acts toward others. This is the reason for those biblical statements instituting capital punishment as a proper response to murder; for instance, "Whoever sheds the blood of man, by man shall his blood be shed" (Gen. 9:6). These verses are not in the Bible as relics of a more barbarous age or because in the biblical outlook man is not valuable. They are there for precisely the opposite reason: man is too valuable to be wantonly destroyed. Thus, the harshest penalties are reserved for such destruction. In a related way, James 3:9, 10 forbid the use of the tongue in cursing others because these others are also made in God's image: "With the tongue we praise our Lord and Father, and with it we curse men, who have been made in God's likeness. . . . This should not be." In these texts murder of another or cursing of another are forbidden on the grounds that the other person (even after the Fall) retains something of God's image and is therefore to be valued by us, as God also values him.

MALE AND FEMALE

Second, man was created male and female, and it is still so. In our day many say that there are no essential differences between men and women, or that whatever differences there are, are accidental. This is understandable from

---

[2]Francis A. Schaeffer, *Death in the City* (Downers Grove, Ill.: InterVarsity Press, 1969), p. 80.

those who think that mindless evolution is the means by which we have become what we are. But it is entirely incomprehensible from the standpoint of the Bible, which tells us that nothing is an accident and that sexuality in particular is the result of the creative act of God. Maleness and femaleness are therefore good and meaningful, just as other aspects of God's creation are good and meaningful. Men are not women. Women are not men. One of the saddest things in the universe is a man who tries to be a woman or a woman who tries to be a man. "But who is superior?" someone asks. I answer: A man is absolutely superior to a woman—at being a man; a woman is absolutely superior to a man—at being a woman. But let a woman try to be a man or a man try to be a woman, and you have a monstrosity.

This is thought to deny equality before God, as if equality means indistinguishability. But this thought is neither biblical nor rational. The man and the woman are equal before God, but they are not indistinguishable. In the economy of the family (and the church), the man is to lead, protect, care for, cherish, act upon, and initiate. The woman is to respond, receive, be acted upon, bear, nurture, follow. In this the human family is a deliberate parallelism to the Trinity. We say in theology that within the Trinity the three persons are "one God, the same in substance, equal in power and glory." But there are also distinctions according to which the second person of the Godhead, the Son, voluntarily subordinates Himself to carry out the wishes of the Father in redemption, and the third person, the Holy Spirit, voluntarily subordinates Himself to the united wills of the Father and Son.

The subordination of the woman to the man in marriage is a voluntary submission. As Gerstner writes, "No woman need accept the proposal of any man. But when she enters voluntarily into holy matrimony with that man, she becomes as 1 Peter 3 demands, 'submissive' and 'obedient' to her husband." In the same way, children are under the divine command to "obey" and "honor" their fathers and mothers. "We know from sorry experience that many of them choose not to do so, but if they do (as they are under a divine mandate to do), they must do so voluntarily. So there is in the economy of the human family, which God made in his own image, a replica of the divine Trinity itself, in which there is a proper and voluntary subordination."[3]

BODY AND SOUL

Third, God made man body and soul, and He still does. There is a debate at this point between those who believe in a three-part construction of man's being and those who believe in a two-part construction (the position Gerstner takes in the address I am following). But the debate is not as significant as it sometimes seems. All parties recognize that the human being consists at least of the physical part that dies and needs to be resurrected and the immaterial part that lives beyond death. The only question is whether this immaterial part can be further distinguished as containing, on the one hand, a soul or personality and, on the other hand, a spirit that alone relates us to God.

Here the linguistic data should be determinative, but unfortunately it is not as clear as one could wish. Sometimes, particularly in the earlier parts of the Old Testament, soul (*nephesh*) and spirit (*ruach*) are used interchangeably. But in other places, particularly in the later parts of the Old Testament, *ruach* increasingly comes to designate that element by which men and women relate to God, in distinction from *nephesh* which

---

[3]Gerstner, "Man as God Made Him," p. 22.

then meant merely the life principle. In conformity to this outlook, "soul" is used in reference to animals, while "spirit" is not. Conversely, the prophets, who heard the voice of God and communed with Him in a special sense, are always said to be animated by the "spirit" (but not the "soul") of God. In the New Testament the linguistic data is similar. While soul *(psyche)* and spirit *(pneuma)* are sometimes freely exchanged for one another, as in the Old Testament, *pneuma* nevertheless also expresses that particular capacity for relating to God which is the redeemed man's glory as opposed to mere *psyche*, which even the unsaved man possesses (1 Cor. 2:9–16).

In this area the particular words are possibly less important than the truths they convey. Those who insist on the unity of man, nevertheless believe that he is more than mere matter. If they adhere to a two-part scheme, they recognize that there is that about him that sets him off from animals.

The body is the part we see, the part that possesses physical life. We have a body in common with every living thing.

The soul is the part of the person we call personality or self-identity. This is not a simple matter to talk about. The soul is related to the body through the brain, a part of the body. It is also related to the qualities we associate with spirit. Nevertheless, in general terms soul refers to what makes an individual unique. We might say that the soul centers in the mind and includes all likes and dislikes, special abilities or weaknesses, emotions, aspirations, and anything else that makes the individual different from all others of his species. It is because we have souls that we are able to have fellowship, love, and communication with one another.

But man does not only have fellowship, love, and communication with others of his species. He also has love and communion with God, and for this he needs a spirit. The spirit is that part of human nature that communes with God and partakes in some measure of God's essence. God is nowhere said to be body or soul. But God is defined as spirit. "God is spirit," said Jesus; therefore, "his worshipers must worship in spirit and in truth" (John 4:24). Because man is spirit (or comes to possess a spirit by means of the new birth) he can have fellowship with God and worship Him.

In speaking of soul and body, Gerstner has a good insight. He notes that "the quirk of human nature in its present state, unlike its original condition, is that we have a tendency to recognize that the other person is a conscious, rational and moral soul, but that we treat ourselves as if we were merely a combination of chemicals and reactions. A boy once said to his mother, 'Mother, why is it that whenever I do anything bad it's because I am a bad boy, but whenever you do anything bad it's because you are nervous?' That is the principle. When the boy does something bad the mother recognizes that he is a spirit. He is a morally responsible individual who can be properly reprimanded for his misbehavior. But when she does the same thing . . . she reminds her son that she is a body of nerves and should somehow not be responsible."[4]

But we are responsible. The soul does have dominion over the body. Consequently, whatever our weaknesses may be, we are responsible to subordinate our fleshly desires and live for God.

Dominion Over the Animals

Fourth, man was created dominant over the animals—the point particularly stressed in these verses. Martin Luther wrote in his lectures on Genesis that in his opinion Adam in his original state

---

[4]"Man As God Made Him," p. 23.

was superior to the animals even in those points where they were strong. "I am fully convinced," he said, "that before Adam's sin his eyes were so sharp and clear that they surpassed those of the lynx and eagle. He was stronger than the lions and the bears, whose strength is very great; and he handled them the way we handle puppies." Later on, as he begins to think of Adam's intellectual powers, he says, "If . . . we are looking for an outstanding philosopher, let us not overlook our first parents while they were still free from sin."[5] It was with such capacities that man ruled creation.

At the present time we have this horrible situation. In his sin man either tends to dominate and thus violate the creation, subjecting it to his own selfish ends, or else he tends to fall down and worship the creation, not realizing that his debasement is brought about in the process. As the Bible describes them, the man and the woman were made "a little lower than the heavenly beings" (Ps. 8:5); that is, they were placed between the highest and lowest beings, between angels and beasts.[6] But it is significant that man is described as being slightly lower than the angels rather than being slightly higher than the beasts. That is, man's privilege is that he is to be a mediating figure, but he is also to be one who looks up rather than down. The unfortunate thing is that when man severs the tie that binds him to God and tries to cast off God's rule, he does not rise up to take God's place, as he desires to do, but rather sinks to a more bestial level. In fact, he comes to think of himself as a beast ("the naked ape") or, even worse, a machine.

HOLY AND STILL IS—NOT

This brings us to the last point: God created man holy, and he still is—not. The other items we have considered remain, though they are distorted by sin in each case. Man is still a created being, though weak and destined to die. He is still male and female. He is still body and soul. He is still dominant over the animals. But man was also created holy as God is holy, and of this original righteousness not a vestige remains. Rather, as the Scriptures say, "Every indication of the thoughts of his heart [is] only evil all the time" (Gen. 6:5).

This is why man needs a Savior. God made man upright, but he sought out his own devices. In turning each to his or her own way man brought ruin on the race. Now, not only is no one holy, none is capable even of regaining that holiness. Before the Fall, to use Augustine's phrase, man was *posse non peccare* ("able not to sin"). But he was also, as Augustine also faithfully declared in accordance with the Bible's teaching, *posse peccare* ("able to sin"), which choice he exploited. Now he is *non posse non peccare* ("not able not to sin"). It is as though he jumped into a pit where he is now trapped. He must remain in that pit until God by grace through the work of Christ and the power of the Holy Spirit lifts him out.

---

[5]Martin Luther, *Luther's Works*, Vol. 1, *Lectures on Genesis Chapters 1-5*, edited by Jaroslav Pelikan (St. Louis: Concordia, 1958), pp. 62, 66.

[6]The reference to being made "a little lower than the angels" applies in the first instance to the person of the coming Messiah, the Lord Jesus Christ. But it is in reference to His incarnation alone that this is said. Therefore, the phrase and, indeed, the entire psalm is also rightly understood as having reference to men and women in general. This is particularly clear in the following verses which refer back to the role of dominion given to Adam and Eve in Genesis: "You made him ruler over the works of your hands; you put everything under his feet" (Ps. 8:6).

13

The Seventh Day

(Genesis 2:1–3)

Thus the heavens and the earth were completed in all their vast array. By the seventh day God had finished the work he had been doing; so on the seventh day he rested from all his work. And God blessed the seventh day and made it holy, because on it he rested from all the work of creating that he had done.

What does it mean, God rested on the seventh day? It does not mean that God closed His eyes and went to sleep. He did not take a nap. It does not mean that God rested in the sense that He became indifferent to what the man and woman were doing. We know God was not indifferent because, when Adam and Eve sinned, He was immediately there in the garden calling them to an accounting. He pronounced judgment and held out hope of a Redeemer to come. Rest is not to be understood in either of those ways.

What is involved here is what St. Augustine had in mind when, with his magnificent use of words, he contrasted the rest of God with our restlessness. He said, "Thou has made us for Thyself, and our hearts are restless until they find their rest in Thee." Augustine was thinking of the turmoil of the human heart. He was saying that our true destiny is to find the rest that is found in God only.

Is it not the case that what is involved here is this kind of rest? God, having completed His work of creation, rests, as if to say, "This is the destiny of those who are My people; to rest as I rest, to rest in Me."

REST AND RESTLESSNESS

One thing that makes our lives restless is the pace of change. I wonder how many people have had the experience of watching a population clock. I did at the first of the world congresses on evangelism in Berlin in 1966 and can report that it is a very disturbing experience. In the Congress Halle in Berlin, where the meetings took place there was a population clock display. It was a printout of numbers that kept increasing at the rate of the increase of the population of this planet. The numbers went by very rapidly. They were literally flipping by in front of our eyes—ten, twenty, thirty, forty, fifty, a hundred, two hundred, three hundred, a thousand, two thousand, three thousand. . . . That is the way they went. As I stood watching this clock, I was overwhelmed by the rapid pace of change. On this occasion even the clock was overwhelmed, because the mechanism was unable to keep up with the increase of the population and the poor thing began to slow down. Toward the end of the assembly someone had to announce from the platform that the clock was not keeping up with the population and if you wanted to know what it was, you had to upgrade the numbers by a certain amount.

If we fail to recognize how disturbing this is, we need to think of this further fact: not only are the numbers increasing, indicating that time is quickly marching on, but even the rate of increase is increasing. The population increases are accelerating. Instead of slowing down, the clock should have been speeding up. The speed at which it was going back in 1966 for the World Congress on Evangelism was much slower than it would have to be if it were keeping pace with the increase of the world's population today.

Moreover, the problem is not just the increase in population. That would not be such a bad thing in itself. It is that everything is changing. This is why Alvin Tofler in his book *Future Shock* speaks of a pending monumental breakdown of people who live in industrialized lands. It is not a case, as some have said, of our choices being increasingly eliminated and industry forcing us into greater and greater uniformity. Rather, our options are increasing and at an ever faster rate of speed. People cannot keep up with the choices they are compelled to make. We look at such things and conclude, rightly and inescapably, that this is an age of great distress and restlessness.

However, we still have not come to the real cause of restlessness. If we were to go back in history before what we regard as the modern age and the quickly accelerating pace of modern life, we would still find people having the kind of restlessness about which St. Augustine wrote. He lived in an age of change. But if we could have asked him, "Augustine, how can it be that you, living back in what we regard as the early periods of western history, can speak of restlessness? We see our problem as having to do with the fast pace of modern life," Augustine would have said, "It's not the fast pace of modern life or the slow pace of life that is your problem; the basic problem is sin, which brings turmoil to the heart." Perhaps he would have pointed us to those words of Scripture that speak of the wicked having lives that are like the churning sea that never rests. That is what sin causes.

The devil was the first one to sin, and he has as one of his names, *Diabolos*, which means "the disrupter." The word *diabolos* is based on two Greek words:

dia which means "through" or "among," and *ballo* which means "to throw." We get our word "bowling" from it. Together the words describe one who is always throwing something into the middle of things. He is the one who throws the monkey wrench into the machinery. He disrupts. And so does sin! If we were sinless we would have the peace of the Lord Jesus Christ within. But because we do not, we are at odds with God (who has become our enemy), with others (with whom we are in constant conflict), and ourselves. Even when we sit by ourselves we are unable to be at peace. An author once said, "The greatest problem with men and women is that they do not know how to sit and be still."

Sabbath Rest

What is the cure for restlessness? It is interesting that these verses in Genesis are picked up by the author of Hebrews in a chapter that is entirely given over to this subject. He begins in chapter 3, but it is really in chapter 4 that he talks about what he calls "Sabbath-rest" (v. 9). He calls attention to the fact that although God has created rest for His people, we are not at rest. He points out that when God led Israel out of Egypt into the wilderness in their days of wandering He had as a goal to bring them into the Promised Land. It was to be a place where they would find rest from their wandering. It was a symbol of heaven. But the people rebelled, as we do, and God judged that generation. The author quotes Psalm 95:11 in which God says, "I declared on oath in my anger, 'They shall never enter my rest.'" The author asks how this can be. Here is God, who creates a day of rest and promises rest and yet swears that His people will never enter into that rest. He replies that we do not enter into rest because we will not come to God at that point at which rest may be found, namely, in the Lord Jesus Christ.

The author exhorts the people of his

day. He says, in effect, "Don't go on as those people did who perished in the wilderness, about whom these things were said. Rather strive to enter into God's rest. Cast off sin. Cast off everything that keeps you from Christ. Come in the fullness of faith to rest in Him."

Jesus Himself made that offer. Before His crucifixion when He was with His disciples in the upper room, He recognized that they were bothered by what was happening. They had heard His prophecies of His death, and although they did not understand them fully they knew that things were going to change. They were troubled, but He said, "Do not let your hearts be troubled. Trust in God; trust also in me" (John 14:1). He went on to talk about heaven and the giving of the Holy Spirit and the privilege of prayer, and when He got to the end He gave them something that can rightly be regarded as His legacy: peace. He said, "My peace I give you. I do not give to you as the world gives. Do not let your hearts be troubled and do not be afraid" (v. 27).

How does that come about? It is by finding Christ who has done what we need. Sin is the basic cause of restlessness, and sin is the problem with which we must deal. We cannot handle it. We are the sinners. But the Lord Jesus Christ not only can, He does. He comes; He dies; He pays the penalty for our sin. He opens the door into the presence of God for all who believe in Him. Then God, on the basis of the death of Christ, pronounces the believing one justified. That one now stands before the presence of God clothed in the righteousness of Jesus Christ.

As long as we live we will be troubled by sin. But we can begin to enter into God's rest now and can look forward to that day when we will be made like Jesus and stand before God in holiness.

HOLINESS AND SIN

That leads to the second point. God not only promises rest in these verses; He promises holiness as well. Holiness means to be set apart. So God sets the Sabbath day apart to teach that we are to enter not only into rest but also into holiness.

The two go together, because holiness is the opposite of sin, and sin is what makes us restless. Why is it that when we go out into the world with the gospel the world is not willing to respond to Christ's teaching? Why is it that when we talk about rest, the world, which is restless, does not rush with open arms to embrace the gospel? The answer is that rest is connected with holiness and the world does not want holiness.

The attributes of God are always an offense to men and women. God is sovereign. That is offensive because we want to be our own sovereign. We want to be lords of our lives. We want to say, as one of the poets did, "I am the master of my fate; I am the captain of my soul."

God is also omniscient. He knows everything. This is troublesome, too, because it means that God knows us. We do not want to be known, certainly not well. We want to be noticed. We want to be praised, built up. But we do not want to be known as we are because we are ashamed of what we are. Yet God knows us as no other man or woman will ever know us, and to be exposed in the sight of a holy God is frightening.

The most troublesome of all the attributes of God is holiness. God is absolutely holy. He has no place for sin. There is not a sinful thought, not a sinful wish, not a sinful deed or emotion in God. Yet everything we do is marred by sin. It says a little later in the Book of Genesis that the thoughts of people had become "only evil all the time" (Gen. 6:5). We may resist the judgment of God and say that this is not true, but this is the way God sees it. We tend to minimize sin. We say, "Of course, there are times when I do not do everything I should, but generally I'm pretty good."

God says, "Even those good times are so infused with sin that, if you could see as I see, you would abhor yourself in ashes."

Men and women do not like God for His holiness, and it is this that makes the gospel so hard to preach. People need rest, yes. But they need it in the way it is to be found: by having sin's penalty removed through the work of Christ; sin's power broken through the power of the Holy Spirit; sin's presence eradicated by Christ's return, when those who believe on Him shall be made like Him in all His perfections.

For believers there is a sense in which the seventh day is fulfilled in us now. We enter by degrees into the rest and holiness Christ provides. But the ultimate realization of the Sabbath is to be at Christ's return when we go to be with Him and rest with Him in holiness forever.

To the Work

In spite of the promise of the seventh day, it is nevertheless the case that the seventh day is succeeded by the first day which also has importance for us. Donald Grey Barnhouse in his devotional study of the Book of Genesis has an interesting word at this point. Each segment of Genesis is followed by a devotional comment, and at this point, after the words "on the seventh day God finished the work which he had done and rested," Barnhouse remarks, "But not for long." Sin entered, and God was soon at work again in Christ to bring redemption. Jesus said, "The Father worketh hitherto, and I work." That work is still going on. So if God the Father, the Lord Jesus Christ, and the Holy Spirit are working, then we had better be working too, because there is much work to be done.

It is significant that the Christian day of worship is not the Sabbath day of rest (characteristic of the Old Testament period) but the first day of the week,

Sunday, which is a day of joy, activity, and expectation. Why is it a day of *joy?* Because we see the culmination of the gospel in Jesus Christ. Before, God's people lived in expectation. They looked for the coming of the Messiah. Now the Messiah has come, and we rejoice in Him. Christ's first word to the women after his resurrection was "Rejoice." They were to rejoice because there was much to rejoice about.

Then let us be done with the long faces and solemn demeanors that so often characterize the people of God on the Lord's Day. And let us be done with the type of worshiper who comes to church only to go home. If you do not enjoy the worship of God and the fellowship of God's people, if you do not enjoy the preaching of the Word and the response of the congregation in word and song, stay home! In the early days of the church the apostles did not have to go around ringing doorbells to get people to come out to the service. They did not have to maintain every-member visitation plans to renew flagging interest. In fact, the opposite was true. We read in the second chapter of Acts that the Christians "devoted themselves to the apostles' teaching and to the fellowship, to the breaking of bread and to prayer. . . . Every day they continued to meet together in the temple courts. They broke bread in their homes and ate together with glad and sincere hearts, praising God and enjoying the favor of all the people. And the Lord added to their number daily those who were being saved" (vv. 42, 46, 47).

These were happy Christians. Other people liked to be with them, perhaps most of all because they were happy. Friendships developed. Then on the basis of these friendships the Lord moved and added to the church daily those who were being saved.

The second characteristic of the Lord's Day is *activity.* The first Lord's Day was a day of activity: the women on the way to the tomb, the appearances of Jesus, the return to Jerusalem of the Emmaus disciples, the sharing of experiences, communion, the Lord's commission. It is possible that if you have been working hard for the other six days of the week, Sunday might have to be a "day of rest" for you. But this is not an integral part of the Lord's Day. The Sabbath was the day of rest. If you need to rest, try resting on Saturday. The Lord's Day should be a day of activity.

This does not mean that just any old activity will reflect the fullest significance of the day. You may mow your grass, if you wish. You are not under law. But this does not have much to do with Christ, nor does it help to express your joy in His resurrection.

Worship is significant. It may strike some persons as strange to speak of worship as an activity; for in many minds worship is conceived in a passive sense, that is, sitting in a pew and letting the words of the day run through one's head like water. But this is a travesty of real worship. The Lord said that real worship is done "in spirit and in truth" (John 4:24). Truth involves content. So worship is above all else an active, rational activity.

Why do we have Scripture readings in the speech of the people instead of in Hebrew, Greek, or Latin? Why are the words of the music in common speech? Why does a sermon stand at the heart of each service? The answer is: to engage our minds.

"We must therefore beware of all forms of emotional, aesthetic or ecstatic worship in which the mind is not fully engaged, and especially of those which even claim that they are superior forms of worship," writes John R. W. Stott, rector of All Souls Church in London. "The only worship pleasing to God is heart-worship, and heart-worship is ra-

tional worship. It is the worship of a rational God who has made us rational beings and given us a rational revelation so that we may worship Him rationally, even 'with all our mind.' "[1]

Another activity that ought to characterize the Lord's Day is witness. Jesus revealed this characteristic when He instructed the women, "Go tell my brethren," and later informed the disciples that they were to carry the good news of His life, death, and resurrection into all the world. You can do that on any day, of course. It is of the essence of our day that anything done on Sunday can also be done (and perhaps should be done) on other days also. But do you at least bear witness on Sunday? This is a day on which to invite your friends to go with you to hear God's Word. At the very least it is a day on which you should teach what you know about Christ to your children.

There is one thing more: the first day should be characterized by *expectation.* I love Sunday, and one of the reasons why I love Sunday is that I never know in advance what will happen. As I leave my house on the way to church I never know precisely whom I will meet. I never know who will be present in church or who will respond to the preaching. I never plan messages to preach at problems that I imagine to be present in the congregation, yet it is often the case that what I say is used of the Lord to speak precisely to some problem. Lives are changed. Not infrequently, the day is the turning point in someone's entire spiritual experience.

We who know the reality of the rest and holiness of God should of all people be most joyful, active, and expectant as we take the gospel's glorious message to a world that knows neither rest nor holiness, but needs them desperately.

---

[1]John R. W. Stott, *Christ the Controversialist* (Downers Grove, Ill.: InterVarsity Press, 1978), p. 165.

14

Are There Two Creations?

(Genesis 2:4–6)

This is the account of the heavens and the earth when they were created. When the LORD God made the earth and the heavens, no shrub of the field had yet appeared on the earth and no plant of the field had yet sprung up; the LORD God had not sent rain on the earth and there was no man to work the ground, but streams came up from the earth and watered the whole surface of the ground.

When the Pharisees asked the Lord Jesus Christ about divorce He replied by quoting from the early chapters of Genesis. First, He referred to the statement that God had made man male and female—"Haven't you read . . . that at the beginning the Creator 'made them male and female'?" Then, he referred to a specific statement about marriage—"For this reason a man will leave his father and mother and be united to his wife, and the two will become one flesh" (Matt. 19:4, 5). Since one of these quotations comes from Genesis 1 and the other from Genesis 2 (Gen. 1:27 and 2:24 respectively), it would seem that Jesus regarded the two chapters as belonging to one harmonious account.

For many years, liberal scholars have argued that Genesis 1 and 2 represent different and even contradictory accounts of creation.

It is hard to tell at which point this liberal view originated, but it was underway by the time of Jean Astruc's monumental work on the literary sources of Genesis, published in 1753. He noted that "in the Hebrew text of Genesis, God is designated by two different names. The first is Elohim. . . . The other is Jehovah,"[1] and he explained this by arguing that the material

containing these names came from two (or even more) sources. Since the name used for God in Genesis 1 is Elohim and the name Jehovah is introduced in chapter 2, it followed that these had different origins and represented different points of view.

Today the source theories of Genesis are considerably more elaborate, but the idea is the same. Scholars speak of four types of documents, processes, or schools lying behind our current texts. There are documents containing the names Jehovah or Elohim. They are designated J and E respectively. There is a priestly document or process designated P. Finally, there is a source attributable to a deuteronomic school or D. It is argued that Genesis 1 is a priestly document and therefore reflects the outlook of that school, while the second chapter is a combination of a Jehovah and an Elohim text and consequently reflects the outlooks of those documents.

Are there two accounts of creation? Was Christ naïve, or are we mistaken in thinking that He held to one authorship?

CRITICAL PROBLEMS

One obvious problem with the critical theory has already been suggested, although indirectly. When we read Astruc

---

[1]*Encyclopedia of Religion and Ethics*, Vol. 4, edited by James Hastings (New York: Charles Scribner's Sons, 1912), p. 315.

we might assume that use of the names for God in Genesis is a clear-cut affair. This is not actually the case, and our reference to the use of the name Jehovah in Genesis 2 has already suggested the problem. The word for God occuring there is actually Jehovah Elohim, not Jehovah alone. In other words, the use of the names is not so simple a matter as some scholars imply. True, in Genesis 1 the name for God is Elohim, the most general of all names and therefore the most appropriate one for a general account of creation. But when the second chapter introduces its remarks by a reference to Jehovah Elohim (v. 4), this is not so much an evidence of Genesis 2 being a separate document as it is a further elaboration of the account already given in chapter 1. It is as much as to say that the Elohim already mentioned in chapter 1 is none other than Jehovah about whom the remainder of the book will speak. Since Jehovah is the personal name of God, it is appropriate that it is introduced at the point at which the personal relation between man and God is developed.

Reasons for use of the various names of God—there are others besides Jehovah and Elohim—can be suggested for differences similar to those in Genesis 1 and 2 occurring elsewhere.

There is another problem with this critical theory, especially where the early chapters of Genesis are concerned. E. J. Young calls it "a psychological difficulty." He develops his thoughts in this way. "If it is correct that the Pentateuch does consist of a number of documents which were finally pieced together by a redactor [the person or persons who finally got the book into the shape in which we now find it], then it must be acknowledged that the Pentateuch is a very remarkable work. It is not the kind of writing that very many people could produce. Undoubtedly it is one of the greatest writings in existence, and whoever was responsible for it was an artist and a genius. . . . But if [this] is so, then why did he make such a blunder at the very beginning as to put together two contradictory accounts of creation? If he was such a genius, would he not have realized that it was not very sensible to put two conflicting accounts of creation together?"[2]

The problem should encourage a person to take a closer look at the two accounts to see if there is not a good reason, perhaps several reasons, why they exist in the form we find them. Indeed, we should be encouraged when we realize that until the rise of modern critical scholarship no one seemed to have noticed that these two accounts were "conflicting."

ACCOUNT OF CREATION

Let us be a bit more precise. We have been speaking of the accounts in Genesis 1 and 2, but, strictly speaking, the account in Genesis 2 does not begin until verse 4. Genesis 2:1–3 tells of the seventh day of creation and therefore properly belongs with Genesis 1 in which the acts of God on the various days are chronicled. The second account (whether "contradictory" or not) begins with verse 4, which tells us, "This is the account of the heavens and the earth when they were created."

This verse seems simple and even unimportant, but it is actually a key verse for understanding Genesis. Unfortunately, it has been a battleground for at least two conflicting opinions. On the one hand, some regard it as a conclusion to what has gone before. The technical term for this is a subscription (from *sub* meaning "under" and *scriptus* meaning "written"). On the other hand, there are people who regard it as an introduction to what follows. The technical term is superscription (from *super*

---

[2]Young, *In the Beginning*, p. 59.

meaning "over" and *scriptus*, "written"). In other words, it is either a summarizing statement for Genesis 1:1—2:3, or it is a descriptive caption for Genesis 2:4—4:26. The reason this is a key verse for understanding Genesis is that there are eleven such verses scattered throughout the book (2:4, 5:1; 6:9; 10:1; 11:10, 27; 25:12, 19; 36:1, 9; 37:2), and these are either intended to summarize or introduce sections.

A person who takes the first view is Henry M. Morris. He notes that with the exception of the first instance (Gen. 2:4, the verse we are considering), each of these eleven references involves a name—the account of Adam, the account of Noah, the account of Shem, Ham and Japheth, and so on—and that the story of each of these people is given in the verses that come before these references. He thinks it self-evident that they are a summary and even suggests that they may be something like a signature, indicating that the preceding section is verified by and may even have been written down by the one whose name is given.

The trouble with this view is that it neglects the precise meaning of the word that the New International Version renders "account" and the older Authorized Version renders "generations." No doubt the translators of the NIV felt that the word "generations" was too old-fashioned and would probably be meaningless to most modern readers. But the Hebrew word is *toledoth*, which comes from a root meaning "to bear" or "to beget," and this means that the word "generations" is, in fact, more accurate. What is involved is the descendants of the person named. So, strictly speaking, the sentences in which this word occurs introduce descendants. The reference in 5:1 introduces the descendants of Adam. The reference in 6:9 introduces Noah and his descendants (both being taken together since their stories are linked by the Flood). The reference in 10:1 introduces the descendants of Shem, Ham, and Japheth. So on through Genesis. Because of this feature, we could say that the book is divided into two parts. The first, very short, part runs from 1:1 to 2:3. It is the account of creation. The second, much longer, part runs from 2:4 to 50:26. It is the account of the "generations," showing what came from each of the key personalities around whom the story of the race develops.

The bearing of this on the problem of whether or not there are two accounts of creation is that the sentence "This is the account [generations] of the heavens and the earth when they were created" settles it for us. The words are a superscription, as are the other similar references later on. They tell us that what follows is not a second account of creation, but rather the account of something that came from the creation of the heavens and the earth, namely man. From here on the orientation will be to the human race and the problems created by the sin of the first man and woman. (It is interesting to note that although the NIV uses the word "account" for the probable reason suggested, it nevertheless places the phrases or sentences in which *toledoth* occurs at the beginning of the following sections, rather than at the end of the preceding.)

GOD AND MAN

With this clue we can return to Genesis 2. When we do we immediately discover that the emphasis is indeed on man and not on other aspects of the creation. We can see this in two ways. First, there is more detail about the creation of man, both male and female. Second, there is an emphasis on God's special provision for the man and woman. This is where references to the other parts of creation come in.

Emphasis on the man and woman is seen in several ways. We notice almost at once that the chronological sequence followed so clearly in Genesis 1, with its succession of seven key days, is dropped and a more topical sequence is adopted. Of course, some critical scholars have pointed to the order of things in Genesis 2 as being evidence that the two creation "accounts" are contradictory: the first gives one order for things, the second gives a different order. But this is surely nonsense. If you take Genesis 2 as teaching a chronological sequence, you have first the creation of man, then the planting of a garden, then God putting the man in the garden, then God causing trees to grow in the garden. After this there is a description of the rivers of the garden. Then man is put in the garden again. Problems like this should tell us that something is wrong with that approach. They tell us that chronology is not in view here at all. What matters in this chapter is man. Everything else is introduced for its relationship to him.

Another way in which we notice the special emphasis in Genesis 2 is the further detail as to man's nature. Significant points have already been made in chapter 1. He is said to have been created in God's image and to have been given rule over all the earth. Each of these points is repeated several times over. But in chapter 2 we are told in addition that "the LORD God formed man from the dust of the ground and breathed into his nostrils the breath of life, and man became a living being" (v. 7). Here we are beginning to learn what being created in God's image means.

There is also a suggestion of God's special interest in and special care for the man. God was interested in all creation and even pronounced a benediction after each stage of its completion ("God saw that it was good"). But the earlier chapter does not give us anything comparable to the picture of God bending down to form Adam from the dust of the earth and then gently placing His mouth next to Adam's face in order to blow into him the breath of life. I marvel at how

the critical scholars go astray at this point. They see this portrait and call it "anthropomorphic," meaning that someone with very limited understanding of the grandeur and transcendence of God has imagined Him to be like man, having a human form. They dismiss this conception. They prefer the distant, formless God of Genesis 1. How much they lose by their rejection! Certainly God is transcendent; He does not have a human body. But this does not mean that He does not relate to and care for man in a personal and intimate way. God is personal. He does care. He is intimate. How was the author of Genesis to say that—in addition to portraying God in His transcendence—if not by the type of description he has given us? Moreover, as we are to learn in Genesis 3, God actually communicated with man face to face in those halcyon days—perhaps through a preincarnate manifestation of the second person of the Trinity. Who are we to say that God did not literally form man from the dust of the earth or literally breathe the breath of life into his nostrils?

Each of these points—the ordering of events, the additional information regarding man's nature and the special attention of God to His creation—shows that we are not dealing with a mere second account of creation but with that creature about whom and for whom the book is written.

The second way in which we see the particular emphasis of Genesis 2 is God's special provision for the man and woman. Here again there are three elements. First, there is God's special preparation of the garden in which Adam and Eve were to dwell. We cannot emphasize enough that when this chapter speaks of the trees, the water of the four great rivers and the animals, it is not speaking of these as various stages of creation, as was the case in chapter 1. Each of these parts of creation is spoken of in the past tense as something God had already formed. Again, it is not the waters, plants, and animals of the entire globe that are in view, but only those waters, plants, and animals that had bearing on Adam's life in Eden. The point is that these were made for man's special delight and benefit.

When we say delight, we take special note of the garden. To those who live in lush, well-watered lands, the existence of a garden is not remarkable. But Genesis was originally written, not to those who live in lush climates, but to people who lived in extremely arid or desert countries and for whom a garden was therefore an exquisite delight—virtually a symbol of heaven. To say that God prepared Adam a special garden complete with trees (not merely shrubs) and rivers (not merely brooks) was to say to the near-eastern reader, clearer than anything else could possibly say, that Adam was beloved of God and was the receiver of His bounty.

The second element showing God's special provision for the man was God's giving Adam special work to do, namely, the naming or classifying of the animals. This was no small blessing, nor is it to be taken lightly, as so many have done and do. We have heard jokes like the one Mark Twain told about Adam coming home one night to a somewhat critical Eve. "What did you call that big animal out there?" she asks.

"I called it an elephant."

"Why did you call it an elephant?"

"Because it looked like an elephant," Adam answers testily.

Actually, it was no small job to name the animals and (presumably) all the other parts of creation. To name something is in a sense to know it. So if Adam was to name the animals wisely—which we must assume he certainly was called upon to do—then he had his work cut out for him. He was to be the first and greatest of all biologists and botanists.

He was to survey creation and divide up everything he found by genus, subgenus, species, subspecies, and variety.

John Gerstner tells of a German ditty that Cornelius Van Til used to teach his students to explain the problem Adam would have had trying to name the animals. *Warum heisst der Loewe, Loewe?* ("Why is a lion called a lion?") *Weil er durch den Walde lauft.* ("Because he runs through the forest.") The thought hinges on a pun between *Loewe* and *lauft.* You call him a *Loewe* because he *lauft.* That seems reasonable. But then the ditty continues. *Warum heisst der Tiger, Tiger?* ("Why is the tiger called a tiger?") *Donner wetter! Sie kannte ja nicht alle Loewe heissen.* ("You can't call them all lions.") Gerstner continues by observing that "classification is no mean problem" and that "the most fundamental knowledge of the human species ultimately is in the dictionary. When we have a definition for anything, when we really have studied its nature to the point where we can say that it is *this* and not *that*, we have achieved knowledge."[3]

This was the nature of the work given to Adam. We have a tendency today to rebel against work, regarding it as undesirable and onerous, and it is true that since the Fall work has acquired burdensome overtones ("By the sweat of your brow you will eat your food until you return to the ground," Gen. 3:19). But even now work is a good thing—it is good to work—and in Eden it was another perfect element in God's wise and gracious provision for Adam.

The third element in God's provision was Eve, the point with which the chapter closes. Already we have been told that man was created male and female and that the dominion over creation given to the man was given to the woman also (Gen. 1:28). Now we are told how the creation of the woman

---

[3]Gerstner, "Man as God Made Him," p. 24.

came about. The two were not made in the same instant, though we might wrongly assume that from the first chapter. Rather the man was first made, then the woman. Moreover, we are told that when man existed alone (whether long or short, we do not know) God said, "It is not good for the man to be alone. I will make a helper suitable for him" (Gen. 2:18). Up to this point, as God had looked out over His creation, He had declared that everything was good. But now for the first time He sees something that is not good: "It is not good for man to be alone." So God made woman from man and brought her to him as the greatest and most precious of His gifts.

Shadows Over Eden

The chapter concludes with man as the pinnacle of creation ensconced in the place of God's choosing. He is the apple of God's eye. He exists in a special relationship to him. He has a place to live, has work to do, and has an ideal companion. All is well. Yes, but there are forebodings. For chapter 2 is not only a development from chapter 1, it is a preparation for chapter 3 also.

Everything in the chapter seems foreboding in view of chapter 3. Man is formed from the dust of the ground and receives God's breath of life. But he is soon to lose that life and return to the dust from which he came. He has been placed in a garden, a symbol of heaven. But he is soon to be driven from it. The garden is abundant with trees. But among those many from which he is permitted to eat, there is the tree of the knowledge of good and evil from which he is not to eat, lest eating, he die. And he does eat! Most tragic perhaps is the fact that she who was to be his helper, no doubt in spiritual things as well as in the mere running of the garden, became a channel of temptation and so was instrumental in the Fall. He who was to be her head and guardian also rebelled and thus drew the woman as well as all their posterity into the agony of sin and death.

The only bright spot is God, who always remains the same ("I the LORD do not change," Mal. 3:6). He continued to love the man and woman and provided for them even in their sin and depravity. So also does God provide for us—through Christ, the second Adam, who did not fall but who triumphed to bring "God's abundant provision of grace and of the gift of righteousness" to all His people (Rom. 5:17).

15

Dust and Glory

(Genesis 2:7)

And the LORD God formed man from the dust of the ground and breathed into his nostrils the breath of life, and man became a living being.

Alexander Pope was not being particularly biblical when he wrote, "The chief study of mankind is man." He was not even being original, for the obligation to "know thyself" was an axiom of Greek thought thousands of years before him. Still, Pope was expressing an obligation felt by most men and women in nearly every age of history. We want to know who or what we are, why we are here, and where we are going.

Unfortunately, it is impossible for us to answer these questions apart from the biblical revelation. The reason is that we see parts of the answer, but only parts, and are therefore constantly distorting the picture. Zoologists, like Desmond Morris, who calls man "the naked ape," tell us that man is essentially an animal. Karl Marx says that the essence of man is in his labor, what he does. Existentialists tell us that man is essentially volition. That is, his uniqueness is found in his will. Hugh Hefner tells us that we are sensuous creatures and are therefore to be understood largely in terms of our passions or sexual performance. Common today is the view that man is essentially a machine, a large computer. At the Carnegie Mellon Institute in Pittsburgh there is a research project in which scientists are asking whether there is any essential difference between a human being and a computer. Each of these attempts to define man has ele-

ments of truth. But in the final analysis each fails because it is reductionistic. It sees part of the picture, but it lacks a comprehensive view of the whole. Consequently, in this age as in previous ages of human history man is "his own most vexing problem," as Reinhold Niebuhr reminds us.[1]

What are we to do? The only wise course is to ask who we are from God. When we do that we find that there is no profounder statement of who we are than Genesis 2:7.

FORMED FROM THE DUST

The profundity of this verse is that it describes man as a combination of what is low and what is high. On the one hand, he is described as being formed from the dust of the ground—an image of lowness though not of evil, as the Greeks thought, for even the dust is made by God and is good because He made it. On the other hand, man has been breathed into by God—an image of glory. It is man's unique role to combine both dust and glory.

Dust is one of the most fascinating images of Scripture, and a study of it amply repays the time invested. It is a symbol of that which is of *little worth*, of low or humble origin. We see this in a number of passages. For instance, when Abraham is pleading with God over Sodom and wishes to emphasize his

---

[1]Reinhold Niebuhr, *The Nature and Destiny of Man*, one-volume edition of the Gifford Lectures on "Human Nature" and "Human Destiny" (New York: Charles Scribner's Sons, 1949), Part 1, p. 1.

own littleness to engage in such pleading, he says, "Now that I have been so bold as to speak to the Lord, though I am nothing but dust and ashes, what if the number of the righteous is five less than fifty?" (Gen. 18:27). Or again, Hannah, in praising God for hearing her request for a son, says, "He raises the poor from the dust and lifts the needy from the ash heap" (1 Sam. 2:8; cf. Ps. 113:7). On one occasion God reminds King Baasha of Israel that it was He who lifted him "up from the dust" and made him "leader of my people Israel" (1 Kings 16:2). But because he did not obey or honor God, God removed him and brought him down to dust again. Dust is used as a symbol of the total defeat of one's enemies ("the king of Aram had destroyed the rest and made them like the dust at threshing time," 2 Kings 13:7; cf. Ps. 18:42; 72:9). It is a sign of mourning ("Then Joshua tore his clothes and fell facedown to the ground before the ark of the LORD, remaining there till evening. The elders of Israel did the same, and sprinkled dust on their heads," Josh. 7:6; cf. Job 2:12; 16:15; Lam. 2:10; 3:29; Ezek. 27:30; Mic. 1:10; Rev. 18:19). Job used the word twenty-two times to speak of the littleness of man in his misery. In a classic passage near the end of his book, this suffering saint declares, "My ears had heard of you but now my eyes have seen you. Therefore I despise myself and repent in dust and ashes" (Job 42:5, 6).

We repeat that dust is not evil, nor is it nothing. But it is "next to nothing," as Matthew Henry notes. He adds that man "was not made of gold-dust, powder of pearl, or diamond dust, but common dust, dust of the ground."[2] In describing man as being formed from the dust Moses undoubtedly wished to stress man's humble origin and show that he can aspire to glory only by the grace of God, who made him.

There is something else to be noted about dust: it is a symbol of *frustration.* The greatest example is the frustration of Satan whose curse, related in Genesis 3:14, was in part that "you will crawl on your belly and you will eat dust all the days of your life." This passage does not mean that snakes literally eat dust, nor does it imply that the author of the passage thought so. Dust in the mouth is a figure for defeat and humiliation.

Before his fall Satan was an intelligent and extremely powerful being, chief of all the angels. Somewhere along the line—we do not know when or how—this supremely intelligent creature conceived a most unintelligent thought, namely, that he could get along without God. He said, "I will ascend to heaven; I will raise my throne above the stars of God; I will sit enthroned on the mount of assembly, on the utmost heights of the sacred mountain. I will ascend above the tops of the clouds; I will make myself like the Most High" (Isa. 14:13, 14). He rebelled. But God brought him down from the lofty heights of his own sinful imaginations, and instead of finding himself in heaven replacing God he found himself a fugitive in God's universe. In God's initial judgment on Satan the fallen cherub had his first taste of dust.

He had another in Eden. No doubt, after having suffered God's instantaneous judgment on himself for his sin, Satan thought that Adam and Eve would experience the same—if he only could get them likewise to rebel against their Creator. So Satan tempted first Eve, then through her, Adam. Satan got them to sin. But instead of the immediate judgment he expected he found God coming graciously to clothe the first man and woman in skins taken from the first animal sacrifices and heard God promising an eventual and full deliverance by him who was to crush the head of Satan (Gen. 3:15).

---

[2]Matthew Henry, *Commentary on the Whole Bible* (Grand Rapids: Zondervan, 1960), p. 5.

Satan's most bitter mouthful of dust was at the cross of Christ when he, who undoubtedly engineered Christ's death, thinking thereby to strike back at God, found to his dismay that he had unwittingly been instrumental in furthering God's great plan of redemption. Certainly God was correct when He said, "You will eat dust all the days of your life." Satan ate dust then. He will always eat it. For even in Isaiah's great description of the earth's golden age it is said, "The wolf and the lamb will feed together, and the lion will eat straw like the ox, but dust will be the serpent's food" (Isa. 65:25).

In his discussion of the frustrations of Satan (and of others who follow in his path of rebellion), Donald Grey Barnhouse refers to a cartoon published in the London *Star* during World War II. The forces of Germany were at their farthest point of advance. Axis armies were in the foothills of the Caucasus mountains. Rommel's troops were standing within the borders of Egypt. Rommel boasted that he would be in Cairo in two weeks. But then the Russian power began to stir, and the armies under Montgomery began that victorious march across Egypt that was to result in the total defeat of the German forces in North Africa. This cartoon showed Hitler standing on tiptoe on a heap of skulls, reaching into the sky where his fingers were just barely missing a cloud in the shape of the word "Victory." The caption said, "It is always just out of reach." So it is for Satan, and for all who think they can succeed in their rebellion against the true God.[3]

The third truth symbolized by dust is *death*, which for unbelievers is the ultimate frustration (cf. Eccl. 3:19–21). It appears in Genesis. In the same judgments in which it is said of Satan, "You will eat dust all the days of your life," it is said of man, "By the sweat of your

brow you will eat your food until you return to the ground, since from it you were taken; for dust you are and to dust you will return" (Gen. 3:19). This was a thought often on Job's mind. He said in his misery, "I will soon lie down in the dust; you will search for me, but I will be no more" (Job 7:21; cf. 17:16; 20:11; 21:26). It is spoken prophetically of Christ: "My strength is dried up like a potsherd, and my tongue sticks to the roof of my mouth; you lay me in the dust of death" (Ps. 22:15; cf. v. 29).

This image speaks of increasing despair: from littleness to frustration to death. But it is not so for believers. Although we are formed from the dust, we remember that it is God who has formed us and who "remembers that we are dust" (Ps. 103:14). True it is, as the psalm goes on to say, "As for man, his days are like grass, he flourishes like a flower of the field; the wind blows over it and it is gone . . ." (vv. 15, 16). But it is also true, as the psalm adds, "From everlasting to everlasting the LORD's love is with those who fear him, and his righteousness with their children's children—with those who keep his covenant and remember to obey his precepts" (vv. 17, 18). The author of Psalm 119 declares, "I am laid low in the dust." But he adds, "renew my life according to your word" (v. 25).

THE BREATH OF LIFE

The reason why it is possible for men to call on God for renewal or even to remember that God remembers their origin is that they are more than dust. They are also spirit, which Genesis 2:7 indicates by saying that after God had formed man from the dust of the ground He continued His work by breathing "into his nostrils the breath of life." This is man's glory.

To appreciate this verse fully we must recognize the close connection between

---

[3]Donald Grey Barnhouse, *The Invisible War* (Grand Rapids: Zondervan, 1965), p. 60.

God's Spirit and the word for "breath." It comes from the fact that in nearly all ancient languages, particularly Latin, Greek, and Hebrew, the words for spirit and breath are identical. In Latin the word for spirit or breath is *spiritus*, which has obviously given us our word "spirit." But *spiritus* also means breath, as we recognize in many of our Latin derivatives. *Spiritus* has given us: aspire, conspire, inspire, perspire, and expire. They all refer to different ways of using one's breath. When men aspire, they take a deep breath and try harder. When they conspire, they put their heads together and breathe in and out with one another. A man is inspired when another man (or God) blows some of his breath into him. A person perspires by breathing out through the skin. When we expire, we breathe out for the last time. We die.

In Greek, the language in which the New Testament is written, the corresponding word is *pneuma*. It refers to breath also. This word is harder for English-speaking people to pronounce than the Latin word *spiritus* because of the initial two consonants, *pn*, so we do not have so many words based on it. Nevertheless, we have pneumatic and pneumonia. The first word refers to any tool that is air operated, like a pneumatic drill. The second refers to a disease of the breath box or lungs.

Finally, just as the Latin and Greek words for "spirit" refer to breath, wind, or air, so also does the Hebrew word. This word is *ruach*, which you cannot even say properly without exhaling. *Ruach!* It is the sound of a breath. When we understand this, we have some sense of the poetry of the opening verses of the Bible in which the creative Spirit of God blows over the waters like a troubling wind. No one English version can capture both ideas—the ideas of wind and spirit—but the New English Bible at leasts suggests the idea of the wind, with a reference to God's Spirit pre-

served in a footnote. The NEB declares: "In the beginning of creation, when God made heaven and earth, the earth was without form and void, with darkness over the face of the abyss, and a mighty wind that swept over the surface of the waters" (Gen. 1:1, 2).

It is this word that occurs in Genesis 2:7 with the implication, readily seen by any Hebrew reader, that man was specially created by God's breathing some of His own breath into him. Man has a special relationship to God by virtue of the divine spirit. Hence, although like the animals in certain respects, he is also above them and is to excel them in his love of and obedience to the Creator.

We know to our sorrow that man did not excel the animals in fulfilling this high destiny. He rebelled against God and thereby sadly effaced the image of God that had been given to him. Now, though retaining vestiges of that former glory, he is nevertheless thoroughly depraved in the sense that he can do no good acceptable to God, can no longer understand spiritual truth unless aided by the Holy Spirit, and cannot seek the true God against whom he has rebelled. That is why Paul writes of man in his fallen state saying, "There is no one righteous, not even one; there is no one who understands, no one who seeks God. All have turned away, they have together become worthless; there is no one who does good, not even one" (Rom. 3:10–12).

Fortunately, this is not the whole story. Although man cannot seek God, God does seek man and even recreates him according to the pattern originally set in Genesis. It is what Jesus spoke about to Nicodemus when He told that leader of Israel, "You must be born again" (John 3:7). Nicodemus did not understand Christ's meaning. So Jesus explained that the birth He was referring to was a birth from above by means of God's Spirit: "I tell you the truth, unless a man is born of water and the Spirit, he cannot enter the kingdom of God. Flesh gives birth to flesh, but the Spirit gives birth to spirit" (vv. 5, 6). Jesus was saying, not that a man must be born again of his mother (which is what Nicodemus first thought), but that he must be born again of God—just as Adam was born of God originally (cf. Luke 3:37). Flesh gives birth to flesh, fallen man to fallen man. But God gives new life now through His spirit, breathing into us as He once breathed into Adam. Without that necessary rebirth or recreation a person "cannot see the kingdom of God."

A LIVING BEING

Genesis 2:7 adds one final thought. As a result of God's forming man from the dust of the ground and breathing some of His own breath into him, man became a "living being." The phrase translated "a living being" (actually, "living soul") in Genesis 2:7 is also used in Genesis 1:24 of the animals. But as a result of the particulars of man's creation given in the second chapter, a distinction is undoubtedly implied. Man is not only alive. He knows he is alive. Even more important, he knows from whom that life has come and of his duties to the God who breathed His own breath into him.

Man also knows that he depends on God for physical life and that he must come to Him for spiritual life, as Jesus indicated. Isaiah teaches the physical dependence of man on God in a fascinating verse. It plays on the idea of man's breath by saying, "Stop trusting in man, who has but a breath in his nostrils. Of what account is he?" (Isa. 2:22). We might paraphrase Isaiah's command by saying, "Why trust in man who is able to take only one noseful of breath at a time? Trust God, whose breath is inexhaustible." The breath of God in us may be our glory, but it is still received by us only one breath at a time. We breathe in. We hold our breath. We breathe out. But then we must breathe in

again, or die. Nothing could better characterize our utter dependence on God.

And what if God should withhold His breath? Job answers by saying, "If it were his intention and he withdrew his spirit and breath, all mankind would perish together and man would return to the dust" (Job 34:14, 15). So did the psalmist: "When you hide your face, they are terrified; when you take away their breath, they die and return to the dust" (Ps. 104:29).

I give two closing verses. There is a verse in 1 Corinthians which, by its contrast between the first Adam in his littleness and Christ in His greatness, summarizes most of what this study has been saying. Paul writes, "So it is written: 'The first man Adam became a living being' [a clear reference to our text in Genesis]; the last Adam, a life-giving spirit" (1 Cor. 15:45). What does Paul mean? Simply this: Adam existed by breathing in, and the breath he breathed in was from God. He could not sustain himself. Christ, on the other hand, is the One who breathes out, for He is "a life-*giving* spirit." We are to live physically and spiritually only as we turn to and are united to Him.

The last verse is in the form of a concluding challenge, particularly to any who are not yet Christ's. It comes from the little-known Book of Ecclesiastes: "Remember him [that is, remember God]—before the silver cord is severed, or the golden bowl is broken; before the pitcher is shattered at the spring, or the wheel broken at the well, and the dust returns to the ground it came from, and the spirit returns to God who gave it" (Eccl. 12:6, 7). It is the preacher's way of saying, "I tell you, now is the time of God's favor, now is the day of salvation" (2 Cor. 6:2).

When death comes it is too late. Now, while you still have life, come to Him who is able to give eternal life, and find yourself accepted in the Savior.

16

East, in Eden

(Genesis 2:8–17)

Now the LORD God had planted a garden in the east, in Eden; and there he put the man he had formed. And the LORD God made all kinds of trees grow out of the ground—trees that were pleasing to the eye and good for food. In the middle of the garden were the tree of life and the tree of the knowledge of good and evil.

A river watering the garden flowed from Eden, and from there it divided; it had four headstreams. The name of the first is the Pishon; it winds through the entire land of Havilah, where there is gold. (The gold of that land is good; aromatic resin and onyx are also there.) The name of the second river is the Gihon; it winds through the entire land of Cush. The name of the third river is the Tigris; it runs along the east side of Asshur. And the fourth river is the Euphrates.

The LORD God took the man and put him in the Garden of Eden to work it and take care of it. And the LORD God commanded the man, "You are free to eat from any tree in the garden; but you must not eat from the tree of the knowledge of good and evil, for when you eat of it you will surely die."

The word Eden has almost faded from our vocabularies in these prosaic times, except as a name for honeymoon resorts or cottages. It needs to be revived, because it is a proper and constant reminder of two truths basic to Christianity. First, Christianity is an historical religion. It is not a religion of mere metaphysical concepts and ideas, as many of the non-Christian religions are. It deals with real people who lived in real places and who experienced the very real redemptive acts of God in history. Second, it is the story of man's fall from perfection and the subsequent redemption of certain men and women by God for their good and the praise of His glory.

Occasionally in my preparation of studies like this I turn to reference books in which the various literary uses of a word such as Eden are recorded. On this occasion I looked up "Eden" in Roget's *International Thesaurus,* and was surprised to find it, not under a section dealing with historical names and places, but under the section dealing with "imagination." It was listed with such terms as "utopia," "paradise," "heaven," "Atlantis," "Happy Valley," "fairyland," "cloudland," "dreamland," "Land of Promise" and "kingdom come." The quotations, which in Roget accompany each word section, contained such gems as "Imagination rules the world" (Napoleon), "The center of every man's existence is a dream" (Chesterton) and "All dreams are lies" (French proverb). Apparently, for the compiler of the thesaurus Eden was no more real than fairyland.

Is this the Christian view? Many would like it to be, because if Eden is not real, then the Fall is not real and we can all entertain the comfortable secular notions that there is really not much wrong with the human race and that whatever imperfections may be said to exist they are all inevitably being wiped out by time. Unfortunately for secular man, the

Bible opposes such optimism and declares instead that man's state apart from God is desperate.

NAMES AND PLACES

All along in our study of the opening chapters of Genesis we have insisted that the accounts before us are historical. We asked, "Is Genesis fact or fiction?" We answered that it is clearly fact, defending this from the nature of the material itself as well as from the attitude of the other biblical figures toward Genesis, including that of the Lord Jesus Christ. But if it is true that Genesis 1:1–2:3 is fact—verses that give an account of creation in the briefest possible language—it is many times more evident that Genesis 2:4–17 is fact, for in these verses Moses sets Eden before his Jewish readers as a place they would recognize.

Two features are striking. First, Eden is said to have been located in "the east"—a directional notation. We must remember that Genesis, being the first of the five books of Moses, was initially written to the people of Israel during the days of their wilderness wandering in Sinai. So when Moses says that "God had planted a garden in the east, in Eden" (Gen. 2:8), he is giving the location from the point of view of Sinai. Although the reference is not sharply specific, it means that Eden was located somewhere across the great Arabian desert toward the area we know as the valleys of the Tigris and Euphrates rivers.

The second feature of this description is the extraordinary collection of place names found in verses 10–14, including the names of the rivers just mentioned. The text says, "A river watering the garden flowed from Eden, and from there it divided; it had four headstreams. The name of the first is the Pishon; it winds through the entire land of Havilah, where there is gold. (The gold of that land is good; aromatic resin and onyx are also there.) The name of the second

river is the Gihon; it winds through the entire land of Cush. The name of the third river is the Tigris; it runs along the east side of Asshur. And the fourth river is the Euphrates." As we study this we must admit that quite a few of these places are unknown today. It may be, as some have suggested, that the geography of the area of Eden has changed as a result of the Flood so that today only two rivers, the Tigris and the Euphrates, are found where four were found originally. Or it may be, as Calvin believed, that the names of the "unknown" rivers have simply changed in time and therefore do actually exist today, though the course of the rivers has undoubtedly changed considerably. Calvin regarded the Pishon and Gihon as ancient names for tributaries to the Tigris and Euphrates and believed, on the basis of the Genesis account, that they all flowed together into one river and then divided again into a delta as they flowed from Eden into the Red Sea.

Whatever the solution to this particular geological problem, there is no doubt that Moses was using names and places at least partially known to his contemporaries. The Tigris and Euphrates were known then and are known to this day. Moses speaks of Havilah as a land of gold, resin, and onyx. He speaks of Cush, generally regarded as a section of Arabia and Ethiopia. Asshur is the land of Assyria. Moses is telling the people that at a specific period in past history and in a place well known to them, God placed the first man and woman and that the fall of man, which has effected all subsequent life so drastically, was as real as the acts they themselves were committing in a different but not totally unrelated environment.

Since Genesis is about to speak of the Fall this comparison cuts two ways. On the one hand, it means that the disobedience of Adam and Eve was as real, comprehensible, and evil as the sins the people themselves were committing. On the other hand, it means that their sin was as real, comprehensible, and evil as the sin of our first parents.

Human beings always tend to treat sin lightly, and one way of doing this is to dismiss it to a mystical realm in which it becomes merely part of the human dilemma or, as is sometimes said, a symbol of the fact that things are not as good as they can and may yet be. In this perspective sin is not a particular thing that I do. It is just an old word for a general and blameless imperfection. This is not what Genesis teaches, and at this point Christianity stands radically opposed to the non-Christian view. Sin is rebellion against God. It is "any want of conformity unto, or transgression of, the law of God," as the Westminster Shorter Catechism states (A. 14). This means that although it is also a flaw in the human constitution resulting from Adam's first sin, it is also nothing less than specific acts, performed by particular persons at particular points and places in history. Therefore the solution to sin must also be a specific act performed by a particular person at a particular point and place in history, namely, the atonement made by the Lord Jesus Christ in Israel in the days of Pontius Pilate.

GOD'S GARDEN

A person might argue that the mere historicity of Eden does not in itself prove the historical nature of the fall of man, and that is true. But, of course, this is not all that we are told of Eden. Eden is described as a real place, but in addition to this it is also described as an idyllic place perfectly suited to the man in his unfallen state. Just as Genesis 2:7 describes man's nature and portrays it as perfect, so does Genesis 2:8–17 describe man's environment before the Fall and portrays it as perfect.

These two things go together and make the Fall dreadful. Man could claim some excuse for his sin were he made imperfect, on the one hand, or placed in an imperfect, sinful or degrading environment, on the other. But neither is the case. His nature was perfect; his environment was perfect. So when he sinned, as we know sadly he did, it was not because of some deficiency either of nature or environment for which God might be thought responsible.

There are three striking things about Eden. First, it was a *beautiful* place. This is evident throughout the narrative, but it is explicit in the matter of the trees which, the text says, were "pleasing to the eye" (v. 9). This is an understatement, of course. We remember that throughout the account of creation God has been described as making beautiful things and pronouncing the creative acts of each of the days of creation "good" (Gen. 1:3, 10, 12, 18, 21, 25, 31). Outside Eden there was an abundant and exceedingly beautiful world. Yet here, in the place that is to be the abode of the man and woman, God had poured out beauty in a special measure. Calvin says, "No corner of the earth was then barren, nor was there even any which was not exceedingly rich and fertile; but that benediction of God, which was elsewhere comparatively moderate, had in this place poured itself wonderfully forth. For not only was there an abundant supply of food, but with it was added sweetness for the gratification of the palate, and beauty to feast the eyes. Therefore, from such benignant indulgence, it is more than sufficiently evident, how inexplicable had been the cupidity of man."[1]

God intended that the environment of man be a thing of great beauty, and in many areas the beauty of man's God-given environment is still evident. On the other hand, we can hardly read this and then turn without weeping to the many distorted and ugly environments that men have made for themselves. God

[1]Calvin *Commentaries on Genesis,* p. 116.

made a garden, but we litter that garden. In our cities we often eliminate the garden entirely. In place of beauty we have the junk, garbage, and sometimes terribly mangled lives of men and women. How terrible sin is! How abnormal is the environment of man today, as we find it!

The second striking thing about Eden is that it was a *useful* place. It had a utilitarian value to it, for we are told that the trees were not only pleasing to the eye but also "good for food" (v. 9).

Here we must stop for a moment. In recognizing the value of what God had made we must not make the mistake of linking value to the beautiful as if to say that the thing made by God was beautiful only because it had some utilitarian value. We sometimes think that way in our fallen state or, which is much the same thing, fail to recognize that something is beautiful in itself just because it is not immediately useful to us. But these early chapters of Genesis alone should warn us against that kind of thinking. At this point we are in Genesis 2. But we remember that even before the creation of the man and woman God created a beautiful and varied world and pronounced all that He created good. It was good, first of all, because He made it. It had value in itself. But in addition to that, the creation of God was also beautiful, and some parts of it (from the perspective of Adam and Eve) were useful also.

The third striking thing about Eden is that it was *perfectly suited* to the nature and responsibilities of Adam. In the verse immediately before this section we are told that "God formed man from the dust of the ground and breathed into his nostrils the breath of life, and man became a living being" (v. 7). By nature man was related both to the ground, from which he was made, and to God, whose breath gave him both life and God-consciousness. Now he is placed in an environment where his task is to "work [the ground] and take care of it"

(2:15). Thus, every day of his life Adam would be reminded of his origin and at the same time of his responsibility, for he would know that he was working the ground at the direction of God and for God's glory.

God kept these matters before Adam by another device too: the command regarding the tree of the knowledge of good and evil. God said, "You are free to eat from any tree in the garden; but you must not eat from the tree of the knowledge of good and evil, for when you eat of it you will surely die" (vv. 16, 17). The existence of this tree would have reminded Adam that he was not his own god and that he was responsible at all times to his maker.

Unfortunately, as we know very well, Adam determined to be his own god anyhow and so rebelled by doing what God had commanded him not to do.

Two Gardens

In time we are going to study the Fall of man thoroughly. But here we should not overlook the obvious contrast between the situation and conduct of Adam in this garden and the situation and conduct of the second Adam, Jesus Christ, in the Garden of Gethsemane before His arrest and crucifixion.

The first contrast is between the good that stretched out before our first parents in Eden and the evil that lay before Christ. Adam and Eve had entered Eden at the peak of God's creative activity. Theirs was a world that God declared unequivocally to be good. He had made our first parents vice-regents over this world, giving them dominion over "the fish of the sea and the birds of the air, over the livestock, over all the earth, and over all the creatures that move along the ground" (Gen. 1:26). Moreover, He had blessed them, saying, "Be fruitful and increase in number; fill the earth and subdue it. Rule over the fish of the sea and the birds of the air and over every living creature that moves on the ground. . . . I give you every seed-bearing plant on the face of the whole earth and every tree that has fruit with seed in it. They will be yours for food. And to all the beasts of the earth and all the birds of the air and all the creatures that move on the ground—everything that has the breath of life in it—I give every green plant for food'' (Gen. 1:28–30). Adam and Eve had all this before them without even a suggestion of a lessening of God's great favors. Yet they turned from this overwhelming and delightful prospect and sinned.

By contrast Jesus faced what Adam and Eve could not even begin to conceive: first, physical death in what is probably the most prolonged and excruciating form known to man, and second, spiritual death from which even His highly disciplined and divinely motivated soul shrank in deep horror. The full measure of what was before Christ is seen in His great agony, bloody sweat and heart-breaking prayer (''My Father, if it is possible, may this cup be taken from me,'' Matt. 26:39; cf. Mark 14:36; Luke 22:42). Nevertheless, Jesus did not turn from this suffering but rather embraced it willingly for our salvation.

The second contrast between Adam and Eve's conduct in Eden and Christ's conduct in Gethsemane is that our first parents spent their time talking to Satan while Jesus spent His time talking with God. The need for prayer was very much on Christ's mind, for all His actions seemed geared to meeting it. He left Jerusalem to pray (John 18:2). He separated Himself from the larger number of His disciples, admonishing them to pray (Luke 22:40). Then He Himself earnestly prayed, returning to pray twice, after interrupting Himself to encourage the disciples in their own vigil. Jesus clearly felt the need for prayer. But Adam and Eve, though on the brink of that sin that would condemn the race, did not pray. Rather, they seemed ob-

livious to the danger as they blithely communed with Satan.

The third point of contrast between Adam and Eve on the one hand, and the Lord Jesus Christ on the other, is obvious. They fell while He conquered. How soon did they fall? Almost instantly, it would appear. Satan presented his arguments, and they quickly ate the forbidden fruit. Jesus, on the other hand, wrestled in prayer and only prevailed at the end.

Finally, we notice that by their sin Adam and Eve plunged the race into misery. They fell and carried their descendants over the cliff of sin to destruction. On the other hand, Jesus stood firm. He did not sin, nor did he shrink from the work before Him, as a result of which he saved all whom the Father had given Him. In Adam all were lost. But Jesus could say, ''None has been lost'' (John 17:12).

The apostle Paul makes this contrast in that magnificent fifth chapter of the Book of Romans. ''Therefore, just as sin entered the world through one man, and death through sin, and in this way death came to all men, because all sinned—for before the law was given, sin was in the world. But sin is not taken into account when there is no law. Nevertheless, death reigned from the time of Adam to the time of Moses, even over those who did not sin by breaking a command, as did Adam, who was a pattern of the one to come. But the gift is not like the trespass. For if the many died by the trespass of the one man, how much more did God's grace and the gift that came by the grace of the one man, Jesus Christ, overflow to the many! Again, the gift of God is not like the result of the one man's sin: The judgment followed one sin and brought condemnation, but the gift followed many trespasses and brought justification. For if, by the trespass of the one man, death reigned through that one man, how much more will those who receive God's abundant provision of grace and of the gift of righteousness reign in life through the one man, Jesus Christ. Consequently, just as the result of one trespass was condemnation for all men, so also the result of one act of righteousness was justification that brings life for all men. For just as through the disobedience of the one man the many were made sinners, so also through the obedience of the one man the many will be made righteous. The law was added so that the trespass might increase. But where sin increased, grace increased all the more, so that, just as sin reigned in death, so also grace might reign through righteousness to bring eternal life through Jesus Christ our Lord" (vv. 12–21).

That is precisely it. One writer declares, "Sin, death, and judgment flowed from the act of Adam. Righteousness, life and kingship flow from the cross of Christ. The sin of Adam was a stone cast into a pool which sent ripples to every inlet. The cross of Christ was the rock of ages cast into the ocean of the love of God, and it is the destiny of all who are in Christ to be carried on the swell of his majestic love and life and power both now and forever."[2]

---

[2]Donald Grey Barnhouse, *God's Grace*, Vol. 5 of the series on *Romans* (Grand Rapids: Eerdmans, 1959), p. 14.

17

A Wife for Adam

(Genesis 2:18–22)

The Lord God said, "It is not good for the man to be alone. I will make a helper suitable for him."

Now the Lord God had formed out of the ground all the beasts of the field and all the birds of the air. He brought them to the man to see what he would name them; and whatever the man called each living creature, that was its name. So the man gave names to all the livestock, the birds of the air and all the beasts of the field.

But for Adam no suitable helper was found. So the Lord God caused the man to fall into a deep sleep; and while he was sleeping, he took one of the man's ribs and closed up the place with flesh. Then the Lord God made a woman from the rib he had taken out of the man, and he brought her to the man.

Our passage begins with a statement which by now should be shocking to any careful student of Genesis. Up to this point everything God has done has been good, and God has pronounced his own benediction on it. Here for the first time we find a malediction, something that is not good. God looks at Adam and says, "It is not good for the man to be alone" (Gen. 2:18). Out of this judgment comes the creation of one who is to be Adam's wife and companion. The passage concludes, "So the Lord God caused the man to fall into a deep sleep; and while he was sleeping, he took one of the man's ribs and closed up the place with flesh. Then the Lord God made a woman from the rib he had taken out of the man, and he brought her to the man" (vv. 21, 22).

In these verses we learn that the woman was made *for* man; she was made *from* man; and she was given *to* man—the greatest of all God's gifts. In the next section we find that she was named *by* man. On the basis of this created order, the later, New Testament instructions for the relationship of a woman and man within marriage and the function of a man and woman within the church are constructed.

Preparation of Adam

God's creation of Eve is given in the context of a story, and the first part of that story is the preparation of Adam for Eve's arrival. Adam had been made in God's image. In his pristine glory he must have had a brain surpassing Aristotle's. Nevertheless, God needed to show Adam that in all the created order, with all its variety, there was still at this time no creature suited to be his companion. Adam's first lesson was to learn to appreciate his wife.

What an interesting way God chose to go about it! Apparently God and Adam stood shoulder to shoulder while God caused a great variety of animals and birds to pass before Adam. As they passed by—from the aardvark to the zebra—Adam was to study and name the animals. We have already seen that this was no arbitrary naming, as if Adam had merely pulled names out of the back of his mind and slapped them on the animals that went by. Adam was being asked to study the animals, note their nature and relationships, and then name them accordingly. That is, he was being asked to do what is even today one aspect of the work of a biologist. He was to study and categorize and see whether among this vast array of animals there might be one suited to be a helper for him. The results were negative, as God knew they would be: "For Adam no suitable helper was found" (v. 20).

The reason for this negative result, as Adam no doubt quickly saw, was that none of the animals had been created in the image of God as he had been. They had bodies. In a certain sense they could be said to have souls, for animals have personalities and are aware of their individualities. But the animals did not have spirits and so could not commune with Adam on the spiritual level.

In the tenth volume of his great work on history, Arnold Toynbee has an interesting comment on the nature of the fellowship that exists between a man and a dog. He says that it is possible for a man and a dog to have great fellowship. They can spend many enjoyable hours. They can play games. They can show and share affection. But, says Toynbee, the fellowship must be on the dog's level because the dog can only communicate on that level. Adam undoubtedly saw this in the parade of animals and realized that if he was to have a companion, the companion would have to be specially created by God and in the image of God, as he was.

It is somewhat peripheral to our theme, but still worth noting, that the radical discontinuity between Adam and the animal kingdom is an additional refutation of pure evolutionary theory. We do not question that in many ways Adam and the animals were similar. All breathed air and participated in certain basic life processes. All could move, act, relate, and react to certain stimuli. But the point of the passage is that there

were even greater dissimilarities. Although similar in some respects, none of the animals was *like* Adam. Henry Morris says, "It is abundantly clear and certain that he had not recently evolved from them! If the latter were true, and his body were still essentially an ape's body (or the body of whatever 'hominoid' form may have been his immediate progenitor), it seems strange that he could have found nothing in common with either parents or siblings. On this point, as on many others, the notion of human evolution confronts and contradicts the plain teaching of Scripture."[1]

There is an additional problem for evolution in the creation of woman, as Morris also notes, but this is even more of an aside. What is clear from these verses is that *Adam was no evolutionist*, at least not after he had carefully examined the animals.

WHAT A WOMAN!

So Adam was prepared for Eve, and Eve was now to be prepared for Adam. She was to be made for him as his ideal counterpart in this world.

Children often get into stages in which they are immensely intrigued by riddles, and one of the riddles that intrigues them—and which therefore passes down from generation to generation—is: What is most like half of the moon? If you had a normal childhood, you probably heard that when you were three. Nevertheless, if a child asks that riddle, the thing to do is guess everything you can possibly think of without guessing the answer. What is most like half of the moon? "Half of an orange?" No. "Half of a basketball?" No. "Half of an Edam cheese?" No. You have to mention everything round and orange colored that you can think of. At last you say, "I give up; what is most like half of the moon?" The answer comes

---

[1]Morris, *The Genesis Record*, p. 98.

back, "The other half of the moon."

Well, that is right. The thing most like one half of the moon is the other half of the moon. So we ask, "What is most like a man?" The answer is: a woman. "And what is most like a woman?" The answer is: a man. Men and women are different, and long live the difference (as the French say). But they are also more alike than anything else in creation.

I wish I could have been there to have seen that first woman. What a woman she must have been! When we were dealing with the creation of the man in our study of Genesis 1:28–31, we pointed out that man in his original state must have been a most extraordinary specimen. Luther thought he must have excelled the animals even in those points where they were strong—power greater than the lion's or bear's, eyesight sharper than a lynx's or eagle's. But if that was true of Adam, what are we to say of the companion God now created for him? Luther thought Eve would have been as strong, fast, clear-sighted, and brilliant as the man,[2] and in addition to that she must have had a beauty and grace that excelled him. What a woman! In her pristine glory Eve would have made Wonder Woman or the Bionic Woman look sick.

Made for Adam

Yet in spite of this physical, mental, and moral excellence—far surpassing that of any woman today—Eve was made *for* the man, as a "helper suitable for him." In this, among other things, the woman has a clue to her unique position in marriage.

This is a point that greatly incenses today's radical feminist and is sometimes a cause for anxiety even for other women. To speak of woman being made for man, even more to speak of her need to be obedient to the man in marriage, seems to such persons to reek of rank prejudice, inequality, and injustice. These outmoded and obnoxious ideas need to be thrown off; women (like men) need to become autonomous, such persons feel. Here we need clear thinking, and one of the things we need to think clearly about is the meaning of the word "equality." You cannot talk about this word in general terms. You need specifics. In a similar discussion of this theme Elisabeth Elliot asks, "In what sense is red equal to blue? They are equal only in the sense that both are colors in the spectrum. Apart from that they are different. In what sense is hot equal to cold? They are both temperatures, but beyond this it is almost meaningless to talk about equality."[3]

Are men and women equal? It depends on what you are talking about. There are important ways in which men and women *are* equal. First, they are both created in the image of God. It is this that makes the woman a fit companion for the man (and the man for the woman), and which explains why the animals are not fit companions. Second, they were both placed under the moral command of God and thus given moral responsibility. Third, they were both guilty of disobeying the command of God and were therefore judged by God for their disobedience. Fourth, men and women are alike objects of God's grace in Jesus Christ. Elliot observes at this point, "In Galatians 3:28, which is the magna charta of those who call themselves biblical feminists, we find Paul saying that 'there is neither male nor female, neither bond nor free, neither Jew nor Greek,' referring to the qualifications for baptism. Social status, nationality and sexuality are all irrelevant to our qualifications for being

---

[2]Luther, *Luther's Works*, Vol. 1, p. 115.

[3]Elisabeth Elliot, "Masculinity and Femininity Under God" in *Our Savior God: Studies on Man, Christ and the Atonement*, edited by James M. Boice (Grand Rapids: Baker, 1980), p. 41.

members of Christ's body."[4] Beyond these items, however, equality is nearly an irrelevant concept.

In the Bible the human family is introduced as a deliberate parallel to the divine Trinity, and the relationships of husband, wife, and children are similar. Theologians speak of the *essential* Trinity, which the Westminster Confession of Faith defines as "three persons in the Godhead . . . the same in substance, equal in power and glory." They also speak of the *economic* Trinity in which, although "one in substance, equal in power and glory," various members of the Godhead deliberately and willingly submit themselves to another in the work of redemption. The Son submits to the Father. The Holy Spirit submits both to the Father and the Son. This relationship is parallel to that of the man and woman within marriage, for as Paul says, "The head of every man is Christ, and the head of the woman is man, and the head of Christ is God" (1 Cor. 11:3). He says the same in Ephesians: "Wives, submit to your husbands as to the Lord. For the husband is the head of the wife as Christ is the head of the church, his body, of which he is the Savior. Now as the church submits to Christ, so also wives should submit to their husbands in everything" (Eph. 5:22–24).

In view of these texts it is difficult to see how so-called "biblical" feminists can insist that these relationships are abolished. They argue that submission is part of the curse, now abrogated by Christ's atonement. But it is significant that the subordinate relationship of wife to husband is found in Genesis first, not after the Fall but before it—in Genesis 2, as we have indicated.

We must stress that this relationship is between a man and woman *within marriage* and, because of the deliberate divine parallels, *within the church* which is the family of God. Nothing in Genesis

implies that every woman is to exist for every man, still less be obedient to him. Moreover, even in the case of marriage the submission involved is voluntary. No woman is obliged to accept a proposal. But if she does and if she is a Christian woman, she must know that the pattern for her relationship to that man is found in Genesis 2 where God said that He would make a "helper suitable for" Adam. If she cannot be a helper to her man or does not want to be, the woman should not marry him.

FLESH OF MY FLESH

The woman is not only made for man, however. She is also made *from* man, as the account goes on to show: "So the LORD God caused the man to fall into a deep sleep; and while he was sleeping, he took one of the man's ribs and closed up the place with flesh. Then the LORD God made a woman from the rib he had taken out of the man, and he brought her to the man" (vv. 21, 22). Apparently, Adam recognized at once what had happened and declared, "This is now bone of my bones and flesh of my flesh; she shall be called 'woman,' for she was taken out of man" (v. 23).

There is something particularly poignant and even poetic about this creation. The woman had been made for man and might therefore be thought by us (thinking now in our fallen, sinful state) to be man's servant. But Genesis has nothing of this. Instead Adam immediately perceives Eve to be his companion—the other half of the moon—and so breaks into verse in celebration of their essential similarity and union.

Like most ministers I am constantly engaged in marriage and premarital counseling, and one of the points I always try to make in my counseling is that God intends a husband and wife to be one—on each level of their being. If

---

[4]"Masculinity and Femininity," p. 41.

man is created a trinity of body, soul, and spirit, as I believe he is, then a husband and wife are to be united on each of those levels—body, soul, and spirit—if the marriage is to be all that God intends for them. A union of body with body is a sexual union. This is important, for if a physical union does not or cannot take place, then the marriage is not a true marriage and it can rightly be annulled.

On the other hand, if the relationship is based on nothing but sex, if it is a marriage of body with body alone and not of soul with soul and spirit with spirit, then the marriage is weak and is headed for the divorce courts. When the glamour wears off, as it always does if there is nothing more to sustain it, the relationship is finished, and there is either total indifference, a divorce, or adultery. This is the result of a marriage that is based purely on physical attraction.

A better marriage is one that is also a union of soul with soul. This refers to the intellectual and emotional side of a person's nature, involving the characteristics we normally associate with the functioning of the mind. A marriage that involves a union of souls is one in which the couple shares an interest in the same things—the same books, the same shows, the same friends—and establishes a meeting of minds (as it were) both intellectually and emotionally.

At this point a special word needs to be said to Christians who are married. Whenever a minister speaks like this, many are already racing ahead of him to point three and are concluding that because their marriages are marriages of spirit with spirit, therefore they do not need to worry very much about a union of their minds or souls. This is not right. Not only do they need to worry about it, they also need to work toward it, for an emotional and intellectual union does not in itself come naturally.

What does a girl have in her mind when she marries a man? What is her vision of her new husband? It has something to do with her father and whether she liked him or rebelled against him. It has a little bit of Cary Grant mixed up in it, and perhaps a little of James Bond or Johnny Carson. What is the vision of the husband? Keith Miller, who wrote the best-seller *The Taste of New Wine,* said that his vision was probably a combination of Saint Theresa, Elizabeth Taylor and . . . Betty Crocker.

What happens when a woman with a vision of Cary Grant and a man with a vision of Elizabeth Taylor get married and begin to find out that the other person is not much like their vision? One of two things! Either they center their minds on the difference between the ideal and what they are increasingly finding the other person to be like and then try, either openly or subversively, to push their spouse into that image, or else by the grace of God they increasingly come to accept the other person as he or she is, including his or her own standards of how *they* should be, and then under God seek to conform to the best and most uplifting of those standards. If we are to have the latter in our marriages, we must work toward it by cultivating the interests and aspirations of the other party.

Finally, a true union must also be a marriage of spirit with spirit, and this means that both the husband and wife must be Christians. If you are a Christian, you must marry another Christian or not marry at all. If you marry a non-Christian, you are willfully choosing much unhappiness, for God's blessing will not be on the marriage and you will be unable to share what is most precious to you.

What will happen to you may be illustrated graphically from the case of Solomon. Solomon had been the recipient of many blessings from God, first because of God's promises to his father David and then because of the fact that

Solomon had himself determined to walk in the Lord's way. However, after the temple was finished and Solomon was at ease in Jerusalem, he began to marry foreign women, one of whom was the daughter of the Pharaoh of Egypt. This was not God's will for him, for the Egyptian princess did not worship Jehovah. And Solomon knew it! In 2 Chronicles 8:11 we read, "Solomon brought Pharaoh's daughter up from the City of David to the palace he had built for her, for he said, 'My wife must not live in the palace of David king of Israel, because the places the ark of the LORD has entered are holy.'" Solomon was saying, "I recognize that this woman does not fit in with the things I know to be true about God, and whenever I bring her around the palace of David or the temple I feel guilty and my conscience bothers me. The only solution is to build her another house and hereafter to live my life in as nearly separate compartments as is possible."

If you marry a non-Christian, that is what will happen with you. Do not think that you will lift the non-Christian up, that he or she will become a Christian. That may happen eventually because of God's great grace, but even if it does there will still be years of heartbreak and sorrow. If you are obeying God, make sure your partner becomes a Christian before the wedding or do not get married. If the other person is not a Christian or does not become one some time before the engagement, I tell you on the authority of God's Word that he or she is not the husband or wife for you. The Bible says, "Do not be yoked together with unbelievers. For what do righteousness and wickedness have in common? Or what fellowship can light have with darkness?" (2 Cor. 6:14). You will have a marriage of body with body and perhaps even of soul with soul. But you will never have a marriage of spirit with spirit and so will fall short of true union.[5]

---

[5]I have borrowed a portion of this discussion from James Montgomery Boice, *The Sermon on the Mount* (Grand Rapids: Zondervan, 1972), pp. 121–24.

18

The First Wedding

(Genesis 2:22–24)

Then the LORD *God made a woman from the rib he had taken out of the man, and he brought her to the man.*
The man said,

"This is now bone of my bones
and flesh of my flesh;
she shall be called 'woman,'
for she was taken out of man."

For this reason a man will leave his father and mother and be united to his wife, and they will become one flesh.

When God brought the first woman to the first man, as we are told in the second chapter of Genesis He did, He did not merely provide Adam with a suitable helper and companion. He also established marriage as the first and most basic of all human institutions. Long before there were governments or churches or schools or any other social structures God established a home based on the mutual respect and love of a husband and wife, and all other human institutions came from it. From the authority of the father there developed the patriarchal and later tribal systems of human government. These gave rise to monarchical systems and then democracies. From the responsibility of parents to raise and educate their children came more formal systems of education: academies, institutes, colleges, and centers of higher learning. From the need to care for the family's health came hospitals. From the obligation of parents to educate their children in the knowledge of God and the ways to worship came synagogues and then churches. One cannot think of a contemporary social or cultural organization that does not have a derivative relationship to the home and marriage.

And that is the problem! Today marriage is under attack. It is being destroyed, and if marriage falls then all these other institutions—churches, schools, businesses, hospitals, and governments—will inevitably fall with it.

FOUR-PRONGED ATTACK

It is not difficult to discern directions from which the contemporary attack against marriage comes. There are four. First, marriage is attacked by the *rampant hedonism of our age*. It has been called the "new" hedonism or the "Playboy" philosophy. But it is new only in the sense that it is being accepted as never before, and it is "play" only in the sense that a child can play with matches or a pagan can play around with sacred things.

Hedonism says that the chief goal in life is pleasure and that this is to be pursued regardless of whatever long-range detrimental effects there may be. Generally it denies them. Sex is for fun, says hedonism, and the more of it with the greater variety of partners there may be, the better. Certainly one does not have to be married to enjoy a sexual relationship. In a strange way, this new hedonism has been supported by so-called Christian theologians through what has come to be called the "new morality," though it is actually no more new than the new hedonism. The new morality has been popularized by such well-known churchmen as Bishop John A. T. Robinson of England, Joseph Fletcher, Harvey Cox, and others. It says that there are no ethical norms except for the one rather vague norm of love. Anything goes. Anything is permissible "as long as it does not hurt the other person." Whether it will or not is to be determined solely from the situation.

The difficulty, of course, is that it is not so easy to define a situation. A couple in the privacy of a living room or bedroom may decide that intercourse outside marriage will not hurt them and that no one else need know. But they cannot be sure that it will not hurt them, and they cannot foresee the consequences that go beyond their own relationship. If nothing else, their decision will change their attitude toward marriage, and that, as I am pointing out, has consequences for the whole of society.

A second direction from which an attack on marriage comes is the *widespread acceptance of adultery*. Indeed, it is worse than acceptance. There is a sophisticated justification for it in the argument that adultery is often a tonic for a lackluster marriage and may well revive it. I have noticed a strange thing about this, however. People who are having affairs readily buy this argument as a defense of their own activity. They feel they are better lovers or at least happier and more interesting spouses to be married to. But when they discover that their spouse has been doing the same thing they are shocked, outraged, wounded, and often quickly on the way to the divorce courts.

It does not require a great deal of effort to think clearly on this matter. A person simply has to put the burgeoning divorce statistics next to the justification of adultery to see what is wrong. If adultery is good, if it is a tonic to faltering marriages, if it helps to hold homes together (as is so often claimed), if it is common (as we know it is), why are there so many divorces? The divorce rate has been rising for decades. In some areas of America more than half the marriages do not make it. One does not have to be brilliant to see that the fault is in the theory. It is *not* true that adultery helps failing marriages. Adultery actually destroys them, though by the grace of God (particularly in the case of Christians who sometimes also sin along these lines) it does not have to. The theory is a lie. No doubt those who want to sin this way and need to justify their conduct will go on believing the lie. Eve believed the devil's lie when she wanted to eat of the fruit of the tree of the knowledge of good and evil ("You will not surely die," Gen. 3:4). But Christians at least should not believe it. Let us stand by the truth and warn even non-Christians of where their sin will lead them.

A third source of attack on marriage is the *ease of divorce itself*, for which our changing social mores and laws are responsible. A generation ago, when divorce was still considered a disgrace, it was not nearly so easy to get a divorce and there was enormous social pressure to hold the home together. No one would be so foolish as to say that all such homes became happy homes. Many were terribly unhappy. But the homes did hold together, and the children did grow up with the benefit of both parents. Besides, in other cases the need to live together and work things out, in spite of what may have been their first desires, did lead many couples to do precisely that with the result that their home became stronger.

Which is the better of the two ways? An approach to marriage that recognizes that it is often hard to live together and which therefore determines to work hard to make the marriage viable? Or an approach that demands easy perfection and which is prepared to dissolve the marriage if the perfection is not immediately forthcoming? The second is increasingly common, but it is not for the good of the couple or society.

The fourth attack on marriage is more recent and more subtle. It is the *legalization of abortion on demand* in which abortion is made an exclusively private affair between a woman and her doctor. Why is this detrimental to marriage? It is detrimental because it excludes the father from a decision affecting his as well as the woman's offspring and, even more importantly, excludes him from the time-honored obligation and right to defend his child.

Not long ago Dr. Bernard Nathanson, a New York doctor who had probably performed more abortions in the country than anyone else, published a book in which he turned his back on his past and called for a reversal of the 1973 Supreme Court decision permitting abortion on demand, which he had worked for. One of his reasons for this change was a gradually dawning realization of what he had done. He had considered himself working in utilitarian fashion for "the greatest good of the greatest number." But he came to see that, whatever his justifications may have been, he was actually presiding over multiple murders—75,000 by his direct action, and countless others indirectly. He now argues that each human life, however small, is precious. A second reason for this change of mind is the family. It is being dissolved, he maintains. By fiat of the high court the father has been denied the natural right to defend his child. And if he has, then he cannot reasonably be saddled with any other responsibility toward it—to society's detriment.

The conclusion is clear. By upholding the right to kill the newest member of a family, the court makes the state a foe of the family. Marriage, pregnancy, and childbirth act as cohesives holding the family together. Sexual activity separated from the family and from childbearing tend to dissolve the family and destroy other social institutions.[1]

Dr. Mildred Jefferson, a general surgeon at Boston University Medical Center and a foe of abortion, agrees with Nathanson. In an interview published in connection with her appearance in the film seminar *Whatever Happened to the Human Race?* she said, "The omission of the father in the 1973 decision implied that he was considered to have no rights in the matter. Later, when the court spoke directly, striking down the Missouri laws in 1976, the courts further denied the father any rights to protect the life of his child before birth."[2]

Nor is this only a problem for the father. It concerns a mother too, in a case involving the pregnancy of an unmarried minor daughter. According to many state laws, a daughter who is a minor has a right to an abortion without even the requirement of informing, let alone obtaining the consent of, her parents. In this case parents are put in an inferior position even to the abortionist. As Jefferson says, "The abortionist has complete and direct access to the teenagers walking in and out of their clinics; whereas the parents are denied the opportunity of even knowing what is happening."[3] We have not seen the full effect of these decisions yet. But we will undoubtedly see them in an intensifying weakening of the family and other social relationships, unless such tragedies are reversed and America undergoes a genuine spiritual recovery.

[1] Bernard Nathanson with Richard Ostling, *Aborting America* (New York: Doubleday, 1979).

[2] "A Look at Life with Dr. Mildred Jefferson" in *Life Times* (Los Gatos, Calif.: Franky Schaeffer V Productions, 1979), p. 7.

[3] "A Look at Dr. Jefferson."

CAN WE RECOVER?

Is a recovery possible? I do not know. With God all things are possible, but given a fixed set of historical circumstances not all things are—unless there are changes. What I do know is that there will be no recovery unless Christians first recover a sense of what God intends marriage to be and then set about to achieve that in their own lives and communities.

The reason I say that Christians are the key to recovery is that only they have a gospel adequate to do what needs to be done. More than anything the innate selfishness of the human heart must be broken. It is a poisonous weed that must be attacked at the root and struck down. That does not happen naturally. It happens supernaturally and then only through the *surrender of self* to God in salvation.

What is most wrong with marriages today, in my opinion, is the love of self that our culture encourages. We put ourselves first. Consequently, if the other person does not contribute to my sense of well-being, serve my goals, and bolster my ego, I am ready to dissolve the relationship. An article by Margaret Halsey in *Newsweek* magazine entitled, "What's Wrong with Me, Me, Me?" is very perceptive. It begins by identifying ours as the "me" generation and analyzes its foundations as the belief that "inside every human being, however unprepossessing, there is a glorious, talented and overwhelmingly attractive personality [which] will be revealed in all its splendor if the individual just forgets about courtesy, cooperativeness and consideration for others and proceeds to do exactly what he or she feels like doing."[4] Halsey denies this assumption on the grounds that most people are just normal human beings and then calls on them, not to intensify the search for this elusive, wonderful person to whom all others should defer, but rather to get down to the rather difficult and demanding task of constructing a personality that is desirable.

All in all, Halsey's analysis is quite good. But it does not go far enough at the point of a solution. It is true that so long as we put ourselves first all relationships will suffer, including marriage. But how does one overcome what is apparently an innate human desire to put oneself first? Humanly speaking, we cannot. But when the love of self is broken at the cross of Christ—when we see ourselves as sinners in rebellion against God and bow before Him—then something happens that inevitably spills over into other relationships. We are less inclined to be self-centered.

The second thing that Christians have and others do not, at least to the same degree, is a *proper sense of service*. We live to serve, not to be served, and for this reason we are willing to submit ourselves to one another within marriage.

When Paul writes about marriage in that great fifth chapter of Ephesians he instructs wives to be submissive to their husbands. "Wives, submit to your husbands as to the Lord. For the husband is the head of the wife as Christ is the head of the church, his body, of which he is the Savior. Now as the church submits to Christ, so also wives should submit to their husbands in everything" (vv. 22–24). He tells husbands that they are to love their wives. "Husbands, love your wives, just as Christ loved the church and gave himself up for her to make her holy, cleansing her by the washing with water through the word, and to present her to himself as a radiant church, without stain or wrinkle or any other blemish, but holy and blameless. In this same way, husbands ought to love their wives as their own bodies" (vv. 25–28). Clearly this is a relationship

---

[4]*Newsweek*, April 17, 1978, p. 25.

in which husbands are to love their wives and be true heads to their homes and wives are to thrive in this relationship. There is a true headship "as Christ is the head of the church," and there is a true submission "as the church submits to Christ." Nothing can deny this. But it is significant that the verse immediately before this calls on Christians to "submit to one another out of reverence for Christ" (v. 21).

Is this contradictory? Are we faced with two different models from which we may choose, taking one and rejecting the other? Not at all. It is merely that the husband and wife submit to and serve one another in different ways. The husband serves his wife by loving her as Christ loves the church, building her up, and leaving his father and mother in order to live with her exclusively. The wife serves her husband by submitting to him as head of her home. The place husbands and wives learn to do this is in fellowship with Christ, who served us by taking the nature of a servant, assuming human likeness, and humbling himself and becoming "obedient to death—even death on a cross" (Phil. 2:7, 8). This is why Paul can say of marriage, "This is a profound mystery—but I am talking about Christ and the church" (Eph. 5:32).

Because of Christ, Christians understand service differently from non-Christians. To most non-Christians service means servility; it implies that the one serving is of little or lesser worth. Christians can never think this way. Christ, who has the greatest worth of all ("God exalted him to the highest place and gave him the name that is above every name," Phil 2:9), is at the same time the servant. We remember that in the upper room, at the very time He was giving His last instructions to His disciples, Jesus took off His outer clothing, wrapped a towel around His waist, poured water into a basin, knelt down and washed His disciples' feet. He then said, "Now that I, your Lord and Teacher, have washed your feet, you also should wash one another's feet. I have set you an example that you should do as I have done for you" (John 13:14, 15). We are being most Christlike when we serve the other person.

We can sum up by this statement: A marriage does not exist for *me*, but for *us*—for the children and society and for the glory of God.

GOD'S GLORY

That brings me to my last point, namely, that marriage exists for God's glory This is why God instituted marriage. During the week I was preparing this message I attended a membership class at Tenth Presbyterian Church in which the teacher, one of our elders, said that God created sheep so that Christians might understand how they act and what they are. I had never thought of it that way, although I should have. I had thought of it the other way around, that God had created sheep and that Jesus came along and discovered that they made a good illustration. Our elder meant that God had created sheep with this end in view—that Jesus would have the illustration when He should come to this important part of His teaching. The point is: if this is true of sheep, it is even truer of marriage, for the Bible tells us explicitly that God created marriage in order that by marriage we might understand the most important of spiritual relationships.

That is why Jesus is portrayed to us in the Bible as the great bridegroom and husband of the church. It is why we who believe on Him are portrayed as His bride. How are we going to communicate this greatest of all relationships if we who are Christians do not demonstrate it in our marriages? On the other hand, if we do demonstrate it there, then the world around will have a real-life illustration of how God works toward us in Christ to bring us to faith and save us from our sins.

19

Camelot, O Camelot

(Genesis 2:25)

The man and his wife were both naked, and they felt no shame.

In the stage version of the King Arthur story, *Camelot*, there's a plaintive scene in which the aging king sings the glories of his once perfect Camelot. It was a paradise, "a most convenient spot," he says. But Camelot was marred by the adultery of Guinevere and Lancelot and by the civil wars that followed and destroyed the kingdom. As the sad monarch sings, Camelot exists only as a memory.

I think of that scene as I read the last verse of Genesis 2, for Genesis 2:25 is a eulogy to the glory of Adam and Eve in Paradise before the Fall. The text says, "The man and his wife were both naked, and they felt no shame." This seems like an anticlimax at first reading. The earlier verses describe the preparation of Eve for Adam and Adam's reaction as God brought this first glorious bride to him and performed the first wedding. If this were Hollywood, the music would swell up at this point and the action would end. Everyone would know that the virile young man and the glamorous young woman would now live happily ever after. But this is not Hollywood. This is the Word of God—reality. Therefore, the text describes the scene in anticipation of the loss to come.

The verse is a bridge to chapter 3. Adam and Eve were naked. We are all born naked—Job said, "Naked I came from my mother's womb, and naked I will depart" (Job 1:21)—but for us nakedness involves shame. Adam and Eve had no shame even though they were soon to acquire it through the Fall.

SIN AND NAKEDNESS

I do not doubt for a minute that the nakedness of the man and woman was true nakedness. Unless it was true nakedness we cannot understand their later attempt to clothe themselves with fig leaves or understand God's provision of clothing by the skin of an animal. Nevertheless, if we are to understand this and the verses that follow, we must know that the nakedness of our first parents was more than physical nakedness and that their awareness of their nakedness after the Fall was more than mere fear of exposure.

What is the significance of their nakedness? The answer emerges in the next chapter where the shame of nakedness is linked unmistakably to sin. In the account of their fall we read that Satan deceived the woman, that the woman presented the forbidden fruit to Adam, and that he ate. Then, immediately after this, we read, "The eyes of both of them were opened, and they realized they were naked" (Gen. 3:7). What is involved here? It is not a matter of physical sight. Adam and Eve were not blind before the Fall. Adam's eyes were not opened physically for the first time so that he saw Eve's nakedness now, though not before, and became aware of his own nakedness also. What is involved is spiritual nakedness, that is, nakedness before the eyes of that holy God against whom they had sinned. It was their sinful state they were aware of, which their nakedness symbolized.

118

In a number of his works Ligonier Valley Study Center's R. C. Sproul analyzes nakedness from the perspective of our culture and shows how we too fear exposure. He analyzes "staring" and shows our ambiguity in being looked at by other persons. On the one hand, we want to be noticed. If someone comes into a room where we are sitting and then passes through it without even glancing at us, we are offended. "Hey, didn't you notice I'm here?" we want to ask. But if that same person comes into the room, sits down and stares at us, we are also offended—only more so. This time our reaction is, "Why are you staring? What do you want? Why don't you mind your own business?"

Why do we react this way? The reason we want to be noticed is that we are persons, made in the image of the personal God. It is a human characteristic grounded deep within that we want to be noticed. But the reason why we do not like staring is that we associate staring with prying and are ashamed to have anyone pry into what we actually are like. So we hide ourselves. We wear masks, pretending to be what we think other people will respect and admire. In a psychologically related manner, we project these false images but reveal our true psychological and spiritual nakedness through the choice and use of clothes. So did Adam and Eve. They made fig-leaf clothes. And when they heard God coming toward them in the garden they hid, knowing that their clothes were inadequate to disguise their true selves.

Before Both God and Man

This gives us the clue to understanding our text, for it tells us that at this time, before the Fall, neither the man nor woman was guilty of sin and therefore neither was aware of shame. They stood naked before both God and themselves and had no cause for embarrassment. They had done nothing wrong, and there was nothing about which they could possibly be ashamed or embarrassed.

There is no way we can understand the beauty of this moment except by contrast with our experience in our own embarrassed state. The point of greatest contrast is in our *relationships to God.* Adam and Eve stood before God fully exposed and yet shameless. They conversed with God freely. We cannot stand before God, nor do we want to. Instead we run and hide from Him, fearing exposure.

This is why some people, such as the existentialist philosopher Jean Paul Sartre, try to deny God's existence. Sartre confesses this openly. In *Being and Nothingness,* Sartre devotes a section of his discussion to what he calls "The Look." He pictures himself in the attitude of looking through a keyhole at someone but being caught in that act by someone else. He does not mind looking so long as he is in the position of power, so long as he is the unseen seer. But as soon as he is seen his whole being is affected. He is overcome with feelings of fear, pride, or shame. He stands up, turns around, pretends he was not looking. So it is with thoughts of the existence of God, Sartre feels. I can see and be seen. But God cannot be seen; He can only see. Therefore, if God exists, I am reduced from the level of a person who can engage with another as an equal, to being a mere object of that one's gaze. I am made less than human. Consequently, for me to be truly human (says Sartre) there must be no God.

It is interesting how Sartre's interpretation of exposure has shifted from that of Scripture. In Scripture we fear to stand before God because we are sinners. In Sartre, objective sin is denied and the problem becomes one of being or becoming an object. Rather than acknowledging true guilt and true exposure, God is denied.

Christians do this too, of course,

though not in philosophical terms in most cases. They do it practically. Donald Grey Barnhouse tells this personal story. He had been preaching on a college campus and was invited to speak in one of the girls' dorms following a meeting held elsewhere earlier in the evening. He spoke briefly and then answered questions. When he had finished a girl remained behind obviously very offended at what he had said. Her face was scowling. "I used to believe all that, but I don't believe it anymore," she said.

Barnhouse asked, "What class are you in?"

"I'm a freshman."

"And what kind of a family do you have?" The girl said that she came from a Christian family.

"Do you have a Bible?"

"Yes."

"Do you read it?"

"I used to read it," the girl said, "but I don't read it anymore. I told you I no longer believe that stuff."

"Can you remember when you stopped reading it?" Barnhouse asked. The girl said that she stopped reading it around Thanksgiving. "Tell me," said Barnhouse, "what happened in your life around November the tenth?" The girl began to cry, and it soon came out that at that time she had started to live in sin with a young man, and it was because of this that she could no longer tolerate the gaze of God that confronted her when she read her Bible. Wesley said it well: "The Bible will keep you from sin, or sin will keep you from the Bible." The God who confronts us in our sin through Scripture is the holy God before whom all sinful hearts are open and all base desires known. If we are not running from sin, we will be running from Him and will be trying to cover our spiritual nakedness by whatever fig leaves are at our disposal.

Adam and Eve knew none of this in those glorious hours before their disobedience. In those hours they approached God openly and fearlessly for, being sinless, they knew no shame.

There was a second area in which they were also without shame: in their *relationships to one another*. They were naked before each other and knew no shame. Here again we can understand the beauty of such a desirable state only by contrast. One of the great wonders of a Christian marriage is that a man and woman can allow themselves to be known by each other and can know that each is accepted in spite of his or her sin and imperfections. The knowledge that a husband and wife have of the other's nakedness is a symbol of this truth. To be naked before one's husband or wife and to be accepted as seen is beautiful. But we must also note that even in the best of such marriages there is still a part of the partners that fears exposure.

We see the principle on a humorous level when a young man and woman are just getting to know one another. When they go out on their first date each is very much concerned with making a good impression. She washes her hair, applies her make-up, brushes her dress, and then tries to appear as beautiful, sophisticated, and charming as possible. For his part, the young man combs his hair and tries to be as "cool" as Fonzi. We must assume for the sake of our illustration that this first date goes well. The young man and the girl each go to their homes and begin to think about their next date. Each has this problem. He asks himself, "What is going to happen when she finds out that I am not quite as cool as I pictured myself tonight?" She asks, "What will he think of me if he learns that I am not really sophisticated or even consistently charming?"

Then they begin, ever so slowly, to reveal their true selves. On the second date he will say somthing like this: "You know, you probably think of me as a pretty cool person, and it's true, I am.

But I wasn't always this way. About ten years ago, when I was just a kid in grade school, I was a little bit awkward. And (can you believe it?) I was even ill at ease with girls.'' Then he stops. He does not confess anything else. Because he is waiting for the girl to say, ''That's funny. When I was a kid in high school I wasn't very sophisticated either. I even wore braces, and I was afraid to go out with boys.'' He is waiting for that because he knows that if she makes a confession to match his, then she has accepted him insofar as he has revealed himself, and he can open up more.

On their next date the fellow and girl may confess what they were like as recently as five years ago, on the following date they get closer to ''now.'' Perhaps, if the relationship goes very well, they may really let their hair down and share what are almost their innermost thoughts. It's a beautiful thing. Still, even in the best of relationships, even in the best of marriages, there is much of inner feelings and past deeds that is never revealed to the other person.

Isn't that a shame? Even in the best of relationships we cannot fully be ourselves. Yet Adam and Eve knew none of this. They were perfectly open and unashamed with one another. They had no sin. There was nothing in either one to hide.

The third area in which Adam and Eve were naked and yet shameless was in *their relationships to themselves.* Adam could look at himself in those days, and when he did he had nothing of which to be ashamed. Eve could look at herself, and she had nothing of which to be ashamed. We in our day hardly dare to stop our mad race through life long enough even to begin to consider who we are. The evidence of our guilt on this, the deepest and most personal of all psychological levels is the hectic pace of our lives. Generations ago people lived slower lives. But life has intensified. People today cannot even come into a room and sit down without snapping on the television in order to fill their heads with something, anything, to keep them from thinking. If they are out on the street where they cannot carry a television, they carry a radio. They fill their heads with the drivel that comes in over the airways constantly. ''All the news all the time!'' It is to keep us from thinking.

The reason we tolerate this and even encourage it by our listening and working habits is that we do not want to think. And the reason we do not want to think is that we suspect (even without confessing it openly) that the God who made our minds might through our minds just get through to us to show us the kind of people we are, and we cannot take that. Oh that we could! If we could see who we are, in all our spiritual nakedness before the holy God, we just might stop to consider and receive the solution that He provides.

Naked Yet Clothed

This brings us to the climax toward which our train of thought has been moving: God provides the remedy. When we understand what it means when we are told that the man and woman ''were both naked'' and ''felt no shame'' we experience the deepest of all pangs of nostalgia. We see that this is a bygone day. It will never come back. You and I will never be able to say, ''Here we stand naked before both God and man, and we know no shame.'' We do know shame, and we cannot return to the days of primal innocence.

But by the grace of God we can go forward. We can go forward because God, who is the God of the future as well as the God of our present and our past, has provided a way by which we can go forward and once again stand before Him and one another. We find it in the continuing story of Genesis. As we come to the next chapter with its account of the Fall and God's confrontation of the man and woman, we find God providing, not innocence, which is now gone, but clothing by which the guilt is covered. We find God taking animals, killing them in what was the first sacrifice for sin, and then clothing Adam and Eve with their skins. The text says, "The LORD God made garments of skin for Adam and his wife and clothed them" (Gen. 3:21).

This is a pattern for what must be done for us as well. We cannot deny guilt because the guilt is there. We can try to deny it. But everything in our way of life, culture, and psychological makeup will deny the denial. We show our guilt by doors and blinds and shower curtains and the clothing industry, and also by our attempts to hide who we are from one another. These behavior patterns testify to the truthfulness of the Word of God, whether we like it or not. "Let God be true, and every man a liar" (Rom. 3:4). But the glory of the gospel is that God deals with the guilt. He deals with it in Jesus Christ, who died for our sins, which is what the killing of the animals and the clothing of the man and the woman with their skins anticipate. Sin is real. But the Atonement is also real. There has been a true restitution. The penalty accruing to sin has been paid. Now God clothes those who have believed in Christ with Christ's righteousness.

This means that we are known by God in all our sin and guiltiness. But we are also loved and received and covered over by grace. We sing about it in a number of our finest hymns.

> Nothing in my hands I bring,
> Simply to thy cross I cling;
> Naked, come to thee for dress.

Or again:

> Jesus, thy blood and righteousness
> My beauty are, my glorious dress;
> 'Midst flaming worlds, in these arrayed,
> With joy shall I lift up my head.
>
> Bold shall I stand in thy great day;
> For who aught to my charge shall lay?
> Fully absolved through these I am,
> From sin and fear, from guilt and
>   shame.
>
> O let the dead now hear thy voice;
> Now bid thy banished ones rejoice;
> Their beauty this, their glorious dress,
> Jesus, thy blood and righteousness.

Child of Adam, whoever you are, know that one day you will stand before the judgment bar of God. You will stand there in one of two ways. Either you will be clothed in the righteousness of Jesus Christ and therefore as one for whom He died. Or you will stand there in the horror of your spiritual and moral nakedness and will be condemned for your sin. The Book of Revelation speaks of that day and of such people, "Then the kings of the earth, the princes, the generals, the rich, the mighty, and every slave and every free man hid in the caves and among the rocks of the mountains. They called to the mountains and the rocks, 'Fall on us and hide us from the face of him who sits on the throne and from the wrath of the Lamb! For the great day of their wrath has come, and who can stand?'" (Rev. 6:15–17). Do not wait until the day of God's wrath overtakes you, when you will vainly attempt to flee from Him. Flee to Christ now! The Bible says, "I tell you, now is the time of God's favor, now is the day of salvation" (2 Cor. 6:2).

20

The Snake in the Garden

(Genesis 3:1)

Now the serpent was more crafty than any of the wild animals the LORD God had made. He said to the woman, "Did God really say, 'You must not eat from any tree in the garden'?"

Step by step the second chapter of Genesis has been preparing the reader for the third chapter, but coming to it for the first time we find we are still unprepared. We have been told that God made everything good. The universe was orderly. But suddenly we come upon a creature whose existence has not even been hinted at until now and we discover, as we read about him, that far from being good he is actually an evil being whose temptation of Adam and Eve brings evil on the human race.

He is described as "the serpent" (Gen. 3:1). Since Revelation 12:9 speaks of "that ancient serpent called the devil or Satan, who leads the whole world astray" we are no doubt right in identifying him as Satan, the ancient adversary of God. But where did Satan come from? Did God create him? Did God create evil? Few would maintain that God could or did create evil. But if not, where did evil come from? Some speak of God creating beings with a free choice, which He undoubtedly did, and therefore with the inherent possibility of choosing evil. But that does not solve the problem. If God created the angelic beings and then later the man and the woman, all with a fullness of virtue and every possible incentive to continue in virtue, as again He undoubtedly did, how could such beings possibly find disobedience to God or opposition to God attractive? To my knowledge no one

has ever satisfactorily explained how such a thing was possible. But explained or not, it obviously was possible, for Satan first fell and then the man and woman.

What we know—from Genesis 3 and other passages—is that there is such a being as Satan, who was created perfect but fell away from virtue through pride, that he carried many other angelic beings with him in his rebellion against God, and that he presented himself here in the garden at the beginning of the history of the human race to tempt the first man and woman.

WHO IS SATAN?

Although there are great and seemingly impenetrable mysteries connected with the fall of Satan and man, there are nevertheless several passages in the Bible that probably refer to Satan's fall and therefore throw light on it and on sin in general. I acknowledge that they do not necessarily refer to Satan; our observations on them must be tentative. Still they seem to refer to Satan and are not inconsistent with what we either know or can conjecture about him.

The first such passage is Ezekiel 28:12–15. Earlier in this chapter there is a prophecy against the prince or ruler of Tyre, an important ancient city on the Mediterranean coast. The person involved is obviously a human ruler. In fact, it is said of him, "You are a man and not a god" (v. 2), though he boasted of being one. But after this prophecy there is a heightened or extended prophecy against the *king* of Tyre, which does not at all appear to be dealing with a mere mortal. It seems to be dealing with Satan or a satanic power that stood behind the earthly throne just as, by contrast, God Himself may be said to stand behind a godly ruler. It is from this section of the chapter that verses 12–15 come.

"Take up a lament concerning the king of Tyre and say to him: 'This is what the Sovereign LORD says: You were the model of perfection, full of wisdom and perfect in beauty. You were in Eden, the garden of God; every precious stone adorned you: ruby, topaz and emerald, chrysolite, onyx and jasper, sapphire, turquoise and beryl. Your settings and mountings were made of gold; on the day you were created they were prepared. You were anointed as a guardian cherub, for so I ordained you. You were on the holy mount of God; you walked among the fiery stones. You were blameless in your ways from the day you were created till wickedness was found in you.'"

Obviously there is much about these verses that we probably will not understand until we get to heaven. But if they describe the original state and subsequent fall of Satan, as we may assume they do (though not with total certainty), they do tell us some important things about him. First, they describe him as being the wisest of all God's created beings, for he was "the model of perfection, full of wisdom." Presumably he used this wisdom to occupy the highest and most important post in the administration of the universe. Second, he is said to have been the most beautiful of God's creatures, for he was "perfect in beauty." The imagery by which this beauty is elaborated is that of precious stones—ruby, topaz, emerald and so on. Gems are valuable, lasting, brilliant

and—most important of all—reflective of light. In a dark room gems are nothing; they do not glow by themselves. But they are brilliant when the sun's light shines on them. We are probably right in supposing that by this imagery the prophet is suggesting what we know to be true in other ways, namely, that Satan, like any other created being, was made to reflect God's glory and that the failure to do this plunged him into moral and spiritual darkness.

Satan was probably what we would call God's prime minister, to use a human analogy. He was to speak for God, administering the universe in God's name. He was to direct the worship and obedience of all created beings back to God. This was a very high position, indeed the highest possible position save that of God Himself. But he was still a creature rather than the Creator, and when he aspired to be more than a creature he sinned. The text says tersely and without any further explanation, "You were blameless in your ways from the day you were created till wickedness was found in you" (v. 15).

LIKE THE MOST HIGH

The second passage that throws light on the nature and fall of Satan is Isaiah 14:12–15. Again, this is a difficult passage to be sure of. Like Ezekiel 28:12–15, it occurs in the midst of a chapter dealing with the wickedness of an earthly king, in this case the king of Babylon. But the language of these particular verses seems to have a greater reference than this, and a quotation of verse 12 by Jesus in reference to Satan in Luke 10:18 seems to link these verses to him. They say, "How you have fallen from heaven, O morning star, son of the dawn! You have been cast down to the earth, you who once laid low the nations! You said in your heart, 'I will ascend to heaven; I will raise my throne above the stars of God; I will sit enthroned on the mount of assembly, on the utmost heights of the sacred mountain. I will ascend above the tops of the clouds; I will make myself like the Most High.' But you are brought down to the grave, to the depths of the pit."

Two characteristics of these verses strike us. First, there is an ascending chain of ambition leading from the lower heavens through the stars to the mount of the congregation, to the utmost heights of the mountain above the stars to the very throne of God. Satan was attempting to displace God. Second, there is a fivefold repetition of the words "I will"—three times in verse 13 and twice in verse 14. Before this all was at harmony in the universe. There was one mind or one will. Now there was a second, dissonant will, and there has been a multiplicity of wills and disharmony since.

In Scripture the word "heaven" is used to refer to three different spheres. The first heaven is what we call the sky or atmosphere. It is where the birds fly. The second is what we would call space. It is where the created universe has been situated. The third heaven envelops everything and yet is more than all we can possibly see or know. It is the abode of God Himself and is beyond our full understanding. Satan dwelt in the second heaven, though he also had access to the third (cf. Job 1:6; 2:1). When we read of his desire to ascend "into heaven," what is probably in view is his sinful and base desire to take God's abode away from Him.

When Satan says, "I will raise my throne above the stars of God," we are probably to understand this as a reference to the other angels. Job 38:7 uses the phrase this way ("while the morning stars sang together and all the angels shouted for joy"). Satan was probably saying that he would usurp authority over the rest of the angelic creation.

Isaiah 2:2 and Psalm 48:2 throw light on "the mount of assembly." This has an earthly reference to Jerusalem in which

the people of God would gather to worship. It also apparently has reference to a heavenly gathering of God's people. When Satan said that he wanted to be enthroned on this mountain he was saying that he wanted to receive their worship.

Finally, there is a reference to the "clouds" of God. If this is referring to mere atmospheric clouds, the progression of these verses is broken. But it may refer to that special "glory cloud," the Shekinah, which appeared to and was with Israel during the days of her wilderness wandering. It moved before the people to indicate the direction they should be going and spread out over them to give shade during the daytime and warmth at night. It symbolized God's presence with the people. In my judgment the reference to "the tops of the clouds" in Isaiah 14:14 is to this cloud, which symbolizes God.

Immediately after this Satan declares with emphasis, "I will make myself like the Most High." Why "the Most High"? God has many names. Why did Satan choose this particular name to express his ambitions? Donald Grey Barnhouse answers, "In the story of Abram we have the record of an incident revealing the inwardness of the name 'the Most High.' Abram was returning home after the battle with the kings and the deliverance of Lot. We read that 'Melchizedek, king of Salem, brought forth bread and wine [the communion elements]; and he was the priest of the most high God. And he blessed him, and said, Blessed be Abram of the most high God, possessor of heaven and earth . . .' (Gen. 14:18, 19). Here is the key to the pride of Satan. God is revealed as *El Elyon*, the Most High God, and in this character he is 'the possessor of heaven and earth.' This is what Lucifer wanted to be. His rebellion was not a request for God to move over so that he might share God's throne. It was a thrust at God himself. It was an attempt to put God out so that Satan might take his place as possessor of the heavens and the earth."[1]

Clearly, when Satan appears in Eden in the guise of the serpent to tempt Eve and Adam, it is a renewed attempt to further this ambition. Having failed to take heaven, he is nevertheless determined to consolidate his hold on earth through earth's inhabitants.

The second prominent feature of the Isaiah passage is Satan's fivefold repetition of the words "I will." He said, "I will . . . I will . . . I will . . . I will . . . I will . . . ." This feature gives insight into the nature of sin and possibly into the reason why God permits it and its accompanying evils in His universe.

Suppose for some reason that the word "sin" was suddenly eradicated from the English vocabulary, and suppose we still had the task of telling men and women about their need of God and of God's work of restoration through Christ. How could we go about it? One way we could go about it would be to speak of "sin" as the existence of a contrary "will" in God's universe. Before Satan's fall there was only one will. It was God's will; it was perfect. After Satan's rebellion there were two wills— Satan's and God's—but, of course, only one of the two was perfect—God's. When Adam and Eve were created there was an immediate problem as to which of the two they would follow. Satan thought he would get Adam and Eve to follow him. Although he got them to rebel against God, he did not succeed in getting them to follow his will. So, there were now four wills, each going its own way and only one of them (God's will) remaining perfect. In time there were six wills, as Abel and Cain were added. Then there were sixteen wills and thirty-two and sixty-four. Today there are billions of wills, which explains the constant conflicts in the human race. But it is still the case that only one, the will of

God almighty, is perfect and totally desirable.

Satan has been trying to fashion these rebellious and mutually hostile wills into a kingdom, but with very few exceptions he has been monumentally unsuccessful. God's permission of evil allows this truth to become increasingly evident.

But what Satan cannot do, God does. In Christ He is drawing the wills of His people back to Himself and establishing harmony where there was chaos before. That is why Paul admonishes us to be "transformed by the renewing of" our minds so that we will be able "to test and approve what God's will is" (Rom. 12:2). It is why he says, "We demolish arguments and every pretension that sets itself up against the knowledge of God, and we take captive every thought to make it obedient to Christ" (2 Cor. 10:4, 5).

Only God can give harmony. Satan cannot. Satan has power to tear down, but he cannot build up. He can divide, but he cannot bring together again. Actually, even his names show this. "Lucifer"—his name before his fall— means "the bringer [or bearer] of light," a reference to his role as reflector of God's glory. But "Satan" means "adversary," and "devil" means "disrupter." The last name is based on two Greek words: *dia*, meaning "through" or "among," and *ballo*, meaning "to throw." The devil is the one who from the beginning has been attempting to throw a monkey wrench into the machinery of the universe.

READING THE BOOK

Satan has been "unsuccessful," but this is in terms of his ultimate goals only. In many cases, as in the temptation of Eve and Adam, he has succeeded. He is a dangerous foe, "a roaring lion looking for someone to devour" (1 Peter 5:8).

---

[1]Barnhouse, *The Invisible War*, p. 50.

The Christian must be on guard against him.

How shall we do that? One thing we must do is learn about him. In the movie *Patton* there is a scene in which for the first time the American general encounters the tank corps of Germany's North African army under command of the brilliant German war strategist Rommel, the "Desert Fox." Rommel's tanks have been destroying the western armies. But Patton outthinks him and is waiting for Rommel with an ambush. The "Desert Fox" is routed, and Patton, who has succeeded by studying Rommel's writing, is jubilant. He laughs and says, "Rommel, you son-of-a-gun, I read your book." Patton defeated Rommel because he knew his enemy. In the same way, although Satan has not given us a war manual, God has; and we are therefore forewarned against Satan and his strategies.

Satan's strategies are going to emerge in part in our study of the fall of Eve and Adam. What we should note here is that Satan is a creature, as Ezekiel 28:15 makes abundantly clear, and therefore he does not possess the divine attributes. He is powerful, but limited.

The limitations of Satan are worth talking about in detail. To begin with, he is not omniscient. God knows all things, but Satan does not. Above all, he does not know the future. No doubt he can make shrewd guesses because he knows the nature of man and has observed history. The so-called revelations of mediums and fortune-tellers—when they are not outright deceits—fall in this category. But this is not true knowledge of what is to come. God stated this in a challenge to all false gods, saying, "Present your case. . . . Set forth your arguments. . . . Bring in your idols to tell us what is going to happen. . . . Declare to us the things to come, tell us what the future holds, so we may know that you are gods. Do something, whether good or bad, so that we will be dismayed and filled with fear. But you are less than nothing and your works are utterly worthless" (Isa. 41:21–24).

Satan is not omnipotent. He cannot do everything he wants to do, and in the case of believers he can do only what God will permit. The great example here is Job, who was safe until God lowered the hedge He had thrown up about him, and even then God did this for His own worthwhile purposes and kept Job from sinning.

Satan is not omnipresent. He cannot be everywhere at the same time tempting everyone. God is omnipresent. He can help all who call on Him, all at one time. But Satan must tempt one individual at a time or else operate through one or more of those angels, now demons, who fell with him.

This means that while the Christian must never ignore or underestimate Satan and his stratagems, neither must he overestimate him. Above all, he must never do this to the point of taking his eyes away from God. God is our strength and our tower. He limits Satan. He will never permit a Christian to be tempted above that which he is able and will always with the temptation provide the way of escape that he may be able to bear it (1 Cor. 10:13). We will stand against the temptations of Satan only if we are united to God through the Savior and draw near to Him. Apparently neither Eve nor Adam sought such union; so they fell. But we, though far weaker than they, may stand because we stand in the power of Him who defeated Satan by His victory on the cross and who will return one day to judge him and confine him to the lake of fire forever (Matt. 25:41).

21

Is the Fall a Fact?

(Genesis 3:1–6)

Now the serpent was more crafty than any of the wild animals the LORD God had made. He said to the woman, "Did God really say, 'You must not eat from any tree in the garden'?"

The woman said to the serpent, "We may eat fruit from the trees in the garden, but God did say, 'You must not eat fruit from the tree that is in the middle of the garden, and you must not touch it, or you will die.'"

"You will not surely die," the serpent said to the woman. "For God knows that when you eat of it your eyes will be opened, and you will be like God, knowing good and evil."

When the woman saw that the fruit of the tree was good for food and pleasing to the eye, and also desirable for gaining wisdom, she took some and ate it. She also gave some to her husband, who was with her, and he ate it.

For the third time in our study of Genesis—once in considering the nature of the book itself ("Fact or Fiction"), once in studying Eden ("East, In Eden") and also now—we must ask whether the material we are dealing with is historical or merely something to be relegated to some special literary genre such as fiction. The inquiry is not demanded by the nature of the material itself. As we have seen, the narratives purport to be history. The reason is that these accounts have been attacked by others as being fictitious because, as I believe, they do not want to face the truths they are teaching.

There has been a concerted effort to dismiss the first two chapters of Genesis. But what has been true of Genesis 1 and 2 is true many times over of the third chapter in that it is even more offensive to the carnal mind. Once, when I was in the beginning stages of my study of Genesis, someone chided me for beginning a book that was "so long and had so little real doctrine in it." But, as I tried to show that person and will try to show anyone who is inclined to think along

such lines, nothing could be farther from the case. Genesis is literally crammed with doctrine—the deep doctrines of the Word of God—and Genesis 3 is particularly notable in this regard. It is for this that so many have been strong in their attacks upon it.

Arthur W. Pink has some perceptive words on this subject: "The third chapter in Genesis is one of the most important in all the Word of God. What has often been said of Genesis as a whole is peculiarly true of this chapter: it is the 'seed-plot of the Bible.' Here are the foundations upon which rest many of the cardinal doctrines of our faith. . . . Here we find the divine explanation of the present fallen and ruined condition of our race. Here we learn of the subtle devices of our enemy, the Devil. Here we behold the utter powerlessness of man to walk in the path of righteousness when divine grace is withheld from him. Here we discover the spiritual effects of sin—man seeking to flee from God. Here we discern the attitude of God toward the guilty sinner. Here we mark the universal tendency of human

128

nature to cover its own moral shame by a device of man's own handiwork. Here we are taught of the gracious provision which God has made to meet our great need. Here begins that marvelous stream of prophecy which runs all through the Holy Scriptures. Here we learn that man cannot approach God except through a mediator."[1]

It would be possible to extend even this rather extensive list, but the point is already well made. Genesis 3 deals with important and disturbing doctrines, and for this it has been subject to the sharp and continuing attacks of those who do not like these teachings.

Fables, Legends, Myths, Parables

E. J. Young, a former professor of Old Testament at Westminster Theological Seminary, has examined the views of those who would consider Genesis 3 to be either a fable, legend, myth, or parable, and has concluded that not one of these views is credible.

On the surface there do seem to be grounds for thinking of Genesis 3 as a *fable*. As soon as we begin to read the chapter we encounter a talking snake, but since everyone knows that snakes do not really talk and that the only place they do appear as talking is in fables, the natural but quite superficial conclusion is that Genesis 3 is a fable. Is this the case? Should the chapter be assigned to this particular literary genre? The interesting thing about fables, which Young carefully points out, is that they all have a moral. Aesop's fables are the best known—though there are other collections of fables also—and in all Aesop's fables a very clear moral is drawn. Young relates one in which a lamb was drinking water downstream and a wolf was drinking water upstream. The wolf accused the lamb of

muddying the water, which gave him an excuse to pounce upon the lamb and devour it. The moral is that evil persons will always find an excuse to do wrong. The story of the wolf and lamb is a story created to communicate that moral. Is Genesis 3 like that?

Young answers, "We realize immediately that such is not the case. In the Old Testament animals do not speak. We have the special case of Balaam's ass, but no other cases than that and the speaking of the serpent in Genesis ever occur. Furthermore, if you are going to dismiss this as being a fable, you would have to find some kind of moral. A fable has moral, but there is no moral attached here at all. So to say that the third chapter of Genesis is just a fable is really not to begin to do justice to it."[2]

There is also this additional problem: the idea that Genesis 3 presents us with a talking snake is based on an inaccurate reading of the passage. I know that this is the way the passage is generally taken. We have all seen pictures in which Eve is seen standing demurely in the bushes while overhead a snake is slithering down out of a tree to tempt her to eat the forbidden "apple." But Genesis does not say that Eve was tempted by a talking serpent. The creature that tempted Eve became a serpent as a result of God's judgment on it, and it went slithering away into the bushes to the intense horror of Adam and Eve, who wondered if God's just judgment on the serpent might also be their own. But when the creature spoke to Eve there is no reason for thinking that this was any other than an upright creature, not totally dissimilar to Adam and Eve themselves. We must not press this too far, of course, for in chapter 2 we have been told that Adam did not find a creature suitable to be his companion and helper until God made Eve. Still, it was not a snake and

[1]Pink, *Gleanings in Genesis,* p. 33.

[2]Young, *In the Beginning,* p. 82.

was undoubtedly an extraordinary and beautiful creature.

Some people would say that Genesis 3 is not a fable but a *legend*. A legend is different from a fable. It does not involve talking animals but rather involves heroic individuals who do heroic deeds. In English literature the best-known legends are those surrounding the figure of King Arthur and his Round Table. Everyone is willing to recognize that there might be some sort of historical basis for these tales. There may have been a king in England by the name of Arthur. But these stories are obviously blown out of all human proportions. The people in them may not be exactly supermen, but they were the supermen of their day. Is Genesis 3 like that? There might be cause for finding material for legend in the deeds of Adam and Eve before their fall, if any were recorded. Then they had powers of mind and body that undoubtedly excel our own. If any beings in the whole of literature have the qualification for legend, certainly they are Adam and Eve before their fall. But we do not find those elements in Genesis. We do not find Adam slaying any dragons. We do not find Eve going off to find a Holy Grail—nothing of the sort. We have an apparently normal man and woman in a normal garden setting, sinning, unfortunately, in an all too normal way.

In recent days it has been popular to regard much of the Bible as *myth*. Myth is a little harder to define than either fable or legend, and this is probably one reason why it has become so popular with some liberal theologians. Broadly stated, a myth is a story meant to tell a religious truth. It does not necessarily have to do with gods and goddesses or heroes and heroines. It often does; the pagan myths did. But this is not essential. What is essential is that it not be

taken literally. That is the point of the liberal scholars.

But whenever I come to a judgment like that, I think of a corresponding judgment by C. S. Lewis, who made his reputation dealing with mythology. He wrote, "A man who has spent his youth and manhood in the minute study of New Testament texts and of other people's studies of them, whose literary experiences of those texts lacks any standard of comparison such as can only grow from a wide and deep and genial experience of literature in general, is, I should think, very likely to miss the obvious things about them. If he tells me that something in a gospel is legend or romance, I want to know how many legends and romances he has read, how well his palate is trained in detecting them by the flavor; not how many years he has spent on that gospel." Lewis then introduced the Gospel of John as an example of biblical material often considered to be mythology and concluded: "I have been reading poems, romances, vision-literature, legends, myths all my life. I know what they are like. I know that not one of them is like this."[3]

Nor are they like Genesis. If Genesis is a "myth," then we are going to have to find another word for myths, for they are different.

Finally, we come to the category of *parable* and ask, "Is the Fall like the parables of our Lord?" On one occasion the Lord told the story of an unjust judge. It involved a widow who had been wronged. She came to the judge to get justice, but he did not want to bother with her. She had no money to bribe him. He turned a deaf ear to her cries. But she kept coming back. She came back again and again and again, and finally the judge said, "Even though I don't fear God or care about men, yet because this widow keeps bothering

---

[3]C. S. Lewis, "Faulting the Bible Critics," *Christianity Today*, June 9, 1967, p. 895. The article later appeared in *Christian Reflections* (Grand Rapids: Eerdmans, 1967).

me, I will see that she gets justice, so that she won't eventually wear me out with her coming" (Luke 18:4, 5). The point of the parable is not that God is an unjust judge—God is just—but simply that if even an unjust judge may be importuned in such a way, certainly God, who is anxious to hear the cries of His people, will do justice to those who call on Him. That is a parable. So we ask, "Is Genesis 3 a parable?" If it is, what is the point? What is the conclusion? What is the lesson that we are supposed to learn?

By contrast we have what is apparently a simple unfolding of the events of the early days of the history of the race and of the consequences that came from them. The biblical teaching is that the man and woman were made upright by God, who Himself is upright. They fell into sin and did so as representatives of the human race, Adam in particular being so designated. As a result of that fall, the judgment of God in the form of death passed on everyone.

Here is the way it is stated elsewhere in the Word of God. Paul writes, "Many died by the trespass of the one man" (Rom. 5:15). Again, two verses later: "By the trespass of the one man, death reigned" (v. 17). In 1 Corinthians 15:21, 22, the same author writes, "Death came through a man. . . . In Adam all die." The verses are teaching that sin and the consequences of sin go back to the act of Adam.

GUILT BY IMPUTATION

A careful reading of the passages from which these verses are taken will show that something more is involved here than simply a description of the fact that all human beings sin. It is true that we sin, but what is also said is that there is a necessary connection between all these individual occurrences of sin. In other words, it is not merely that all sin and are therefore sinners; it is that men sin because they are sinners, and this is to say that the original sin of Adam in some

inevitable way passed on the entire human race. Moreover, it is not only the fact of sin that passed on the race so that there is no one who is able not to sin— *non posse non pecare,* as Augustine expressed it. It is the guilt of sin as well. The biblical view is that God holds the entire race to be guilty because of Adam's transgression.

Is anything harder for the natural man to accept? Guilt by imputation? It is hard to imagine anything more offensive to most human ideas of justice and fair play. This doctrine is thought to be unworthy of God, outrageous, revolting, a valid reason for despising such a God forever if it should be shown that this is in fact the way He operates. It is thought to be so unjust that no possible defense of it could be given. But is this so? Before the doctrine of original sin is rejected outright, it would be well to think through it clearly to see if it does not, in fact, both represent the true state of affairs (whatever we may think of them) and also hold forth the only possible hope of salvation (as strange as this may seem to the lost).

The truth or falsity of original sin may be settled by the answer given to this simple question: Where does sin come from if it does not come as the Bible declares? We see the results of sin in the various forms of human misery and death. We may agree that in many cases these are the direct result of our own sin or failings. The chain smoker cannot really blame anyone but himself for his lung cancer. The overeater is to blame for the weakened condition of his heart. But it is not only the chain smoker who develops cancer or the overeater who has a weak heart. Those who do nothing to bring such things upon themselves are also affected. Children, even infants, suffer. What about these things? How may birth defects, colic, cancer in the newborn or other forms of suffering in the innocent be explained if not by the biblical teaching?

To the knowledge of the present writer, in the whole history of ideas of the human race there have been only two other answers given, and one of them is not really an answer at all while the other is inadequate. The first answer is the eternity of evil. That is, evil has existed from the very beginning of things, just as good has existed from the beginning; therefore, all life is characterized by this mixture. But this is actually no answer because, as we can easily understand, it is simply a denial of the problem. It is the denial that sin or evil had a beginning.

The other explanation is known most popularly as reincarnation. It is the idea that each of us has had a previous existence and, presumably, an existence before that and another before that, and that the evil we inherit in this life is due to what we have done in those previous incarnations. It should be said in defense of this view that it is at least a serious attempt to account for our present state on the basis of specific individual actions and thereby satisfy the basic idea of justice that we all share, namely, that each must suffer for his or her own sins and not those of another. But as an ultimate solution it is clearly unsatisfactory, for we immediately want to ask: But how did individuals get to be wrongdoers in their previous existence? This approach merely pushes the question back and back without resolving the difficulty.

So what other answer is there? There is none, save that of the Bible which explains the universality of sin as the result of God's judgment on the race because of Adam's transgression. Adam was the representative of the race. He stood before God for us so that, as Paul says, when he fell we fell and were involved inevitably in the results of his rebellion.

God's Grace

We should not be angry at God for this state of affairs. We sometimes think we should be angry at a God who is so arbitrary as to visit the judgment of sin on all because of one man's transgression. But we show by that judgment that we do not really understand what is involved. Actually, the opposite is the case. The fact that Adam was made a representative of the race is proof of God's grace.

In the first place, it was an example of His grace toward Adam. For what could be better calculated to bring forth an exalted sense of responsibility and obedience in Adam than the knowledge that what he would do in regard to God's command would affect untold billions of his descendants? We know this even in the more limited area of one human family. What father and mother are there who are not influenced for good by the thought that what he or she does for good or evil inevitably affects the offspring? The man who is inclined to drink may hold back at least somewhat if he knows that his children will be hurt by his drinking. The man who has a chance to steal might not steal if he reflects that the act, should he be caught at it, will inevitably injure his family. In any given case it may well be that the thought of the effect of his action on his family may not be enough to insure a virtuous life, as we well know. However, it cannot help but have some effect on him for good. Thus, it is impossible but that the knowledge of the inevitable effect of his sin on the entire race should have acted as a restraint on Adam. This must have been the most powerful of incentives for good. So if he fell, it was in spite of the grace of God toward him and not as a justified reaction to an arbitrary action.

Even more important, the representative nature of Adam's sin is also an example of the grace of God toward us, for it is on the basis of representation that God is able to save us. Paul says "For just as through the disobedience of the one man the many were made sinners, so also through the obedience of the one man the many will be made righteous" (Rom. 5:19). If you and I and all human beings were as the angels, who have no family or representative relationships, and if we were judged as the angels were judged when they fell—immediately and individually, each for his own sin (which is how most men and women think they would like to be judged)—there would be no hope of salvation, just as there is none for the fallen angels. But because we are beings who live in relationships and because God has chosen to deal with us in that way, both in regard to Adam and his sin and to Jesus and His righteousness, there can be salvation. In Adam we are made sinners. In Jesus we who are sinners can be made righteous. We who are "dead in . . . trespasses and sins" can be made alive spiritually.

The blessings of salvation come, not by fighting against God's ways or by hating Him for what we consider to be an injustice, but rather by accepting His verdict on our true nature as fallen beings and turning to Christ in faith for that salvation which God alone provides.

22

The Fall

(Genesis 3:1–6)

Now the serpent was more crafty than any of the wild animals the LORD God had made. He said to the woman, "Did God really say, 'You must not eat from any tree in the garden'?"
The woman said to the serpent, "We may eat fruit from the trees in the garden, but God did say, 'You must not eat fruit from the tree that is in the middle of the garden, and you must not touch it, or you will die.'"
"You will not surely die," the serpent said to the woman. "For God knows that when you eat of it your eyes will be opened, and you will be like God, knowing good and evil."
When the woman saw that the fruit of the tree was good for food and pleasing to the eye, and also desirable for gaining wisdom, she took some and ate it. She also gave some to her husband, who was with her, and he ate it.

When God placed the man and woman in Eden to be His vice-regents on earth He gave them a maximum of freedom and dominion. They were to rule the earth. There were no restrictions as to how they were to do it, except in the matter of the tree of the knowledge of good and evil, of which they were not to eat.

Many foolish things have been said about this tree. It has been called an apple tree and the forbidden fruit an apple, without justification and with no apparent reason. One writer has conjectured that the fruit was the grape and the sin that of making wine. Many today perceive the fruit to be sex, which throws light on the barely suppressed guilt with which our contemporaries consider this subject but does not at all illuminate Genesis. We know that this is not the meaning of the tree, because God instructed the first couple to be fruitful and multiply even before warning them about the fruit of the knowledge of good and evil (in Gen. 1:28). What does the fruit symbolize? It symbolizes the fact that, although the man and woman had maximum freedom and dominion in the earth, they were nevertheless God's creatures and enjoyed their freedom and exercised their dominion as a result of God's gift. It was a restraint on them. It was to remind them that they were not God and that they were responsible to Him.

Has God Said?

We do not know how long Adam and Eve lived in the Garden of Eden in an unfallen state. But as we read Genesis we gain the impression that the assault on them by Satan came quite early, before they had been confirmed in any good pattern of obedience. Certainly Satan had heard God's warning: "You are free to eat from any tree in the garden; but you must not eat from the tree of the knowledge of good and evil, for when you eat of it you will surely die" (Gen. 2:16, 17). Now he comes—immediately it seems—to suggest that God is not benevolent and that His word cannot be trusted.

This validity of the word of God is the issue in Satan's temptation. For Satan's

134

first words end in a question mark designed to cast doubt on God's veracity: "Did God really say . . . ?" This is the first question mark in the Bible. We know, of course, that in the original text there are no punctuation marks of any kind, but the questioning is in the thought and, therefore, the question mark is well applied in our Bibles. "Did God really say . . . ? Has God said . . . ?" The origin of sin is involved in that speculation.

The exact words of Satan are of special interest, for the sentence beginning "Did God really say . . . ?" goes on to specify the matter that Satan is questioning. It reads, "Did God really say, 'You must not eat from any tree in the garden'?" But that is *not* what God said. God had said, "You are free to eat from any tree in the garden; but [here is the exception] you must not eat from the tree of the knowledge of good and evil, for when you eat of it you will surely die" (Gen. 2:16, 17). Satan changes this positive invitation to eat of every tree (with only one exception) into a negative prohibition designed to cast doubt on God's goodness. Can we see what is involved here? God gives the man and the woman all creation to enjoy, with but one exception—everything they have and see is from Him—and even the one prohibition is explained by means of the penalty attached to it. But Satan suggests that God is essentially prohibitive, that He is not good, that He does not wish the very best of all worlds for His creatures.

The woman did not agree with the force of this initially. But Satan's skillful question put her on the defensive, and she replied with a correct (or at least mostly correct) reiteration of what God had said, ending with the warning, "You must not eat fruit from the tree that is in the middle of the garden, and you must not touch it, or you will die" (v. 3).

At this point Satan replied with an outright denial: "You will not surely die. . . . For God knows that when you eat of it your eyes will be opened, and you will be like God, knowing good and evil" (vv. 4, 5). What is at stake in this denial? Is it food? Apples? Inebriation? Sex? Freedom? It is none of these things. The issue in this first part of the temptation is the integrity of the word of God. Having begun to cast doubt on the essential benevolence of God, which the first pair had no reason for doubting, Satan now blatantly contradicts God's testimony. The issue is simply: Does God speak truth? Can the righteous Judge of the universe be trusted? Sadly we are told, the woman looked at the fruit and saw that it was "good for food and pleasing to the eye, and also desirable for gaining wisdom" (v. 6). She therefore took some and ate it; then she gave it to her husband, and he ate too.

This is the first great revelation of sin's nature. Sin is unbelief. It is a rejection of God's good will and truthfulness, leading inevitably to an act of outright rebellion. There is proof in man's instinctive attempt to blame God for the tragedy.

In one episode from the popular television series of a few years ago, *All in the Family*, Archie Bunker is arguing about Christianity with his atheistic son-in-law Michael because Archie wants to get Michael's son baptized and Michael will have none of it. They argue about a number of unessential things. But at last Michael asks, "Tell me this, Archie, if there is a God, why is the world in such a mess?"

Archie is dumbfounded. He stands stock-still for a moment. Then he tries to bluff his way through. He turns to his wife Edith and says, "Why do I always have to give the answers, Edith? Tell this dumb Polack why, if God has created the world, the world is in such a mess."

Edith answers, "Well, I suppose it is to make us appreciate heaven better when we get there." The exchange is entertaining. But there is a touch of sadness too, for it apparently never occurred to Michael, Archie, Edith, or any of the writers that the mess in the world might just possibly be our fault rather than God's. Rather than acknowledge this simple but unpleasant truth, men say, as H. G. Wells once did, that faced with the world's evil we must conclude that a good God either has the power but does not care or cares but does not have the power. Or they say that He does not exist. These expressions fail to recognize that the cause of the problem is in men and women.

Outright Rebellion

The most important fact about sin is seen in the fall of the man, and the basis for understanding this is to note that it is nowhere even suggested that Adam fell through the deception of Satan. The woman did fall as a result of Satan's arguments. In fact, she fell with good will; for she had come to believe that the tree of the knowledge of good and evil would make one wise—that was what the name signified after all—and she wanted both herself and her husband to enjoy that imagined blessing. That is why she gave the fruit to Adam. She wanted to help him if she could. Eve erred and sinned in her error. But her error, serious as it was, was not duplicated in the case of Adam, nor was it as reprehensible. Adam sinned out of pure rebellion against God.

We see this distinction in Paul's interpretation of the Fall in 1 Timothy, where he writes, "Adam was not the one deceived; it was the woman who was deceived and became a sinner" (1 Tim. 2:14). This may be explained as follows. We must assume for a moment, erroneously, that Adam had sinned first and then the woman. We may suppose that God then came to the couple in the garden saying, "What have you done? I told you not to eat of the tree of the knowledge of good and evil, and you have eaten of it." If that had taken place, the woman might have answered, "But You

also created me to be a helper for my husband, indicating that I am to follow his lead. He is to be the head of our home. So when he ate of the tree, I properly obeyed him and ate also." This is what the woman could have said if Adam had sinned first, and she would have had at least a partial excuse for her transgression. But, says Paul, in actual fact she sinned first and so was in the transgression as much as Adam.

But though Eve was in the sin she did not fall for the same reason. She was deceived; but Adam sinned in utter rebellion. We may remember here that God had placed Adam in the garden as lord of creation and had given him the fruit of all the trees of the garden, except one. He had said that Adam could eat of all the trees north, east, south, and west of where he stood; but one tree, one tree only, was forbidden to him. If he ate of it, he would die. Adam, in full knowledge of what he was doing, looked at that one tree and said in effect, "I do not care if I am allowed to eat of all the trees north of here, east of here, south of here and west of here. So long as that one tree stands in the garden as a symbol of my creaturehood, so long as it is there to remind me that I am not God, that I am not perfectly autonomous—so long as it is there, I hate it! So I will eat of it and die."

This is why the Bible never places the blame for the fall of the race on the woman. Our jokes and much of our popular literature blame Eve for getting us into sin—it is another example of male chauvinism—but there is never a word of blame placed on Eve in Scripture. Instead we read, "For since death came through a man. . . . In Adam all die" (1 Cor. 15:21, 22); "As sin entered the world through one man, and death through sin. . . . By the trespass of the one man, death reigned. . . . Through the disobedience of the one man the many were made sinners" (Rom. 5:12, 17, 19).

The nature of Adam's fall says something else important. It says that sin is apostasy, that is, a falling away from something that existed formerly and which was good. It is the reversal of God's good intentions for the race. We see this in nearly all the synonyms for sin found in the Scriptures: *pesha* ("transgression"), *chata* ("to miss the mark"), *shagag* ("to go astray"), *harmartia* ("shortcoming") and *paraptōma* ("offense"). Each of these involves a departure from a higher standard or from a state enjoyed originally.

Emil Brunner notes that in the Greek view the essence of evil is to be found in matter or, as it can more fully be stated, in the life of the senses. That is, "The conception of sin in Greek philosophy . . . is based upon the fact that the sense instincts paralyze the will, or at least hinder or suppress it. Evil is thus due to the dual nature of man. . . . If this evil is to be brought into relation to time, it has to be described as that which is 'not yet good,' or has 'not yet reached the plane of spirit,' or is 'not yet' dominated by spirit.''[1] The biblical view reverses the matter, replacing the "not yet" by "no longer." Man *was* without sin, as was all creation. God created all things perfect. But man rebelled against God and perfection, and so fell away from that sublime destiny God had for him.

This is the essential biblical note regarding sin, as Brunner points out. "Whenever the prophets reproach Israel for its sin, this is the decisive conception: 'You have fallen away, you have strayed, you have been unfaithful. You have forsaken God; you have broken the covenant, you have left him for other gods. You have turned your backs upon him!' Similarly, the parables of Jesus speak of sin as rebellion, as leaving God.

The prodigal son leaves home, goes away from the Father, turns his back upon him. The wicked husbandmen usurp the master's rights and wrongly seize the land which they only held on a rental. They are actually rebels, usurpers. The lost sheep has strayed away from the flock and from the Shepherd; it has gone astray.''[2]

Sin is rebellion because it is not the primary element. It is only the secondary element. The primary element is that "good, pleasing and perfect will" of God from which we have strayed but to which we are restored by the power of the grace of God in Christ.

PRIDE

In our analysis of Genesis 3 we have taken time to isolate the sin of the woman and the sin of the man, and contrast them in order to define the two root elements of sin as "unbelief" and "rebellion." This has been valuable. But there is additional value, not merely in contrasting the fall of the man and the woman, but in comparing them for similarities. When we do, we discover a great similarity which is at the same time a third and highly important part of sin's nature. It is pride.

What lay at the root of the woman's determination to eat the forbidden fruit and give some to her husband Adam, if it was not pride? What lay at the root of Adam's determination to go his own way rather than adhere to the path God placed before him, if this was not pride? In the woman's case it was the conviction that she knew what was better for herself and her husband than God did. God had said that the eating of the tree of the knowledge of good and evil would bring death. But she was convinced by her own empirical observation—after Satan had raised the doubt—that the

[1]Emil Brunner, *The Christian Doctrine of Creation and Redemption: Dogmatics*, Vol. 2, trans. by Olive Wyon (Philadelphia: Westminster Press, 1952), p. 91.

[2]Ibid.

tree would actually be good for her and that God was mistaken. In the man's case pride is also present, for he repeated the sin of Satan, saying in effect, "I will cast off God's rule. I am too great to be bound by it. I shall declare myself autonomous. I will be like the Most High" (cf. Isa. 14:14).

How terrible pride is! And how pervasive; for, of course, it did not vanish in the death of the first man and woman. Pride lies at the heart of our sinful race. It is the "center" of immorality, "the utmost evil," that which "leads to every other vice," as C. S. Lewis warns us.[3] It is that which makes us all want to be more than we are or can be and, consequently, causes us to fall short of that truly great destiny for which we were created.

This brings us back to what we have already suggested, namely, that we are fallen beings. We are not on the way up, as today's optimistic humanists would indicate. We are not sinful by the very nature of things, as the ancient Greeks would argue. We are not even machines, as if we could be excused on the grounds of such an analysis. We are fallen. We are faithless, rebellious, filled with pride. As a result our only hope is in that grace of God by which He sends a Redeemer, who instead of being faithless was faithful, instead of being rebellious was obedient, and instead of being filled with pride was one who actually humbled Himself to "even death on a cross" (Phil. 2:8). God promises that Redeemer in this chapter. But before we go on to the good news, we must explore further the results of the fall of man that make it necessary.[4]

---

[3]Lewis, *Mere Christianity*, p. 94.

[4]This chapter has already appeared in substantially this form as part of a chapter on "The Fall" in *God the Redeemer* (Downers Grove, Ill.: InterVarsity Press, 1978), pp. 18–25.

23

The Results of the Fall

(Genesis 3:1–6)

Now the serpent was more crafty than any of the wild animals the LORD God had made. He said to the woman, "Did God really say, 'You must not eat from any tree in the garden'?"

The woman said to the serpent, "We may eat fruit from the trees in the garden, but God did say, 'You must not eat fruit from the tree that is in the middle of the garden, and you must not touch it, or you will die.'"

"You will not surely die," the serpent said to the woman. "For God knows that when you eat of it your eyes will be opened, and you will be like God, knowing good and evil."

When the woman saw that the fruit of the tree was good for food and pleasing to the eye, and also desirable for gaining wisdom, she took some and ate it. She also gave some to her husband, who was with her, and he ate it.

In a certain sense, everything that follows Genesis 3:6 in the Bible is a part of our topic—the results of the Fall—particularly the verses that immediately follow. But I want to anticipate that matter in a general way so that, when we come to the remainder of this chapter (and, indeed, to the rest of Genesis), we can focus on specific problems and the cure for these through the work of Christ. We begin with the question: How bad is sin? Or, to express it differently, How serious are sin's consequences?

One result of our being sinners is that we treat sin lightly. But right here we must stop and grapple with this tendency of our natures. Without a true and humbling knowledge of our unfaithfulness and rebellion against God we will never come to know God's grace. Without a knowledge of our pride we will never know His greatness. Nor will we come to Him for that healing we need. If we are sick physically and know we are sick, we will probably seek out a doctor and follow his prescription for a cure. At least we are foolish not to. But if we do not know that we are sick, we will not seek help and may perish from the illness. It is the same spiritually. If we think we are well, we will never accept God's cure; we think we do not need it. But if by God's grace we become aware of our sickness—actually, of the fact that in spiritual terms we are worse than sick, that we are dead so far as any meaningful response to God is concerned—then the base is laid on which we can understand the meaning of Christ's work on our behalf, embrace Him as Savior and be transformed by Him.

How Bad Is It?

In facing this tendency of human nature and in attempting to understand sin better we must be on guard particularly against the argument that, although something is obviously wrong with human nature, surely it is not as bad as the Bible, written by those melancholy prophets of a bygone age, imagines it to be. After all, we are told, the biblical writers lived in grim times; we can understand how they might have been a bit pessimistic. Their world was filled with wars, starvation, disease, and many forms of economic hardship. But this is not 2000 B.C. It is almost A.D. 2000! We do not have those things today! We have reason to be more optimistic. Man is not perfect. But is it not true that his imperfections are just that, imperfections, and that they should rather be considered merely the flaws, short-comings, or peccadilloes of the race?

One answer to this is that if man's nature is really as slightly flawed as the argument supposes, then surely it should have been perfected by now. Those little flaws should have been eliminated long ago. That they have not suggests that the matter is quite a bit more serious.

But an even greater answer is that this is totally unrealistic, as the Bible points out. Man's state is desperate, and we can see it to be such. For one thing, sin is linked to death in the biblical perspective, and death is the ultimate enemy and inevitable victor over all. We must escape death if we are to achieve that immortality we sense is our rightful destiny. For another thing, the tragedy of human existence is overwhelming even here, and it is visible to any who will honestly view the mounting starvation, suffering, hatred, selfishness, and indifference on our planet.

The uniqueness of the biblical position can be seen by noting that in the long history of the race there have been only three basic views of human nature. They may be summarized as the views that man is well, that man is sick, and that man is dead. (There are variations in these views, of course. Optimists will unite in saying that man is well, but some will admit that he is perhaps not so well as he possibly could be. More realistic persons will differ as to how sick he is—acute, grave, critically, mortally, and so on.)

The first view, that man is well, says

that all man really needs, if he needs anything, is just a little exercise, some vitamins, checkups once a year, and so on. "I'm all right, Jack," is the optimists' cry.

The second view is agreed on the diagnosis that man is sick. He is not well. He may even be mortally sick, as some would say. But the situation is still not hopeless; therefore with proper care, drugs, miracles of modern spiritual medicine and the will to live, who can tell what might happen? What we need is to work hard at our ills and solve them. We must remember, so we are told, that even if some of our diseases are beyond our ability to cure now, not all are, and even these remaining ills may be solved eventually. The situation may be bad, but . . . well, "where there's life, there's hope." There is no need to call the mortician yet.

The biblical view, the third, is that man is not well; nor is he sick. Actually, he is dead so far as his relationship to God is concerned. He is "dead in [his] transgressions and sins" (Eph. 2:1), as God warned he would be when He spoke of the consequences of sin before the Fall: "But you must not eat from the tree of the knowledge of good and evil, for when you eat of it you will surely die" (Gen. 2:17).

DEAD TO GOD

Here we are helped by the discussion of the threefold nature of man's being that occurred toward the beginning of these studies.[1] There we pointed out that one thing the Bible means when it says that man was created in the image of God is that man was created a trinity, analogous to the way in which God is a Trinity. God exists in three persons: God the Father, God the Son, and God the Holy Spirit. Yet God is one. In the same manner, man is a trinity in that he possesses a body, soul, and spirit, and these are one. There is an important debate at this point between those who believe in a two-part division of human nature and those who believe in a three-part division, as an earlier study noted. But this is not as significant as it seems. All the three-part division is intended to imply is that man is separated from the plant world, along with the animals, by virtue of possessing a distinct, self-conscious personality. He is separated from the animals by that which makes him aware of God. The soul is that with which man thinks, feels, reacts, and aspires. The spirit, or capacity for spirit, is that with which man prays. Man worships while the animals do not.

This is the being that God created, a being perfect in regard to his spirit, soul, and body. He was the apex of creation. When he fell, on the other hand, he fell lower than the rest of creation, for the Fall affected each part of this magnificent threefold nature. Specifically, his spirit died, for the fellowship that he had with God was broken; his soul began to die, for he began to lie and cheat and kill; his body died eventually, for, as God said, "Dust you are and to dust you will return" (Gen. 3:19).

In the area of the spirit the effect of Adam's sin was instantaneous and total. The spirit was that part of man's being that had communion with God. So when the spirit died, that communication was broken, and Adam proved it by running away when God came to him in the garden. In contemporary language this is described as alienation—alienation from God—and it is the first result of that death which came into human experience as the result of sin. John Stott calls it "the most dreadful of all sin's consequences," writing, "Man's highest destiny is to know God and to be in personal relationship with God. Man's chief claim to nobility is that he was made in the image of God and is therefore capa-

ble of knowing Him. But this God whom we are meant to know and whom we ought to know is a moral Being," and we are sinners. Consequently, "our sins blot out God's face from us as effectively as the clouds do the sun. . . . We have no communication with God. We are 'dead through trespasses and sins' (Eph. 2:1) which we have committed."[2]

This alienation is so total in its effect that it has plunged us into a state in which it is simply not possible for us to find our way back to God unless aided by God Himself. This is the meaning of Romans 3:10–12, in which the apostle Paul writes, "As it is written: 'There is no one righteous, not even one; there is no one who understands, no one who seeks God. All have turned away, they have together become worthless; there is no one who does good, not even one.'"

It is important to understand this text in relation to God, for each of the three main terms—righteousness, understanding and seeking—must be defined in terms of that relationship. If we do not do this, we distort the teaching of Scripture and affirm that which is not true. For example, if we fail to define righteousness in terms of God and His righteousness, we end by saying that there is no good in man at all, and that is not true if we are considering the matter from the human point of view. Humanly speaking, not all persons are as bad as they possibly could be, and even the worst have at times what we would call some spark of goodness. We acknowledge that at times there is even "honor among thieves." But this is not what this verse is talking about. It is talking about righteousness as God sees righteousness, and from that perspective it is perfectly true that "there is no one righteous, not even one." It means that the death of the spirit has affected us deeply

---

[1]See "The Sixth Day" (Gen. 1:24–27), pp. 59–63.
[2]John R. W. Stott, *Basic Christianity* (Grand Rapids: Eerdmans, 1958), pp. 72, 75.

and permanently in the area of our moral nature.

It has also affected us in the area of our intellect. Again, we must not make the mistake of explaining the phrase "no one who understands" on the human level, although it is true that sin has affected our understanding even there. If we said that, we would be affirming that men and women never understand anything, and that would be false. Human beings do have understanding in many things, and some excel in this area. We do have great philosophers, scientists, and statesmen. Paul's words do not deny this. What they do deny is that we have understanding in spiritual things apart from the workings of the Spirit of God who alone gives understanding. He expresses this in 1 Corinthians by saying, "The man without the Spirit does not accept the things that come from the Spirit of God, for they are foolishness to him, and he cannot understand them, because they are spiritually discerned" (1 Cor. 2:14).

The third area of our relationship to God affected by the death of the spirit is our will. It is involved in the phrase "no one who seeks God." The meaning here is that, not only are we incapable of coming to God because of our sin and His righteousness and not only are we incapable of understanding Him because His way may only be discerned by the aid of the Spirit of God. In addition, it is also true that we do not even want to. We must point out that there is a sense in which nearly all men and women do seek "a god," that is, a god of their own making who might, they hope, fill the spiritual vacuum of their lives. But they do not seek God, if by that we mean the true God who reveals Himself to us in the Scriptures and in the person of Christ. It is because of this that Jesus said, "No one can come to me unless the Father who sent me draws him" (John 6:44).

The way in which the death of the spirit has affected us may be seen in the following illustration. In medicine there is a condition known as *myasthenia gravis,* in which the muscles of the body cannot respond to the signals being sent to them by the brain and therefore wither away. In a normal patient the brain signals the muscles to contract by sending electrical impulses along the nerves to the muscles where they are received by a special apparatus known as the motor-end-plate. The motor-end-plate receives the signal and passes it along to the muscle. In those afflicted by *myasthenia gravis* the end-plates are missing. Consequently, although the brain sends the signal, it is never received by the muscle. Because it is not received, the muscle does not respond and it eventually shrivels up.

This is exactly what has happened in the human personality due to the death of the spirit. In the human system the spirit was meant to play the part of the motor-end-plates. It was meant to receive the signals sent to it from God. However, when man sinned the motor-end-plate died. Thus, although the signals are still there, although God is still speaking, the signal is not received and the spiritual life withers.

Soul and Body

The illustration of *myasthenia gravis* also suggests a second result of the Fall. It is not just that the fellowship the human being was meant to have with God is broken and that, with that one exception, things nevertheless are all right. Rather it is the case that this one deficiency affects other areas as well. In the illustration the fact that the muscle cannot receive the brain's signals does not only mean that the muscle fails to respond as the brain wishes. It also means that the muscle itself suffers, for it withers in its inactive state and dies eventually. In terms of the human constitution this means that the death of the spirit affects the soul, with the result that men and women become depraved in this area.

If we go back to the story of the fall of Adam and Eve in Eden, we see precisely how this operates. Following the Fall and the subsequent appearance of God in the garden, we are told that the man and woman hid, thereby attempting to escape the encounter. It was an example of their alienation from God, the first visible effect of their sin. However, immediately after this God called them forth to meet Him and began to interrogate them as to what they had done. God asked Adam, "Have you eaten from the tree that I commanded you not to eat from?" (Gen. 3:11).

Adam replied, "The woman you put here with me—she gave me some fruit from the tree, and I ate it" (v. 12).

What is the full sense of Adam's reply? On the surface it is simply a statement, and a true one at that. The woman had given him the fruit. God had given him the woman. But this is not the real meaning of the fallen man's reply. The real meaning is that Adam was attempting to shift the blame away from himself, where it primarily belonged, to others. He was trying to blame the woman—hardly a chivalrous thing to do, not to mention the more basic need to be honest. Beyond that he was also trying to blame God. What he was really saying was that the Fall would not have taken place if God had not been so mistaken in His judgment as to have provided him with Eve.

In a similar way Eve also shifted the blame, for when God asked what she had done, she replied, "The serpent deceived me, and I ate" (v. 13).

The point of this is that the shifting of blame is typical of the sinful nature and well illustrates what happens once the connection with God has been broken. God is the source of all good, as James says (James 1:17). When the connection with God is broken, irresponsibility, cowardice, lying, jealousy, hatred, and every other evil descend on the race.

But there is more than this. When personal decay takes place this inevitably has social implications. Thus, it must also be said that a further result of the Fall is conflict. Are we to think that the relationship between Adam and Eve was as harmonious after Adam had tried to blame his wife for the Fall as it was beforehand? Of course not! It was the beginning of marital conflict. Similarly, the wish to blame others, plus self-interest and the desire for self-advancement, produce the conflict between individuals, races, social stratifications, institutions, and nations which so mar human history.

Finally, the deaths of the spirit and soul, which have such dire effects, are accompanied by the death of the body. When Adam sinned, the spirit died instantly, with the result that men and women since are born with what we may call dead spirits. The soul began to die. In this area the contagion may be said to be spreading, with the result that we are increasingly captivated by sin. The remaining part of man's nature, the body, dies at last. This is universal. All die. Paul even uses this to prove the extent of sin, for he writes in Romans, "Death came to all men, because all sinned" (Rom. 5:12).[3]

ROBES OF RIGHTEOUSNESS

What is to be done? If sin really is as bad as the Bible declares it to be and if we are unable to set ourselves free from sin's consequences, how can any of us be saved? We cannot save ourselves. That is certain. But the good news of the Christian gospel is that God comes to us in our sin and sets us free, providing precisely what we need. The reason why

---

[3]Parts of this chapter are drawn from James Montgomery Boice, *God the Redeemer* (Downers Grove, Ill.: InterVarsity Press, 1978), pp. 27–34.

these painful truths are elaborated in the Bible as they are is that we might recognize our need and turn to God and His provision.

A number of years ago I had an experience that illustrates these points. I was talking with a young man who had a very low image of himself due in part to his upbringing and his lack of education. He was a shipping clerk for one of the Philadelphia newspapers, and I had occasion to talk to him about sin. Unlike most people, he had an acute sense of sin and was burdened by it. This was the reason why he had come to me. He said that coming to church made him feel worse than he had beforehand, and he was considering not coming any more. He wanted to know what I thought of it. We talked about sin for a bit, and in the course of our discussion I gave him an illustration that Donald Grey Barnhouse had once used, the point being that as we get closer to Jesus Christ we become aware, not of how good we are becoming (though we are, in fact, improving), but rather of how sinful we are.

It concerned a man who was all dressed up and on his way to a party. A car came by, ran through a mud puddle by the side of the road and drenched the man's clothes. It was dark outside, so at first the man thought the damage might be slight. He could tell he was wet, but since it did not look too bad, he thought he would just go on to the party. Ahead of him was a street light. When he got about halfway toward it he looked down at his clothes again and realized that the damage was greater than he had thought. He was worried but thought he would still go on. At last he came and stood beneath the light and now saw the damage with the full illumination of the light upon it. And he said, "My goodness, it's *much* worse than I thought. I'm going to have to go home and change my clothes."

I told this story to make the point about sanctification. But when I got to the end and repeated the party goer's last comment—"My goodness, it's much worse than I thought. I'm going to have to go home and change my clothes"—this young man responded in a wistful voice, "But I don't have any clean clothes."

It was the point to which the Scriptures—whether in Genesis or Romans or any other part—would have us come. They would have us see that we do not have any clean clothes in order that we might come to Christ who alone is able to provide them. These clothes are the clothes of Christ's own righteousness. In them we are able to stand before God. Have you come to Him for those clothes? Have you asked Jesus for that righteousness? If not, do so now and find, as others have found, that He will indeed meet your need and enable you to stand before Him as one of His redeemed children.

24

Carnal Knowledge

(Genesis 3:7)

Then the eyes of both of them were opened, and they realized they were naked; so they sewed fig leaves together and made coverings for themselves.

The most dangerous lie is one that contains some truth, and by this standard the lie of the devil in tempting Eve to sin was very dangerous. He had encouraged Eve to disobey God and eat of the tree of the knowledge of good and evil, arguing, "You will not surely die. . . . For God knows that when you eat of it your eyes will be opened, and you will be like God, knowing good and evil" (Gen. 3:4, 5).

This was partially true. Up to this moment Adam and Eve did not know good *and* evil. They knew the good but *not* the evil. (God knows both, of course. He knows good because it is an expression of His own nature. He knows evil because it is all that is opposed to His nature.) By sinning, our first parents came to know evil as well as good, which is what Satan had said. But they came to know it, not from the standpoint of God, who loves good and hates the evil, but as fallen creatures, who love evil and hate the good. Satan would have been perfectly truthful if he had said, "For God knows that when you eat of it your eyes will be opened, and you will be *like me,* knowing good and evil." It was as Satan that they knew.

Matthew Henry has some well-written words on this subject. He notes that their eyes were opened. "Now, when it was too late, they saw the folly of eating forbidden fruit. They saw the happiness they had fallen from, and the misery they had fallen into. They saw a loving God provoked, his grace and favor forfeited, his likeness and image lost, dominion over the creatures gone. They saw their natures corrupted and depraved, and felt a disorder in their own spirits of which they had never before been conscious. They saw a law in their members warring against the law of their minds, and captivating them both to sin and wrath. They saw, as Balaam, when his eyes were opened (Num. 22:31), the angel of the Lord standing in the way, and his sword drawn in his hand. . . . They saw themselves disrobed of all their ornaments and ensigns of honor, degraded from their dignity and disgraced in the highest degree, laid open to the contempt and reproach of heaven and earth, and their own consciences."[1]

This knowledge is painful, as we can see it to have been in the case of Eve and Adam and know it to be in ours. It was so painful for them that they immediately took steps to deny it or at least cover it up. They tried to cover it up by denial, flight, and fig leaves. Their denial is an example of why the accumulation of greater and greater knowledge often makes it more difficult, rather than easier, for people to come to that true knowledge of self and God which is salvation (John 17:3).

---

[1]Matthew Henry, *Commentary on the Whole Bible,* Vol. 1, *Genesis to Deuteronomy* (New York: Fleming H. Revell, n.d.), p. 25, 26.

GUILT AND GUILT FEELINGS

One painful effect of the knowledge gained by sin is *guilt,* and the most common attempt to get rid of it is by *denial* through shifting the blame to other persons. Adam and Eve did this when God came to them in the garden to confront them with their sin. Adam blamed Eve and ultimately God Himself ("The woman you put here with me— she gave me some fruit from the tree, and I ate it," v. 12). Eve blamed the serpent ("The serpent deceived me, and I ate," v. 13). Today people blame their parents (or children), society, the establishment, or whatever—rather than admit their own responsibility and guilt before God and each other.

With a cunning sharpened by time and desperation, we have today gone even farther and have denied the wrong itself. What I mean by this is that (in the majority of cases) we have made unwarranted distinction between guilt and guilt feelings—a distinction that we owe to psychiatry—and have tried heroically to bring these "feelings" out into the open where they can be disposed of by public approval of our acts and where the acts that caused them can then be done freely. C. S. Lewis writes of this tendency, saying that "we have laboured to overcome that sense of shrinking, that desire to conceal, which either Nature herself or the tradition of almost all mankind has attached to cowardice, unchastity, falsehood, and envy. We are told to 'get things out into the open,' not for the sake of self-humiliation, but on the ground that these 'things' are very natural and we need not be ashamed of them." He says that in doing this "we have broken down one of the ramparts of the human spirit, madly exulting in the work as the Trojans exulted when they broke their walls and pulled the horse into Troy."[2]

To deny that wrong is wrong is no doubt thought to be a great gain by those who are engaged in the wrong. But according to the Bible, the opposite is the case. It is actually the end of the line, the nadir of a darkened mind. This is what Paul indicates in Romans 1, in that threefold repetition of the phrase "God gave them over (or up)." Each repetition represents a degeneration or downward step from the actions described before. In the first case (v. 24) Paul says that when men and women rejected the knowledge of God, and so became fools, "God gave them over in the sinful desires of their hearts to *sexual impurity* for the degrading of their bodies with one another." He is talking about illicit sex—fornication and adultery—as the following verses show. In the second case (v. 26), he says that "God gave them over to *shameful lusts.*" Here he is talking about unnatural sex—homosexuality and lesbianism—as the verses following this also make clear. This is degeneration. Finally (v. 28), Paul says, "God gave them over to a *depraved mind,*" as a result of which "although they know God's righteous decree that those who do such things deserve death, they not only continue to do these very things but also approve of those who practice them" (v. 32).

At first glance, the third step in this sequence seems wrong. It is talking about the mind, and we would reason that, since sin enters the mind before it expresses itself in outward acts, the third step should actually be the first one. But while it is true that sin does begin in the mind, this is not the matter that is involved here and the order is right. What Paul is talking about is not that initial contemplation of sin, as a result of which we do sin, but rather that further rational justification of it by which we deny sin's sinfulness and attempt to gain approval for sin both in ourselves and others. That is the worst

---

[2]C. S. Lewis, *The Problem of Pain* (London: Geoffrey Bles, 1940), pp. 44, 45.

thing we can do. It is the bottom step. Therefore, although it seems a natural attempt to avoid the pain of guilt, which sin has caused, we must reject this attempt and allow ourselves to feel guilt's pain, in order that we might come to the great Physician for the healing that He alone can provide.

The reason we have guilt feelings is that we have real guilt. And the reason we have guilt is that we are in a rebellion against the real God.

NAKED AND ASHAMED

A second painful effect of that knowledge of good and evil gained by doing evil is *shame*, and the standard attempt to get rid of shame is *concealment*. We think back to that beautiful verse that ended chapter 2 ("The man and his wife were both naked, and they felt no shame"), and we realize how much has been lost by disobedience. Before, there was no shame, none at all; there was nothing to be ashamed of. Now there is enormous shame, focused in Adam and Eve's sense of nakedness before God, each other, and themselves. The proof of this acute sense of shame was their attempt to cover themselves with garments made of fig leaves, probably the closest thing at hand.

Concealment ties in nicely with some things C. S. Lewis has written in *The Problem of Pain*, from which I quoted earlier. In this section of his book he has been writing of our need to see sin as sin and thereby realize how bad we are in the sight of the holy God. Now he shows that there are difficulties to be overcome in that we have all tried to conceal these facts both from ourselves and one another.

1. The first way we have done this is by *looking on the outside of things* rather than on what is within. Adam and Eve did this by their makeshift attempts at clothing, a tradition that the modern fashion industries carry on. What Lewis focuses on is our tendency to compare ourselves externally and favorably with other persons. He writes, "We suppose ourselves to be roughly not much worse than Y, whom all acknowledge for a decent sort of person, and certainly (though we should not claim it out loud) better than the abominable X. Even on the superficial level we are probably deceived about this. Don't be too sure that your friends think you as good as Y. The very fact that you selected him for the comparison is suspicious: he is probably head and shoulders above you and your circle. But let us suppose that Y and yourself both appear 'not bad.' How far Y's appearance is deceptive, is between Y and God. His may not be deceptive: you know that yours is. Does this seem to you a mere trick, because I could say the same to Y and so to every man in turn? But that is just the point. Every man, not very holy or very arrogant, has to 'live up to' the outward appearance of other men: he knows there is that within him which falls far below even his most careless public behaviour, even his loosest talk. In an instant of time—while your friend hesitates for a word—what things pass through your mind? We have never told the whole truth. We may confess ugly *facts*—the meanest cowardice or the shabbiest and most prosaic impurity—but the *tone* is false. The very act of confessing—an infinitesimally hypocritical glance—a dash of humour —all this contrives to dissociate the facts from your very self."[3]

What Lewis is saying is that we use an external and superficial comparison of ourselves with other persons to cover up what we really are. And we even cover up in the act of confessing wrongs. We are ashamed of ourselves, and will use any device as a disguise.

2. A second way we have tried to escape seeing how bad things are, and

---

[3]*Problem of Pain*, pp. 47, 48.

thus find relief from our shame, is by *focusing on corporate sin* rather than our wrongdoing. To be sure, there is such a thing as corporate or social guilt. This needs to be addressed. But institutions of government, business, and society have not emerged apart from us. They are projections of what we are and are sinful because we are sinful. It is at the point of our own sin that we must begin to face reality. As Lewis says, "When we have really learned to know our individual corruption, then indeed we can go on to think of the corporate guilt and can hardly think of it too much. But we must learn to walk before we can run."[4]

3. A third way we try to conceal our guilt and cover the shame of sin is by *assuming that time cancels sin*, as Lewis also indicates. We see this in the way we talk about some wrong done in childhood or some nearly equally distant period in our past. We act as if this was of no present concern. At times we even laugh about it. Is God laughing? Is God unconcerned? One of our problems is that we are creatures of time, who possess highly selective memories. Thus, although we may remember the wrong itself, we tend to forget the hurt it caused other people. God is not a creature of time. Everything, including the wrong that we so easily dismiss, is present to Him and is an abomination to Him. Time does not eradicate it. The only thing that does is the blood of Christ which "purifies us from every sin" (1 John 1:7).

4. Finally, we cover our sin by *thinking that there is safety in numbers*. We know how this works. It is based on the simple but illogical conclusion that if everyone fails the exam, then the exam must somehow have been too hard. If *all* people are as bad as Christianity says, then their badness must be excusable.

In human terms it may, of course, be possible that the exam was too hard. But this is not the case when we are talking about God, nor does it always work as an excuse even in regard to human society. Lewis paints this picture: "Many of us have had the experience of living in some local pocket of human society—some particular school, college, regiment or profession where the tone was bad. And inside that pocket certain actions were regarded as merely normal ('Everyone does it') and certain others as impracticably virtuous and Quixotic. But when we emerged from that bad society we made the horrible discovery that in the outer world our 'normal' was the kind of thing that no decent person ever dreamed of doing, and our 'Quixotic' was taken for granted as the minimum standard of decency. What had seemed to us morbid and fantastic scruples so long as we were in the 'pocket' now turned out to be the only moments of sanity we there enjoyed. It is wise to face the possibility that the whole human race (being a small thing in the universe) is, in fact, just such a local pocket of evil—an isolated bad school or regiment inside which minimum decency passes for heroic virtue and utter corruption for pardonable imperfection."[5]

There are doubtless many more ways in which we seek to cover up the shame of our sin, but the point is sufficiently made. What we need to see is that the attempt is wrong and ultimately ineffective. As long as we live in God's universe, as we do (there is no other), we will eventually have to face reality as Adam and Eve did when they were confronted by God in the garden. God has told us these things so we will confront reality now and turn to Him while there is still hope.

FEAR AND FLIGHT

In speaking of the knowledge of evil

---

[4]*Problem of Pain*, p. 49.

[5]*Problem of Pain*, p. 50.

gained by doing evil, we have already spoken of two painful effects of such knowledge and of the most common attempt to escape the pain of each one: guilt, which we attempt to escape by denial, and shame, which we attempt to escape by concealment. There is a third effect also. It is *fear*, and the attempt to escape from it is *flight*.

It is a pathetic picture that we are given of Adam and Eve in the moments following their rebellion. They had become aware of their spiritual as well as physical nakedness, had found it intolerable, and had immediately begun to fashion clothing for themselves from whatever material lay closest at hand. We can imagine them working quickly and grimly, perhaps also none too well because it was work to which they were unaccustomed. But at last they are done and stand up to look at their work. They are fairly pleased with themselves. "Not bad for a first attempt," says Adam. They are thinking that in time they may get rid of the painful effects of shame entirely. They have forgotten about God. Suddenly they hear the voice of God in the garden. They are petrified. Then, like a child who hears his father coming moments after he has broken the antique vase in the living room, they spring into action. They run back into the shrubbery, perhaps even losing their inadequate and fragile clothes in the process. And there they stand, clinging to each other, hearts beating wildly, afraid for their lives. They know He will find them, but they are hoping He will not.

This is the picture of all of us as we are apart from Jesus Christ. We ought to run *to* God, as Adam and Eve should have run to Him. He has not changed. He has not harmed us. He has done us no wrong. On the contrary, we have received nothing but good from His hand. No, we have wronged Him. We have returned evil for good, and now we flee.

This is why Paul says in Romans that there is "no one who seeks God" (Rom. 3:11). It is not that God is not there. It is not that He cannot be found. He has revealed Himself so clearly in nature, in Jesus, and in the Scriptures, that a person is guilty three times over for a failure to seek Him out and find Him. God is there, and He can be found. But we will not seek Him because we do not want to find Him. We fear to come upon Him and therefore hide in the midst of whatever intellectual or psychological shrubbery we can find. Why is it that for all the Bibles and Bible translations in circulation the Bible is so much neglected? It is because the voice of God is heard in that book, calling "Where are you?" and men and women fear the voice of God and run from Him. Why is it that the preaching of the Word is so badly attended? People will give many different excuses—busy schedules, inadequate preaching, hypocrisy among believers—but the real reason is that the voice of God is heard even through the inadequate means of preaching and God's voice makes such persons uncomfortable in their sin. How evident it is that we all share in the sin of our first parents.

What can be done? We cannot undo what is done. But we can allow God to do what is necessary to deal with sin and its consequences. Sin? That has been dealt with at the cross of Christ, for Jesus died in our place to take the guilt, shame, and fear of our sin on Himself. Sin's consequences? These are dealt with as God draws us to Himself through the person and power of the Holy Spirit. He overcomes our fear and clothes us with the righteousness of Christ. And this is knowledge—not that carnal knowledge of good and evil that comes through doing evil, but that spiritual knowledge taught by God's Spirit to all His people.

25

Hiding From Thee

(Genesis 3:8)

Then the man and his wife heard the sound of the LORD God as he was walking in the garden in the cool of the day, and they hid from the LORD God among the trees of the garden.

Someone has said, "The most pleasant of all sounds is the human voice." But if that is true of a human voice, how much truer should it be of the voice of God. God's voice is the most wonderful of all sounds. Yet when the voice of God was heard in the garden following Adam and Eve's sin, the man and his wife were not drawn to it as they had been previously. They were terrified of God and hid themselves.

The problem was not in the voice, of course, for the voice of God was gentle and filled with love. God sometimes speaks in judgment; then the voice is terrifying. But this was not the case in Eden. Everything in God's manner was as before. He came in the garden rather than descending from heaven in some spectacular show of displeasure. He was walking, not running. He arrived in the cool of the day, the most pleasant time, rather than in the heat of the afternoon or in the dark of night, when all human fears seem doubly fearful. He did not come suddenly. He came by degrees, calling as He came. No, it was not the voice or manner of God's coming that was terrifying to Adam and Eve. It was the fact that they had sinned, and when one has sinned against God even the tenderest of voices can be frightening. So they hid! We have a hymn which says,

O safe to the rock that is higher than I,
My soul in its conflicts and sorrows
  would fly;

So sinful, so weary, Thine, Thine would
  I be;
Thou blest Rock of Ages, I'm hiding in
  Thee.

Hiding in Thee, hiding in Thee,
Thou blest Rock of Ages, I'm hiding in
  Thee.

But those sentiments are true only after a person has repented of sin and turned to the Lord Jesus Christ in saving faith. At this point Adam and Eve were not hiding *in* Christ. They were hiding *from* Him, as so many do who today also fear God's face.

NO ESCAPE

I want you to see how foolish any attempt to hide from God is. It is foolish for three reasons. First, it is certain to be unsuccessful, because no one can escape from God. David thought about it and asked, "Where can I go from your Spirit? Where can I flee from your presence?" He answered, "If I go up to the heavens, you are there; if I make my bed in the depths, you are there. If I rise on the wings of the dawn, if I settle on the far side of the sea, even there your hand will guide me, your right hand will hold me fast. If I say, 'Surely the darkness will hide me and the light become night around me,' even the darkness will not be dark to you; the night will shine like the day, for darkness is as light to you" (Ps. 139:7–12).

Why can't we hide from God successfully? The answer is in the nature of

150

God and in who we are, as the psalm indicates. God is the eternal One— "infinite, eternal and unchangeable." He is everywhere, because He is omnipresent. He knows all things, because He is omniscient. On our part, we are merely His creatures (vv. 13–15), and we exist in His universe by His express permission (v. 16). How could we possibly escape Him?

Jonah tried. God came to Jonah with a command to do something he did not want to do. He told him to "go to the great city of Nineveh and preach against it" (Jonah 1:2). But Nineveh was the capital of Assyria, and the people of Assyria were enemies of Jonah's people, the Jews. Jonah reasoned that God was "a gracious and compassionate God, slow to anger and abounding in love, a God who relents from sending calamity" (4:2; cf. Exod. 34:5–7). So if God was sending him to Nineveh with a message of judgment, it was not so He might send the Ninevites to hell—He could do that without the benefit of Jonah's preaching. It was so He could turn them from sin, lead them to repentance and bless them. Jonah determined that literally he would be damned before he would be a part of blessing such enemies.

He determined to run away. The story tells us that he went down to Joppa, where he found a ship bound for the port of Tarshish, and "he went aboard and sailed for Tarshish to flee from the Lord" (1:3).

I wonder what he could have been thinking of. Jonah was not ignorant of spiritual things. He was a Jew. He was a prophet. He even knew the Old Testament Scriptures, for he had the temerity to quote Exodus 34:5–7 back to God in defense of his disobedience (4:2). Did he not know the 139th psalm? He must have known it, for he lived relatively late in Old Testament history and this psalm would have been known and sung for hundreds of years before his own period

of ministry. He would have known the words: "If I rise on the wings of the dawn, if I settle on the far side of the sea, even there your hand will guide me, your right hand will hold me fast." The only reason Jonah could have attempted to hide from God is that sin, once it is conceived, tends to blind the mind and desensitize us to God's presence.

Still, blind and desensitized or not, Jonah could not escape from God's presence. Jonah had his say: the Bible says, "But Jonah . . . ," pointing to his disobedience. But then it goes on to talk about the Lord, and it shows us that God did three things. First, he sent *a great storm*. The storm was so great that even the experienced sailors who were sailing the ship on which Jonah had embarked were frightened. They feared for their lives, and God worked through their fear to bring Jonah to the end of himself and (eventually) to repentance. I seldom think of that storm that I do not also think of that other storm that frightened similarly experienced men on the lake of Galilee. These men were Christ's disciples, and Christ was with them, although asleep in the boat. They rowed for awhile, but they were unsuccessful in bringing the boat to the shore. At last in their great fear they awoke Jesus, crying, "Lord, save us!"

Jesus answered, "You of little faith, why are you so afraid?" Then He got up and rebuked the winds and the waves, and the sea became calm (Matt. 8:23–27).

The comparison with this story of Jonah is obvious. The Lord, who is the Lord of storms as well as all else besides, can either calm the troubled waters of your life or else stir them up to great frenzy. What He does depends on whether or not He is with you in the boat or, to say it a better way, on whether or not you are with Him. If Jesus is in your boat—if you are "hiding in him"— then, when the storms come, you can cry out, "Lord, save me!" and He will calm the storm or see you safely through it. But if you are running away—if you are "hiding from him"—then He will stir up the waves until you repent of your sin.

The second thing God did was send *a great fish* to swallow Jonah and deliver him back to the place from which he had set out. He then gave Jonah the same commission the prophet had received originally: "Go to the great city of Nineveh and proclaim to it the message I give you" (3:2). Farther on in the story we read that God also prepared a small worm to eat the root and thereby destroy a plant that had been shading Jonah. So we notice that, on the one hand, God used one of the largest creatures to do His bidding and that, on the other hand, He used one of the smallest creatures. Apparently it makes no difference to God. He will use whatever it takes to get a disobedient child back into the place of blessing.

Finally, God saved *a great city*. This was His purpose with Jonah originally. Jonah did not want to go to Nineveh. He did not want to be part of anything that would result in blessing on the enemies of His people. But God saved Nineveh in spite of Jonah and preserved it for a time.

Increase Our Misery

The first reason why it is foolish to run away from God is that it is impossible to escape Him, as we have seen. But there is a second reason also: we increase our misery by so doing. This is easy enough to understand. The Bible tells us that "Every good and perfect gift is from above, coming down from the Father of the heavenly lights, who does not change like shifting shadows" (James 1:17). All good is from God. If we will not have God, if we run from Him, the only thing we can hope to find is misery.

We do not admit that, of course; for just as sin blinds us to our inability to escape from God, so does it blind us to

misery. I think here of the prodigal son. At the beginning, when he was home with his father, he was very well off. But he thought himself miserable and longed to be off on his own enjoying the life he was sure his inheritance would provide. He asked for his share of the father's estate, and the father granted it reluctantly. We are told that he then "got together all he had, set off for a distant country and there squandered his wealth in wild living" (Luke 15:13).

The course of sin is downhill, however. So the time came when the money ran out. When this happened the young man hired himself out to a citizen of the foreign country who sent him into the fields to feed pigs. He was hungry. The story says, "He longed to fill his stomach with the pods that the pigs were eating, but no one gave him anything" (v. 16). What happened? Well, when he had money and was enjoying the good life his money was able to buy, he had no thoughts for his father. But at last, with the pangs of hunger gnawing at his insides, he came to his senses, remembered the days of his youth in his father's house and decided to return to him. He said, "How many of my father's hired men have food to spare, and here I am starving to death! I will set out and go back to my father and say to him: Father, I have sinned against heaven and against you. I am no longer worthy to be called your son; make me like one of your hired men" (vv. 17–19).

It is a sad fact that not every case of want awakens a sense of sin and drives the miserable one back to the father. But it often does—this is one reason why God has arranged things this way—and in either case, the story illustrates the misery we bring on ourselves by disobedience. How foolish to run from Him who is our Father and our only true home!

Even When We Run

There is a third reason why it is foolish

to try to hide from God, and the story of the prodigal has already suggested it: God loves us and cares for us even when we run away. The best illustration of this is the story of Hosea and his unfaithful wife Gomer.

God had told Hosea to marry Gomer in order to provide an illustration of how He loves His unfaithful people. For God prophesied in advance that Gomer would prove unfaithful and yet asked Hosea to marry her, explaining, "Go, take to yourself an adulterous wife and children of unfaithfulness, because the land is guilty of the vilest adultery in departing from the LORD" (Hos. 1:2). Hosea did as God commanded him. He married Gomer and loved her. But the time came when she embarked on the path of sin that God had spoken of earlier. She caught the eye of another man, began to flirt with him, and eventually left Hosea for the other man. She left him, as the text says, for pleasure and for the material things she imagined her lover could provide. Hosea quotes her as saying, "I will go after my lovers, who give me my food and my water, my wool and my linen, my oil and my drink" (Hos. 2:5).

What a pity that this poor woman had not learned to value the pure and faithful love of Hosea above these earthly treasures! For not valuing such love, she was bound to lose it . . . and the material things too. What happens to the person who lives this kind of life? The answer is that the way is downhill, as we have seen in the case of Jonah and the prodigal. One year Gomer was living with a man who was able to take care of her fairly well. In contemporary terms we would say that he was able to provide her with a Cadillac and a mink coat. But the year after that, after the first lover had grown tired of her and she was a bit jaded, she was living with a man who was able to provide her with only an Oldsmobile and an artificial fur coat with a mink collar. The year after that it

was a Toyota and a tweed. Eventually she was pulling something out of the trash heap. Hosea's wife sank lower and lower in the social scale of the city of Samaria until the time came when she was living with a man who was not even able to take care of her. He could not provide her with enough food to eat or clothes to wear. She was hungry and was clothed in rags.

We say at that point, "I get the idea: when we run away from God things get bad. Here's the point at which God is going to say, 'You ran away from Me. Aren't you sorry you ran away? I hope you're miserable.'" That is the way we think. It seems to be logical. But that is not the way God thinks, even though in time sin does lead to such consequences. Later on in the story Gomer will be deprived of things. But the first thing God does is intervene in order that she might not lack necessities.

Here is how the events must have unfolded in Hosea's story, though I admit that we have to reconstruct it from the incidental things the prophet says. God must have spoken to Hosea to ask, "Hosea, do you know that your wife is living in the poorest area of the city and that she is living with a man who is not even able to take care of her?"

"Yes," said Hosea.

"Well," God said, "I want you to go down to the marketplace, buy the food and clothing she needs and see that she gets them, because that is the way I deal with My people when they run from Me."

It might have been hard, but Hosea did what God commanded. As we read the story carefully we are struck with the poignancy of this moment. Hosea must have bought the food, gone to the area of the city where his wife was living and then looked up, not his wife, but the lover. "Are you the man who is currently living with Gomer the daughter of Diblaim?"

"What business is it of yours?"

"I am Hosea, her husband."

The man must have drawn back, thinking that Hosea was there to cause trouble. But Hosea said, "No, I'm not here to cause trouble. I understand that you're not able to take care of her. So I bought these things because I love her. Here, take them and see that she doesn't lack anything."

The lover would have thought, "What a fool this man is!" But he took the groceries—scoundrel that he was—and then went to Gomer and said, "Look what I've brought you!" She, foolish woman, believed him and threw her arms around his neck to thank him, giving him the love she should have given Hosea. I think Hosea must have been lingering in the shadows to make sure Gomer actually got what he had provided, for he comments on the nature of her folly. "She said, 'I will go after my lovers, who give me my food and my water, my wool and my linen, my oil and my drink.' . . . She has not acknowledged ['did not know,' KJV] that I was the one who gave her the grain, the new wine and oil, who lavished on her the silver and gold—which they used for Baal" (2:5, 8).

Does love act like that? Does love take valuable money and spend it on a worthless woman? In this life, perhaps not very often. But this is the way God acts constantly. We spurn His love and squander His resources, but still He loves us and provides for us. Donald Grey Barnhouse, who has written well on this story, asks, "Who can explain the sanity of true love? Love is of God, and it is infinite. Love is sovereign. Love is apart from reason; love exists for its own reasons. Love is not according to logic; love is according to love. Thus it was with Hosea, for he was playing the part that God has played with you, all of your life, and with me."[1]

In the end of the story Gomer falls into slavery and Hosea buys her back as an illustration of what the Lord Jesus Christ has done for us in redemption, for redemption means "to buy out of" slavery. But that is an anticipation of themes yet to come. What I have tried to show here is just the folly of trying to run away from God. It is folly because we cannot succeed, because we bring misery on ourselves by so doing and because God loves even when we run from Him. God loved Adam and Eve, as He shows in the verses to which we come next. He loved them and provided for them. He even pointed forward to that ultimate means of salvation through the seed of the woman who would crush the serpent's head.

Why run from God, then—if you are running? Stop running and hear His still, small voice as He calls to you in the garden. It is not an angry voice. It is a gentle, loving, patient, yearning voice. It offers you salvation through Christ.

---

[1]Donald Grey Barnhouse, "Epistle to the Romans," Part 37 (Philadelphia: The Bible Study Hour, 1952), p. 1841.

26

God in the Garden

(Genesis 3:9–14)

But the LORD God called to the man, "Where are you?"
He answered, "I heard you in the garden and I was afraid because I was naked; so I hid."
And he said, "Who told you that you were naked? Have you eaten from the tree that I commanded you not to eat from?"
The man said, "The woman you put here with me—she gave me some fruit from the tree, and I ate it."
Then the LORD God said to the woman, "What is this you have done?"
The woman said, "The serpent deceived me, and I ate."
So the LORD God said to the serpent, "Because you have done this,
  "Cursed are you above all the livestock
  and all the wild animals!
You will crawl on your belly
  and you will eat dust
  all the days of your life."

If we were rewriting the early chapters of Genesis to prepare the book for the stage, our play would already have had several important scenes—each with its own characters and characteristics. The first scene is *creation,* in which God alone is active. He speaks and the worlds come into being. The second scene is *domestic.* It involves God, Adam, and Eve, as God makes a place for the man and woman and prepares each of them for the other. This scene fills chapter 2 and ends on the notation: "the man and his wife were both naked, and they felt no shame" (v. 25). The third scene is *the temptation.* In it the characters are Adam, Eve, and Satan. It ends with the Fall. Beginning with chapter 3, verse 8, we come to a fourth scene in which God now enters the garden to confront the other three. This is *a judicial scene,* a scene of judgment.

Like any true judicial proceeding it has four clearly defined parts: 1) the ar-raignment, 2) the examination, 3) the verdict, and 4) the passing of sentence. The terror of this scene is found in its being a foretaste of that moment when we shall each die and stand before the judgment bar of God.

THE ARRAIGNMENT

The first words spoken by God after man's fall into sin are a question designed to get the man to face up to what he and Eve had done. God asked, "Where are you?" (v. 9).

In the history of the interpretation of this passage these words have been taken in a number of ways. Some have imagined them to be a bemoaning question, as if God were asking, "Poor Adam, what has become of you? How far have you fallen?" Others have seen them as an upbraiding question: "Look what you have done to yourself! Where now is your glory? Where is that inno-cent person who used to meet me joyfully?"[1] I think, in view of the overall tone of the passage, that God is merely calling the man and woman forward to the judicial proceeding. He does not need to ask where they are, for He already knows that. He does not need to berate Adam and Eve, for their corruption becomes all too apparent in the following examination. It is simply that God has proceeded to the dais, so to speak, and has intoned, "We are now ready to open the case of Adam and Eve versus God. Where is Adam? Will Adam and Eve please approach the bench."

Notice that when God called Adam, Adam answered! When God summoned Adam and Eve, they approached the bench! They may not have wanted to. They had been hiding, and they would have preferred to go on hiding. But God called. The will of God was that they come forward. And because this was the sovereign, mighty, efficacious will of God, Adam and Eve did respond, just as all men and women will respond when the trumpet of God sounds to summon them to the last assize.

You may be running away from God, hiding from Him. But the day is coming when God will call your name, and His call will *make* you come before Him. God called Moses from the burning bush, and Moses responded. God called Lazarus, and Lazarus responded even from the tomb. One day the call of judgment will go out and all will appear for sentencing. We read in Jeremiah, "But now I will send for many fishermen . . . and they will catch them. After that I will send for many hunters, and they will hunt them down on every mountain and hill and from the crevices of the rocks. My eyes are on all their ways; they are not hidden from me, nor is their sin concealed from my eyes" (Jer. 16:16, 17). In Revelation we read, "And I saw the dead, great and small, standing before the throne, and books were opened. . . .

The dead were judged according to what they had done as recorded in the books. The sea gave up the dead that were in it, and death and Hades gave up the dead that were in them, and each person was judged according to what he had done" (Rev. 20:12, 13). There is no escape from the judgment call of God. So the first lesson of this passage is to prepare for that judgment while there is yet time.

THE EXAMINATION

Having summoned Adam and Eve from their place of hiding, God now proceeds to the examination. Once again He asks questions: "Who told you that you were naked? Have you eaten from the tree that I commanded you not to eat from? . . . What is this you have done?" (vv. 11, 13). Why does God ask such questions? It is not to gain information any more than God was trying to gain information when He asked, "Where are you?" It was to bring Adam and Eve to the point of personal confession of the wrong done. It was not that God might be informed but that Adam and Eve might be humbled.

Oh, the terrible nature of sin! Adam and Eve were asked questions designed to bring them to the point of confession and repentance. But far from doing as they should have done, our first parents actually compounded the sin by trying to excuse themselves and shift the blame to others. Adam tried to shift the blame to Eve and eventually to God, as we have already seen. He said, "The woman you put here with me—she gave me some fruit from the tree, and I ate it" (v. 12). The woman tried to shift the blame to the serpent: "The serpent deceived me, and I ate" (v. 13). This is not the Adam we have seen in the earlier chapters. This is not the Eve who rated one hundred on a scale of one to ten. Here are miserable sinners, like ourselves, who lie and squirm and shift the blame,

---

[1]These earlier views are discussed by Matthew Henry, *Commentary*, Vol. 1, p. 27.

rather than acknowledge their own deep guilt and moral responsibility.

Martin Luther must have appreciated this passage more than most commentators, for his comments on it are rich and profound. He notes three important things. First, *sin is progressive*. It constantly extends and compounds itself, no less in making excuses for its deeds than in openly running away from God. Luther writes, "Let us learn, then, that this perversion and stupidity always accompany sin and that sinners accuse themselves by their excuses and betray themselves by their defense, especially before God. . . . This is the nature of sin: unless God immediately provides a cure and calls the sinner back, he flees endlessly from God and, by excusing his sin with lies, heaps sin upon sin until he arrives at blasphemy and despair. Thus sin by its own gravitation always draws with it another sin and brings on eternal destruction, till finally the sinful person would rather accuse God than acknowledge his own sin. Adam should have said: 'Lord, I have sinned.' But he does not do this. He accuses God of sin and says in reality: 'Thou, Lord, hast sinned. For I would have remained holy in Paradise after eating of the fruit if Thou hadst kept quiet.' This is in reality the meaning of his words when he says: 'I would not have fled if Thy voice had not frightened me.'"[2]

We can compound our sin even when we appear to be confessing it—so terrible is this malady. On the surface Adam acknowledged that he had indeed eaten of the forbidden fruit: "I ate it" (v. 12). Eve said the same: "I ate" (v. 13). But though they give the appearance of confessing their sin, they are not actually confessing it at all. They are admitting only what cannot be denied. And even while admitting this, they are pleading extenuating circumstances. In law this would be called a plea of "con-

fession and avoidance." It admits the fact but denies guilt on the basis of the circumstances.

When we attempt to deny our guilt by pleading circumstances, we are ultimately blaming one of only two possible individuals: God or the devil. Adam blamed God: "The woman *you* put here with me—she gave me some fruit from the tree" (v. 12). The woman blamed the devil: "The serpent deceived me" (v. 13). But having done this they had exhausted all the possibilities. If they would not acknowledge their own culpability, the only possible beings left to blame were God and Satan. We might argue that this is not quite the case, that it is possible to blame *mere* circumstances. "It's a matter of genes, environment, or conditioning," we might argue. Again, "It's the fault of the other person." But those excuses ultimately boil down to the same thing. Conditions are not moral agents. They are amoral, neutral. Or even if they may be considered to have moral overtones or propensities, we still have to ask who has determined or controls the conditions. If we look at other persons, we have to ask, "But who made those persons (Eve, Adam or whomever)? Who made them the way they are?" It is either God or the devil, and therefore: "Either God or the devil is culpable."

Someone might still argue that there is nevertheless a great difference here, for blaming the devil is far less serious than blaming God. But we tend to blame God even for the devil. Certainly Eve could have gone on to say, "And the serpent who deceived me was the one You allowed into the garden!" It is the case, then, that ultimately every attempt to excuse ourselves is an attempt to blame God. And if that is the case, Luther is profoundly accurate when he views Adam as saying in reality, "*Thou*, Lord, hast sinned." I can think of nothing

---

[2]*Works*, Vol. 1, pp. 174, 175.

more able to show sin's horror than this miserable tendency of men to blame the holy, all-wise God for our own transgressions.

The second point Luther makes in his discussion of this passage is that *sin is the same everywhere.* He writes, "Eve, too, is put before us as an example; and when she is corrupted by sin, she is not one whit better than Adam. Adam wanted to appear innocent; he passed on his guilt from himself to God, who had given him his wife. Eve also tries to excuse herself and accuses the serpent. . . . So we see that sin is and acts the same everywhere. It does not want to be sin; it does not want to be punished because of sin. It wants to be righteous. When it cannot achieve this, it puts the guilt on God, so that it accuses God of a lie when he accuses sin. Thus out of a human sin comes a sin that is clearly demonic; unbelief turns into blasphemy, disobedience into contempt of the Creator."[3]

It is important to see this, because we look only on the outside of things and therefore tend to judge sin to be worse in one person than another because of circumstances. Donald Grey Barnhouse tells of traveling in India along the old Great North Road that leads from Calcutta through the United Provinces and the Punjab to the northwest frontier. It was a hard, paved road. But alongside the paved road was a dirt road used by caravan camels, as their feet cannot stand a paved surface. In the rainy season this dirt road became a quagmire where it was far more difficult to walk than on the paved highway. Barnhouse imagines a man walking along the camel road up to his knees in mud. Another man comes along and says, "Come up here out of the mud; you'll do much better on the paved road." The man

does. There is a great change. His circumstances are now much more pleasant. But, as Barnhouse points out, he is still the same man on the same road headed to the same destination.

In spiritual terms we must acknowledge that the broad road that leads to destruction does have a muddy side and a paved side. But it is still the road to destruction, and sin is sin whether it is dressed in fine linen or rags.[4]

Luther's third point is that *sin blinds us even to God's goodness.* He notes that Adam and Eve are not immediately condemned to death for their sin, as they deserve, but rather experience the great kindness and mercy of God. This is seen at the end of the affair and at the beginning. "The beginnings of this affair, if we evaluate them properly, are more lenient than what Adam deserved. There is not that terrible sight as on Mt. Sinai, where trumpet blasts were mingled with flashes of lightning and peals of thunder. But God comes in a very soft breeze to indicate that the reprimand will be fatherly. He does not drive Adam away from himself because of his sin, but he calls him and calls him back from his sin. Yet Adam does not understand or see this fatherly concern, since he is overwhelmed by his sin and terror."[5]

Nothing so blinds the heart and mind as sin, but the blindness is all on man's part. God knows us. But we are so blinded by sin that we know neither God nor ourselves properly. John Keble has written:

Sun of my soul, Thou Savior dear,
It is not night if Thou be near;
O may no earth-born cloud arise
To hide Thee from Thy servant's eyes.

But the clouds of sin do hide God from our eyes, though they do not come from heaven. These clouds are "earth-born."

---

[3]*Works,* Vol. 1, pp. 178, 179.
[4]Donald Grey Barnhouse, *God's Methods for Holy Living* (Grand Rapids: Eerdmans, 1951), p. 175.
[5]*Works,* Vol. 1, pp. 180, 181.

When man sins he wraps these clouds around himself and goes on in darkness.

THE VERDICT

Every trial has a verdict, and the verdict is not missing here, though it is unspoken by God. The verdict is: GUILTY. It is spoken by Adam and Eve themselves ("I ate it. . . . I ate"); it is illustrated by every word the two speak. They seek to excuse themselves. But their excuses are of no avail, and they are silenced before the God they have offended.

Will this not be our case also in the day in which we stand before God—unless our sin has been dealt with at the cross of Christ? Paul evidently thought so, for he included all persons, both Jews and Gentiles, in his indictment of humanity, saying, "There is no one righteous, not even one; there is no one who understands, no one who seeks God. All have turned away, they have together become worthless; there is no one who does good" (Rom. 3:10–12). He then concludes, "Now we know that whatever the law says, it says to those who are under the law, so that every mouth may be silenced and the whole world held accountable to God" (v. 19). Clearly, there will be no excuses in the day of God's final judgment. Evil will be brought to light. Sin will be uncovered, and every mouth will be silenced.

THE PASSING OF SENTENCE

The last phase of the trial comes quickly as God proceeds to pass sentence. He begins with the serpent through whom the sin originated: "Because you have done this, cursed are you above all the livestock and all the wild animals! You will crawl on your belly and you will eat dust all the days of your life" (v. 14). The curse on the serpent is in two parts, of which this is the first. It applies particularly to the serpent, whom the devil used, just as the second part (involving the enmity between this one and the woman) applies particularly to Satan. But there is a connection. The second part concerns the devil, but it also deals with man's natural fear of snakes, which illustrates the greater animosity. In the same way, although the first part deals with the serpent crawling on its belly and eating "dust," the reference is also to Satan who is forced to eat the dust of frustration.

This is the answer to those ignorant readers of Genesis who imagine the Bible to be in error here because, as they point out, "Snakes do not actually eat dust." "To eat dust is to know defeat, and that is God's prophetic judgment upon the enemy. He will always reach for his desires and fall just short of them. There will be continuous aspiration, but never any attainment."[6] Critics who do not know how to read adult books should be careful how they comment on them.

And yet, there is something very striking in this literal judgment. We do not know what the serpent looked like before this judgment, though he must have been a beautiful and upright creature, perhaps the most splendid of all the creatures. Nor do we know precisely when the judgment here pronounced was executed, though it was probably at this point. What we can know—because we can put ourselves in their place—is the horror of Adam and Eve as they heard the voice of God and witnessed the terrifying transformation of this once beautiful creature into the hissing, slithering, dangerous creature we know as a snake today. They must have recoiled in mortal fear, recognizing that God had every right to pronounce this same or even a more terrible judgment on themselves. They must have expected that He would do so, and the devil must also have expected this judgment. It was for this that he had tempted the man and the woman.

[6]Donald Grey Barnhouse, *Genesis: A Devotional Commentary* (Grand Rapids: Zondervan, 1970), p. 22.

But instead—how unsearchable are the judgments and ways of God—grace intervenes. It is true that there is judgment, of a sort. The woman is given pain in childbearing; the man is to gain a livelihood through the sweat of his brow. But immediate physical death is postponed. And before even these more limited judgments are pronounced, God speaks the promise of a coming one who shall be the deliverer: "I will put enmity between you and the woman, and between your offspring and hers; he will crush your head, and you will strike his heel" (v. 15).

Moments ago I said that although God Himself did not speak the verdict of "guilty" on the man and woman, it was nevertheless spoken by them and illustrated by their feeble excuses. At the time, I passed over the fact that God did not actually pronounce that word. But I want to return to this, because it may well be significant. I may be reading too much into the conversation, but it seems

to me that the fact that God does not actually say "guilty" is of great importance. Had He declared our two parents to be guilty at that point, judgment in its fullest form must inevitably have followed. The man and woman would have suffered immediate banishment from God to hell, and their torment would have been endless. But God did not pronounce that verdict. He postponed it, as courts sometimes do. And when He pronounced it later, He did so not on Adam and Eve or their descendants, but on Jesus Christ who bore the punishment for all who would believe on Him as Savior.

If you are in Christ by saving faith, the verdict of guilty that should have been pronounced on you has been pronounced on Christ. He bore your punishment. He "descended into hell" in your place. If you are not in Christ, that verdict remains to be spoken and indeed will be spoken against you at the final judgment.

27

The First Messianic Prophecy

(Genesis 3:15)

And I will put enmity
between you and the woman,
and between your offspring and hers;
he will crush your head,
and you will strike his heel.

There is always something unexpected about Christmas, even when you have been expecting it for months. It is not just the presents, which you somehow anticipate anyway. It is the grace of God in sending His Son as our Savior. Grace is always unexpected. So whenever we capture even a small part of what Christmas means, the message of grace is somehow always there and surprises us.

We should not be surprised that this is the case, however, for all biblical references to the coming and birth of Jesus, including all the prophecies of His coming in the Old Testament, have this characteristic. This is particularly true of the first messianic prophecy, occuring as early in the Bible as chapter 3 of Genesis. It is unexpected because the scene in which it occurs is of judgment. Satan had tempted Eve to sin. She had believed Satan rather than God and then had sinned in eating of the tree of the knowledge of good and evil, which both she and Adam had been instructed not to eat from. Adam had also sinned in eating of the tree. Now God had come into the garden to call them to task for their sin and to mete out judgment. What fears they must have had! How terrified they must have been as they waited for a punishment perfectly suited to their crime! Do you remember that song from Gilbert and Sullivan's *Mikado*

in which the Lord High Executioner sings of his desire to have each punishment perfectly suit the crime? He sings:

My object all sublime I shall achieve in
  time:
To make the punishment fit the crime,
  the punishment fit the crime.

My favorite verse is the one about billiard players.

The billiard shark, whom anyone
  catches,
  His doom's extremely hard.
He's made to dwell in a dungeon cell
  In a spot that's always barred.
And there he plays extravagant matches
  In fitless finger stalls,
On a cloth untrue with a twisted cue
  And eliptical billiard balls.

Well might we shudder as we think of a punishment suited to the greater crime of Adam and Eve in their unjustified and totally heinous sin against the Creator. But we find only a token judgment—pain upon the woman in childbirth, grief for the man in earning a living—and, wonder of all wonders, a promise of a deliverer to come.

This is the unexpected wonder of Christmas in its very first form: "And I will put enmity between you and the woman, and between your offspring and hers; he will crush your head, and you will strike his heel" (Gen. 3:15).

GOD OF CONFLICT

At first glance this verse does not seem particularly wonderful, for it is talking about a conflict that began between the devil and Eve and continues up to the time of Christ and beyond. The verse speaks of "enmity," which means "ill will on one side or on both; hatred; especially mutual antagonism" (Webster's *New Collegiate Dictionary*). It is hard to see how this can be good. But this enmity *is* good, and we should be alerted to this by the fact that it is God who creates it.

A person might ask how evil can be good or how God can be the author of enmity in any form. But the context readily explains this. We remember that Satan is a fallen angel whose original sin consisted in trying to replace God as the chief being in the universe and in trying to gather the worship of the creatures about himself rather than about God. His attempt proved unsuccessful. Now he had appeared on earth to attempt to do among the new race of human beings what he failed to do earlier. Undoubtedly, his temptation of Eve and Adam had in mind, first, seducing our parents away from the worship of God and, second, winning their allegiance and worship for himself. We know sadly that he succeeded in the first objective. He did break the fellowship of the man and the woman with God. But he did not succeed in his second objective, for God announces here that He is putting enmity between Lucifer and the woman.

It is significant that these words are spoken to Satan. For the new thing was not Satan's hatred of Eve. Satan hated Eve from the moment of her creation, even when he was pretending to be her friend and confidant in tempting her to eat of the forbidden tree. The new thing was to be Eve's (and Adam's and all their true offspring's) hatred of Satan as one aspect of God's gracious preservation of and provision for the race.

What a blessing that was! We think at Christmas of the love, joy, and happiness that the coming of Jesus Christ brought us, and we thank God rightly for those things. But we should not forget to thank Him for a corresponding hatred of sin, sorrow at sin's ways, and increasing misery when we find ourselves ensnared in sin's tentacles. When we sin, we often find that we like the sin but want to escape sin's consequences. We would like to destroy ourselves in comfort, like the addict destroying himself in the dreamlike stupor of debilitating drugs or booze. We would like to go to hell happy. But it is one aspect of grace that God does not allow that to happen. God makes sin miserable and sets up an antagonism between ourselves and Satan which modifies the hold of sin and makes it possible for us to hear God's loving voice, even in our misery.

THE TWO HUMANITIES

The enmity established by God was not only to be between the woman and Satan, however—that is, an enmity merely on the personal or individual level. It was also to be an enmity between her offspring and his. This could presumably mean between human beings and the demons, but it is unlikely that it does. For one thing, Satan does not really have offspring. He is not engendering little devils. The demons were created once by God, before their fall, and they are not now increasing in number. For another thing, the passage moves in the direction of one specific descendant of the woman, Jesus Christ, who shall defeat Satan. That is, it is moving from the general to the specific. In view of these facts, the verse probably refers to the godly descendants of the man and woman, influenced by God Himself, and the ungodly descendants of the man and woman, influenced by Satan. Certainly, the Book of Genesis goes on to distinguish between the two humanities (chapters 4 and 5).

If this is so, this is a message for the godly in every age. There is a divinely created animosity between the people of God and those who are not His people, and it is for our good. It is to sharpen our will to serve God. One of Isaac Watt's great hymns ("Am I a soldier of the cross") asks:

> Are there no foes for me to face?
> Must I not stem the flood?
> Is this vile world a friend of grace,
> To help me on to God?

In the context of that hymn the answer is clearly no. Watts wants us to fight against the world for Christ's sake, which we must certainly do. But there is also a sense in which the world *is* a "friend of grace," for its animosity toward us pushes us to a greater measure of dependence on God.

There is also a more specific meaning to this verse. As the Book of Genesis unfolds we see God calling out Israel as a special nation through whom He would work, and we see the animosity of Satan (who heard and well understood this prophecy) directed particularly against the Jews. Here is the birth of anti-Semitism. It begins in Genesis and stretches all through history even to the end times described in the Book of Revelation. "A great and wondrous sign appeared in heaven: a woman clothed with the sun, with the moon under her feet and a crown of twelve stars on her head. She was pregnant and cried out in pain as she was about to give birth. Then another sign appeared in heaven: an enormous red dragon with seven heads and ten horns and seven crowns on his heads. His tail swept a third of the stars out of the sky and flung them to the earth. The dragon stood in front of the woman who was about to give birth, so that he might devour her child the moment it was born. She gave birth to a son, a male child, who will rule all the nations with an iron scepter. And her child was snatched up to God and to his throne" (Rev. 12:1–5). In this passage the dragon is certainly Satan, the woman Israel, and her child the Lord Jesus Christ.

Satan's strategy is to destroy Israel in order to destroy Christ. This is the reason for anti-Semitism, and also the reason why no Christian should ever have a part in it.

CHRIST VERSUS SATAN

There is a third antagonism in these verses, more beneficial even than the others. The first two give us room for hope; they tell us that God has not abandoned us, that He has established a beneficial enmity between those who desire good and those who desire evil. This last enmity assures us, not only of hope, but also of victory. It is the antagonism between Jesus, as the specific and climactic seed of the woman, and Satan himself. It was to result in the bruising of Jesus but also in the crushing of Satan and his power.

Donald Grey Barnhouse traces the conflict like this: "When the Lord Jesus Christ was born Satan's hatred came to white heat. We can see the hatred of Satan at every point in the earthly story of the life of our Lord. Joseph was moved to cast off Mary because he knew that she had not been his wife as yet and drew the natural conclusion that there was sin on her part. But the Lord manifested himself and Joseph accepted Mary because of this divine revelation. The child of promise, the seed of the woman, the branch of David, was born, the Eternal Word was made flesh. Satan moved Herod to kill all of the babies from two years old and under according to the time which he had diligently inquired of the wise men. But God had arranged escape in advance, and had brought gifts of gold to the family of the young child so that a flight into Egypt was made possible.

"At twelve years of age he was left

behind in Jerusalem among the followers of Satan and the enemies of God. The child was growing up before his Father as a tender plant and the heavenly care was about him.

"As soon as our Lord was publicly manifested, Satan immediately confronted him and sought in the three temptations to turn him aside from the path laid down for him in the counsels with the Father. When he had been routed with the sword of the Word, Satan left the Lord, but returned again and again, both personally and through the religious leaders who had become veritable children of the devil, to destroy the Lord before he could come to the hour of the cross. It was Satan who stirred up the people of Nazareth to take Christ to the brow of the hill and thrust him to his death on the occasion of his first public sermon. He had announced the doctrine of salvation by grace apart from works on the basis of the sovereign will of God (Luke 4), and the heart of man rebelled against it and turned easily to the enemy who would exalt the flesh. 'But he, passing through the midst of them, went his way.'

"Again and again Satan played the old plot with different scenes and characters. Sometimes they picked up stones to stone him; they sent officers to arrest him; their leaders attempted to incite the people against him. Always the nerve of their action was paralyzed. Their desire was that of the carnal mind which is enmity against God. Now, for the first time in history, God was visibly before them as the object of their hatred. They were the sons of those who had killed the prophets, but they themselves would have killed their God. He described them fully in the parable of the tenants who killed the messengers and when the owner, last of all, sent his son, cried, 'This is the heir; come, let us kill him, and let us seize on his inheritance'

(Matt. 21:38). Always he escaped unhurt. He was master of every situation. He said, 'No man taketh it [my life] from me; but I lay it down of myself' (John 10:18).

"When human allies failed, Satan moved directly to kill the Son of God. On one occasion the Lord's disciples were with him in a boat on the sea of Galilee. They were lifelong fishermen who were in their home waters. They had thought that there was not a wave that could be unfamiliar to them. But suddenly a storm of such fury broke out that even these hardened mariners were chilled with fright. They rushed to the Lord as he lay asleep in the boat and roused him with their cry of anguish, as they deemed themselves on the point of death, 'Master, save us; we perish!' The gospel narrative states that the Lord arose at the call of the frightened disciples and 'rebuked the wind.' Let the deniers of Scripture realize that if Satan were not behind the power of the storm, then the action of Christ must be compared with that of a child who, hurt by stumbling against a chair, begins to kick at the chair, crying out with petulance against it. But if we understand that Satan had raised that storm to kill the Lord Jesus, . . . we see the whole pattern of these attacks, and understand the force of the words addressed to the storm, 'Peace, be still' (Mark 4:35–41). The verb in Greek means 'to muzzle,' and in ancient domestic life was sometimes addressed to a dog to silence him.

"Finally, the prophecies were fulfilled and Satan bruised the heel of the Lord Jesus Christ and had his own head crushed in the bruising."[1]

TWO VICTORIES

We know how the bruising of the Lord Jesus Christ took place. It happened at the cross as Satan finally succeeded, so it seemed, at striking back at God and

---

[1]Barnhouse, *The Invisible War*, pp. 107, 108.

silencing his meddling in human affairs forever. It was bruising with a vengeance. It included the hatred of the religious leaders, the mocking of the crowds, the beatings, eventually the crucifixion with its great agony. And yet, it was only a bruising, not a defeat, for on the third day after the crucifixion Jesus rose from the tomb triumphantly.

On the other hand, although Satan achieved what he believed to be a true victory, it proved to be a Pyhrric victory, for his power over us was broken. I do not know precisely what Satan was thinking of as he finally achieved his goal of having Christ crucified, but I am sure he had at least forgotten this prophecy or else had dismissed it as applying to other times and circumstances. He failed to see how even his moment of triumph was to be turned to defeat in accord with this prophecy. John Gerstner declares, "Satan was majestically triumphant in this . . . battle. He had nailed Jesus to the cross. The prime object of all his striving through all the ages was achieved. But he failed. For the prophecy which had said that he would indeed bruise the seed of the woman had also said that his head would be crushed by Christ's heel. Thus, while Satan was celebrating his triumph in battle over the Son of God, the full weight of the Atonement accomplished by the Crucifixion (which the devil had effected) came down on him, and he realized that all this time, so far from successfully battling against the Almighty, he had actually been carrying out the purposes of the all-wise God."[2]

Satan's only true power—quite unlike his pretensions to power—comes from the character of God that declares that sin must be punished. Satan's power consists in working within the laws of that character. He reasoned that if he could get the man and woman to sin, which he did, the wrath of God against sin must inevitably come down on them. God's good designs would be thwarted. What Satan failed to see (and what no one ever did see clearly before the death of Christ) is how God could be both just and the justifier of the ungodly (Rom. 3:26). He failed to see how Jesus would take the place of sinners, bearing their punishment, and how he, Satan, would have his power broken in the process.

But now we do see it, if we will, for Christ's was an open triumph. Paul says, "Christ . . . canceled the written code, with its regulations, that was against us and that stood opposed to us; he took it away, nailing it to the cross. And having disarmed the powers and authorities, he made a public spectacle of them, triumphing over them by the cross" (Col. 2:13–15).

In view of this victory (and echoing the language of Jonathan Edwards), Gerstner calls Satan "the greatest blockhead the world has ever known." He says, "The very fact that he is probably the most intelligent being ever created makes him the greatest blockhead, for he was supremely stupid to suppose that he could outthink the All-wise or overpower the Almighty."[3]

Although the victory has been won for us by the Lord Jesus Christ, there is nevertheless still another to be won by those who follow Jesus. It is a victory certain of being achieved, but it is still in the process of being achieved and will be achieved only as we who profess the name of Jesus actually draw close to Him and fight in His power. Paul referred to this victory when he wrote to the Romans, "The God of peace will soon crush Satan under your feet" (Rom. 16:20). John referred to it in Revelation saying, "They overcame him [the accuser of our brothers] by the blood of the Lamb and by the word of their testimony" (Rev. 12:11).

---

[2]Gerstner, "The Language of the Battlefield," in *Our Savior God*, pp. 159, 160.

[3]"Language of the Battlefield," p. 160.

28

Christid and Adam

Christ and Adam

(Genesis 3:15)

And I will put enmity
between you and the woman,
and between your offspring and hers;
he will crush your head,
and you will strike his heel.

In Romans 5:14 the first man, Adam, is called a "pattern" (NIV) or "figure" (KJV) of the Lord Jesus Christ, who was to come. That statement encourages us to think of Adam and Christ together, both for similarities and contrasts, as Paul himself does in Romans 5 and in 1 Corinthians 15. Since Genesis 3:15 is the first text in the Bible in which Adam and Christ appear in proximity, it seems unwise to pass it without looking at this theme carefully.

The theme has figured prominently in Christian theology. Indeed, it is the basis of what is sometimes called "covenant" theology. According to this system, God established an agreement or covenant with Adam according to which he was to stand as the representative of the race of men and women who were to follow him. He was to stand before God on the basis of his obedience. If he continued in obedience, all who followed would also be established in obedience and would be blessed by God. If he fell, all who followed him would fall in his transgression, and sin and death would pass on them because of Adam's sin. We know what happened. Adam did fall,

and we fell in Adam (cf. Rom. 5:12–21). On the other hand, God also established a covenant with the Lord Jesus Christ according to which he was to be representative of the great company of the redeemed. They would be joined to Christ, as all were once joined to Adam, and they—the redeemed—would be saved by Christ's sacrifice.

To be sure, there are no explicit texts concerning the establishing of the covenant with Adam. There is very little written about Adam in the Bible at all. But there are many texts that speak of God's covenant with Jesus (Isa. 53:10–12; Pss. 22:25–31; 40:6–8; cf. Heb. 10:8–10; 12:22–24; 13:20; John 6:37, etc.), and the explicit comparison of Christ and Adam in Romans 5 and 1 Corinthians 15 clearly establishes this doctrine. In most books of theology the first covenant is called a "covenant of works" and the second a "covenant of grace (or redemption)."[1]

WHAT ADAM DID

With this theological background, we turn to the first Adam, our ancestor, and consider his covenant with God in two

---

[1]Charles Hodge distinguishes more precisely between the "covenant of grace," which he sees to be established between God and man, and the "covenant of redemption," which is established between God the Father and Christ (cf. *Systematic Theology*, Vol. 2, pp. 58, 59; the full discussion is on pp. 117–22 and 354–77). This is a valid distinction, but it goes beyond the scope of this chapter and is extraneous to the points we are making.

parts: first, what Adam did in breaking it, and, second, what the consequences of his transgression were.

It has been suggested by various commentators that in eating of the forbidden fruit Adam cast reproach upon "God's love, God's truth and God's majesty."[2] We have already looked at these in one form or another in considering the nature and effects of the fall, but we look at them again now in order to contrast what Adam did when he sinned and what Christ did in obedience. It is clear how Adam cast reproach on God's *love*. God had created him in His own blessed image and had placed him in a garden of earthly delights. Adam had every pleasure he could desire. He had rule over the animal world. Moreover, he had valuable work to do both in ruling and in studying and cataloging the animals. He had every incentive to continue in obedience to such a loving God. Yet when Satan came with the suggestion that perhaps God was not essentially good, that He was essentially prohibitive in withholding the fruit of the tree of the knowledge of good and evil that had power to make one wise, "knowing good and evil," Adam (as well as Eve) began to doubt God's goodness and eventually repudiated His love by eating of the forbidden fruit.

Again, Adam cast reproach on God's *truth*. God had said, "You must not eat from the tree of the knowledge of good and evil, for when you eat of it you will surely die" (Gen. 2:17). God taught that blessing was by way of obedience. But Satan said, "You will not surely die. . . . For God knows that when you eat of it your eyes will be opened, and you will be like God, knowing good and evil" (Gen. 3:4, 5). Adam may not have been deceived, as the woman was, thinking that he could disobey God and escape the consequences of death. But he certainly felt that he could improve his condition by rebellion. In so thinking he slanderously called the God of all truth a liar.

Third, Adam cast reproach on God's *majesty* by an attempt to throw off His authority. Arthur Pink writes wisely: "As the Creator, God possesses the inherent right to issue commands, and to demand from his creatures implicit obedience. It is his prerogative to act as Law-giver, Controller, Governor, and to define the limits of his subjects' freedom. And in Eden he exercised his prerogative and expressed his will. But Adam imagined he had a better friend than God. He regarded him as austere and despotic, as One who begrudged him that which would promote his best interests. He felt that in being denied the fruit of this tree which was pleasant to the eyes and capable of making one wise God was acting arbitrarily, cruelly, so he determined to assert himself, claim his rights and throw off the restraint of the divine government. He substitutes the Devil's word for God's law: he puts his own desire before Jehovah's command."[3]

What were the results of Adam's disobedience? Paul spells it out in Romans 5 and 1 Corinthians 15, showing that sin and death entered the experience of all because of his transgression: "Sin entered the world through one man" (Rom. 5:12), "Many died by the trespass of the one man" (Rom. 5:15), "By the trespass of the one man, death reigned" (Rom. 5:17), "The result of one trespass was condemnation for all men" (Rom. 5:18), "Through the disobedience of the one man the many were made sinners" (Rom. 5:19), "In Adam all die" (1 Cor. 15:22). God passed judgment on all for Adam's sin.

People have questioned why the sin of Adam should involve his posterity, even

---

[2]Cf. Pink, *Gleanings in Genesis,* p. 51.
[3]*Gleanings in Genesis,* p. 52.

to our time. They have judged it wrong for God to hold unborn generations accountable for the sin of their first parent. But regardless of how we may choose to judge, it is evident from observation of our own lives as well as the history of those who have lived before us that this is precisely how God operated. When Adam sinned he died. He died in his relationship to God; his fellowship with God was broken, which he proved by hiding when God came looking for him in the garden. He died in respect to his own personality; he tried to shift the blame for his sin to Eve, his companion. In time, he and those who followed did things that were much worse. At last Adam died in body and returned to the dust from which he came. Each of these results of sin has passed on to us. Consequently, we see in the universal reign of death, even over infants who have not reached the point of being able to commit any personally guilty act, proof that we are all looked on by God as guilty and are judged for it.

We may recognize these things to be true and still resent them. We may consider God to be arbitrary and cruel in so acting. But before we make this judgment we must ask whether we would not choose to live in precisely the same condition in which Adam lived and fell, if the choice were offered to us (as, in fact, it may even have been offered to Adam). Would any of us have chosen to have it differently?

Charles Simeon of Cambridge, England, wrote about this more than a hundred years ago. "How deep and unsearchable are the ways of God! That ever our first parent should be constituted a federal head to his posterity, so that they should stand or fall in him, is in itself a stupendous mystery. And it may appear to have been an arbitrary appointment, injurious to the whole race of mankind. But we do not hesitate to say, that if the whole race of mankind had been created at once in precisely the same state and circumstances as Adam was, they would have been as willing to stand or fall in Adam, as to have their lot depend upon themselves; because they would have felt, that, whilst he possessed every advantage that they did, he had a strong inducement to steadfastness which they could not have felt, namely, the dependence of all his posterity upon his fidelity to God; and consequently, that their happiness would be more secure in his hands than in their own."

Simeon then shows that if each human being were asked whether he should prefer to be judged in Adam or in himself, the thinking person would choose to be judged in Adam. For Adam faced but one temptation, and that so small as hardly to deserve the name. Besides, he was surrounded with every possible incentive to do good. We, by contrast, are beset by many temptations and certainly do not have the fullness of Adam's incentives for obedience. None of us would fault God's arrangements if only we could think clearly.[4]

THE SECOND ADAM

Still, the fullness of God's grace in dealing with Adam is not seen even in these matters. It is seen only when we turn to the person of Christ and see His victory on behalf of those who are joined to Him by saving faith.

When we were studying the works of Adam, we saw how Adam terribly dishonored the love, truth, and majesty of God. How different is the case of the Lord Jesus Christ! Arthur Pink writes: "How [Jesus] vindicated the *love* of God! Adam harbored the wicked thought that God begrudged him that which was beneficial, and thereby questioned his goodness. But how the Lord Jesus has reversed that decision! In

---

[4]The references to Charles Simeon are from Barnhouse, *God's Grace*, pp. 54, 55.

coming down to this earth to seek and to save that which was lost, he fully revealed the compassion of deity for humanity. In his sympathy for the afflicted, in his miracles of healing, in his tears over Jerusalem, in his unselfish and unwearied works of mercy, he has openly displayed the beneficence and benevolence of God. And what shall we say of his sufferings and death on the cross? In laying down his life for us, in dying upon the cross he unveiled the heart of the Father as nothing else could. 'God commendeth his love toward us, in that, while we were yet sinners, Christ died for us.' In the light of Calvary we can never more doubt the goodness and grace of God.

"How Christ vindicated the *truth* of God! When tempted by Satan to doubt God's goodness, question his truth and repudiate his majesty, he answered each time, 'It is written.' When he entered the synagogue on the Sabbath day it was to read out of the Holy Oracles. When selecting the twelve apostles he designedly chose Judas in order that the Scriptures 'might be fulfilled.' When censuring his critics, he declared that by their traditions they made void 'the Word of God.' In his last moments upon the cross, knowing that all things had been accomplished, in order that the Scriptures might be fulfilled he said, 'I thirst.' After he had risen from the dead and was journeying with the two disciples to Emmaus, he 'expounded unto them in all the Scriptures the things concerning himself.' At every point, and in every detail of his life he honored and magnified God's truth.

"Finally, Christ completely vindicated the *majesty* of God. The creature had aspired to be equal with the Creator. Adam chafed against the governmental restraint which Jehovah had placed upon him. He despised God's law, insulted his majesty, defied his authority.

How different with our blessed Savior! Though he was the Lord of Glory and equal with God, yet he made himself of no reputation, and took upon him the form of a servant. O matchless grace! He condescended to be 'made under the law,' and during the whole of his stay here upon earth he refused to assert his rights, and was ever subject to the Father. 'Not my will' was his holy cry. Nay, more: 'He became obedient unto death, even the death of the cross.' Never was God's law so magnified, never was God's authority so honored, never were God's government claims so illustriously upheld, as during the thirty-three years when his own Son tabernacled among men."[5]

What was the result of this obedience? We have already seen the results of Adam's disobedience. It was death for himself and all who followed him. In the case of Christ, God's judgment is reversed. Adam brought death; Christ brings life. Adam brought condemnation; Christ brings justification. And all by the same principle—the principle of representation, the one for the many! "For just as through the disobedience of the one man [Adam] the many were made sinners, so also through the obedience of the one man [Jesus] the many will be made righteous" (Rom. 5:19).

Thus it is that, far from being an example of an arbitrary injustice on the part of God, the principle of the covenant is actually a means of grace. For it is only by considering all as condemned in the first Adam that God can also consider believers to be justified in the second Adam, the Lord Jesus Christ.

GOD'S GRACE

There is one thing more. Paul compares the effects of sin and grace and concludes that the effects of grace through the obedience of Christ are far

---

[5]Pink, *Gleanings in Genesis*, pp. 52, 53.

greater than those of sin through Adam: "For if the many died by the trespass of the one man, how much more did God's grace and the gift that came by the grace of the one man, Jesus Christ, overflow to the many!" (Rom. 5:15). How is this possible, particularly since not all are saved? How are the effects of Christ's work greater than the inheritance from Adam? One writer suggests the following:

1. The work of Christ is superior to that of Adam in respect to *time*. When measured by time the effect of Adam's disobedience is temporary so far as the redeemed are concerned, while the effect of Jesus' victory is permanent. From the perspective of earth the reign of sin seems long. But the history of earth is but a small thing in the infinitely greater expanse of eternity, and the time is coming when we who are now far too prone to sin will be freed from it and will be made like Jesus.

2. The *effect* of Christ's work is superior to Adam's. It is true that when Adam sinned, death came to Adam and through him to all men and women. But the power of death could be broken. This Christ did. He "has destroyed death and has brought life and immortality to light through the gospel" (2 Tim. 1:10). By contrast, Christ's work cannot be undone, for Satan has no power to reclaim those who have been redeemed by Christ. They are Christ's forever.

3. The work of Jesus is superior to the work of Adam in that it will ultimately affect a far greater *number of people*. These are described as a "great assembly" (Ps. 22:25), "a great multitude that no one could count" (Rev. 7:9).

When we look about us we may well wonder how this can be true. It seems that the majority do not believe in Christ, and we even remember the words of our Lord, who said, "Wide is

the gate and broad is the road that leads to destruction, and many enter through it. But small is the gate and narrow the road that leads to life, and only a few find it" (Matt. 7:13, 14). It is probably the case that we just do not see the whole story. Christ's words are undoubtedly true of adults living in this present age. But what of children? It is possible that those dying in infancy are reckoned among the elect. And what of the future reign of Christ on earth? It is possible that those born in that age may also be among the redeemed and may even be used by God to populate the universe with innumerable, godly offspring.

4. The victory of the Lord Jesus Christ is greater than the disobedience of Adam in respect to the *territory affected*. Adam's sin affected only this earth. Even though men and women may spread the contagion of their disobedience more widely through planetary travel, it is impossible that they can spread it far. On the other hand, the victory of Christ is to be celebrated throughout the universe.

5. Finally, the victory of Jesus exceeds the work of Adam because Christ's is the *work of God* and Adam's is the work of a mere man. As men, we have such high opinions of ourselves that we imagine we can do just about anything. But actually we can do very little when measured by the activity of God. In salvation we can do nothing. By contrast, Christ does all that needs to be done, and what he has begun to perform he will certainly bring to completion (Phil. 1:6).[6]

Apart from the story of the Fall, little is told about Adam, as we noted earlier. But it is enough. We are told that he was created by God, placed in perfect surroundings, given a charge of obedience as representative of the race. We are told that he fell and that the effects of his fall passed on all. We may summarize by saying that Adam was the first man and

---

[6]Cf. Barnhouse, *God's Grace*, pp. 58–62.

the first sinner and that we have been judged for his sin. (Lest we think too harshly of Adam, we are reminded that we would have done precisely what he did had we been in his place.) It is in Adam, way back at the beginning, that we learn the principle of the one standing for the many and see the means by which God has provided salvation through the second Adam.

Every one of us is in Adam. Some, by the grace of God, are also in Christ. Can you look to the cross of Christ and know that you are in Him? You become "in him" by faith, by believing in what He has done and by committing yourself to Him.

29

Grace Abounding

(Genesis 3:15)

And I will put enmity
between you and the woman,
and between your offspring and hers;
he will crush his head,
and you will strike his heel.

It is common to define grace as "God's unmerited favor" or even "God's provision for the undeserving." But those definitions are almost too weak. They are weak because God's grace is shown, not merely to those who do not deserve it, but to those who deserve precisely the opposite.

There is a sense in which everything God does is gracious, because none of us deserves anything. Adam deserved nothing even before his fall. The gift of life was gracious. So was God's gift of the garden, of a wife, of meaningful work to do. But this is not the way the Bible usually speaks of God's grace for the simple reason that the fullness of grace is seen only against the black backdrop of sin. In Adam's case it is seen in God's gentle dealing with him following the Fall and in the promise of a deliverer to come. Later it is seen in God's continuing care of the people of Israel in spite of their constant wandering from Him. Above all, it is seen at the cross of Christ where, in spite of the sin of man in hounding the Lord Jesus Christ to death by crucifixion, God was nevertheless providing the basis by which all who call on the name of the Lord might be saved. Grace actually means that God has provided for us in every possible way, both physically and spiritually, in spite of the condemnation we deserve.

Then, too, there is the matter of the abundant or overflowing nature of grace, which may be stated as: believers gain more through the work of Christ than they lost in Adam. A poet wrote,

Marvelous grace of our loving Lord,
Grace that *exceeds* our sin and our guilt!
Yonder on Calvary's mount out-
poured—
There where the blood of the Lamb was
spilt.

The Bible says, "Where sin increased, grace increased all the more, so that, just as sin reigned in death, so also grace might reign through righteousness to bring eternal life through Jesus Christ our Lord" (Rom. 5:20, 21).

THE LIFE OF GOD

Since Genesis 3:15 is the first verse in the Bible to speak about the grace of God in this sense and since it compares the great and total triumph of Christ to the lesser and ultimately ineffective blow of Satan against both Christ and Adam, it leads us to think about some of the great verses of the Bible that amplify on Genesis 3:15 by speaking of the fullness of Christ's victory. These verses show why grace is abundant and why we have gained more in Christ, the second Adam, than we lost in the first Adam.

The first verse is Colossians 1:27, which says, "To them [that is, the saints]

172

God has chosen to make known among the Gentiles the glorious riches of this mystery, which is *Christ in you,* the hope of glory." We know from the way Paul speaks elsewhere that he is referring here to the fact that those who have believed in Christ have been made alive in Him so that the life of Christ Himself may be said to be within them. In Galatians he writes, "I have been crucified with Christ and I no longer live, but Christ lives in me. The life I live in the body, I live by faith in the Son of God, who loved me and gave himself for me" (Gal. 2:20). Or again in Romans, "The Spirit of him who raised Jesus from the dead is living in you" (Rom. 8:11).

This has two important consequences. First, the divine life within us is eternal. It will not die. Second, the divine life will always strive after righteousness, for that is its nature. It will abhor sin. It will cleave to the good. It is on this basis that the apostle John appeals to the presence of righteousness within the life of a Christian as proof that he or she has been born of God. "The man who says, 'I know him,' but does not do what he commands is a liar, and the truth is not in him. But if anyone obeys his word, God's love is truly made complete in him. This is how we know we are in him: Whoever claims to live in him must walk as Jesus did" (1 John 2:4–6). "No one who is born of God will continue to sin, because God's seed remains in him; he cannot go on sinning, because he has been born of God" (1 John 3:9). John does not mean that Christians never sin. That would be untrue, and John explicitly denies this conclusion (cf. 1 John 1:8). But he does mean that the new life of Christ within any true child of God will inevitably yearn after righteousness and lead the believer in that direction day by day throughout his or her life.

This is a great improvement over the case of Adam, for the natural life of Adam (even though without any moral flaw) did not apparently so lead. On the contrary, Adam chose rebellion and death. In granting us divine life, the grace of God in Christ has abounded.

GIFT OF JUSTIFICATION

The second text is Romans 5:16, which says, "The gift of God is not like the result of the one man's sin: The judgment followed one sin and brought condemnation, but the gift followed many trespasses and brought justification." This verse is from that great passage in Romans (which we have looked at in the last chapter as well as this one) in which Paul is comparing the entrance of death into the world through Adam and the entry of eternal life through the work of Christ. It is making the chief comparison: sin and grace (the gift), condemnation and justification. But how is it that the grace of God in Christ to justification is greater than the working of sin in Adam to condemnation? Paul answers that the condemnation was based on just one sin. But justification is God's answer, not only for that one, original sin, but for all the *many* sins committed down through the *many* ages since Adam by the *many* multitudes of God's people.

Justification is a legal term, referring to the work of God in dealing with the most basic of all religious questions: How can a man or woman become right with God? We are not right with Him in ourselves; this is what the doctrine of sin means. Sin means that we are in rebellion against God, and if we are against God we cannot be right with Him. We are transgressors. Moreover, we are *all* transgressors, as Paul says elsewhere: "All have sinned and fall short of the glory of God" (Rom. 3:23). The doctrine of justification is the most important of all Christian doctrines because it tells how one who is in rebellion against God may become right with Him. It says that we may be justified from all sin by the work of Christ alone received by faith, and not by our own works-righteousness.

Paul puts it like this: "All who believe . . . are justified freely by his [that is, God's] grace through the redemption that came by Christ Jesus" (Rom. 3:22–24); "a man is justified by faith apart from observing the law" (v. 28); "to the man who does not work but trusts God who justifies the wicked, his faith is credited as righteousness" (Rom. 4:5). These verses teach that justification is God's work and that it flows from grace. As Paul says later on in the letter to the Romans, "It is God who justifies. Who is he that condemns?" (Rom. 8:33, 34).

In God's justification of the sinner there is an entirely unique factor that does not enter into any other case of justification. That unique factor is Christ's atonement for our sin coupled to God's provision for our need of a divine righteousness through him. In justification God declares that He has accepted the sacrifice of Christ as the payment of our debt to the divine justice and has imputed Christ's righteousness to us in place of the sin. Because Christ's atonement satisfied the justice of God in regard to all our sins, God's grace clearly abounds in justification.

There is another way in which the grace of God in our justification exceeds the sinful work of Adam. When Adam fell, he fell from a position of innocence, which is a neutral position, to that of being a sinner. But the work of Christ does not merely restore us to a state of innocence but lifts up and beyond that to make us people who know both good and evil but who choose the good. We can understand this as a scale. Imagine a scale running from plus 100 down through zero to minus 100. We may say that Adam started at zero and fell to minus 100. That is, he lost 100 points. The work of Christ may be portrayed as double that work, for He restores His people not merely to the zero point but

to the plus 100, disposing of the many sins by a superabundance of righteousness.

JOINT HEIRS WITH CHRIST

The third text is Romans 8:17, which tells us that the redeemed are "heirs of God and co-heirs with Christ." This is an improvement on Adam's state, for at best Adam was merely God's regent over an earthly paradise. We, by contrast, are to inherit all that is Christ's and actually rule with Him over creation (2 Tim. 2:12).

In law there is an important difference between being an heir and being a joint (or co-) heir. Suppose a certain man dies and leaves a $400,000 estate to his four children. If they are designated his heirs, the estate will be divided equally among them. Each will receive twenty-five percent or $100,000. But suppose the children are designated co-heirs. In this case, the estate is not divided, and together they possess the $400,000. Each one can say, "I am worth $400,000." In human affairs things are rarely done this way, because human beings have a hard time getting along, and children finding themselves in the position of those in our illustration would probably argue. But what does not work well in human affairs will work in divine affairs, because the co-heirs of Christ will have the spirit of Christ and will always work together for the good of all.

What is our inheritance? It is all that is Christ's. Donald Barnhouse writes, "Shall the King possess something and not share it with his bride? 'Blessed be the God and Father of our Lord Jesus Christ, who hath blessed us with all spiritual blessings in heavenly places in Christ' (Eph. 1:3). Does he have riches? Then 'ye know the grace of our Lord Jesus Christ, that, though he was rich, yet for your sakes he became poor, that ye through his poverty might be rich' (2 Cor. 8:9). Does he have love and fellowship with the Father? In showing forth this portion of our inheritance it would be possible to cite the whole of his great high priestly prayer in the garden on the Mount of Olives the night before he died. . . .

"There are three verses in the New Testament, each wonderful in its own right, which, when taken together give us a startling picture of our association with our Savior Lord. It was on the Mount of Olives that he prayed, 'And now, O Father, glorify thou me with thine own self with the glory which I had with thee before the world was' (John 17:5). We know that he says that all his prayers are answered, but to Peter was given a special revelation concerning this particular prayer asking for glory. Speaking of the death and resurrection of our Lord, Peter writes, 'Christ [was the] lamb without blemish and without spot, who verily was foreordained before the foundation of the world, but was manifest in these last times for you, who by him do believe in God, that raised him up from the dead, and gave him glory' (1 Peter 1:19–21). Did you note those last words? God raised him from the dead *and gave him glory*—the glory that he had prayed for, particularly the night before he was crucified.

"But what did he do with the glory which he received in the triumph of his resurrection? Go back to the Mount of Olives and listen to him pray, 'And the glory which thou gavest me, *I have given them*' (John 17:22).

"How incalculably wonderful! Partakers of his glory! Fellow-heirs with his resurrection triumphs! We are become 'the fullness of him that filleth all in all' (Eph. 1:23)."[1]

Moreover, ours is an inheritance that can never depreciate in value or be lost. It is, as Peter said, "an inheritance that can never perish, spoil or fade—kept in heaven for you" (1 Peter 1:4). We know that Adam lost his inheritance through sin. But we cannot lose our inheritance because it is given on a different basis. Adam's inheritance was based on a covenant of works. If he remained in obedience, the inheritance would be his. If he rebelled, it would be forfeit. Our inheritance is based on the covenant of grace, and since grace is neither earned nor deserved—it is based purely on the will of the unchangeable God—our inheritance is secure and certain.

Romans 8:17 says this in other language, arguing, "If we are children, then we are heirs." We become children by the grace of God, for we are born "not of natural descent, nor of human decision or a husband's will, but born of God" (John 1:13). Since our inheritance is based on our being children and since we become children not by our own will but by the will of God, nothing can alter it. In this the grace of God in Christ also abounds over the sin of Adam.

EXCEEDING GREAT JOY

Our fourth text is the benediction which ends the Book of Jude: "To him who is able to keep you from falling and to present you before his glorious presence without fault and with great joy" (v. 24). This teaches that our joy in God, in the future and also now, is greater than the joy Adam had in God before his fall. Although Adam's joy was great, he had nothing to compare his state of sinlessness to and therefore undoubtedly did not value it as much as the redeemed. Nor did it run the gamut of their experience. We know what it is to be lost and to be brought from that darkness into God's marvelous light.

We see the principle illustrated even among the redeemed, for those who have been forgiven much, love much. Take the case of John Newton. Newton

---

[1]Donald Grey Barnhouse, *God's Heirs*, Vol. 7 of the series on *Romans* (Grand Rapids: Eerdmans, 1963), pp. 115, 116.

had been raised in a Christian home in England in his early years, but he became orphaned when he was seven and was sent to live with a non-Christian relative. There Christianity was mocked, and he was persecuted. At last, in order to escape the conditions in the home, Newton ran away to sea and became an apprentice in the British navy. Debauched and rebellious, at last he deserted and ran away to Africa. He tells in his own words that he went there for just one purpose: "that I might sin my fill." In Africa Newton joined forces with a Portuguese slave trader in whose home he was cruelly treated. At times the slave trader went away on expeditions, and the young man was left in the charge of the slave trader's African wife, the head of his harem. She hated all men and took her hatred out on Newton. He tells that she exercised such power in her husband's absence that he was compelled to eat his food off the dusty floor like a dog.

At last the young Newton fled from this treatment and made his way to the coast where he lit a signal fire and was picked up by a slave ship on its way to England. The captain was disappointed that Newton had no ivory to sell, but because the young man knew something about navigation he was made a ship's mate. He could not keep even this position. During the voyage he broke into the ship's supply of rum and distributed it to the crew so that the crew became drunk. In a stupor Newton fell into the sea and was saved from drowning only when one of the officers speared him with a harpoon, leaving a fist-sized scar in his thigh.

Near the end of the voyage, as they were nearing Scotland, the ship on which Newton was riding encountered heavy winds. It was blown off course and began to sink. Newton was sent down into the hold with the slaves who were being transported and told to man the pumps. He was frightened to death, feeling sure that the ship would sink and

he would drown. He worked the pumps for days, and as he worked he began to cry out to God from the hold of the ship. He began to remember verses he had been taught as a child. As he remembered them he was miraculously transformed. He was born again. He went on to become a great teacher of the Word of God in England. Of this storm William Cowper, the poet, wrote:

God moves in a mysterious way
  His wonders to perform;
He plants His footsteps in the sea
  And rides upon the storm.

Newton himself wrote many poems, among them:

How sweet the name of Jesus sounds
  In a believer's ear!
It soothes his sorrows, heals his
    wounds,
  And drives away his fear.

He wrote this classic.

Amazing grace—how sweet the
    sound—
  That saved a wretch like me!
I once was lost but now am found,
  Was blind but now I see.
'Twas grace that taught my heart to fear,
  And grace my fears relieved;
How precious did that grace appear
  The hour I first believed!
Through many dangers, toils and snares
  I have already come;
'Tis grace has brought me safe thus far,
  And grace will lead me home.
And when this flesh and heart shall fail,
  And mortal life shall cease,
I shall possess within the veil
  A life of joy and peace.
When we've been there ten thousand
    years,
  Bright shining as the sun,
We've no less days to sing God's praise
  Than when we've first begun.

Newton was a great preacher of grace, and it is no wonder, for he had been lost and was found. He had been blind, but by the abounding grace of God in Christ he had come to see.

30

The Curse of God

(Genesis 3:16–19)

> To the woman he said,
>> "I will greatly increase your pains in childbearing;
>> with pain you will give birth to children.
>> Your desire will be for your husband,
>> and he will rule over you."
>
> To Adam he said, "Because you listened to your wife and ate from the tree about which I commanded you, 'You must not eat of it,'
>> "Cursed is the ground because of you;
>> through painful toil you will eat of it
>> all the days of your life.
>> It will produce thorns and thistles for you,
>> and you will eat the plants of the field.
>> By the sweat of your brow
>> you will eat your food
>> until you return to the ground,
>> since from it you were taken;
>> for dust you are
>> and to dust you will return."

When we hear the word "curse" in our day we tend to think lightly and perhaps even humorously of a voodoo witch doctor sticking pins in a small wax doll. Or we think of "Jewish" curses like: "May your brain surgeon have the palsey" or "May God let everything happen to you that you're thinking about asking Him to let happen to me." There is nothing funny about a curse in the Bible.

We think that when God forgives a sin (or even fails to bring down the full measure of His wrath on the sinner) the effects of sin should be removed altogether. But this is not the way God thinks. We have seen how God graciously came to Adam and Eve in the garden following their fall and held out hope of a final glorious deliverance: "I will put enmity between you and the woman, and between your offspring and hers; he will crush your head, and you will strike his heel" (Gen. 3:15). But we are not to think, just because God is gracious in failing to visit the full measure of punishment on Adam and Eve immediately, that He is indifferent to sin or will allow our first parents to escape its consequences. On the contrary, we are now to see God's judgments on the man and woman.

It is significant that neither Adam nor Eve are said to have been cursed personally. God does curse Satan (v. 14) and the ground for Adam's sake (v. 17). Although they are not cursed personally —being objects still of God's tender concerns and mercy—Adam and Eve nevertheless experience the doleful effects of sin and thus participate in the curse of God against sin directly.

The Woman's Desire

God's judgment on the woman is in two parts, the first an "increase" of pain in childbearing, the second a change in her relationship to her husband here said to have "rule over" her.

We do not need to say much about the first of these two judgments except to note that it probably concerns more than mere childbearing. We ask in this regard whether there is any difference between the first part of the judgment ("I will greatly increase your pains in child-bearing") and the second ("with pain you will give birth to children"). This is a parallel construction, of course; it may be only that the second part repeats the first with slight variation. But it may also be that the second part gives a particular example of a more general first statement, the chief idea of that part being an "increase" of trouble in everything having to do with children. This is the only way I can understand the word "increase." Are we to think that Eve would have had pain in childbirth even before the Fall and that it is now only made greater? Hardly! Is it not rather that the pain associated with children's births will continue in other ways throughout the mother's (and father's) life as these who are now born in sin dishonor their parents and experience in their own lives the consequences of their own disobedience?

If this is the case—if the reference is to the lifelong pain children cause parents—then we may apply it by urging parents to be understanding and patient with their children, for it is because of our sin and that of our forebears that a sinful and rebellious nature has come on them. Our duty is to train them in the Lord (Eph. 6:4).

The second of the two judgments of God on the woman must chiefly concern us, for there is disagreement as to what it means. It reads: "Your desire will be for

your husband, and he will rule over you" (v. 16). In what sense is the woman's desire to be for her husband? And what is the relationship of this part of the judgment to the second, which deals with the husband's rule? Typically there have been three interpretations. First, a woman's sexual desire for her husband will be so strong that she will be willing to accept the results of sexual intercourse, namely conception and the bearing of children. Second, a woman has such an immense psychological dependence on man that she is willing to submit to what is often the man's insensitive and tyrannical rule within marriage. Third, a woman's desires become wholly subservient to those of her husband as a result of this judgment.

With the exception of the last of these three views, which (although it is the view of John Calvin) any honest husband and wife would question, there is a measure of truth about them. Certainly a woman does submit to sexual intercourse in spite of the known pain of childbearing, in most cases desiring it. There is also a psychological dependence of women on men that many acknowledge, even in this age of increased female self-consciousness. A male writer must be careful in what he says in dealing with a subject that often provokes extreme reactions. But it is worth noting that in one contemporary novel dealing with woman's liberation, *The Women's Room*, a character who has been deeply hurt by men and is now trying to make an independent life for herself observes to a friend in the same situation that although they have been hurt by men they still spend most of their time talking about them: "They're still at the center of our conversation," she says.[1] A fact like this might support one or more of these interpretations.

The problem with these views, however, is that they do not quite fit with the

---

[1]Marilyn French, *The Women's Room* (New York: Jove Publications, 1978), p. 427.

whole of what we are told concerning the relation of the man and woman in Genesis. To begin with, the headship of the husband in marriage is not something that enters subsequent to the Fall—in spite of the opinion of some "liberated" evangelical women writers —but is, in fact, already present in the second chapter of Genesis. In that chapter the woman is described as being "a helper" made "for" the man and given "to" him (vv. 18, 22). His sin consists in part in being led by his wife rather than leading her (Gen. 3:17). Again, each of these interpretations, though differing in some respects, agrees that in some way the woman's "desire" for her husband makes her willing to endure his rule. But is that really a result of sin, an aspect of God's judgment on it? Is it not actually the reverse? Would it not be more correct to say that the woman willingly submitted to the leadership of the man *before* the Fall but has been characterized both in her original sin and since by a *rebellion against* that rule, just as Adam and all his descendants are characterized by their rebellion against God?

One person who has felt the full weight of these problems and who has tried to find the solution to them in Scripture is Susan T. Foh, who writes on the subject "What Is the Woman's Desire?" in a recent issue of the *Westminster Theological Journal.* She outlines the problems I have cited but then finds a possible solution in the use of the word "desire" in the next chapter of Genesis. This verse is part of God's warning to Cain on the occasion of his anger about God's acceptance of his brother Abel's sacrifice and the rejection of his own. It says, "If you do what is right, will you not be accepted? But if you do not do what is right, sin is crouching at your door; it *desires* to have you, but you must

master it" (4:7). According to the traditional interpretations of Genesis 3:15, this use of the word "desire" would be entirely different from its use just fifteen verses earlier—a desire to submit in chapter 3 versus a desire to rule in chapter 4. But Foh suggests that the use is actually the same and that the verses are strikingly parallel.

She views it like this: "The woman has the same sort of desire for her husband that sin has for Cain, a desire to possess or control him. This desire disputes the headship of the husband. As the Lord tells Cain what he should do, i.e., master or rule sin, the Lord also states what the husband should do, rule over his wife. The words of the Lord in Genesis 3:16b, as in the case of the battle between sin and Cain, do not determine the victor of the conflict between husband and wife. These words mark the beginning of the battle of the sexes. As a result of the fall, man no longer rules easily; he must fight for his headship. Sin has corrupted both the willing submission of the wife and the loving headship of the husband. The woman's desire is to control her husband (to usurp his divinely appointed headship), and he must master her, if he can. So the rule of love founded in paradise is replaced by struggle, tyranny and domination."[2] Support for this view is in the fact that not all husbands rule their wives and that a woman's "desire" does not generally contribute to that headship.

What is the solution? Well, it is not the abolishing of the man's place as head of the home, as some women's liberation spokespersons suggest. It is rather the transformation of the attitudes and aspirations of both the man and woman through the indwelling Spirit of Christ, so that, as Paul clearly writes, wives will be able to "submit to [their] husbands as to the Lord" and husbands will be able

---

[2]Susan T. Foh, "What Is the Woman's Desire?", *Westminster Theological Journal*, Vol. 37, Spring, 1975, pp. 376–83. Quotation from pages 381, 382.

to "love [their] wives, just as Christ loved the church and gave himself up for her" (Eph. 5:22, 25). In this life each of these will always be done imperfectly, but they are better accomplished imperfectly than not at all.

THE MAN'S JUDGMENT

After God has pronounced judgment on Eve He turns to the man, judging him last because he had sinned last. God says, "Cursed is the ground because of you; through painful toil you will eat of it all the days of your life. It will produce thorns and thistles for you, and you will eat the plants of the field. By the sweat of your brow you will eat your food until you return to the ground, since from it you were taken; for dust you are and to dust you will return" (vv. 17–19).

"It is interesting," as Francis Schaeffer notes, "that almost all of the results of God's judgment because of man's rebellion relate in some way to the external world. They are not just bound up in man's thought life; they are not merely psychological. Profound changes make the external, objective world abnormal."[3]

This is of great importance, for if the effects of sin are solely in the mind, then we may imagine that sin (or at least the effects of it) may be cured by thought. We do not need God. We do not need a deliverer. In actuality, however, the effects of sin are not merely psychological, though sin does affect the mind and personality; they are also external—in the very nature of things, we might say—so the cure must be found in the God who made these things and brought these specific aspects of His judgment on the world. God has acted this way in order to keep the fact and nature of sin before us and remind us by every manifestation of it that we need a Savior.

The judgment on Adam has three parts. First, the ground is cursed be-cause of him. Before, it had produced fruit and every good plant in abundance. Now, although it will still produce what is good, it will produce thorns and thistles faster, and growing the food necessary for survival will become a chore. Second, Adam is condemned to live by the sweat of his brow. Before, his work had been pleasure. Now, although the nature of work is in itself still good, it will be accompanied by pain and weariness so that Adam might well say, as Job did later, "Does not man have hard service on earth? Are not his days like those of a hired man? Like a slave longing for the evening shadows, or a hired man waiting eagerly for his wages" (Job. 7:1, 2). Third, there is an end decreed, an end that is not release but disaster. It is death, the dissolution of the total man. God speaks of it saying, "You [will] return to the ground, since from it you were taken; for dust you are and to dust you will return" (Gen. 3:19). We acknowledge this sad end at every funeral service.

There are two things that we should see about this: 1) that life is filled with pain and sorrow, and 2) that in many respects it grows continually worse.

We live in an age that is accustomed (at least until quite recently) to think optimistically. Our thinking is infused with the idea of progress. This means in practice that we tend to deny what is unpleasant or, if we actually do acknowledge it, we assume that eventually and inevitably it will go away. The trouble with this attitude is that life is filled with countless unpleasantries, whether we acknowledge them or not, and they do not go away. Consequently, we must either acknowledge this, recognizing the unpleasant things and looking to God for strength to bear up through them and occasionally change them, or else be lost in frustration. I believe this is the cause of the frustration of many of

---

[3]Schaeffer, *Genesis in Space and Time,* p. 95.

the young. They have been told that life does not or should not have troubles. But it does, and when they experience them they are surprised and do not know what to do. Sometimes they cease to function.

Augustine knew differently. In *The City of God* he has provided us with an optimistic view of history. He ends with "the beatific vision" and "the eternal felicity" of believers. But just before he discusses those subjects he speaks "of the miseries and ills to which the human race is justly exposed through the first sin, and from which none can be delivered save by Christ's grace."

He writes, "Who can describe, who can conceive the number and severity of the punishments which afflict the human race—pains which are not only the accompaniment of the wickedness of godless men, but are a part of the human condition and the common misery—what fear and what grief are caused by bereavement and mourning, by losses and condemnations, by fraud and falsehood, by false suspicions, and all the crimes and wicked deeds of other men? For at their hands we suffer robbery, captivity, chains, imprisonment, exile, torture, mutilation, loss of sight, the violation of chastity to satisfy the lust of the oppressor, and many other dreadful evils. What numberless casualties threaten our bodies from without—extremes of heat and cold, storms, floods, inundations, lightning, thunder, hail, earthquakes, houses falling; or from the stumbling, or shying, or vice of horses; from countless poisons in fruits, water, air, animals; from the painful or even deadly bites of wild animals; from the madness which a mad dog communicates, so that even the animal which of all others is most gentle and friendly to its own master, becomes an object of intenser fear than a lion or dragon, and the man whom it has by chance infected with this pestilential contagion becomes so rabid, that his parents, wife, children, dread him more than any wild beast! What disasters are suffered by those who travel by land or sea! What man can go out of his own house without being exposed on all hands to unforeseen accidents? Returning home sound in limb, he slips on his own doorstep, breaks his leg, and never recovers. What can seem safer than a man sitting in his chair? Eli the priest fell from his, and broke his neck."[4] Augustine goes on in this vein for about three times that length, but the point is already well made. Our melodies might be different, but the song is the same.

Again, might it not be the case that such evils actually increase with time rather than decrease, as optimists would have us believe? Martin Luther lived at the time of the Renaissance, a great period, but he did not think things were getting better. On the contrary, in his lectures on Genesis he argues for several pages that as sin has increased, so have troubles. He writes, "The world is deteriorating from day to day."[5]

GOD OF ALL GRACE

But all is not lost, though at times it may seem to be. Although sin grows worse and with it sin's troubles, God is unchanged and His mercy endures from generation to generation.

We see it in the judgment of Eve and Adam. It is true that Eve and those women who follow her were subjected to pain in childbearing, but sorrow is afterward forgotten for "joy that a child is born into the world" (John 16:21). One of those births produced the Savior.

[4]Saint Augustine, *The City of God*, Book 22, Chapter 22, in *A Select Library of the Nicene and Post-Nicene Fathers of the Christian Church*, Vol. 2, edited by Philip Schaff (Grand Rapids: Eerdmans, 1977), p. 500.

[5]Luther, *Works*, Vol. 1, p. 206.

Again, a woman enters into conflict with her husband, but this is not with one who is a stranger or even her enemy but one who loves her and to whom submission is often sweet. As for man, though the ground is cursed for his sake, the land is nevertheless not made entirely unproductive but rather "yields its fruit in season" (Ps. 1:3). Although God curses the ground, He also sends rains and snows to water it "making it bud and flourish, so that it yields seed for the sower and bread for the eater" (Isa. 55:10). Man sweats, but he revives again. He dies, but he rises to life everlasting.

In the final analysis, the greatest mercy of God is seen, not in God's mitigation of our punishment, but in His taking the full curse of the punishment of our sin on Himself at Calvary, which is why Adam and Eve were not cursed.

Did sin bring pain in childbirth? No pain is equal to that of Jesus who travailed in pain in order that He might bring forth many children into glory (Heb. 2:10). Did sin bring conflict? Jesus endured even greater conflict of sinners against Himself for our salvation (Heb. 12:3). Did thorns come in with sin? Jesus was crowned with thorns (John 19:2). Did sin bring sweat? He sweat, as it were, great drops of blood (Luke 22:44). Do we know sorrow? He was "a man of sorrows, and familiar with suffering" (Isa. 53:3). Did sin bring death? Jesus tasted "death for everyone" (Heb. 2:9).

In short, Jesus took our curse, as Paul says in writing to the Galatians: "Christ redeemed us from the curse of the law by becoming a curse for us" (Gal. 3:13). He became a curse so that we might be set free to live to God through Him.

31

Living by Faith

(Genesis 3:20)

Adam named his wife Eve, because she would become the mother of all the living.

Genesis 3:20 seems to have no connection with what has gone before. It stands apart. And so does the next verse! Genesis 3:16–19 deals with God's judgment on Eve and Adam for their sin of eating of the forbidden tree; it follows the preceding verses nicely. In fact, every sequence of events and verses in chapters 1 through 3 is apparent . . . until now. But now we read, "Adam named his wife Eve, because she would become the mother of all the living" (v. 20), and in the next verse we find, "The LORD God made garments of skin for Adam and his wife and clothed them" (v. 21).

Once, when Donald Grey Barnhouse was preaching on these verses, he called attention to this apparent problem and told this story. In the early days of push-button radios the children in his family used to amuse themselves by listening to one program and then pushing the button that would quickly switch them to another station. The first station might be broadcasting a political speech: "Vote for me and I'll . . ." The button would be pushed and the radio would continue: "A pop fly! Out on third!" Barnhouse told of one incident that occurred when the family was listening to the radio broadcast of the marriage of Queen Elizabeth of England to Philip, when Elizabeth was just a princess. The minister said, "Do you, Philip, take this woman to be your lawfully wedded wife . . ." The button was pushed, and (believe it or not) the radio continued with a prize fight: "Shake hands, go to your corners and come out fighting at the bell." Sometimes Scripture seems like that. One verse follows another with no apparent connection. But when we study the Bible we must never forget that the Bible is not like radio with many unrelated stations broadcasting in total disregard of one another. On the contrary, although it is composed of many books, the Bible has only one author: God. He is a God of order. So whenever we come to a verse that seems unrelated to what has gone before or comes after, we must simply re-examine the text more closely.

"Adam named his wife Eve, because she would become the mother of all the living." This verse is right where God wanted it, and it is there for a purpose.

He Called Them "Adam"

The place to begin in attempting to understand this verse is with the fact that "Eve" was Adam's name for his wife and not God's name for Adam's wife. We are so used to speaking of Adam and Eve—we have often spoken of Adam and Eve in these studies—that we generally fail to notice that not once in the story of the Creation and the Fall, up to this point, has Adam's wife been called Eve. She has been called a "female" (1:27), a "helper suitable" for Adam (2:18), a "woman" (2:22, 23), a "wife" (2:24, 25; 3:8). But those are all descriptive or generic terms, not names. We do not find the name "Eve."

This does not mean that God did not

183

name the woman, however. He did. But the name God gave her is not found in these chapters. It is found in chapter 5. There, in verses 1 and 2, we read, "When God created man, he made him in the likeness of God. He created *them* male and female; at the time they were created, he blessed *them* and called *them* 'man' [or 'Adam,' because 'Adam' means man]." In other words, the name that God gave the woman was "man" or "Adam," which was the name of her husband.

This has a number of interesting facets apart from the significance of the name "Eve." For one thing, it says something about the current desire of some spokespersons for the women's liberation movement to alter language so that "man" is no longer used to refer to both male and female. Such people want to eliminate words like "humanity." They want to say "human kind." They do not want to say "chairman." They want to say "chairperson" or simply "the chair." But according to this text, such efforts are actually opposed to God's revelation.

We never want to offend unnecessarily, and I confess that in my own public speaking I have adjusted my use of language to say "men and women" when I am referring to both male and female. But when we are doing that, let us not forget that "man" is God's word for the race and that those in a previous age who used the words "man" and "humanity" were actually closer to the language of Scripture than we are.

The really significant point about this divine naming of the woman is the psychological fact that in most marriages the woman inevitably gets a large share of her identity from her husband, which is what is symbolized by the woman taking the man's name in marriage rather than it being the other way around. Many modern women react strongly against this, as if it is unjust. But they often acknowledge it unconsciously anyway. Barnhouse, whom I mentioned

earlier, told of a conversation he once had with a woman who protested angrily against what she termed "the Bible's degrading view of women." She did not like the idea that a wife's identity is derived in large measure from her husband. The conversation went on and the name of a certain woman came up. Barnhouse asked, "Who is she?"

The woman answered, "Oh, she's the wife of Senator So-and-So."

Barnhouse asked, "But who is she?"

The woman said, "I told you, she's the wife of Senator So-and-So."

Barnhouse said, "I heard that, but I asked 'Who is *she?*'"

The woman replied, "I said, 'She's the wife . . .'"

Barnhouse interrupted, "That's precisely what I was telling you five minutes ago. The wife gets her identity from her husband." This does not mean that a wife has no identity of her own, of course. But it does mean that there is this special feature in marriage, which is of God and which should cause every godly woman to take particular care about whom she marries. If you have two sisters from a wealthy family and one marries a congressman and the other a chauffeur, what are the two sisters known as from that time on? The answer is obvious. So a woman should take particular care whom she marries.

Adam Called Her "Eve"

God called the woman "Adam." But that immediately raises the question, "Why, if God called Eve 'Adam,' did Adam call Eve 'Eve'?" The answer is not that Adam was contradicting God or changing the name of his wife on his own authority. Her name remained "Adam." What Adam was actually doing was giving Eve a title. For "Eve" is a title; it means "life" in the sense of being a "life-giver." We would say "mother." The text says, "Adam named his wife Eve, *because* she would become the *mother* of all the living."

It is sometimes the case in studying the Bible that the solution to one problem introduces another—that is what makes the study of the Bible so fascinating—and that is precisely what happens here. Yet it is at this point that we really come to the heart of the text. The problem is that, although Adam called his wife's name Eve, meaning "life-giver" or "mother," Eve was not a mother. In fact, if we read this and the next chapter closely, we have reason to believe that she had not even conceived. Her first child was Cain, and we are told not only of the birth but also the conception of Cain in chapter 4: "Adam lay with his wife Eve, and she *conceived* and gave birth to Cain" (v. 1). So we ask: Why did Adam name his wife "mother" when she was not yet a mother and, in fact, had not even become pregnant?

There is only one answer to that question, and it comes from the context. Five verses before this Adam and Eve had heard the judgment of God against Satan in which God said, "I will put enmity between you and the woman, and between your offspring and hers; he will crush your head, and you will strike his heel" (Gen. 3:15). This verse mentioned the woman's offspring and said flatly that her seed would crush the head of Satan.

God had said that the punishment for eating of the tree of the knowledge of good and evil was death. Adam and Eve had seen the judgment of God against Satan. Satan had appeared to them in the guise of the serpent, which was most assuredly not the slithering, lowly creature we know as a snake today. The Hebrew word translated "serpent" in Genesis 3:1 is *nahash,* which in its early and primary use probably meant "a shining one" (Gesenius). The serpent stood upright and was perhaps the most glorious of all God's creatures. Suddenly, however, Adam and Eve heard God's judgment on Satan and saw this beautiful animal turn into a snake and slide away into the bushes. They must have been paralyzed with fear. They had seen the serpent's judgment, and they were next. What would God do to them? Would they become snakes also? Would they die?

As they thought about this and heard the greatly reduced words of the judgment of God on themselves, the deliberately hopeful words contained in God's reference to the woman's offspring must have gotten through. The fact that Eve would have offspring was itself significant. Since she had not yet given birth it meant that she would not die physically, at least not then. Since she had not yet conceived it meant that Adam would not die either. Moreover, there was the nature of the one to come. He would be a deliverer. He would crush the head of Satan. This was their hope. God had said that Eve would give birth to one who in some manner would be the deliverer. So when Adam named his wife Eve, mother, she not even being pregnant, it was an act of faith, by which he testified to his belief that God would keep His promise and that the deliverer would come.

Genesis 3:20 is not the only place in Genesis that would lead us to think this way. In time we are coming to chapter 4, where we will look at this next matter in some detail. But we may note even here that when Eve finally conceived and brought forth Cain, both she and Adam thought that he was the deliverer. They thought Cain was Jesus, which is why they named him "Cain," meaning "brought forth" or "acquired." In colloquial language we would say, "I've got him" or "Here he is." Indeed, when we get to chapter 4, I am going to show that Eve's words were even stronger than this. For she did not merely say, "I have brought forth [there is the meaning of 'Cain'] a man," that is, the man who was promised. She said (so I believe), "I have brought forth a man, even Jehovah [the 'Redeemer']."

We know, of course, that Eve and Adam were mistaken. They thought they had brought forth the deliverer when actually they had brought forth a murderer, for Cain killed his brother Abel. But up to this point their perceptions were right. God had promised a deliverer, and they believed Him, showing their belief by the naming of Eve by Adam and Cain by Eve. By this they showed that they were staking their hope on the word of God.

ABRAM AND ABRAHAM

I think in this connection of another naming that was equally an act of faith and which, because of its significance in the history of salvation, also belongs in this context. It is the change of Abraham's name from Abram, which was his name originally, to Abraham, by which we know the father of the Jewish people today.

The original form of the patriarch's name means "father of many," and the key to the story is that this man, even though he had a name like that, was actually the father of none. This may not be a particular disaster in our day, but in Abram's day in the East it must have been particularly galling. Orientals are a most polite people, and their politeness manifests itself in asking many personal questions that would be considered impolite in our culture but which must be asked in theirs. Abram was an oriental. Furthermore, he was located at Hebron, at the crossroads of the most important caravan routes of the ancient world. When the caravans of the rich merchants came into his land on their way east or west, they stopped for rest and provender. Abram's servants took care of the needs of the camels and the servants of the traders. Food was sold to the travelers. In the evening the merchants would have come to Abram's tent to pay their respects. The questions would have followed a set pattern. How old are you? Who are you? How long have you been

here? When the trader had introduced himself, Abram was forced to name himself: Abram, father of many.

Donald Barnhouse writes particularly well on this passage. "It must have happened a hundred times, a thousand times, and each time more galling than the time before. 'Oh, father of many! Congratulations! And how many sons do you have?' The answer was so humiliating to Abram: 'None.' And many a time there must have been the half concealed snort of humor at the incongruity of the name and the fact that there were no children to back up such a name. Abram must have steeled himself for the question and the reply and have hated the situation with great bitterness."

Besides, there was probably much gossip about the situation. It was a world of skins and cloth, where all lived in tents, and there was little privacy from the eyes and none in the realm of the ears. Think of the many conversations on the subject: Who was sterile, Abram or Sarah? Was Abram really a man? Oh, he was the patriarch, the ruler of the oasis. His word was law. He was rich. But he had no children, and his name was "father of many."

Barnhouse continues, "If someone thinks that I am imagining all this, let me present in proof the psychology of his wife, Sarah, who finally came to him and suggested that he take her servant girl, Hagar, and have a child by her. Sarah must have sensed that it was she herself who was barren. She was a very proud woman, and very sensitive, as the sequel shows, and she must have been goaded to her action by a desperation which forced her to push her husband into the arms of another woman.

"Remember, I say, that it was a world of cloth and skins—they lived in tents, surrounded by servants. The offer is made—Abram is presented with the slave girl as a concubine. The news must have spread with rapidity; the tent was prepared for the master and the slave girl; the servants who did the work and who surrounded the group, must have greeted one another with smirks and winks—old Abram, father of many, father of none, had gone into the tent with a concubine.

"Days passed, while the idle speculation of the women-folk fanned into greater gossip as the news was finally confirmed that Hagar was with child by Abram. Sarah saw herself despised in the eyes of the women of Egypt. The news spread in the camp, for it was a matter of great importance, involving the inheritance of great riches. There was going to be an heir. Abram was looked at with a little more respect—at least it was now certain that he was a real man—here was the proof of it. And he had fathered a child in advanced age. Then it was Sarah after all—it was she who was sterile—a woman who could not fulfill the functions of a woman.

"And then the child was born—it was a boy, and his name was Ishmael. . . . Now when the travelers came to the wells to camp and came to call upon Abram, the question of the name was not quite so difficult as before. What is your name? Abram, father of many. Oh, congratulations! And how many sons do you have? I have one son. True, it was not very many, but it was enough to keep the smirk off the faces of the strangers and the winks from the glance of the servants who stood nearby.

"Thirteen years passed thus. Abram had declined in health and was now feeble. He was ninety-nine years old when God appeared to him and reminded him of the promsie which had been made to him. Abram's first reaction was to remind God, after all, he did have a son, Ishmael, and that the existence of this one son was enough to keep God from being a liar. Even if Abram died then, God could give Ishmael a multitude of sons and fulfill the promises. But God does not work in that fashion. . . .

"God said unto Abram, 'I am the Almighty God; walk thou before me, and be thou perfect. And I will make my covenant between me and thee, and will multiply thee exceedingly' (Gen. 17:1, 2, KJV). . . . Abram fell on his face before God, and God continued, saying, 'As for me, behold my covenant is with thee, and thou shalt be a father of many nations. Neither shall thy name any more be called Abram, but thy name shall be Abraham; for a father of many nations have I made thee' (17:4, 5).

"There are some things in the Bible that cause me to chuckle, and there is a thought in connection with this verse that always has had that effect on me. I cannot help but think of what must have happened when Abraham broke the news to his family and servants that he was now changing his name. They all knew that his former name was Abram, father of many, and they knew it had been somewhat of a thorn to him. So we can imagine the stir of interest and curiosity when he announced, 'I am going to change my name.' Were there some who said to themselves with a laugh, 'The old man couldn't take it. It got under his skin. After all, to be father of nobody for eighty-six years and then to be the father of only one, with a name like he has must have its rough moments.'

"And then the old man spoke. 'I am to be known as Abraham—father of a multitude.' We can almost hear the silence of the stunned moment as the truth breaks upon them. Father of a multitude? Then the laughter broke forth behind the scenes. 'The old man has gone crazy. He had one child when he was eighty-six, and now at ninety-nine he is beginning to get ideas.'"[1]

---

[1]Donald Grey Barnhouse, *God's Remedy*, Vol. 3 of the series on *Romans* (Grand Rapids: Eerdmans, 1954), pp. 310–16.

FAITH IN GOD

From a human point of view it may have been ridiculous for a man of ninety-nine to think like this, but it was not ridiculous from God's point of view. And Abram saw things from the viewpoint of God, who had given the promises. This is why Paul says of Abram's faith in Romans, "Without weakening in his faith, he faced the fact that his body was as good as dead—since he was about a hundred years old—and that Sarah's womb was also dead. Yet he did not waver through unbelief regarding the promise of God, but was strengthened in his faith and gave glory to God, being fully persuaded that God had power to do what he had promised" (Rom. 4:19–21).

I am sure you see the progression: Adam names his wife Eve, Eve names her son Cain, and Abram renames himself Abraham—all in faithful response to God, who gave the promise of salvation. Names do not have quite this significance for us today, but there is one name that does. It is a name that all believers in the Lord Jesus Christ bear, the name "Christian." It is His name; it means "Christ-one." The reason we have His name is that we take it on ourselves in the moment of our surrender to Jesus as our Savior and Lord. It is to say, "From this time forward I am no longer my own, but rather I belong to Him who loved me and gave Himself for me." Have you done that? If not, I challenge you to commit yourself to Christ, taking His name on you, and follow in the steps of Adam and Eve and Abram and all who have believed God.

32

Skin or Fig Leaves

(Genesis 3:21)

The LORD God made garments of skin for Adam and his wife and clothed them.

We have already seen that there are no unrelated thoughts in the Word of God, only in our own understanding of those thoughts, and we have looked at Genesis 3:20 as an example. At first glance, the naming of Eve by Adam seems to be entirely unconnected with what has gone before; it does not seem to follow on God's judgment of the serpent, Eve, and Adam. Yet it is related, as we have seen, and so is the verse to which we come now. In fact, taken together these verses contain the first example in the Bible of what has come to be called in theology the *ordo salutis* or "steps of salvation."

In its full form the *ordo salutis* has many parts, for the steps by which a man or woman is brought to faith and is sustained in faith are many. The beginning point is election. Verses like John 1:13 and James 1:18 put the determination of God to save a particular individual before the person's rebirth. John 3:3, 5 speak of "seeing" and "entering" the kingdom of God and show that these are not possible until one is born again. They correspond to conviction of sin and quickening of faith in Christ. In 1 John 3:9 we read of sanctification. Romans 8:28–30 add justification and glorification, and these verses say, "And we know that in all things God works for the good of those who love him, who have been called according to his purpose. For those God foreknew he also predestined to be conformed to the likeness of his Son, that he might be the firstborn

among many brothers. And those he predestined, he also called; those he called, he also justified; those he justified, he also glorified." If these various steps are put together, the sequence is: foreknowledge, predestination, effectual calling, rebirth, faith and repentance, justification, sanctification and glorification.

Not all these steps are present in Genesis 3, of course. But the suggestion of a sequence is there, as I have indicated. The sequence is: conviction of sin, following on the pronouncement of judgment by God; faith, expressed in the naming of Eve by Adam; and now, finally, justification, symbolized by the clothing of Adam and Eve with the skins of animals. It is because of the faith of Adam, disclosed in verse 20, that God does what verse 21 records.

NEED FOR CLOTHING

There are four points to be made about God's clothing of Adam and his wife in skins. First, a covering of some sort was needed. We hear people speak of prostitution as the oldest human profession, but they are wrong when they say this. Their view throws light on the guilt with which our contemporaries view many sexual relations, but it is misleading. The oldest of all professions is not prostitution but the clothing industry. Later, sin showed itself in sexual sins among others. But we are told in Genesis that the first effect of sin was the opening of the eyes of Adam and Eve to perceive

189

their nakedness, in response to which "they sewed fig leaves together and made coverings for themselves" (Gen. 3:7). God confirmed this need when He made garments from the skins of animals.

I do not need to repeat the details of this principle, which we considered earlier in our treatment of Genesis 2:25 ("Camelot, O Camelot") and Genesis 3:7 ("Carnal Knowledge"), except to say that the nakedness of Adam and Eve, which required clothing, was psychological as well as physical. That is, it was related to sin and the fact that as a result of sin the man and woman now stood in a wrong relationship to God, one another, and themselves. They felt exposed. The psychological exposure was intolerable. So they tried to cover themselves up. In the beginning they used fig leaves. Later, when God appeared in the garden to confront them with their sin, they used evasions, excuses, and at last tried to put the blame on God.

People do the same today. They use clothes and other means, but the underlying desire is to appear as something they are not. They want to hide their shame and put on a front before others.

Fig Leaves

The second point to be made about this verse is that the coverings we are capable of making for ourselves are inadequate. This is seen in the case of Adam and Eve, but it is evident of us all.

The most common covering is good works. We have many people coming to God like the moralist described by Paul in the second chapter of Romans (vv. 1–16). He is one who would readily agree with Paul's description of the need of the pagan world. He would agree that it is indeed corrupt, in need of renewal. But he would exclude himself from Paul's description claiming that he is better by virtue of his moral attain-

ments. "I am not corrupt," he would maintain. "I want to be accepted by God on the basis of my good works."

God's judgment is that a man's good works are fig leaves (Eph. 2:8, 9).

It is not that good works are without value from a human point of view. It is just that they are no good from God's point of view, and that is because they do not deal with the basic sin problem. Good works are a bit like Monopoly© money. It is good for the game of Monopoly©, but it is no good in the real world. Suppose your family has a good Monopoly© player and that every time you play the game this person tends to accumulate all the property and collect all the money. Suppose further that after one of these games he takes his Monopoly© money and goes down to the First National Bank to open an account. He steps up to the teller and says, "I'd like to open an account in your bank."

"Very good," says the teller. "How much would you like to deposit?"

"$472,984!" He pushes the Monopoly© money across the counter. If that ever happened, I am sure the teller would quickly call someone to come and take this person away. Monopoly© money serves well in the game of Monopoly©, but it has no value in the real world. In the same way, although good works are sufficient to make ourselves acceptable before other men and women, they are not sufficient to gain an acceptable standing before God.

There is another type of person, which Paul also discusses (Rom. 2:17–29). He is a religious person. His confidence is in the careful performance of his religious duties. "I keep the law," he would say. "I have been baptized, confirmed. I teach in Sunday school; I serve on the church boards; I pay my tithe."

God says that these are fig leaves too, no less than the pagan's good works.

"But why?" someone asks. "Aren't the sacraments, Christian education, tithing, and service good things?" Yes, they are. Later in Romans Paul is going to say, using the most eminently religious person of his day, the Jew, as an example, "Theirs is the adoption as sons; theirs the divine glory, the covenants, the receiving of the law, the temple worship and the promises. Theirs are the patriarchs, and from them is traced the human ancestry of Christ, who is God over all, forever praised" (Rom. 9:4, 5). Paul means that there are great advantages in the outward forms of true religion, primarily because they are intended to lead us to Christ. But they are useless so far as our standing before God is concerned, because they do nothing about the state of our heart. ("A man is not a Jew if he is only one outwardly, nor is circumcision merely outward and physical. No, a man is a Jew if he is one inwardly; and circumcision is circumcision of the heart, by the Spirit," Rom. 2:28, 29.)

Years ago, when I lived in Switzerland, I got an illustration of this principle from the Salvation Army. Each year at Fashnacht, the Swiss equivalent of the Mardi Gras, the citizens of Basel (where I lived) donned masks and costumes and presumably did things, covered by their masks, that they would not normally do at other times of the year. I say "presumably" because the Swiss themselves presumed so and made many jokes about it. They would joke about how many illegitimate babies would be born nine months after Fashnacht, to give just one example. Each year at this time the Salvation Army would advertise on billboards throughout the city. The advertisements would display the Salvation Army seal, a number where it could be reached, and then in large letters this inscription: *Gott sieht hinter deine Maske.* That means "God sees behind your mask." And it is true. He does. Therefore, the outward acts of religion without Christ are just fig leaves.

"But," says someone, "I have worked hard at self-reformation. I used to be a drunkard, and I shook the habit of drink and now have a good job and . . ."

"Fig leaves," says God.

"But I read my Bible every day and I go to church twice on Sunday and I always try to say hello to the person sitting next to me in the pew and. . . ."

"Fig leaves," says God.

"But I give to the United Fund."

"Fig leaves."

"I give blood."

"Fig leaves."

"I . . . I . . ."

"Fig leaves," says God. "These are all fig leaves. None of them deal adequately with sin."

COVERING OF SKINS

The third and main point of our text is that God must provide the covering, for only God is adequate to deal with the sin problem. The text says, "The LORD God made garments of skin for Adam and his wife and clothed them" (v. 21).

It does not say here what animals God killed to get the skins with which He then clothed Adam and Eve. But I tend to think, though this is a guess and may well be wrong, that the animals were probably lambs and that the skins were lambskins. This incident is meant to point to Jesus as our only sufficient Savior and to His righteousness as our covering. Jesus is pictured as "the Lamb of God, who takes away the sin of the world" (John 1:29). During those long ages before the coming of Jesus, when the promises of His coming were passed on from generation to generation among those who waited for it, the promises in the words of Scripture were preserved upon skins, generally lambskins, which were carefully prepared and sown together to make large rolls of writing known as scrolls. With this imagery and practical matter to go on, it is reasonable to suppose that God killed lambs to clothe our first parents. But whatever the case, we are to know that God killed animals, made garments from their skins, and then clothed Adam and Eve after taking their inadequate fig-leaf clothes from them.

DEATH FOR LIFE

This brings us to the fourth and final point: in order for Adam and Eve to be clothed in the skins of animals the animals had to die. In a similar way, in order for us to be clothed with the righteousness of Jesus Christ, which is what the skins symbolize, Jesus had to die. The Bible says, "Without the shedding of blood there is no forgiveness" (Heb. 9:22). It was necessary for the innocent One to die in order that the guilty might live.

This truth must have appeared quite wonderful when it was first revealed to Eve and Adam. They had been warned that they were not to eat of the tree of the knowledge of good and evil upon penalty of death. God had said, "You are free to eat from any tree in the garden; but you must not eat from the tree of the knowledge of good and evil, for when you eat of it you will surely die" (Gen. 2:16, 17). Yet up to this point no one had died. Adam and Eve had sinned. They must have expected death as the immediate penalty for their sin. When God came to them in the garden they must have shivered at the prospect of this judgment. But they did not die (though their spirits died, which they showed by attempting to run away from God when He called them). In fact, not even the serpent died. Up to this point there had been no death at all. And now, the death that occurs is not their death, though they richly deserved it, but the death of innocent animals—lambs. And the One who killed those animals was God.

Two thoughts must have gone through Adam and Eve's minds. First, an instinctive horror of death. "So this is what death is," they must have exclaimed as they looked down in horror at the bodies of the slain animals. "How horrible!" In that instant it must have

dawned on them that if death is the result of sin ("the wages of sin is death"), then sin is far worse than they could possibly have imagined it to be. And they must have determined, so far as possible, to refuse to sin and to be obedient to God.

The second thought, mingling with their awareness of sin's horror, must have been a deep and growing wonder at the mercy of God who, though He had every right to take their lives in forfeit of his broken commandment and had said that death must follow sin, was nevertheless showing that it was possible for an innocent victim to die instead.

We know as we look back on this event from the perspective of later revelation that it was not the blood of the slain animals that actually took away the sin of Eve and Adam. It was not the death of animals that permitted God to forgive sin and proclaim sinners just. The only death that could possibly do that was the death of Jesus, and the only blood that could cleanse was His blood. On the other hand, we understand that the death of the animals pointed to His death.

On this occasion, God was showing that it was possible for one animal, an innocent substitute, to die for one sinning *individual*—one animal for Eve, one animal for Adam. Later in Jewish history, at the time of the Exodus from Egypt, God commanded each Jewish family to take a lamb into the house, examine it for the space of three days, kill it, and then spread its blood on the doorposts and lintel of the house as a sign to the angel of death, who that night would pass through the entire land and slay the firstborn of every household that was not so covered. This was the Passover, and the symbolism was now broadened to show how one animal could die for one *family*. A little later, when God gave the law, He also gave instructions for the Day of Atonement, on which day the high priest was to kill an animal on behalf of the nation and then sprinkle its blood on the mercy seat of the ark of the covenant within the Holy of Holies of the Jewish tabernacle. Now it is one animal for one *nation*. At last the day came when John the Baptist was standing beside the Jordan and, seeing Jesus, pointed Him out for the benefit of his disciples, saying, "Look, the Lamb of God, who takes away the sin of the *world*" (John 1:29).

One substitute for one individual, one substitute for one family, one substitute for one nation, one substitute for the world!

Two Religions

That is God's religion. It is the only religion by which anyone is ever going to get to heaven. In the last analysis there really are only two religions, whatever nation, tribe, place or period of history you consider. There is the religion of fig leaves, the religion of works. Or there is the religion of skins, the religion of God's perfect provision through the death of Christ.

Most people come to God with fig leaves. They may not be much; but they are something they have done for themselves, and they want God to recognize them. They will acknowledge His grace, they will accept His help—so long as there is that little bit of their own good works mixed with it. But this is precisely what God will not accept. Good works may please other men and women; fig leaves may look beautiful. But they will not please God because there has been

no death, and "the wages of sin is death." If you have been coming to God with fig leaves—if you are coming with fig leaves now—I urge you to throw them aside, admit they are useless and accept the clothing God offers. Then the nakedness of your sin will be covered, and you will be able to sing with the redeemed from every place and century:

> My hope is built on nothing less
> Than Jesus' blood and righteousness.

And especially the last verse:

> When He shall come with trumpet
>   sound,
> O may I then in Him be found,
> Dressed in His righteousness alone.
> Faultless to stand before the throne.
>
> On Christ, the solid Rock, I stand;
> All other ground is sinking sand.

Do not delay! The Lord told a story about a man who came to a king's feast without a wedding garment. He said, "When the king came in to see the guests, he noticed a man there who was not wearing wedding clothes. 'Friend,' he asked, 'how did you get in here without wedding clothes?' The man was speechless. Then the king told the attendants, 'Tie him hand and foot, and throw him outside, into the darkness, where there will be weeping and gnashing of teeth.' For many are invited, but few are chosen" (Matt. 22:11–14). Actually, *all* are invited. The question is: Are you among the chosen? Are you clothed with the righteousness of Christ?

33

The Way to Life

(Genesis 3:22–24)

And the LORD God said, "The man has now become like one of us, knowing good and evil. He must not be allowed to reach out his hand and take also from the tree of life and eat, and live forever." So the LORD God banished him from the Garden of Eden to work the ground from which he had been taken. After he drove the man out, he placed on the east side of the Garden of Eden cherubim and a flaming sword flashing back and forth to guard the way to the tree of life.

I do not know who said "A picture is worth a thousand words," but the sentence could almost have been taken from Scripture. Why? Because the God who has revealed Himself to us propositionally in a book of words also has disclosed spiritual truths by pictures, and these are valuable. I do not mean literal pictures, of course, the kind you hang on walls. I mean the pictures found in Scripture itself. Some of these are literal: Job sitting in ashes scraping his sores, Peter sinking in the water of the Sea of Galilee while Jesus reaches out to save him. Some are probably symbolic. The Book of Revelation is filled with such pictures as these. The picture painted for us at the end of the third chapter of Genesis is both.

We have probably all seen paintings of this event because many artists have dealt with it. Most of the great Renaissance painters handled this theme. So did William Blake in his well-known illustrations for Milton's *Paradise Lost.* My favorite is the work of Masaccio done in fresco for the wall of the Brancacci Chapel, Church of the Carmine, Florence. The work is called "Expulsion from Paradise" and features bold contrasts of light and darkness that serve to highlight the picture's drama. In it Adam and Eve are being driven away by

an angel who hovers overhead, sword in hand. The human pair are engulfed in anguish. Adam's head is bowed low, hands covering his face. Eve's head is thrown back, her mouth open in a cry of deep personal pain. As Adam and Eve walk away from the Garden of Eden their withering shame is painfully evident in the very motion of their bodies. This fresco, like the verbal portrait given to us in Genesis, at once etches the shame and misery of the human condition on our minds.

LOSS OF LIFE

What does the picture in Genesis 3:22–24 teach us? The first clear teaching is that sin keeps us from life. In Eden in their sinless state, Adam and Eve rightly anticipated an eternity of life with God, who is the source of life. Having sinned, they are now driven out into the world to earn their living by the sweat of their brow, bear children in pain and at last die and return to the dust from which they were made.

This is the meaning of "the tree of life" (v. 22). From the point of view of a simple understanding of this story the tree is puzzling. Commentators have asked whether it is supposed to be the same tree as "the tree of the knowledge of

194

good and evil" (2:17). If there were two trees, what are we to suppose was the purpose of the second one? Would this tree actually impart eternal life? If so, had Adam and Eve eaten of it before they sinned? If they had and if they had lost such life by sinning, how could they be supposed to regain life now? If they had not eaten, why not? Questions of this type could be multiplied indefinitely, but they are actually beside the point. Presumably this was a literal tree, just as the tree of the knowledge of good and evil was also literal. Both involved a real eating or not eating. But the meaning was not in the actual trees or their fruit but rather in what the fruit stood for. In the one case, it was a knowledge of good and evil, which Adam and Eve gained by sinning. In this case, it was an eternal prolongation of life in its sinful state—however it might actually have been communicated. If Adam and Eve had been allowed to live forever, they would have lived as sinners. They were to be set free from sin only by a literal death and resurrection.

I doubt if Adam and Eve were thinking these particular points through. All they would have been aware of is that they were being driven out from the place where life could be sustained and that they were eventually to die.

What a sad picture! There he is, that poor man Adam, head bowed, face covered in shame. There is Eve, head thrown back, crying out in anguish. But it is not just Adam. Or Eve. This is you and I and all who go their own sinful way rather than obeying God. Jesus spoke of His purpose in coming into the world at one point saying, "I have come that they may have life, and have it to the full" (John 10:10). But if we will not have God and Christ, if we will not walk in that way, we will not have life. We will have death even in life, and our death will be the worst of all deaths eventually. The apostle Paul spoke of a widow living in sin by saying, "The widow who lives

for pleasure is dead even while she lives" (1 Tim. 5:6).

Remember this when sin beckons. The devil will call, "Come away with me and enjoy sin's pleasure. Nothing will come of it. No harm will be done." When you hear that voice let your mind run back to God's portrait of Adam and Eve being driven from Eden in shame and remember that the devil has been a liar from the beginning.

Life Without God

There is a second lesson taught by this picture: sin keeps us from God. This is implied in the first lesson, of course, for if God is the source of life and if sin keeps us from life, then sin obviously keeps us from God too. But the lesson is made even more vivid in this passage.

In order to understand how powerful this is we have to learn something about the angels called cherubim, mentioned in verse 24. These are referred to sixty-five times in the Bible. (Only one of these references is in the New Testament, but the "living creatures" of Revelation 4 and 5 and Isaiah 6 are similar if not identical beings, as we will see.) Most of the references are to the figures that occupied either end of the mercy seat of the ark of the covenant of the Jewish temple. The only other large block of references is in a vision of Ezekiel recorded in chapter 10 of that prophecy.

Ezekiel is the place to begin, however, for only here (though possibly also in Revelation and Isaiah) do we have a description of the cherubim themselves. (The figures on the mercy seat were not real cherubs but only representations of them.) Ezekiel describes these as being associated with the throne and glory of God. "I looked, and I saw the likeness of a throne of sapphire above the expanse that was over the heads of the cherubim. The LORD said to the man clothed in linen, 'Go in among the wheels beneath the cherubim. Fill your hands with burning coals from among the cherubim and scatter them over the city.' And as I watched, he went in. Now the cherubim were standing on the south side of the temple when the man went in, and a cloud filled the inner court. Then the glory of the LORD rose from above the cherubim and moved to the threshold of the temple. The cloud filled the temple, and the court was full of the radiance of the glory of the LORD. The sound of the wings of the cherubim could be heard as far away as the outer court, like the voice of God Almighty when he speaks" (Ezek. 10:1–5). The chapter develops the description along those lines, becoming increasingly more elaborate and more glorious, and finally concludes with this observation: "These were the living creatures I had seen beneath the God of Israel by the Kebar River, and I realized that they were cherubim. Each had four faces and four wings, and under their wings was what looked like the hands of a man" (vv. 20, 21). Parts of this vision are hard to understand, but several things are clear. It is a vision of the glory of the presence of God, symbolized by the shekinah cloud, and it is this with which the cherubim are associated.

We can now turn to the similar portraits in Revelation and Isaiah. In Revelation, Ezekiel's phrase "living creatures" is used of otherwise unnamed beings that surround God's throne. It is said of them: "In the center, around the throne, were four living creatures, and they were covered with eyes, in front and in back. The first living creature was like a lion, the second was like an ox, the third had a face like a man, the fourth was like a flying eagle. Each of the four living creatures had six wings and was covered with eyes all around, even under his wings. Day and night they never stop saying:

'Holy, holy, holy
is the Lord God Almighty,
who was, and is, and is to come.'

Whenever the living creatures give glory, honor and thanks to him who sits on the throne and who lives for ever and ever, the twenty-four elders fall down before him who sits on the throne, and worship him who lives for ever and ever" (Rev. 4:6–10).

The text in Isaiah calls these beings seraphs, saying, "In the year that King Uzziah died, I saw the Lord seated on a throne, high and exalted, and the train of his robe filled the temple. Above him were seraphs, each with six wings: With two wings they covered their faces, with two they covered their feet, and with two they were flying. And they were calling to one another:

'Holy, holy, holy is the LORD Almighty;
the whole earth is full of his glory' "
(Isa. 6:1–3).

I do not think this is the place to sort out whether the creatures of Ezekiel, Revelation, and Isaiah are identical. My own opinion, based solely on the descriptions, is that the creatures of Revelation and Isaiah are identical (each has six wings, for example) and that the cherubim of Ezekiel are closely related though not identical (they are said to have four wings). The point I am making for our study of Genesis is merely that these creatures, whether of one type or several, are all nevertheless always associated with the presence and glory of God. That is, they are not as other, "normal," angels who appear here and there on errands of God's bidding but without God's special presence.

At this point the meaning of the appearance of the cherubim in Genesis emerges. For if the cherubim appear and if they drive the man and woman away, then it is God Himself from whom Adam and Eve are barred. The lesson is that sin does that. Sin bars us from God, and this is the greatest of all tragedies.

This was not God's will for us nor our intended destiny. We are created by God. "In him we live and move and have our being" (Acts 17:28). The Westminster Shorter Catechism asks the chief end of man and answers correctly, "Man's chief end is to glorify God, and to enjoy him forever" (Answer to Question 1). But what happens? Adam, having been created to glorify God and enjoy Him forever, is now being driven from God's presence. Eve is banished. What has brought them to such a sorry state? The culprit is sin, and the consequence is separation from the One who is altogether loving. Let us learn, then, that sin does matter and that the devil is wrong when he says that sin will not hurt. Sin disrupts. It disrupts that greatest of all relations: that between a man or a woman and God.

ARK OF MERCY

I come now to my final point. But unlike the first two, which I have approached with heaviness because of their stern and frightening aspect, I turn to this with joy. Even when painting a picture of judgment to warn us of sin and turn us to righteousness, God nevertheless also paints pictures of grace.

I think of an illustration developed with great skill by Donald Grey Barnhouse in a sermon entitled "Falling into Grace." Sir Edward C. Burne-Jones was a prominent artist in England during the latter part of the nineteenth century. One day he was invited to tea at the home of his daughter. On this occasion his little granddaughter was also seated at the table, but she became so naughty that her mother made her stand in the corner with her face to the wall. Sir Edward was a well-trained grandfather, so he did not interfere. But the next morning he arrived at his daughter's home with his paints and palette. He went to the wall where the little girl had been forced to stand, and there he painted pictures—a kitten chasing its tail, lambs in a field, goldfish swimming. The wall on both sides of that corner was decorated with his paintings, all for his granddaughter's delight. Now, if she had to stand in the corner again, at least she would have something to look at.[1]

I think of that story here because, as I study the picture of Adam and Eve being driven from Eden by the cherubim and recoil in sorrow, I remember that God has taken this scene of judgment and transformed it into one of the most wonderful pictures in the Bible of His grace.

You will remember that when I introduced the matter of the cherubim and went to Ezekiel, Revelation, and Isaiah for a study of them, I said that the other great block of references, the majority of them, is to the representations of cherubim on the mercy seat of the ark of the covenant within the Jewish temple. There are several places where these descriptions occur—in Exodus 25 and 36, where the instructions for building the ark are given to Moses and where the actual construction is said to have taken place; in 1 Kings 6–8 and 2 Chronicles 3–5, where the same thing is done again on a grander scale in the building of Solomon's temple; in other, scattered places.

The description in Exodus is worth quoting in full. "Have them make a chest of acacia wood—two and a half cubits long, a cubit and a half wide, and a cubit and a half high. Overlay it with pure gold, both inside and out, and make a gold molding around it. Cast four gold rings for it and fasten them to its four feet, with two rings on one side and two rings on the other. Then make poles of acacia wood and overlay them with gold. Insert the poles into the rings on the sides of the chest to carry it. The poles are to remain in the rings of this ark; they are not to be removed. Then put in the ark the Testimony, which I

---

[1]Donald Grey Barnhouse, "Falling into Grace," *Tragedy or Triumph* (Philadelphia: The Barnhouse Booklet Club, 1967), p. 45.

will give you. Make an atonement cover of pure gold—two and a half cubits long and a cubit and a half wide. And make two cherubim out of hammered gold at the ends of the cover. Make one cherub on one end and the second cherub on the other; make the cherubim of one piece with the cover, at the two ends. The cherubim are to have their wings spread upward, overshadowing the cover with them. The cherubim are to face each other, looking toward the cover. Place the cover on top of the ark and put in the ark the Testimony, which I will give you. There, above the cover between the two cherubim that are over the ark of the Testimony, I will meet with you and give you all my commands for the Israelites" (Exod. 25:10–22).

This is precisely what happened. When the wilderness tabernacle with its furnishing was finished, the shekinah glory cloud of God, which symbolized the presence of God, descended on the tabernacle and took its place between the wings of the cherubim. First Samuel 4:4 and other texts speak of God being "enthroned between the wings of the cherubim" (cf. 2 Sam. 6:2; 2 Kings 19:15; 1 Chron. 13:6; 28:18; Pss. 80:1; 99:1; Isa. 37:16). Numbers 7:89 says explicitly, "When Moses entered the Tent of Meeting to speak with the LORD, he heard the voice speaking to him from between the two cherubim above the atonement cover on the ark of the Testimony. And he spoke with him."

We read this and see immediately that the ark reproduces the essential elements of the scene in Eden: the presence of the glory of God and the cherubim who guard it from the eyes of sinful people. (None could enter the Holy of Holies save the high priest and that only once a year on the Day of Atonement.) It is a scene of wrath, of judgment. But it is changed, for it now has this new and wonderful element: It is designed around the mercy seat, here called the "atonement cover," on which the high priest was to sprinkle the blood of a sacrifice once a year as a sign that a substitute had died for the people's sin.

GRACE FOR ADAM

It may be—though I am not at all sure of this—that God painted the identical scene for Adam. The cherubim stationed at the entrance to the Garden of Eden may not merely have been barring Adam and Eve from the tree of life. They may also have been guarding the way to the appointed place of sacrifice, so that Adam and Eve would be able always to come with their sacrifices and thus find God ready to receive them on the basis of the shed blood.

I say I am uncertain of this because it is hardly the general view of commentators. Neither Luther nor Calvin thought along these lines. But it is the view of Henry Alford (*Genesis,* 1872), Arthur W. Pink (*Gleanings In Genesis,* 1922), Donald Grey Barnhouse (*Genesis,* 1970), Henry Morris (*The Genesis Record,* 1976) and some others. Alford writes: "The placing of these cherubim at the east of Eden was indicative of ordinances of worship and a form of access to the divine presence still open to man, though he was debarred from entrance into paradise."[2] Barnhouse wrote, "As soon as man sinned, God found him and provided him a Savior. He opened a way back to himself and guards that way jealously lest anyone should close it."[3] Perhaps we cannot know for sure whether this last scene was enacted for the benefit of Eve and Adam, but we can know that it has been enacted clearly for us. The lesson for us is to turn from sin and come to God in the way He has appointed.

---

[2]Henry Alford, *The Book of Genesis and Part of the Book of Exodus* (Minneapolis: Klock & Klock Christian Publishers, 1979), p. 19.

[3]Barnhouse, *Genesis,* p. 29.

34

The Story of Two Brothers

(Genesis 4:1–10)

Adam lay with his wife Eve, and she conceived and gave birth to Cain. She said, "With the help of the LORD I have brought forth a man." Later she gave birth to his brother Abel.

Now Abel kept flocks, and Cain worked the soil. In the course of time Cain brought some of the fruits of the soil as an offering to the LORD. But Abel brought fat portions from some of the firstborn of his flock. The LORD looked with favor on Abel and his offering, but on Cain and his offering he did not look with favor. So Cain was very angry, and his face was downcast.

Then the LORD said to Cain, "Why are you angry? Why is your face downcast? If you do what is right, will you not be accepted? But if you do not do what is right, sin is crouching at your door; it desires to have you, but you must master it."

Now Cain said to his brother Abel, "Let's go out to the field." And while they were in the field, Cain attacked his brother Abel and killed him.

Then the LORD said to Cain, "Where is your brother Abel?"

"I don't know," he replied. "Am I my brother's keeper?"

The LORD said, "What have you done? Listen! Your brother's blood cries out to me from the ground."

Under normal circumstances parents expect great things for their children. They want them to be wise, handsome or beautiful, filled with grace, successful. In some cases they look to their children to live out their own more limited successes or overcome their failures. This was the case with Bill, the hero of the well-known stage musical *Carousel*. He is a man of little character who eventually dies in a robbery. But when he learns of the pending birth of his child he sings,

I bet that he'll turn out to be
The spit-an' image of his Dad.
But he'll have more common sense
Than his puddin' headed father ever
    had. . . .

He'll be tall and tough as a tree, will Bill!
Like a tree he'll grow, with his head
    held high
And his feet planted firm on the ground,
And you won't see nobody dare to try
To boss him or toss him around.

In one form or another, every parent has that hope for his or her child. But in the whole history of the human race there has never been a greater measure of hope for any child than the hope of Adam and Eve at the birth of their first child, Cain.

CHRIST OR KILLER

Proof of this statement is by taking the reaction of Adam and Eve to Cain's birth in conjunction with the promise of God to send a deliverer (Gen. 3:15). The first man and woman had expected to die as the result of God's judgment on them for their sin in eating of the forbidden tree. God had said, "You must not eat from the tree of the knowledge of good and evil, for when you eat of it you will surely die" (Gen. 2:17). But they did not die, at least not then. Instead, God promised a deliverer to be born of the woman (Gen. 3:15). Adam and Eve believed God's promise, and Adam showed his faith in God by naming his wife Eve, meaning "life" or "life giver." She was the one through whom the promised salvation would come.

All this happened before Eve had produced any children, as we have seen. In fact, it happened even before she became pregnant. So, later, after they left the Garden of Eden, when Eve did become pregnant, the event was wonderful beyond description. Neither the man or woman had ever seen a pregnancy or birth before. So the wonder of birth was increased many times in their experience. Not only was there to be new life. It was to be the promised life, the One who should destroy the work of Satan and restore people to Paradise once more.

Adam and Eve must have counted the months, weeks, and days. Nine months, eight months, seven, six, five, four, three, two, one, two weeks, one week. . . . At last the child was born, and Eve held in her arms the one whom both she and Adam thought was the deliverer. How delighted they were! They did not know that they actually held in their arms a little murderer and that the tragic history of the human race, written in blood, had begun.

This much of the story is evident from the parts of it we have already considered, but it is expressed in particularly poignant terms at the start of Genesis 4. The story says, "Adam lay with his wife Eve, and she conceived and gave birth to Cain. She said, 'With the help of the LORD I have brought forth a man'" (v. 1). This translation unfortunately does not give the full force of what Eve said. We need to notice two things. First, the word "Cain" either sounds like or is actually based on the Hebrew verb *qanah,* which means "acquired." So when Eve says that she has "brought forth" or "acquired" a man from the Lord, she is either punning on the name Cain or actually explaining why that name was given to her first child. In view of the

promise of a deliverer, the name probably means "Here he is" or "I've gotten him." Eve called her son "Here he is" because she thought the deliverer had been sent by God.

Second, Eve did not actually say, as the New International Version and most other English versions translate, "With the help of the LORD I have brought forth a man." The words "with the help of" are not in the Hebrew text but are merely an English way of rendering what the majority of translators think the text means. Actually, they translate the Hebrew participle or preposition *'eth.* This word is usually the mark of the accusative, though it can also mean "with," the idea the translators followed when they rendered it "with [the help of]" the Lord. If it is the former, *'eth* makes the word following it the object of the action of the sentence. In this case, the sentence would mean "I have brought forth . . . the Lord." In my judgment this meaning should be preferred for linguistic as well as theological reasons, because *'eth* also occurs in front of the word "Cain" earlier in the sentence, which puts the two parts in parallel construction. Together they read, "She bore *'eth-Cain,* and she said, 'I have brought forth a man, *'eth-Jehovah.'*"

The obvious objection to this translation is that Eve could hardly have thought that she was giving birth to God, at least so early in the history of God's revelation. But that very point may well be the answer to the difficulty. Today we read these verses from the perspective of later Christian history and assume that the word "Jehovah" must have meant "Jehovah God" to Eve and Adam. But in Exodus 6:3 we find God saying to Moses, "I appeared to Abraham, to Isaac and to Jacob as God Almighty, but by my name the LORD [Jehovah] I did not make myself known to them." This seems to be saying that God revealed His names to the patriarchs over a period of years and that He was not known as Jehovah in the earliest periods. If so, Eve would not have been claiming to have given birth to God but rather would have been using the word in a broader sense meaning perhaps "the one who brings into being," "gives life" or "delivers."

In this case, the best translation of Eve's words would be, "I have brought forth a man, *even the deliverer.*" Yet she had not, as we know. She had given birth to a killer rather than Christ.

Beauty or Blood

The truth made itself known in time, of course, for the story tells us that one day Cain and Abel, now fully grown, came to present their offerings to the Lord. These words leave out much that we might like to know, but they suggest that God must have given considerable instruction to Adam, Eve, and their descendants concerning the proper place and form of sacrifice. The words read literally "at the end of days," meaning perhaps that God had appointed a particular time when sacrifices were to be offered. At any rate, Abel and Cain had undoubtedly been instructed in these things by Adam.

Cain brought the fruits of the soil as his offering, Abel an offering from the firstborn of the flock. God then received Abel's offering, perhaps by sending down fire on his altar, as He did on Elijah's altar on Mount Carmel. Cain's offering was rejected.

Of the many things about Genesis that trouble modern people, the acceptance of Abel's offering and the rejection of Cain's is high on the list. Because it seems unfair and irrational. "Cain did the best he could," such persons argue. "He gave what he had. Why should his offering be judged inferior to Abel's? In fact, if a choice must be made, why shouldn't Cain's beautiful offering of fruit be judged even more acceptable than Abel's bloody sacrifice?" Ah, but that is just the point. Abel's sacrifice in-

volved blood and therefore testified to the death of a substitute. He was coming to God as God had shown He must be approached. When God killed animals in the Garden of Eden and then clothed Adam and Eve with their skins, God was showing that, because sin means death, innocent victims must die in order that sinners might be pardoned. The sacrifices pointed forward to Christ. When Abel came with the offering of blood he was believing God and was looking forward to the provision of the deliverer. When Cain brought his fruit he was rejecting that provision.

"But wasn't the offering of Cain more beautiful?" someone asks. Yes, it was. "And isn't God the author of all beauty?" Yes, He is; God made the fruit Cain offered. But Cain left out the blood.

The offering of Cain represents all the beautiful things of this world that God has given to us and which you and I would like to offer back to Him. It is possible for us to offer these to God, but only if we have first come to Him on the basis of the sacrifice of Christ. If Cain had first presented the animal sacrifice, thereby confessing that he was a sinner, that sin requires death, that he was thankful to God for having shown that a substitute could die in his place and that he was coming on that basis—if he had done that and then had also presented his offering of fruit, saying, in effect, "God, I love You so much that I just wanted You to have this extra offering too," God would have accepted the fruit without question and would have said, "I love you too, Cain." But when Cain refused to come with the blood offering, God was obliged to reject both him and anything else he might offer.

That is the trouble with so many "good, religious people." They come to God with their heightened sense of esthetics and want to be received by God because of their beautiful offerings. But God rejects them and their godless worship. There is no blood, no Christ and, hence, no true Christianity, however beautiful their service might be. On the other hand, if one comes first through faith in Christ and His shed blood, then he can present all the beautiful things he is capable of finding or creating. And God will be pleased by this, because the person does not trust these things for salvation but rather is offering them to God just because he loves Him and wants to show affection. It is only on the basis of the sacrifice of Christ that one can come.

MASTER OR MASTERED

Here there is a point in the story that always touches me deeply. Although the offering of Cain was rejected, God did not simply walk away from Cain, as it were, but rather approached him and tried to reason with him about his sacrifice and what he needed to do to be accepted. So also would God plead with you, if you are fighting Him.

God reasoned with Cain: "Why are you angry? Why is your face downcast? If you do what is right, will you not be accepted? But if you do not do what is right, sin is crouching at your door; it desires to have you, but you must master it" (vv. 6, 7). There are several important parts to this reasoning. First, there is an indication that God saw Cain in whatever state he was in. Cain may be downcast and turn away. He may withdraw from Abel's society. He may turn his back on Eve and Adam. But God sees him regardless, just as God sees you.

Second, Cain need not have been angry. The fault was not outside himself, as if it were something that could not be changed. It could be changed, and the one to change it was Cain. So too with us. We tend to blame others for our troubles. Although others are sometimes a factor, the true cause is seldom there. It is within. It is as Pogo said in one of his memorable utterances, "We have met the enemy and he is us."

Third, there is a reminder of the right course of action: "If you do what is right, will you not be accepted?" This is another indication that the way of approach to God by sacrifice had been made clear to Adam and Eve long before now. If not, how could God call one course "right" as opposed to another? If Cain was admonished to do the right thing, it was because the right had been made known to him. Consequently, he rejected the right, not for lack of knowledge, but for lack of humility, faith, and obedience. He refused to come with the sacrifice because he considered the confession of his need demeaning.

Finally, God gave a warning, and the warning was that in Cain's refusing to come on God's terms he was flirting with disaster. The cause of his anger was sin, and sin was about to master him. Is that not our case also? Sin is always crouching at our door; indeed, it is sometimes even across the threshold and entrenched on the hearth. It desires to master us and in many cases has. We must master it. But how? How can we drive the demons of sin out and cleanse this old house in which we live? We cannot do it ourselves. The Lord once told a story of a man who was possessed of a devil and drove the devil out. But the devil went and found seven other devils, returned and took possession and "the final condition of that man [was] worse than the first" (Matt. 12:43–45). We are inadequate for such things. If we would master sin, we must first be mastered by Him who mastered it. We must be the Master's.

THE WAY OF CAIN

Cain did not allow himself to be mastered by God and so became enslaved by the devil. Sin had its way with him, and he became the first murderer. What a murderer he became! If we were to speak in modern legal terminology, we would not be able to claim that Cain was guilty only of negligent homicide or second-degree murder or any other category that might lessen his offense. This was absolute, premeditated murder—murder in the first degree, "murder one." Cain plotted Abel's slaughter and then pulled it off. He said, "Let's go out to the field" (v. 8). Then, when they were in the field out of sight of others, "Cain attacked his brother Abel and killed him."

But Cain was not out of sight of God. God sees everything, and God saw Cain. He said to him, "Where is your brother Abel?"

Cain replied, "I don't know. Am I my brother's keeper?" Think how evil this reply is. It contains the first lie and the first human question in the Bible. The lie was Cain's denial that he knew his brother's whereabouts. He knew perfectly well. But so greatly had sin mastered him at this point that he not only lied; he lied to God, no doubt thinking that he could get away with it. How greatly sin had worked in less than one generation! It is true that Adam and Eve had tried to shift the blame when God had confronted them with their sin on the occasion of the Fall. But they did not lie; they told the truth even though they were trying to escape from under it. But now Cain lies, and the lie is to God.

Second, he asks a question—the first human question in the Bible—and this is even worse than the lie. So hard is his heart that he now suggests that his brother, whom he killed, is not his responsibility. If something has happened to Abel, it is his own fault. In this world of dog-eat-dog, it is every man for himself, and the devil take the hindmost.

Do I hear the voice of modern man in Cain's cruel question? I think I do. A woman is murdered in New York while more than thirty neighbors hear her screams and ignore her cries for help. In Oklahoma City a woman gives birth to a baby on the sidewalk while similarly calloused people ignore her cries and merely gaze on her plight from the window of a cozy corner tavern. These stories could be multiplied indefinitely. Although many people do answer such cries for help, this only reinforces the cruelty and sin of the many more who do not.

My final thought is from the New Testament where the Bible speaks not only of Cain, which it does in three places (Heb. 11:4; 1 John 3:12; Jude 11), but of "the way of Cain," which those who are of God must avoid (Jude 11). What does this mean? It means that although Cain's case is a sorry one, it is sorrier even than this in that it has become a pattern for many persons who have followed him. If you are walking in Cain's way—if you have rejected the way of salvation provided for you through the shed blood of Christ, refusing to accept responsibility for your own state or the state of others—heed the warning of God and turn back while there is still time. Reject Cain's way. Take the way of Abel who, though he was killed, nevertheless had testimony of God that he was righteous (Matt. 23:35; Luke 11:51; Heb. 11:4).

God says of Abel, "By faith he was commended as a righteous man, when God spoke well of his offerings. And by faith he still speaks, even though he is dead" (Heb. 11:4). Let Abel speak to you and follow his example.

35

Cain's Curse

(Genesis 4:10–16)

The LORD said, "What have you done? Listen! Your brother's blood cries out to me from the ground. Now you are under a curse and driven from the ground, which opened its mouth to receive your brother's blood from your hand. When you work the ground, it will no longer yield its crops for you. You will be a restless wanderer on the earth."

Cain said to the LORD, "My punishment is more than I can bear. Today you are driving me from the land, and I will be hidden from your presence; I will be a restless wanderer on the earth, and whoever finds me will kill me."

But the LORD said to him, "Not so; if anyone kills Cain, he will suffer vengeance seven times over." Then the LORD put a mark on Cain so that no one who found him would kill him. So Cain went out from the LORD's presence and lived in the land of Nod, east of Eden.

In December, 1863, a little-known American writer named Edward Everett Hale published a story in *Atlantic* magazine entitled "The Man Without a Country." This story, which subsequently made Hale famous, was about a United States Army officer, Philip Nolan, who had been involved in the revolutionary war treachery of Aaron Burr. At his trial he was asked if he wished to say anything in his defense to show that he had always been faithful to the United States. But he cried out, "Damn the United States. I wish I may never hear of the United States again." The judge decided to take Philip Nolan's request seriously. So instead of sentencing him to death for his treason, which he had every right to do, he sentenced him to be imprisoned at sea on government vessels with instruction to the officers that no one was to permit him to hear the name of or receive any information about his country. In this fashion many years go by. He passes from ship to ship, always being transferred just before the one on which he has been traveling returns to a US port. Government red tape keeps him from

being pardoned, and at last he dies at sea—but not before the supposed author of the story, himself a naval officer, breaks orders and tells him about America and its remarkable growth and prosperity during the preceding twenty-five years. Nolan's last words are that no one ever loved his country as much as he.

A man without a country! This is what Cain became as a result of his far more serious crime of first hating and then murdering his brother Abel. But in Cain's case, so far as we can tell, there was no change of heart, softening of temper, or growing love for the land and people he abandoned.

LESS THAN HE DESERVED

The judgment of God on Cain for his murder of Abel is a very serious thing, in fact, the most serious judgment of God on sin yet in this story. Earlier in Genesis, on the occasion of God's judgment on Satan, Eve, and Adam, following the sin of our first parents in eating of the forbidden tree, Satan is cursed (Gen. 3:14) and the ground is cursed for Adam's sake (Gen. 3:17). But Adam and

Eve were not cursed, as we have seen. Now for the first time the curse of God is laid on a mortal. God says, "Now you are under a curse and driven from the ground, which opened its mouth to receive your brother's blood from your hand."

This curse was a fearful thing. Yet in certain ways it was less than Cain deserved. Essentially it was a curse that affected the ground so far as Cain's ever tilling the ground was concerned. It reads, "You are under a curse and driven from the ground." This is explained as meaning "When you work the ground, it will no longer yield its crops for you." It is in this sense that Cain is "driven" from it. The fact that he becomes "a restless wanderer on the earth" is a consequence of the curse but not necessarily a part of the curse itself, as we will see. What has happened is that the curse on the ground for Adam's sake has been intensified in the case of Adam's offspring.

Besides, what Cain really deserved was death. A few chapters farther on in Genesis, God institutes capital punishment, saying to Noah, "Whoever sheds the blood of man, by man shall his blood be shed" (Gen. 9:6). If death is the divinely appointed punishment for murder and if even man is given authority to pronounce this punishment, God certainly had every right to punish Cain in this way. Yet He did not, so great is His mercy to our race.

This says something significant about capital punishment, an issue that is being hotly debated in our time among evangelical Christians as well as among society at large. Recently the death penalty has been reestablished in America, and there have been several executions. Is this right? Should Christians rejoice at the reinstatement of this penalty? Clearly, a case can be made for either

side. According to the Mosaic code of law, "the murderer shall be put to death" (Num. 35:16). In fact, there are eighteen crimes for which one could be executed under the Old Testament legislation. If it is argued that we are not now under this legislation but should be guided rather by the "law of love," a case can be made for capital punishment on the basis even of love—love for all men. It is, as one writer argues, "love that desires through good laws to provide safety and protection for all the people. Because the enforced legal death of a convicted murderer (of whose identity there is no doubt) has removed a menace to life, certain law-abiding citizens will be enabled to live out their full days. Had he been paroled back to society, they would be dead—murdered."[1]

On the other hand, a case can be made for prohibiting the death penalty. It can be claimed that it overlooks the soul of the murderer, which is a very important thing. Sometimes murderers are converted and thereafter lead worthwhile and commendable lives. Even Moses, through whom the death penalty was legislated in Israel, was a murderer. He murdered an Egyptian. David had a man killed. Paul contributed to a lynching.

"But the law of Moses still requires the death penalty," says the advocate. Yes, but it is also most specific. Think of the crimes for which it is required: 1) *murders*—Exodus 21:12–15, 20; 22:2, 3; Leviticus 20:2; 24:17, 21; Numbers 35:11–21, 30; Deuteronomy 19:11–13; 2) *accidentally causing the death of a pregnant woman or her fetus* if injured in a fight—Exodus 21:22–25; 3) *allowing a person to be killed by a dangerous animal that had killed before*—Exodus 21:28–30; 4) *kidnapping*—Exodus 21:16; 5) *rape of a married woman*, but not of a virgin—Deuteronomy 22:25–29; 6) *fornication*—Deuteronomy 22:13–21; Leviticus

[1]Sherwood Eliot Wirt, *The Social Conscience of the Evangelical* (New York, Evanston and London: Harper & Row, 1968), p. 139.

21:9 (an exception in Lev. 19:20–22); 7) *adultery*—Leviticus 20:10; Deuteronomy 22:22–24; Numbers 5:12–30; 8) *incest*—Leviticus 20:11, 12, 14; 9) *homosexuality*—Leviticus 20:13; 10) *sexual intercourse with an animal*—Leviticus 20:15, 16; Exodus 22:19; 11) *striking a parent*—Exodus 21:15; 12) *cursing a parent*—Exodus 21:17; Leviticus 20:9; 13) *rebelling against parents*— Deuteronomy 21:18–21; 14) *sorcery or witchcraft*—Exodus 22:18; Leviticus 20:27; 15) *cursing God*—Leviticus 24:10–16; 16) *leading people to worship other gods*—Deuteronomy 13:1–16; 18:20; 17) *revenging a death in spite of the person having been acquitted by law*— Deuteronomy 17:12; and 18) *intentionally giving false testimony in the trial of one facing the death penalty*—Deuteronomy 19:16–19.[2] For which of these eighteen crimes would we be willing to reinstate the death penalty today? If not all, why not all? On what basis would we choose some and not others?

The difficulty in all this is probably our attempt to treat the penalty in a binding manner, when it is not necessarily to be so taken. To come back to Genesis, we note clearly that God granted man the right to enact the death penalty (Gen. 9:5, 6). But the fact that God Himself did not enact it in the case of the first murder—a crime that would certainly head the list of eighteen possibilities from the Mosaic legislation— should make us extremely careful about imposing it and encourage us to make every possible effort to show mercy instead.

More Than He Can Bear

We have seen, then, that God punished Cain with far less a punishment than he deserved. But in Cain's eyes this was, nevertheless, far more than he could bear. He complained, "My punishment is more than I can bear. Today you are driving me from the land, and I will be hidden from your presence; I will be a restless wanderer on the earth, and whoever finds me will kill me" (vv. 13, 14).

Such is the complaint of the unrepentant, and Cain was certainly unrepentant. We think in this regard of the rich man in Christ's parable. In this life he was dressed in purple and fine linen and lived in luxury every day. Lazarus was a beggar, covered with sores. We are told that he longed "to eat what fell from the rich man's table" (Luke 16:21). But apparently not only did the rich man not feed him; he was even reluctant to drop those crumbs. In time both died. The beggar was transported by angels to be with Abraham. The rich man was sent to hell and was in torment. Looking up he saw Abraham and Lazarus beside him. But he did not think of the wrong he had done to Lazarus. He did not repent of any sin whatever. He was thinking only of himself and of how unfairly he had been treated. He called out, "Father Abraham, have pity on me and send Lazarus to dip the tip of his finger in water and cool my tongue, because I am in agony in this fire" (v. 24). I do not know if John, who probably heard this, was thinking of the story of the rich man and Lazarus as he composed the Book of Revelation. But his observation in Revelation 16:10, 11 would be a fitting commentary on it: "Men gnawed their tongues in agony and cursed the God of heaven because of their pains and their sores, but they refused to repent of what they had done."

How horrible sin is! Cain refused to come to God by the way of sacrifice, which God had graciously provided. Rejected, he plunged into an ever-increasing vortex of hatred and murder. At last, being judged by God in a manner far less rigorous than he deserved or had himself inflicted on Abel, he com-

---

[2]Cf. Dave Llewellyn, "Restoring the Death Penalty: Proceed With Caution," *Christianity Today*, May 23, 1975, pp. 10–17.

plained because the earth was not going to be as kind to him as it was previously and because he would become a wanderer in the earth!

We do this too. One of the clearest marks of sin is our almost innate desire to excuse ourselves and complain if we are judged in any way. How many times have you said, "But that's not fair"? How many times have you complained against God who, if He was only fair and not also merciful, would have sent you to hell before you awoke this morning?

Fortunately, there are other examples than that of the rich man of the parable. I think of the repentant thief. He too was guilty of crimes worthy of death and was, in fact, crucified alongside the Lord Jesus Christ. He was in agony and doubtless cursed his fate. He and another robber who was also being crucified hurled insults at Jesus (Matt. 27:44). But in time he calmed down. Something in the quiet, gracious manner in which Jesus bore His suffering got through to this thief. So turning to the other, he rebuked him, saying, "Don't you fear God . . . since you are under the same sentence? We are punished justly, for we are getting what our deeds deserve. But this man has done nothing wrong" (Luke 23:40, 41). His confession of sin paved the way for greater insight and he eventually turned to Jesus saying, "Remember me when you come into your kingdom" (v. 42).

Jesus told him, "I tell you the truth, today you will be with me in paradise" (v. 43).

Is it not interesting that Jesus told the thief he would be with Him in paradise when, in a sense, it was precisely paradise that Cain was departing from? I say "departing" instead of being "driven" because, as I read the story, it seems that Cain's departure was more his own doing than the Lord's. It is true that Cain had been told that the land would no longer yield its fruit for him and that he would be a wanderer in the earth. I recognize, too, that most commentators assume that God drove Cain away. He may have. But to say that he would be a wanderer in the earth is not exactly the same as saying that God drove him to that fate. Could it not much rather be the case that he was led to wander by his own sense of deep guilt, hardness of heart, and fear of what others might do to him in spite of God's promise of physical protection?

Let me tell you what I think Cain should have done. I am assuming for the sake of this argument (as I only suggested earlier) that God had established a place of meeting and worship for Adam and his descendants at the edge of Eden. He had established an altar there—a place of sacrifice—and had placed the cherubim to guard it. When Cain speaks of the "presence" of the Lord in this story it may well be this place that he is thinking of. What Cain should have done when he heard God's words of judgment is to have fled to God, rather than from Him. He should have fallen on his knees and begged God, however great his sin, to forgive that sin and not allow it or anything else to drive him from God's presence. I will go further. Like Jacob at the river Jabbok, he should have thrown his arms around God and wrestled with Him and refused to let go until God blessed him (cf. Gen. 32:22–32).

I know, of course, that no one can struggle successfully against God. But I tell you this: although we cannot overpower Him, this is the kind of struggle God likes and honors. Did not Jesus say, "From the days of John the Baptist until now, the kingdom of heaven has been forcefully advancing, and forceful men lay hold of it" (Matt. 11:12)? What did He mean? He meant that the kingdom is for those who consider it worth having, whose minds are off themselves and on God, who realize that to win the whole world and lose their souls is folly and who therefore cast all aside and sell everything to obtain that treasure or possess that pearl of great price (Matt. 13:44, 45).

IN HARM'S WAY

If you have never come to the Lord Jesus Christ as your Savior, then you are somewhat like Cain. You are in danger, and you must flee from it. The Navy in wartime uses an expression of ships that sail into danger. They are said to be "in harm's way." That is an expression for you, if you are apart from Christ. You are in harm's way, and you must get back into the safe way before you are lost forever.

There are things that will keep you from it. One is your *pride*, the very thing that got Cain into trouble in the first place. Perhaps as I spoke of those forceful men and women who cast everything aside to obtain God's kingdom, you turned up your lips in scorn, thinking such persons weak. To bow, to scrape, to grovel before God seems too utterly repulsive to you for it ever to be contemplated, let alone performed. You would rather go to hell than bow like that. But that is precisely what you will do if you do not lay your pride aside and come to God on God's terms. You will not even know that it is not the weak but the strong who humble themselves before God or that they are truly the forceful men and women of this world, the conquerors.

You may also be held back by *hate*, though you might not call it that. You think you are a paragon of virtue, but the very fact that you think so poorly of Christians should be a warning that all is not right with you and that you are encumbered with far more irritations and animosities than you imagine. Hate is a terrible thing. You do not possess it; it possesses you. It is truly the sin crouching at the door that desires to master the home's inhabitant.

Again, there are *resentment and self-pity*. No one likes these things in others, but no one is so blind to anything as these when they occur in himself or herself. Cain had killed a man, his own brother. But he was so possessed with resentment against God and others that he could not see the enormity of his crime and so actually felt sorry for himself when God punished him with far less of a judgment than he deserved. I am not saying that you are guilty of murder, though some who hear or read these words may be. Even if you have never committed so great a crime as murder, you have committed a far greater crime against God in refusing to honor Him fully as your Creator and in spurning the very Son whom He sent to die for your salvation.

Can you not see this? Can you not sense your danger? Sin is driving you from God, whom you think to be the cause of your misery. You are failing to see that He is actually being good to you and that His goodness is given precisely so that it might lead you to repentance.

The way of Cain is hard. One commentator writes, "He started with human reason as opposed to divine revelation; he continued in human willfulness instead of divine will; he opposed human pride to divine humility; he sank to human hatred instead of rising to divine love; he presented human excuses instead of seeking divine grace; he went into wandering instead of seeking to return; he ended in human loneliness instead of in divine fellowship. To be alone without God is the worst thing that earth can hold, to go thus into eternity is, indeed, the second death."[3] Cain, we are told, "went out from the LORD's presence and lived in the land of Nod, east of Eden" (v. 16). Do not let it be true of you that you "went out from the LORD's presence." Flee to Him, and find in Him the One you have needed all along.

---

[3]Barnhouse, *Genesis*, pp. 38, 39.

36

Civilization Without God

(Genesis 4:17–24)

Cain lay with his wife, and she became pregnant and gave birth to Enoch. Cain was then building a city, and he named it after his son Enoch. To Enoch was born Irad, and Irad was the father of Mehujael, and Mehujael was the father of Methushael, and Methushael was the father of Lamech.

Lamech married two women, one named Adah and the other Zillah. Adah gave birth to Jabal; he was the father of those who live in tents and raise livestock. His brother's name was Jubal; he was the father of all who play the harp and flute. Zillah also had a son, Tubal-Cain, who forged all kinds of tools out of bronze and iron. Tubal-Cain's sister was Naamah.

Lamech said to his wives,

> *"Adah and Zillah, listen to me;*
> *wives of Lamech, hear my words.*
> *I have killed a man for wounding me,*
> *a young man for injuring me.*
> *If Cain is avenged seven times,*
> *then Lamech seventy-seven times."*

Today in the United States of America civilization seems hellbent on being secular. And that is precisely where it is going, apart from the grace of God in the gospel! The fourth chapter of Genesis exposes this secular culture in its earliest forms as it begins to trace the effects of sin on humanity.

The early chapters of Genesis are extremely logical. They contain an account of God's original, orderly work of creation, including a description of the nature and responsibilities of the man and woman. After this we see Adam and Eve's testing and fall, and then the effects of their sin on themselves, their offspring, and eventually the entire human race. It is to cover these last two points that chapter 4 has been written. Unfortunately, secular and even many Christian scholars ignore this chapter and instead devise an imaginary account that tends to glorify man and minimize his depravity.

One commentator writes, "Having cast off the only reliable account of man's first deeds and achievements, practically all writers of the present then proceed to draw very largely upon their imagination, which happens to be cast into the thought patterns of evolutionistic conceptions. Then they misread the available archaeological hints—for actual archaeological evidence for earliest man is not available—and the result is a highly fantastic and entirely incorrect story of man's development from the cave-man stage, as it is claimed, to the point where the first higher cultural achievements are found and the historical period actually begins. . . . The value of our chapter is completely lost sight of. For man not only did not start on the low anthropoid or simian state that is usually assumed, but as a human being he at once stood on the high intellectual and physical level that the preceding chapters described. . . . Whereas man was not an inferior

209

being on a lower level, such writing of history degrades him without warrant. Whereas he was brought low by the Fall, this pseudo-science ignores his true degradation. In both respects the chapter before us, being strictly historical and entirely correct, serves to set the student of the history of mankind right; and at the same time it gives to all men a clear account as to how man progressed and how sin grew."[1]

Did man and his culture progress? Yes, indeed—if by that we mean from sin to sin. For man even in these early days was not as depraved as he would yet become.

LOSS OF ROOTS

The verses that are the subject matter for this study speak of Cain building a city and of the resulting civilization. But to understand this civilization we have to go back to the previous verses in which Cain is said to have become a wanderer as a result of his sin. We find it in God's words of judgment: "You will be a restless wanderer on the earth" (v. 12). We find it in Cain's complaint: "I will be a restless wanderer on the earth, and whoever finds me will kill me" (v. 14). We even find it in the name of the land to which Cain goes, for Nod ("the land of Nod") means "wandering." The point obviously is that Cain remained a wanderer at heart even when he attempted to settle down. Having rejected God, he had severed his roots and was condemned to restlessness.

Adam and Eve suffered something similar, for they were cut off from Eden. But their roots were in God, and they remained close to the presence of God through the provision of the sacrifices. It is far worse for Cain. He had rejected God and was therefore restless and rootless. It is what Augustine had in mind when he said in his *Confessions*, "Thou hast formed us for thyself, and our hearts are restless till they find their rest in thee."[2]

I think also of Jacques Ellul's book on *The Meaning of the City*. He begins with a discussion of Cain, who built the first city: "He is to be a wanderer and a vagabond. As such he can find no rest. He is therefore condemned to a perpetual searching for God's presence, the God with whom he wanted nothing to do and in whom he does not believe, and his very condition keeps him from ever finding him. Whatever he does, he cannot succeed, and that is the hoplessness of it all."[3]

Rootlessness is the basic ingredient, not only of this first and ancient culture, but of all secular cultures and especially our own. If ever there was a day in which civilization was attempting to form itself without God, it is the day in which we live. But never has the restlessness of the ungodly been more evident. Simone Weil, a brilliant French writer who lived in London during the occupation of France by Germany during the second world war and who died there in 1943, wrote a book entitled *The Need for Roots* in which she analyzed the uprootedness of her day. She discussed uprootedness in the cities and in the countryside. She discussed it in relation to nationhood. She concluded that the only cure for uprootedness is a rediscovery of the human being as God's creature and of God Himself as the source of those basic elements without which a proper civilization cannot function: order, liberty,

---

[1]H. C. Leupold, *Exposition of Genesis*, Vol. 1, *Chapters 1–19* (Grand Rapids: Baker, 1942), pp. 186, 187.

[2]Saint Augustine, "Confessions" in *Basic Writings of Saint Augustine*, Vol. 1, ed. by Whitney J. Oates (New York: Random House, 1948), p. 3.

[3]Jacques Ellul, *The Meaning of the City*, trans. by Dennis Pardee (Grand Rapids: Eerdmans, 1970), p. 4.

obedience, responsibility, equality, the right to express one's opinion, security, private property, truth and others.[4] Weil is right. Our roots are in God; and if we will not have God, we are condemned to be vagabonds.

Perhaps this is why our civilization engages in so much frantic activity—to cover up our lack of roots and consequently our loss of destiny. Years ago the noted English agnostic Thomas Huxley was in Dublin, Ireland, for a speaking engagement, and when it was over he left his hotel in a hurry to catch a train. He jumped into one of the city's famous horse-drawn taxis and, thinking the doorman at the hotel had told the driver where he was going, simply shouted to the driver to drive fast. The taxi set off at a breakneck pace, but after a few minutes Huxley realized that it was headed away from the station. "Do you know where you're going?" he shouted to the driver.

"No, your honor," the driver answered, "but I'm driving fast."

So is our civilization, with similar confusion. For many of our contemporaries the situation is as Franklin Delano Roosevelt described it in his first inaugural address: "We don't know where we are going, but we are on our way."

CLOSENESS WITHOUT COMMUNITY

The second characteristic of civilization without God is closeness without community. We see this in Genesis 4 in Cain's first two acts following God's judgment for his murder of Abel. First, Cain "lay with his wife" so that she became pregnant and gave birth to Enoch. Second, he "was . . . building a city" (v. 17). These two go together. For having been driven from the company of those others who lived at that time, Cain now tries to surround himself with other

people through procreation and the consolidation of these people into the first metropolis.

I have taken part in a number of meetings growing out of the work of the International Council on Biblical Inerrancy, and at a number of them, where the doctrine of the full inspiration and inerrancy of the Bible has been upheld, there have been question and answer periods. I have been surprised to find that at most of these question periods someone sooner or later asks the age-old question: "Where did Cain get his wife?" Many people are interested in that man's wife. And even today, after that question has been answered many times, some people still use it as an excuse for failing to receive the Bible as the Word of God and believe it utterly.

Where *did* Cain get his wife? Well, if you turn over the page of the Bible to chapter 5, you find in verse 4 that "after Seth was born, Adam lived 800 years and had other sons and daughters." Could Cain marry his own sister? Yes, he could—in those early days when the race had not yet suffered the pollution of the succeeding centuries. If you were going to drink directly from the Hudson river, would you not rather drink from it up in the Adirondack mountains where it is fresh and pure than down by New York City after it has picked up the pollution of the scores of cities along its banks? It is the same with the human race. Today close interbreeding brings out harmful genes and results in lower IQ's, among other things. But in the early days it was not so. Abram married his half-sister Sarah, and before that Cain married his full sister as did the others born in those days.

We can be sure that they had many to choose from. One writer has estimated that if during the several hundred years that Adam lived only half of the children

---

[4]Simone Weil, *The Need for Roots; Prelude to a Declaration of Duties Towards Mankind*, trans. by A. F. Wills (London: Routledge & Kegan Paul, 1952).

that would normally be born grew up (and they probably all grew up) and if only half of those who grew up got married (and they probably all got married) and if only half who got married had children (and they probably all had children), that even at the half, half, half rate Adam would have lived to see more than one million of his own descendants. So not only did Cain have a wife, he had a choice that was as great as any have today. Equally important, there were many of his own descendants as well as others to populate the city he was building.

As I read the story, I sense that it must have been an unpleasant city. If we are to take as an indication the only example of Cain's descendants who is pictured for us at length, Lamech, it must have been a culture of hard, arrogant self-seekers. Rootless people are not less rootless for having gathered together in a city. They are not less hard for being together in one place. The loneliest people I know are in the city. The saddest stories I know concern city people. This is one reason why the greatest task facing the Christian church today is winning the city person to Christ.

There are Christians who are opposed to the city for reasons based on the very points I am making. They regard the city as godless. They think of urban cultures as being man's invention and therefore utterly opposed to God, who placed the first man and woman in a garden rather than a city. But while we acknowledge the truthfulness of this as a description, we deny that it is the whole story. The problem with the "godless city" is not the "city" itself but the "godless." The problem of "civilization without God" is not "civilization" but its godless characteristics. Our task is not to abandon earthly kingdoms but to build God's kingdom in the midst of the godless ones and in so doing look forward "to the city with foundations, whose architect and builder is God" (Heb. 11:10).

THE CULT OF BEAUTY

The third characteristic of this early civilization was its worship of beauty, which we see in the names of Lamech's wives. Lamech was the first bigamist in history, and if the names of his wives are to be a guide (these names are all significant), he apparently chose women for their physical attractions rather than their moral stature or spiritual commitments. Adah, the name of the first, means "pleasure, ornament or beauty." Zillah, the second, means "shade," perhaps referring to a luxuriant covering of hair. Lamech's daughter's name, Naamah, means "loveliness." Here was a culture committed to physical pleasure, beauty, and charm and not to those inner qualities that Peter describes as being "the unfading beauty of a gentle and quiet spirit, which is of great worth in God's sight" (1 Peter 3:4).

In my opinion, the description of the accomplishments of Cain's culture is to be viewed in this light. The names of two of the descendants of Cain contain the simple name for God, *el:* Mehujael and Methushael. But this concession to religion is merely a "form of godliness" while denying its power (2 Tim. 3:5). It is the kind of religion Cain chose by his aesthetically pleasing sacrifice. It is all too common today—a religion of beautiful liturgies, words, and music but without the promise of God's forgiveness of sin through the shed blood of Jesus Christ.

The same is true of the professions and arts, suggested here by the occupations of Lamech's children: Jabal, who raised livestock; Jubal, an inventor of music and musical instruments; Tubal-Cain, who worked in bronze and iron. Are these things bad in themselves? Not at all, any more than the city is bad in itself. We remember that Abel was also a herdsman; he was accepted by God on the basis of his sacrifice of an animal. Later in Israel's history God's Spirit came upon certain craftsmen to enable them to create the works of art used in God's temple (Exod. 31:1–11). David was a musician. Clearly it is legitimate to participate in the arts and enjoy the most beautiful things, if you can afford them, provided such participation and such enjoyment is in obedience to God and results in thankfulness to Him for such beauty. But God help the person who enjoys the gifts more than the Giver or who worships and serves the creature rather than the Creator of all! It was this reversal of values that characterized Cain's civilization.

And also our own! Today many rightly protest against the cult of beauty. Women in particular object to such marketing of beauty as the Miss America Beauty Pageant or the sale of items through sexually oriented advertising. They resent being reduced to that level and rightly so. But the marketing goes on. The exploitation continues. Why? Not because it is not seen to be destructive of better values, but because the better values that would drive out the lesser ones are missing. Women (and men) perceive themselves to be exploited and rightly protest against that exploitation, but they will continue to be exploited in the worst way and even willingly submit to that exploitation until they discover that they are creatures made, not in the image of Cheryl Tiggs or Bo Derek or Robert Redford, but in the image of God and that they possess infinite value not because of their outward beauty, which they may or may not have, but because they are capable of communion with God and possess eternal souls.

PRIDE IN PASSION

The last characteristic of Cain's civilization is pride, culminating in an arrogant defense of murder. The boast is even expressed in poetry, which is thus

the first recorded poetry of the human race. It is a song of Lamech:

> Adah and Zillah, listen to me;
>   wives of Lamech, hear my words.
> I have killed a man for wounding me,
>   a young man for injuring me.
> If Cain is avenged seven times,
>   then Lamech seventy-seven times
>   (vv. 23, 24).

Lamech is boasting of his violence in killing a man who merely wounded him, and he is saying that he is better able to take care of himself by murdering others than God was able to take care of Cain. One commentator describes him as saying, "I have been offended and I have judged that the offense is a mortal one, punishable by death. Because the God of the universe, who is supposed to be running things, didn't run them to suit my fancy, but permitted someone to offend me, I have erased that offender from the face of the earth. And no one may call me to account. God put a mark on old grandfather Cain, in order to protect him, but I am perfectly able to take care of myself."[5]

The same commentator continues, "Ponder the white space between that verse and the next in the Bible. For the story of Cain's family ceases abruptly, and that next verse announces the birth to Adam of another son whose line is to forward the purposes of God. Lamech and his civilized, lawless family are never heard of again. In the space that follows his song of the sword, we must see the rising waters of the deluge which devoured them all. They were ungodly, and their ungodliness brought the just recompense of its reward. They were blotted out from under heaven in order to teach us that the day will come when the judgment fires of God will do the same for the entire creation."[6] God's evaluation of the godless in this period was that man's wickedness had become

---

[5]Barnhouse, *God's Grace*, pp. 40, 41.
[6]*God's Grace*, p. 41.

very "great" and that "every inclination of the thoughts of his heart was only evil all the time" (Gen. 6:5).

Yet this is not the whole of what can be said. For after that white space between Genesis 4:24 and Genesis 4:25 there is, as just indicated, the beginning of the history of those who did not merely adopt the name of God in their names as some religious fetish but who truly loved God and began "to call on the name of the LORD" to salvation. Their history began with "righteous" Abel and Seth and all those listed in Genesis 5. It continued through godly Noah and his descendants. It was lost from sight for a time, but it emerged again in Abraham, Isaac, and Jacob. It is seen in the godly within Israel, at times a large number, at other times a remnant. At the time of the birth of Christ that line of history was still flowing on, for we see Mary and Joseph, Zechariah and Elizabeth, Simeon, Anna, and all those who "were looking forward to the redemption of Jerusalem" (Luke 2:38). Today it is seen in those millions who have turned from sin to faith in Jesus Christ and who by the grace of God are determined to serve Him wholly.

We need a transformed civilization. But it will not be built by those who have lost their roots. It will not be built by the lovers of beauty or those who take pride in cruelty and independence. It will be built only by those whose lives have been surrendered to God and been transformed by Him.

37

The Two Humanities

(Genesis 4:25, 26)

Adam lay with his wife again, and she gave birth to a son and named him Seth, saying, "God has granted me another child in place of Abel, since Cain killed him." Seth also had a son, and he named him Enosh.
At that time men began to call on the name of the LORD.

The fourth and fifth chapters of Genesis outline two cultures from the earliest years of earth's history: the culture of the godless and the culture of the godly. But the break does not come between the two chapters, as we find them in our Bibles, but between verses 24 and 25 of chapter 4. The earlier section gives an account of Cain and his descendants. Beginning with 4:25, we have an account of the godly line starting with Seth. The two chapters together give a portrait of what Francis Schaeffer has termed "the two humanities."[1]

Or, since we are dealing with cultures as well as with individuals, "the two cities"! This is the distinction invented by Saint Augustine as the basis for his monumental and highly influential work on the philosophy of history, entitled *The City of God*. According to Augustine, the history of the human race is the history of two groups of people, each having a distinct origin, development, characteristic, and destiny. He wrote that these are "two cities . . . formed by two loves: the earthly by the love of self, even to the contempt of God; the heavenly by the love of God; even to the contempt of self."[2] In Augustine's work "city" means "society." The earthly society has as its highest expression the

city cultures of Babylon and, in what was for Augustine more modern times, Rome. The other is the church, composed of God's elect. The former is destined to pass away. The latter is blessed by God and is to endure forever.

THE TWO CITIES

The fourth and fifth chapters of Genesis discuss these two humanities, as we have already said. But so far as Genesis goes, the origin of the cities is found one chapter earlier in the words of God to the serpent following the temptation and fall of Adam and Eve. God cursed the serpent, then gave this word both of decree and prophecy: "I will put enmity between you and the woman, and between your offspring and hers; he will crush your head, and you will strike his heel." Here are three sets of antagonists: 1) the serpent and the woman, 2) the descendants of the serpent and the descendants of the woman, and 3) Satan himself and the ultimate descendant of the woman, Jesus Christ. These are in conflict. But the victory of the godly seed is to be assured by the ultimate victory of Eve's specific descendant, Jesus.

If Genesis 3:15 were the only text to go on, we might think its second contrast is

---

[1]Schaeffer, *Genesis in Space and Time*, pp. 103–118. "The Two Humanities" is the title of chapter 6.
[2]Augustine, *The City of God*, Book 14, Chapter 28, pp. 282, 283.

215

between the demons, conceived as the seed of the serpent, and mankind. But this is not the case, as the next two chapters of Genesis make plain. It is true that there is antagonism between the fallen angels and *believing* men and women. But there is also conflict between the holy angels and the fallen angels and between believing men and women and those who do not believe. Genesis 4 and 5 show that the antagonism in view in 3:15 is between godly and ungodly men and women.

The first illustration is the conflict between Abel and Cain, which we have already studied. Cain was the first child of Eve (born after the Fall), and the essential meaning of his Hebrew name is "Acquisition," or colloquially, "Here he is!" The name was a mistake on Eve's part. She had heard God's promise of a deliverer who should crush the head of Satan. He was to be born of her. So when Cain was born she assumed that he was this deliverer. She was wrong. Instead of a savior, she had given birth to a murderer. For, as the story shows, Cain grew jealous over God's acceptance of his brother's offering rather than his own, and killed him.

The cause of Cain's jealousy is very important, for it concerned the means of approaching God. Cain had brought an offering from the field, the result of his own labor. Abel had brought a lamb that was then killed and offered as the innocent substitute bearing the guilt that Abel recognized as his own. We do not know how much Abel understood concerning the proper means of approaching God through sacrifice, which anticipated the ultimate sacrifice of Christ. But he must have understood a good bit, for he is praised in Hebrews as having done what he did through faith: "By faith Abel offered God a better sacrifice than Cain did. By faith he was commended as a righteous man, when God spoke well

of his offerings" (Heb. 11:4). Abel came in the right way, and Cain did not. In these brothers we see the first example of the two humanities.

The remainder of Genesis 4 and the next chapter show how these two individuals gave birth to two different societies. Cain is driven away to be a wanderer in the earth, and his descendants are listed: Enoch, whose name Cain gave to the city he was building; Irad, the son of Enoch; Mehujael; and finally Methushael, the father of Lamech. Lamech receives special mention as an illustration of what was happening in the line of these who walked in "the way of Cain" (Jude 11). He had three sons: Jabal, who, we are told, "was the father of those who live in tents and raise livestock"; Jubal, "the father of all who play the harp and flute"; and Tubal-Cain, "who forged all kinds of tools out of bronze and iron" (Gen. 4:20–22). Although brief, these descriptions speak of a well-developed culture, but it was a cruel culture as Lamech's boast to his two wives shows:

Adah and Zillah, listen to me;
  wives of Lamech, hear my words.
I have killed a man for wounding me,
  a young man for injuring me.
If Cain is avenged seven times,
  then Lamech seventy-seven times
              (vv. 23, 24).

This is the story of a man boasting about murder and, since the boast seems to be in poetry, actually writing a song about it. As Francis Schaeffer says in his discussion of this incident, "Here is humanistic culture without God. It is egotism and pride centered in man; this culture has lost the concept not only of God but of man as one who loves his brother."[3]

At this point Genesis introduces the godly line of Seth, which continues through his descendants to Noah. (Noah and his family were the sole survivors of

---

[3]Schaeffer, *Genesis in Time and Space*, p. 114.

the Flood and therefore constitute a new beginning.) The names in this line are: Seth, Enosh, Kenan, Mahalalel, Jared, Enoch, Methuselah, Lamech, and Noah. Two of these are mentioned in Hebrews 11 as examples of those whose lives were marked by faith: Enoch, who is said to have "pleased God" (Heb. 11:5); and Noah, of whom it is written, "By faith Noah, when warned about things not yet seen, in holy fear built an ark to save his family. By his faith he condemned the world and became heir of the righteousness that comes by faith" (v. 7).

These lines may be traced throughout history, as Augustine does in *The City of God*. The godless line is traceable in the world's cities, states, and cultures. The godly line is in Abram and his descendants, the faithful within Israel and eventually the church.

THE GODLY LINE

One proof of the inspiration of the Bible is that much is said in few words, unlike the works of men that usually say little in many words. That characteristic of Scripture is evident in the two verses that end chapter 4 and introduce Adam's godly line. In fifty-five words (thirty-six in Hebrew) the essential characteristics of this line are enumerated.

The first characteristic is the starting point, namely, *God and His preeminence.* It is seen in Eve's statement at the time of Seth's birth: "God has granted me another child in place of Abel, since Cain killed him" (v. 25). Even on the surface it is evident that Eve (and no doubt Adam also) was relating the birth of Seth to God and acknowledging that God was the source of it, something no one in Cain's line is said to have done. But this self-evident testimony is intensified for us when we contrast it with Eve's word on the occasion of the birth of Cain, recorded earlier in the chapter (v. 1). When we looked at that statement we saw that it is correctly translated, "I have brought forth a man, even the de-liverer," and we noticed that it was undoubtedly a profession of faith in God's promise. As such it was commendable. But now, as we look back and contrast it with Eve's later confession at the birth of Seth, we see that it contained a tragic flaw. It was man-centered. Eve said, "*I, I* have brought forth a man." What she had to learn, and what God taught her through Cain's ensuing sad history, is that the deliverer could never come by her or her husband's own doing but would be God's gift. So the second time around she says, "*God* has granted me another child in place of Abel."

Nothing is so characteristic of the diverse natures of the world and Christianity as that contrast. The godless culture begins with man—the very essence of humanism. The other begins with God, though sometimes even the godly have to learn this the hard way, as Eve did.

Someone may say, and many today do, "But what is the significance of that: beginning with God or beginning with man? What difference does it make where you begin since we all come to the same place in the end?" But we do not all come to the same place. That is the point, and it is why the matter is important. We see this in these chapters. In chapter 4, at the beginning of the description of the godless culture, there is some acknowledgment of God. Cain knows of Him as well as does Abel. He even argues with Him. Later, in the fifth and sixth generations, the names of Mehujael and Methushael contain the name of God, *el*, as in Elohim. But having rejected God as a starting place at the beginning, this acknowledgment of God becomes increasingly formal, and the end becomes a bold statement of the superiority of man over God: "If Cain is avenged seven times [i.e., by God], then Lamech seventy-seven times [i.e., by Lamech]" (v. 24). By contrast, even though Seth's line has little detailed knowledge of God, it does begin with

Him and thus goes on to produce a godly culture.

Frances Schaeffer traces the decline of modern humanism in his book *How Should We Then Live?* He traces its origins to René Descartes (1596–1650), who based his philosophy on himself and his own self-awareness: "I think, therefore I am." But he sees it running its modern course through such figures as Jean-Jacques Rousseau (1712–1778), with his romantization of nature; Immanuel Kant (1724–1804), who split the knowledge of things and the knowledge of ideals into two parts; Wilhelm Friedrich Hegel (1770–1831), who relativized all truth and knowledge; and Sören Kierkegaard (1813–1855), who invented "the leap of faith" as the only means of knowing the transcendant. But in this later development, as Schaeffer shows, God increasingly slips out of reach and eventually becomes the "nothing" existentialism perceives Him to be. He quotes his son as summing up the history of humanism (and all godless culture) by saying, "Humanism has changed the Twenty-third Psalm:

> They began—I am my shepherd
> Then—Sheep are my shepherd
> Then—Everything is my shepherd
> Finally—Nothing is my shepherd."

Modern culture, like the culture before the Flood, is at this last point. It has no shepherd and shows it by its lost and increasingly degenerate condition.[4]

GOD AND MAN

The second characteristic of Seth's line is its *view of man*, which is proper in view of the wickedness that now mars the race. This point is not particularly evident in the English translation of these verses, but it is very evident in Hebrew due to the name of Seth's son:

Enosh. Each of these names is important. Seth means "set in place of." He was named Seth because of being given to Adam and Eve by God *in place of* Abel. But now Seth names his son, and Enosh means "frail one" or "mortal." Seth was so impressed with the weakness of mere human beings that he gave his son a name intended to communicate this truth. Instead of boasting about himself, as Lamech did, Seth confessed his need of God.

These two doctrines, the doctrine of man and the doctrine of God, go together and are related in a manner that has sometimes been called the seesaw in theology. The basic idea of a seesaw is that when one end is up the other end is down. You can never have both ends up or both ends down at the same time. That is the way with the doctrines of God and man. If anyone exalts man in his or her theology—if man is thought to be strong and good and well able to take care of his own physical and spiritual affairs—then God is inevitably down, for there is little need of Him. In fact, man becomes equal or even superior to God and eventually imagines himself to be able to do without Him, as we have seen to be the case with humanism. On the other hand, if God is up, then man is inevitably down and is perceived to be the weak and needy creature Seth rightly saw him to be.

The ungodly object to this conclusion, of course, for they think that to lift God up is to debase man and remove his dignity. The case is actually the reverse. It is humanism that debases man and Christianity that elevates him. This is clear in this chapter. The culture of Cain runs on through godless generations and eventually produces Lamech, the epitome of the self-sufficient man. He can take care of himself. He does not need God. But what is his attitude toward other human

---

[4]Francis A. Schaeffer, *How Should We Then Live? The Rise and Decline of Western Thought and Culture* (Old Tappan, N.J.: Fleming H. Revell, 1976), pp. 152–227. The quotation from Franky Schaeffer is on page 226.

beings? Parallel with his exaltation of himself is a lowering of his sense of the value of others, for he is ready to wipe them out for as small an offense as wounding himself. The line of Seth has a far lower view of mankind. It perceives his weakness. But at the same time it also has compassion for those it knows to be made in the image of God and thus of inherent value, in spite of the increasing wickedness.

One of Seth's descendants, Enoch, warned his generation of judgment: "See, the Lord is coming with thousands upon thousands of his holy ones to judge everyone, and to convict all the ungodly of all the ungodly acts they have done in the ungodly way, and of all the harsh words ungodly sinners have spoken against him" (Jude 14, 15). Noah became "a preacher of righteousness" (2 Peter 2:5) as he tried to turn some back from their evil ways.

It is not the godly who have a low view of man—though they have a realistic view and are accused of having a low view by those who reject Christianity. They do not exalt man to an absolute position in the universe. They do not deny his corruption. They speak of his fall. But at the same time they give him the only true grounding for worth that he can possibly have, namely, that man is made in God's own blessed image and is destined for an eternity either with or without Him. The godly care for others so much that they are willing to endure hardship and even suffer personal abuse that those perishing might hear and respond to the gospel of salvation through the work of Christ.

DEPENDENCE ON GOD

That brings us to the last characteristic of Seth's line: *dependence on God*. It is dependence on God for salvation and all other things besides. We have already seen this characteristic in Adam, who

named his wife Eve ("life giver" or "mother") in expectation of God's promise to send a deliverer through her. We have seen it in Eve's mistaken naming of Cain ("here he is . . . the deliverer"). We see it again as chapter 4 ends: "At that time men began to call on the name of the LORD" (v. 26).

There is some question as to how these last words should be taken. They could mean that at this point in history men and women began to call themselves *by* the name of the Lord, thus identifying themselves with Him in a formal way. The importance of names and the fact that many of the names that follow in chapter 5 incorporate one or other of the names for God supports this. On the other hand, it is more likely that these words deal with worship and say rather that at this time those of Seth's line began to call *on* God in a regular way. In either case, there is the idea of dependence. The line of Seth had recognized that sin was no mere imperfection of human nature but something destined to destroy both the individual and culture unless it should be overcome by the grace and power of almighty God. So these individuals now threw themselves on God and trusted Him wholly for their physical and spiritual salvation.

The Reformers were very impressed by this and saw it as an illustration of that utter dependence on God which they themselves had come to value highly. Luther saw Genesis 4:26 as the formation of "a small church . . . in which Adam, as high priest, rules everything by the Word and sound doctrine."[5] Calvin saw it as "a restoration of religion" such as had been effected in his day. He called it "a miracle, that there was at that time a single family in which the worship of God arose."[6] Luther and Calvin were right. The belief of these days did constitute a small church, and it was a miracle.

---

[5]Luther, *Luther's Works*, Vol. 1, p. 327.
[6]Calvin, *Genesis*, p. 224.

38

Like Father, Like Son

(Genesis 5:1–20)

This is the written account of Adam's line.
When God created man, he made him in the likeness of God. He created them male and female; at the time they were created, he blessed them and called them "man."
When Adam had lived 130 years, he had a son in his own likeness, in his own image; and he named him Seth. After Seth was born, Adam lived 800 years and had other sons and daughters. Altogether, Adam lived 930 years, and then he died.
When Seth had lived 105 years, he became the father of Enosh. And after he became the father of Enosh, Seth lived 807 years and had other sons and daughters. Altogether, Seth lived 912 years, and then he died.
When Enosh had lived 90 years, he became the father of Kenan. And after he became the father of Kenan, Enosh lived 815 years and had other sons and daughters. Altogether, Enosh lived 905 years, and then he died.
When Kenan had lived 70 years, he became the father of Mahalalel. And after he became the father of Mahalalel, Kenan lived 840 years and had other sons and daughters. Altogether, Kenan lived 910 years, and then he died.
When Mahalalel had lived 65 years, he became the father of Jared. And after he became the father of Jared, Mahalalel lived 830 years and had other sons and daughters. Altogether, Mahalalel lived 895 years, and then he died.
When Jared had lived 162 years, he became the father of Enoch. And after he became the father of Enoch, Jared lived 800 years and had other sons and daughters. Altogether, Jared lived 962 years, and then he died.

I do not know why it is that in the minds of some people the most boring thing about the Bible is its genealogies. Perhaps it is because they do not read them. People who will pore over pages of fine-print stock quotations or lists of baseball players and their batting averages will not read the Bible's genealogies. Yet these are in the Bible and are therefore part of that revelation of which it is said, *"All* Scripture is God-breathed and is useful for teaching, rebuking, correcting and training in righteousness" (2 Tim. 3:16).

The fifth chapter of Genesis is a genealogy—a list of the descendants of Adam down to the time of Noah and the great Flood. There are not many patri-archs, though there were probably more than are actually listed here. But they were pillars of faith in an increasingly godless age. They stood for God with such tenacity and in such a way that their names have been preserved for future generations.

Martin Luther, who identified with the antediluvian period because of the troubles of his own age, was particularly impressed with these outstanding individuals. He wrote that most were living at the same time and then noted: "This is the greatest glory of the primitive world, that it had so many good, wise, and holy men at the same time. We must not think that these are ordinary names of plain people; but, next to Christ and John the

Baptist, they were the most outstanding heroes this world has ever produced. And on the Last Day we shall behold and admire their grandeur. Likewise, we shall also see their deeds. For then it will be made manifest what Adam, Seth, Methuselah, and the others did; what they endured from the old serpent; how they comforted and maintained themselves by means of the hope of the Seed against the outrages of the world or of the Cainites; how they experienced various kinds of treachery; how much envy, hatred, and contempt they endured on account of the glory of the blessed Seed who would be born from their descendants."[1]

The Bible endorses this period by the fact that two of these individuals—Enoch and Noah—are mentioned in Hebrews 11 as having pleased God by faith. There is no comparable portion of Scripture that yields that many names to the listing.

A History of Persons

In the organization of Genesis by Moses this chapter introduces a new section, for it begins with the Hebrew phrase literally translated, "This is the book *(sepher)* of the generations *(toledoth)* of Adam." The key word in that sentence, "generations," occurs eleven times in Genesis, always as a superscription or title for what follows. Some writers have taken it as a subscription, that is, a summation of what has been narrated. But that is wrong, as we saw in our discussion of Genesis 2:4.[2] The idea is that this is Adam's story in the sense of its being the story of his family. It is the same in each of the other instances: Genesis 2:4; 6:9; 10:1; 11:10, 27; 25:12, 19; 36:1, 9; and 37:2.

The unique feature of Genesis 5:1, which does not occur in any of the other

references, is the addition of the word "book" *(sepher)*, which the New International Version points to by translating, "This is the *written* account of Adam's line." There is no certainty that this is the case, but it may be that by this word Moses acknowledges the existence of a written source, a book however long or short, which he here incorporates into his narrative. If so, this is the oldest written document in all history. And what is it about? It is a record of the godly descendants of Adam. This reminds us that God is particularly concerned to record the names and deeds of those who are faithful to Him and that He will also record our names and deeds if we are faithful. In Malachi 3:16 we are told of such a remembrance: "Then those who feared the LORD talked with each other, and the LORD listened and heard. A scroll of remembrance was written in his presence concerning those who feared the LORD and honored his name." Again, in Revelation we read of those whose names were written in the Lamb's "book of life" (Rev. 20:11–15).

Here is the first real lesson where genealogies are concerned. If we were writing this book, we would probably leave the names out. But God does not. It is because He is more interested in people than we are.

I have been helped a great deal at this point by a chapter of Paul Tournier in his volume *A Doctor's Casebook in the Light of the Bible*. It is entitled "The Personalism of the Bible." Tournier writes, "In the Biblical view, man is not the most highly evolved of the animals; he is a special creation of God. He is not merely a physical and mental machine; he is 'spirit and soul and body' (1 Thess. 5:23), for he has been created in the image and likeness of God (Gen. 1:26). And also, what distinguishes the God of the Bible from the divinities of every

---

[1]Luther, *Luther's Works*, Vol. 1, pp. 334, 335.
[2]See "Are There Two Creations?" (Gen. 2:4–6), pp. 90–95.

other religion is that he is a personal God, who speaks personally to man, who calls upon him (Gen. 3:9–10). . . . Throughout the Bible we see God calling men, and drawing them thus out of the primitive mentality in which they were wallowing. It is a fact that the savage has no consciousness of himself as a person: he identifies himself with his tribe; he identifies himself also with nature, by mystical participation; for him the microcosm that is himself, and the macrocosm that is the world, are confused.

" 'The LORD said unto Abram, Get thee out of thy country, and from thy kindred, and from thy father's house' (Gen. 12:1). God takes him out of his tribe, out of his impersonal existence, conditioned by his environment; he makes a person of him through his personal obedience to a personal command. The personal God makes man into a person. In the view of the Bible, the link between God and man is a link between persons; it is this that makes man a complete being, responsible for himself before God. Right up to the last page of the Bible you will find men called by God out of the prejudices of their tribe, away from the impulses of their own instincts, so that they no longer live the automatic life of animals, but become persons and prophets—prophets in the Biblical sense, but also prophets in the philosophical sense of which Bergson speaks—that is to say, emancipated, adult, creative men, discerning the true meaning of things and teaching it to others.

"God says to Moses: 'I know thee by name' (Ex. 33:17). He says to Cyrus: 'I am the Lord, which call thee by thy name' (Isa. 45:3). These texts express the personalism of the Bible. One is struck, on reading the Bible, by the importance in it of proper names. Whole chapters are devoted to long genealogies. When I was young I used to think that they could well have been dropped from the Biblical canon. But I have since realized that these series of proper names bear witness to the fact that, in the Biblical perspective, man is neither a thing nor an abstraction, neither a species nor an idea, that he is not a fraction of the mass, as the Marxists see him, but that he is a person."[3]

You and I are persons, like the patriarchs of Genesis 5. We are equally noted and remembered in God's book. Let that be an encouragement. The world may not pay much attention to us; in fact, the more like Christ we are, the less the world will be interested. But God is interested, and that fact alone should encourage us to live for Him.

A REMNANT

The second lesson of this genealogy is that it represents a remnant of godly individuals in an ungodly age and that this is often the case. I mean by this, that if there are not many in any given age who believe and serve God, there are at least some, and these will always be an encouragement to each other. Calvin saw this and wrote, "The design with which this catalogue was made, was, to inform us, that in the great, or rather, we might say, prodigious multitude of men, there was always a number, though small, who worshiped God; and that this number was wonderfully preserved by celestial guardianship."[4]

If a person merely compares Genesis 4 with Genesis 5, he might wonder if Calvin is correct at least so far as the numbers are concerned, for these chapters seem very balanced and might therefore be thought to be talking about relatively equal numbers of individuals. There are

---

[3]Paul Tournier, *A Doctor's Casebook in the Light of the Bible,* trans. by Edwin Hudson (New York, Evanston and London: Harper & Row, 1960), pp. 122–24.

[4]Calvin, *Genesis,* p. 227.

six generations in chapter 4, plus the three sons of Lamech. In chapter 5 there are nine generations, plus the three sons of Noah. All presumably had many additional sons and daughters (chapter 5 says so explicitly). We might suppose these to have been disposed in approximately equal numbers. But this was not the case. When we go to chapter 6, which recounts the judgment of God through the Flood, we find that by this time the world had become exceedingly wicked and that, when the Flood finally occurred, there were only eight individuals—Noah, his three sons, and their four wives—who were saved. We read of the majority of this pre-Flood generation, "The LORD saw how great man's wickedness on earth had become, and that every inclination of the thoughts of his heart was only evil all the time" (Gen. 6:5).

The history of this period was not marked by the development of equal numbers of believers and unbelievers, then. It was a period of decline in which all but a few went the way of Cain in spite of the teaching and pleading of Adam, Enoch, Noah, and the other early preachers of God's grace.

Do you find yourself to be a minority—in your family, your neighborhood, your business (even your church)? Do not be discouraged. It has always been this way. Apparently, God does not deal so much in quantity as in quality. Moreover, although the faithful are often few—praise God they are also many at times—there are nevertheless always those few, and they are meant to encourage one another.

This same lesson is taught somewhat later in the Old Testament. Elijah, that greatest of all the prophets, had just come from the victory of God over the priests of Baal on Mount Carmel. In that victory the prophets of Baal had prayed to their god, who had done nothing, while Elijah's God had answered from heaven by fire, which consumed not only the sacrifice but also the wood, stones, soil, and water (1 Kings 18:38). The priests had been rounded up and killed. Then Elijah had prayed for rain and rain had come, ending a three-year drought. The battle was over, the victory won. But the nation still remained unrepentant, and Ahab, the king, sent for Elijah to have him arrested and then executed. In reference to the slain prophets, Jezebel said to Elijah, "May the gods deal with me, be it ever so severely, if by this time tomorrow I do not make your life like that of one of them" (19:2). Elijah, in spite of the recent great victory, was terrified and ran for his life.

The next scene is pitiful. Elijah is tired and discouraged, so much so that he is ready to die. He tells God, "I have had enough, LORD. . . . Take my life; I am no better than my ancestors" (v. 4). A little later he says, "I have been very zealous for the LORD God Almighty. The Israelites have rejected your covenant, broken down your altars, and put your prophets to death with the sword. I am the only one left, and now they are trying to kill me too" (vv. 10, 14).

This certainly seemed to be the case. But what did God reply? God told Elijah to go back; He foretold the overthrow of Ahab and the ascension of Jehu to the throne and then insisted: "Yet I reserve seven thousand in Israel—all whose knees have not bowed down to Baal and all whose mouths have not kissed him" (v. 18). Today you may seem to be alone in your work for God, but you are not alone. God has His thousands here and there in every place who have not bowed down to the gods and goddesses of this age.

A FAMILY RELATIONSHIP

There is a third thing to be noticed about this genealogy of the godly. It is the most obvious of all. The people in this chapter are related to one another, descendants of one another. They are members of one family. This suggests the value of the family and the fact that God generally works in and through families to call people to Himself.

We must be careful at this point, of course. Cain, the founder of the godless line, was also a son of Eve and Adam. This warns us that we cannot presume on God in this matter, as if it were impossible for our children to stray even though they are our children and have been taught correctly. Again, if Adam, Eve, and all the others had many descendants and if, by the time of the Flood, there were only a few who were faithful, there were doubtless others who also walked in Cain's way. Still, all the godly of chapter 5 are in one family and this should not be lost on us. Presumably Adam taught spiritual truths to Seth, Seth taught Enosh, Enosh taught Kenan, and so on from generation to generation. So whatever the problem in the other cases may be, in these cases at least the family relationship was beneficial.

I think this is taught to us in verse 3, where we are told that Adam "had a son in his own likeness, in his own image; and he named him Seth." Why does it say this? Why does Genesis 5:3 say here, as the Bible says nowhere else, that Seth was in the likeness and image of his father? There are three possibilities.

First, there is an obvious link between this verse and verse 1, which reminds us that "When God created man, he made him in the likeness of God." This goes back to the introduction of this idea in chapter 1: "Then God said, 'Let us make man in our image, in our likeness . . .'" (v. 26); "So God created man in his own image, in the image of God he created him . . ." (v. 27). Since Genesis 5:1 and 5:3 appear so close together, the author may be saying that Seth (and all the others) retain this divine image. It is true, as we know, that much if not all of

our image of God was lost in the Fall. But this is still a possible interpretation in that, as late as Genesis 9:6, after the Flood, God reasserts the value of human life by reference to this divine image:

> Whoever sheds the blood of man,
> by man shall his blood be shed;
> for in the image of God
> has God made man.

Moses could mean that although the divine image had been damaged by sin, men and women nevertheless retained something of that image and thus also retained their unique value as the crowning glory of creation.

The second explanation sees the references to "the likeness of God" in verse 1 and the "likeness" of verse 3 as a contrast. That is, Adam was made in God's image. But now the Fall has occurred, and Seth, far from being conceived in God's image, is in the likeness of his fallen father Adam. Those who take this view—Arthur Pink is one of the most articulate[5]—would stress the pronouns referring to Adam ("he had a son in *his own* likeness, in *his own* image") and view the verse as teaching universal depravity. "Every man living in the world today is, through Noah and his three sons, a descendant of Seth; hence it is that care is here taken at the beginning of this new section to trace the spring back to its fountain head, and show how all are, by nature, the fallen offspring of a fallen parent—that we have all been begotten in the image and likeness of a corrupt and sinful father."[6]

The point is true enough, just as the point in the first interpretation is also true. But I wonder if, in the context, another meaning of the phrase is not possible and perhaps even required. I find it significant that the phrase occurs here, at the beginning of the chapter introducing the godly line, and not at the

---

[5]Pink, *Gleanings in Genesis*, pp. 73, 74. Cf. also Calvin, *Genesis*, pp. 228, 229; and Leupold, *Exposition of Genesis*, Vol. 1, pp. 234, 235.

[6]Pink, *Gleanings in Genesis*, p. 74.

beginning of the chapter introducing the ungodly line of Cain (chap. 4). Is this not as much as to say that in spite of the Fall and the increasing depravity and debasement of the race, there were nevertheless some, beginning with Seth, who retained a likeness to Adam in that they followed his lead in worshiping the true God (Gen. 4:26) and in seeking to remain faithful to him in spite of the surrounding wickedness?

If this is the case, we have three likenesses: 1) the full likeness of God that Adam and Eve possessed before the Fall but which exists only in a debased form now, if at all; 2) the likeness of sin that each of us passes on to our posterity; and 3) the likeness of godliness that must be learned. It is our duty to pass this likeness on to others, particularly our children, both by precept and example. We can do nothing about the first two. They are given. But we can live in such a way that God will bless our efforts in the third case. We must be able to say, as Paul did, "Follow my example, as I follow the example of Christ" (1 Cor. 11:1).

Our Faithful God

The final point is the faithfulness of God. It is an important point—perhaps the most important of all—for what does this chapter teach if it is not God's faithfulness? God had promised a deliverer through the seed of the woman. To fulfill that purpose it was necessary to preserve a godly remnant through the faithful testimony of parent to child and the faithful reception of that testimony by those children. All this was taking place while the world about grew increasingly wicked. There were hundreds of dangers and thousands of temptations. Who could be equal to such a task? Not Adam! He was an outstanding human being, but he was a sinner as we also are. Eve was not equal to it. Neither were Seth or Enoch or any of the others. Only God was equal to such a task. And He was not only equal to it; He was faithful to do what He had promised.

That God is our God. The days may be wicked, perhaps nearly as wicked as those before the Flood. But God is no less strong, no less able. He will help us and bless our testimony to our children and others if we do as the godly antediluvians did and call on Him. When our book is written, let it be said of us as it was of them: "At that time men began to call on the name of the LORD" (Gen. 4:26).

39

God's Enoch

(Genesis 5:21–24)

When Enoch had lived 65 years, he became the father of Methuselah. And after he became the father of Methuselah, Enoch walked with God 300 years and had other sons and daughters. Altogether, Enoch lived 365 years. Enoch walked with God; then he was no more, because God took him away.

In the midst of the genealogy of Genesis 5 there is a most interesting man: Enoch. He walked with God in an age when practically no one else did. He is an example of faith when it stands alone.

It is an interesting feature of the biblical references to this person that more is said about Enoch in the New Testament than in the Old. In the whole of the Bible there are only five passages that refer to Enoch. Two of these are genealogies in which only his name is mentioned (1 Chron. 1:3; Luke 3:37), nothing else being said about him. So that leaves only three passages of importance. The first is our text in Genesis. It says, "When Enoch had lived 65 years, he became the father of Methuselah. And after he became the father of Methuselah, Enoch walked with God 300 years and had other sons and daughters. Altogether, Enoch lived 365 years. Enoch walked with God; then he was no more, because God took him away" (Gen. 5:21–24). The second passage is in Hebrews: "By faith Enoch was taken from this life, so that he did not experience death; he could not be found, because God had taken him away. For before he was taken, he was commended as one who pleased God" (Heb. 11:5). The third passage is in Jude. "Enoch, the seventh from Adam, prophesied about these men: 'See, the Lord is coming with thousands upon thousands of his holy ones to judge everyone, and to convict all the ungodly of all the ungodly acts they have done in the ungodly way, and of all the harsh words ungodly sinners have spoken against him" (Jude 14, 15).

That makes four Old Testament verses as opposed to three New Testament verses. But in terms of the number of words, there are only fifty-one words in the Old Testament as opposed to ninety-four words in the New Testament (based on the NIV). More importantly, there are things told us about Enoch in the New Testament that are not even suggested in the Old.

SEVENTH FROM ADAM

I begin with the last of these references, the reference in Jude. It is because of a phrase that is found there: "seventh from Adam." That is a curious phrase. Seventh from Adam! Why does God say that Enoch was the seventh descendant in Adam's line?

At first glance the phrase seems unnecessary, particularly since no similar indication of descent is given for any other biblical character. But it is soon explained when we realize that there were two Enochs in this period, both probably living at the same time, and that one was the seventh descendant from Adam through the line of Seth while the other was the third descendant from Adam through the line of Cain. The Enoch who descended from Adam through the line of Seth was godly. He is our Enoch. The Enoch who descended from Adam through the line of Cain was godless. He is the devil's Enoch. So Jude's identification of Enoch as the seventh from Adam is a way of distinguishing the two. It is as if God is saying, "I want you to follow Enoch. But don't get confused. I don't mean the Enoch who is in the fourth chapter of Genesis, the third from Adam. That's the devil's Enoch. I mean the Enoch who was the seventh from Adam."

There is not much told about the Enoch who descended from Cain, but there is enough. First, he was Cain's son. Presumably he was trained by Cain and participated in the spirit of Cain's rebellion. Second, his name was given to the first city, which we know was a very wicked city. Third, his descendants were ungodly. In time they produced Lamech, the seventh in Cain's line. He boasted of a murder and wrote a song about it. This boast—"I have killed a man for wounding me, a young man for injuring me. If Cain is avenged seven times, then Lamech seventy-seven times"—is the last we hear from this line before the Flood swept it away. By contrast, the Enoch who descended from Seth is said to have "walked with God" and to have preached righteousness.

This has practical applications. It suggests that there is a parallel between those who are God's people and those who are the devil's, and it encourages us always to imitate God's people. Let me spell it out. The devil has his men and women, and God has His men and women. The devil has his doctors; God has His doctors. The devil has his convicts; God has His convicts, who by His grace are lifted out of a life of crime. The devil has his lawyers; God has His lawyers. The devil has his housewives, who gossip and flirt and sometimes commit adultery; God has His housewives, who establish godly homes and raise their children in the knowledge and love of Jesus. The devil has his teachers; God has His teachers. The devil even has his preachers, whose sin against knowledge will produce the greater damnation; God has His preachers, who speak the truth. God wants us to see this contrast and pattern our lives after the lives of the godly.

This contrast even suggests the answer to the continuing existence of evil in this world. God is demonstrating the difference between the lives of those who go their own way, sin and bear the consequences, and those who seek to obey God. God is bringing glory and blessing out of the lives of His people; the devil is not able to do that with his children. Enoch was one in whose life God brought blessing.

Preacher of Righteousness

The reference to Enoch in Jude tells something else about this great antediluvian: he was a preacher. And it gives a hint as to the content of his preaching. Enoch's message had two parts: first a proclamation of the Lord's coming in judgment and, second, a denunciation of the ungodliness that was all too visible in the degenerate culture of those days. He said, "See, the Lord is coming with thousands upon thousands of his holy ones to judge everyone, and to convict all the ungodly of all the ungodly acts they have done in the ungodly way, and of all the harsh words ungodly sinners have spoken against him."

When we read these words we understand rightly that the coming of the Lord referred to here is the second coming of Christ at which time the world will be judged. I do not know whether Enoch fully understood this in the sense that Jesus would come a first time to die and then a second time in judgment. At this early stage of God's revelation of Himself to men and women, probably no one saw this clearly. But Enoch did see something that perhaps even the other godly descendants of Adam did not see.

We remember that the hope of the people of God in this period was the promise of a deliverer to come, preserved in God's words of judgment on the serpent: "I will put enmity between you and the woman, and between your offspring and hers; he will crush your head, and you will strike his heel" (Gen. 3:15). As we studied the verses that follow this promise, we saw how Adam and then also Eve seized on it and lived in hope of that deliverer. Eve named her first child Cain, meaning "here he is," because she mistakenly thought that he was the one who would rescue them from their sad state and return them to Paradise. In this period all God's people presumably lived in hope of this appearance. But now Enoch comes along and preaches that the Lord is indeed coming but that His coming will not be the coming in which Satan is defeated and redemption achieved, but rather a coming in judgment on all the ungodly deeds of men and women. For Enoch's age, this promise was fulfilled in the Deluge. What Enoch saw (and what we need also to see) is that the promises of God to deliver are not blanket promises meant to encompass all, as if all necessarily must be saved, but promises only for those who are God's people and who show that relationship by obedience.

We know how Amos put it. Though living ungodly lives, the people of his day held a fond hope that whenever the Lord came to earth everything would be set right and they would be restored and vindicated. After all, were they not the people of God? Were they not the descendants of Adam and Abram and all the other patriarchs? Amos responded:

Woe to you who long for the day of the Lord!
Why do you long for the day of the Lord?
That day will be darkness, not light.
It will be as though a man fled from a lion
only to meet a bear,

as though he entered his house
and rested his hand on the wall
only to have a snake bite him
(Amos 5:18, 19).

This truth needs to be spoken clearly today. God is a God of mercy, but He is a God of judgment as well. That judgment will surely come on all who walk in the way of Cain, unless they repent and come to God through faith in the sacrifice of Christ, which God has provided.

The second part of Enoch's preaching concerned the ungodliness of his age. He preached that the Lord was coming "to convict all the ungodly of all the ungodly acts they have done in the ungodly way, and of all the harsh words ungodly sinners have spoken against him." If we look carefully at Jude's reference to Enoch, we see that it is actually only one sentence and that the words I have just quoted are only a part of that sentence —approximately half. But in that one-half sentence, containing only twenty-nine words, Enoch uses the word "ungodly" four times. That is, one seventh of his recorded words are the single word "ungodly." What do you think would be the single most spoken word in the sermons of most contemporary preachers? Love? Joy? Peace? Involvement? I assure you that it would not be the word "ungodly." Yet that was the essential theme of Enoch's preaching.

We can apply that easily. Enoch lived just before the Flood, as we have indicated, and this was a sinful age. There is a brief description of it in Genesis 6:1–7 in which God says that "man's wickedness on earth" had become great "and that every inclination of the thoughts of his heart was only evil all the time" (v 5). The age was marked by sexual promiscuity, materialism, demonism, and other things that undoubtedly accompanied such sin. It was a terrible time. We look at it and are appalled. But that age was not essentially different from our own. We too have sexual promiscuity, materialism, spiritism, the occult. Moreover, we have rape and murder and drug addiction, and prostitution. We have wholesale murder of the unborn —even of some who are born but are discovered to have physical defects. How dare we point the finger at the antediluvian culture and say "Ungodly!" when we are so manifestly ungodly ourselves? What would Enoch say if he were here today? Would he not say precisely what he said so many thousand years ago: "Ungodly . . . ungodly . . . ungodly . . . ungodly"? Ungodly is the word most singularly appropriate to our age.

And what is the outcome? In Enoch's day it was the terrible judgment of God by flood, recorded in the next major section of Genesis. Is a similar judgment not in store for our equally godless culture? God is not mocked! Indeed, our Lord has warned us of this explicitly. He said, "As it was in the days of Noah, so it will be at the coming of the Son of Man. For in the days before the flood, people were eating and drinking, marrying and giving in marriage, up to the day Noah entered the ark; and they knew nothing about what would happen until the flood came and took them all away. That is how it will be at the coming of the Son of Man" (Matt. 24:37–39).

If these are such days and if the future coming of the Lord Jesus Christ will be a judgment comparable even to the Flood, should not our preaching and witnessing be as filled with condemnation of sin as was the preaching of Enoch and equally as insistent in warning people to flee from the wrath to come?

He Walked With God

I turn now to the original mention of Enoch in Scripture, which is our text in Genesis. This passage does not record his preaching. On the surface it seems merely to be a record of the years of Enoch's life and the fact that he was the father of Methuselah. In all, it contains only fifty-one words. But in those fifty-one words, strikingly, much as Jude 14 and 15 repeat the one word "ungodly" four times, we are told twice over that Enoch "walked with God." We read, "Enoch walked with God 300 years and had other sons and daughters. Altogether Enoch lived 365 years. Enoch walked with God; then he was no more, because God took him away" (Gen. 5:22–24).

What does it mean "to walk with God"? It means a number of things that various verses in the Bible state quite clearly. First, it means to walk by *faith in God,* not trusting to our own understanding but believing Him when He tells us what we should do and how to do it. Second Corinthians 5:7 states this when it says that we are to "live by faith, not by sight." Enoch lived by faith, for it is for faith that he is praised in Hebrews: "By faith Enoch was taken from this life, so that he did not experience death; he could not be found, because God had taken him away. For before he was taken, he was commended as one who pleased God. And without faith it is impossible to please God, because anyone who comes to him must believe that he exists and that he rewards those who earnestly seek him" (Heb. 11:5, 6).

The second requirement for walking with God is *holiness.* God is holy, and those who would have fellowship with Him must be holy as well. John declares this in his first letter: "This is the message we have heard from him and declare to you: God is light; in him there is no darkness at all. If we claim to have fellowship with him yet walk in the darkness, we lie and do not live by the truth. But if we walk in the light, as he is in the light, we have fellowship with one another, and the blood of Jesus, his Son, purifies us from every sin" (1 John 1:5–7).

Third, there must be *agreement* as to the direction we should go, and this means agreeing with God who has planned the way for us. Amos states this by asking, "Do two walk together unless they have agreed to do so?" (Amos 3:3). Obviously not! So if Enoch walked with God, it was clearly because he was not fighting or resisting God but was delighting to walk as God directed him.

Moreover, he was doing this for a long period of time. You will notice, I am sure, that Genesis 5:21–24 applies one use of the phrase "he walked with God" to the time in Enoch's life immediately after the birth of Methuselah, when Enoch was 65 years old, and the other use of the phrase "he walked with God" to the end of Enoch's life, when God took him to be with Himself. At that time Enoch was 365 years old. The teaching is that Enoch walked with God for 300 years. This was no casual stroll. It was the walk of a lifetime. Moreover, it was a walk and not a sprint or run. Nearly anyone can sprint for a short time or distance, but no one can do it for long. For the long haul you need to walk, and this is what Enoch did. We need people who will walk with God today. Not flashes-in-the-pan. Nor shooting stars who attract you more by their passing brilliance than by their substance. We need steady, faithful people who know God and are coming to know Him better day by day.

At this point the texts in Genesis and Jude come together, for why do you suppose Enoch was so conscious of the ungodliness of his generation and so strong in preaching against it? It was because he walked with God. And what do you suppose was the result of his walking with God? Obviously a growth in holiness as a result of which he perceived the true nature of ungodliness. The two always go together. If you walk with God, you will be opposed to sin. But if you do not walk with God, sin will not seem to be so bad to you and you will inevitably accommodate yourself to it.

One way we accommodate ourselves to sin is by calling it by some other name. We call sin "failure," or we say we've made "a mistake." We call pride "self-esteem," selfishness "fulfillment," lust "an instinct." If we cheat in business, we call it "protecting our own interests." If we commit adultery, we call it "an attempt to save the marriage." We call murdering an unborn child "terminating a pregnancy." What hypocrites we are! How offensive we must be to God, who is obviously not taken in by our reinterpretations but who calls sin, sin and evil, evil. Shakespeare said, "A rose by any other name would smell as sweet." Likewise, sin by any other name will smell as putrid. You and I will never grow in holiness unless we see sin for what it is and call it sin, and we will never learn to do that unless we walk closely with God. It is when we walk with God that we learn to call things by God's vocabulary.

Enoch Pleased God

I turn finally to the third of the three major texts that mention Enoch, Hebrews 11:5, which tells us that "Enoch . . . pleased God." This is the obvious culmination of the account of Enoch's life, for having walked with God and having thereby come to recognize sin as sin and to have turned from it, Enoch inevitably pleased God in what he did. What could be a better testimony for any human life? What could be a better achievement than to have it said that you or I pleased God?

We note that if we please God, we will not be in a position of pleasing most men and women, at least not the ungodly. By the time Enoch died, by the sheer mathematics of birth and reproduction, there were probably several million of Adam's descendants on earth. These were Enoch's relatives, mostly cousins. It was these whom Enoch called "ungodly," and we can be sure that he was not popular with them. Although Enoch may not have pleased his cousins, he has this testimony—that he pleased

God. That is what counted. May it also be true of us. If possible, we wish to grow "in favor with God and men" (cf. Luke 2:52). But if the choice is necessary, as it often is, may it never be said that we choose to please men and women rather than God but that we choose to please God regardless of the consequences.

The end of the story is that the day came in Enoch's life—when he was 365 years old—when God simply took him home to be with Himself. They had been out walking, and God simply said, "Let's not go back to your place tonight. Why don't you just come home with Me?" And so he did.

Martin Luther has fun with this idea in his exposition of Genesis, for he imagines the effect of the translation of Enoch on his godly friends. He notes how Enoch's father and grandfather would have been disturbed. They would have launched a manhunt. They would have been wondering what could have become of this great preacher of righteousness. No doubt they suspected foul play on the part of Cain's descendants. Enoch had preached against their wickedness. Perhaps he had been slain, like Abel, and buried secretly. At last, through the revelation of God they learn that Enoch had not been murdered but had simply been taken away by God and given a place in Paradise. Why should God have acted this way? Luther asks. It was, he says, to show that death is not the end but rather "that there has been prepared and set aside for men another and also a better life than this present life which is replete with so many misfortunes and evils." Enoch was God's testimony to the fact that those who walk with God in this life will also walk with God in a better life hereafter, thanks to the future work "of the promised Seed."[1]

That was the hope of those who lived before the Flood, and it is our hope also. Let us live in that hope and walk with God now so that we may also walk with Him in that blessed age to come.

---

[1] Luther, *Luther's Works,* Vol. 1, pp. 345, 346.

40

The Oldest Man Alive

(Genesis 5:25–27)

When Methuselah had lived 187 years, he became the father of Lamech. And after he became the father of Lamech, Methuselah lived 782 years and had other sons and daughters. Altogether, Methuselah lived 969 years, and then he died.

Our study of Enoch in the last chapter overlooked one important facet of the antediluvian's life: the birth and naming of his son Methuselah and the significance of this for Enoch's ministry. Three things are important about Methuselah. First, it was at the time of his birth, the text seems to indicate, that Enoch began to walk with God in a special way (Gen. 5:22). Second, Methuselah lived a long time, longer than any man who ever lived. Third, his name means "when he is dead, it shall come."

We must acknowledge at the beginning that there is a difference of opinion regarding the meaning of Methuselah's name. This is because two very different translations of it are possible. The name could be composed of the words *math*, meaning "man" or "male," and *shelah*, meaning a "missile" or "weapon." In that case, it would be translated "Man of the weapon" (Gesenius, Leupold) or "Man of the javelin" (Kidner). On the other hand, Methuselah could be made up of the verbs *muth*, meaning "die" or "dead," and *shalah*, meaning "sent."[1] In this case it would be translated "He dies, a sending forth" (Matthew Henry) or, as I have indicated, "When he is dead, it shall come." Of the two translations, the first is most straightforward, but it has no meaning in the context. The

second has great meaning, as I hope to show.

What is the meaning? Simply that Enoch had a revelation at the time of Methuselah's birth of the destruction to come on the earth by flood. God said that the Flood was to come after the death of that son. So either at God's explicit direction or as an act of his own faith, Enoch named the child Methuselah—"when he is dead, it shall come." While Methuselah lived, the Flood would be held back. But when he died, it would come.

Biblical Chronology

This is precisely what happened. I have already indicated one tenuous area of interpretation in regard to Methuselah: the meaning of his name. I want to introduce another one here. But in spite of the difficulties that I am going to suggest, I think you will see how the name Methuselah, the matter of his great longevity, and the Flood go together.

The difficulties (and, hence, the second tenuous area of interpretation) concern attempts to use the genealogies of the Bible to fix strict chronologies. That is, there are problems with simply adding up a list of years, such as those in Genesis 5, and then saying for certain

---

[1] The Assyrian word for die, *matu*, is even closer to the form found in the name Methuselah.

when any one individual was either born or died. The reason for these problems is that the biblical writers apparently did not have quite the same approach to chronology as we do and therefore sometimes skipped over generations in tracing a person's ancestry. For example, in Matthew's genealogy of Jesus, recorded in the first chapter, there are two places at which names are dropped out. In verse 8 Matthew writes of "Jehoshaphat the father of Joram" and "Joram the father of Uzziah." But between Joram and Uzziah three names are missing: Ahaziah, Joash, and Amaziah. We know this by comparing Matthew's genealogy with the full history of these men given in 2 Chronicles 22–25. Three verses later the same thing occurs. Matthew writes of "Josiah the father of Jeconiah." But according to 2 Chronicles 36, Josiah was actually the father of Jehoahaz, who was the father of Jehoiakin, who was the father of Jeconiah. Was Matthew mistaken? No. It is simply that he thought differently about genealogies than we do. Matthew indicates this at the start of the chapter, which he titles "the genealogy of Jesus Christ, the son of David, the son of Abraham" (v. 1). Obviously many generations intervened between each of those three persons.

Here is another example. If we compare 1 Chronicles 6:3–14 with Ezra 7:1–5, we find that Ezra omits six generations between Azariah, whom both accounts identify as the son of Amariah, and Meraioth, the son of Zerahiah. Ezra was a scribe. He above all others should have known the names in a family tree. But he omits six names because it was not his purpose to give a comprehensive listing. It was only necessary to show the general line of descent.

A third example has bearing on the account of Genesis 11. In that chapter Moses gives the descendants of Shem, the most prominent son of Noah. He has this sequence: Shem, Arphaxad, and Shelah (vv. 10–14). But Luke also gives this sequence in his genealogy of Jesus, and his list contains: Shem, Arphaxad, *Cainan,* and Shelah (Luke 3:36). That is, Luke inserts the name Cainan between Arphaxad and Shelah. Because of these variations, scholars hesitate to use genealogies to date events prior to the time of Abram or to take them as inclusive of all the persons involved.[2]

But having said all that, and having therefore cast doubt on the possibility of using the numbers in Genesis 5 for a chronology, I nevertheless want to back up and say two things. First, the names given in Genesis 5 are not challenged at any other point in Scripture. In fact, the opposite is the case. Luke, in the very verses in which he introduces the name of Cainan into Christ's early genealogy, actually reinforces the Genesis 5 chronology by giving its list of names exactly: "Noah, the son of Lamech, the son of Methuselah, the son of Enoch, the son of Jared, the son of Mahalaleel, the son of Cainan [Kenan], the son of Enos, the son of Seth, the son of Adam, the son of God" (Luke 3:36, 37). This encourages us to take the list of names seriously.

Second, there is the matter of the years listed for the lives of each of these patriarchs. Genesis 11, 1 Chronicles 6, Ezra 7, Matthew 1, and Luke 3 do not list years. They give names only. By contrast, Genesis 5 does list years. And these, if they are taken at full value, do tell us when each of the persons was born, when he died, and who was living or who had died at any given period.

It is for this that I have gone into such a

---

[2]On the problem of dating by means of genealogies see Warfield, "On the Antiquity and the Unity of the Human Race," *Biblical and Theological Studies,* pp. 238–61; Whitcomb and Morris, *The Genesis Flood,* Appendix II, pp. 474–89; Fred Kramer, "A Critical Evaluation of the Chronology of Ussher" in Paul A. Zimmerman, editor, *Rock Strata and the Bible Record* (St. Louis: Concordia Publishing House, 1970), pp. 57–67; and Schaeffer, *Genesis in Space and Time,* pp. 122–25.

THE GENESIS 5 CHRONOLOGY

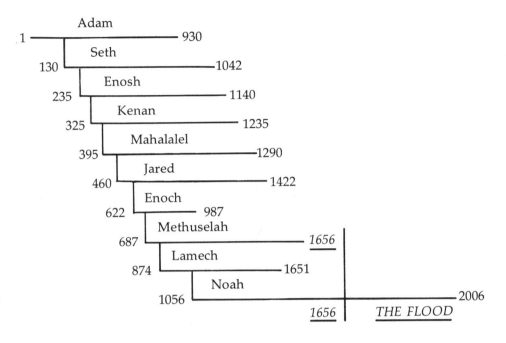

lengthy explanation. Let us put these figures together in sequence, as the numbers encourage us to do. We begin with Adam whose creation must be put in the year 1. He lived until the year 930. Seth was born in the 130th year of Adam's life, which was the year 130, and he lived 912 years or until the year 1042. Enosh was born in the 105th year of Seth's life, which was the year 235, and he lived 905 years or until the year 1140. Kenan was born in the 90th year of Enosh's life, which was the year 325, and he lived 910 years or until the year 1235. Mahalalel was born in the 70th year of Kenan's life, which was the year 395, and he lived 895 years or until the year 1290. Jared was born in the 65th year of Mahalalel's life, which was the year 460, and he lived 962 years or until the year 1422. Enoch was born in the 162nd year of Jared's life, which was the year 622, and he lived 365 years or until the year 987. (Enoch had a relatively short life and died before any of the other patri-

archs except Adam, who had died just 57 years previous.) Methuselah was born in the 65th year of Enoch's life, which was the year 687, and he lived 969 years or until the year 1656. Lamech was born in the 187th year of Methuselah's life, which was the year 874, and he lived 777 years or until the year 1651. (That is, Methuselah's son died 5 years before he did.) The last of the patriarchs was Noah, Lamech's son, who was born in the 182nd year of Lamech's life, which was the year 1056. He lived 950 years, 600 of which were before the Flood and 350 of which were afterward. By this reckoning, the Flood came 600 years after the year 1056 or in the year 1656.

The important thing is this. The Flood came in the year 1656, according to the chronology of Genesis 5. But this is precisely the year in which Methuselah died, by the same reckoning! In other words, the history of the period bears out the meaning of Methusaleh's name. As long as Methuselah lived, the Flood tarried. But when he died, it came.

There is a tradition based on Genesis 6:3 that says that Noah spent 120 years building the ark. Whether or not this is true, it is certain that Noah spent a long time building it and that during this period, however long it was, Methuselah was growing older and older. Here was a man who was 600 years old . . . 700 years old . . . 800 years old . . . 850 years old. . . . By the time Methuselah was 850 years old God had appeared to Noah to tell him to build the ark, and Noah was getting under way. The crowds had gathered to scoff. 900 years old. . . . Noah had laid the keel, constructed the ribbing, fitted the sides. The crowds were smaller because the novelty had worn off. 910 . . . 920 . . . 930 . . . 940 . . . 950 . . . 960. . . . Noah had long since finished the outside and laid the decks. The crowd had now faded away entirely. 965. . . The ark was almost finished. 966 . . . 967 . . . 968. . . The food had been brought on board. *969!* The ark was finished. The animals were taken on. Methuselah died. God closed the door. The Flood came.

"When he dies, it will come!" In this way Methuselah was a living testimony to the fact and inevitability of God's judgment. He was testimony to the truth that the eyes of God "are too pure to look on evil" (Hab. 1:13) and that "he does not leave the guilty unpunished" (Exod. 34:7).

GOD OF PATIENCE

But Methuselah was something else as well. He was a testimony to God's grace. For this is why Methuselah lived longer than any other man on earth. His longevity was no accident. It was not merely that someone had to live longest, and Methuselah just happened to be the one. It was rather that so long as he lived the Flood would not come, and God apparently spared his life year after year, while Noah built the ark to the saving of his family—decade after decade, so re-luctant was he to unleash the destruction. It was precisely as Peter says so clearly in the New Testament, "The Lord is not slow in keeping his promise, as some understand slowness. He is patient with you, not wanting anyone to perish, but everyone to come to repentance" (2 Peter 3:9).

The section of 2 Peter in which this verse occurs deals with the inevitability of God's judgment and has reference to the Flood. This means that it is actually a New Testament commentary on this period. It is proper to close our study of Methuselah by reference to it.

The situation for Peter was as follows. Apparently, 2 Peter was written toward the end of Peter's life, at a time when the believers to whom he was writing were under attack by scoffers who ridiculed the doctrine of Christ's second coming. They were saying, "Where is this 'coming' he promised? Ever since our fathers died, everything goes on as it has since the beginning of creation" (2 Peter 3:4). This has always been the unbeliever's taunt. It is the attitude of our day—on the university campuses, among normal working people, even in some religious circles. A theological professor once told me, "We have got to get it into our heads that Jesus is never coming back, and everything is going to continue on just as it has from the beginning."

But what is Peter's response to such scoffing? He is not intimidated by it. Instead he relates it to the previous judgment of the world by flood and makes the following points.

First, the views of scoffers are based on ignorance, and a willful ignorance at that. That is, they have willfully closed their minds to the abundant evidence that God does not tolerate evil and that He eventually does intervene to judge wickedness. Peter says, "But they deliberately forget that long ago by God's word the heavens existed and the earth was formed out of water and with water. By water also the world of that time was deluged and destroyed. By the same word the present heavens and earth are reserved for fire, being kept for the day of judgment and destruction of ungodly men" (3:5–7). In Romans 1, Paul points out in a discussion of general revelation that people do not know God, not because he cannot be known, but because they do not want to know him. It was because "they did not think it worthwhile to retain the knowledge of God" (Rom. 1:28). Peter says the same thing in reference to the judgment. It is not that the evidence for a coming judgment is not there. It is. It is because people willingly close their minds to what is coming.

Why do they do this? Peter does not hesitate to say that it is so they can follow "their own evil desires" (v. 3). Like the people of Methuselah's day, they reject warnings of judgment in order to continue on their own evil way. Most people do not admit this, of course. They invent intellectual reasons for their unbelief. But from time to time a person will acknowledge this quite openly. Aldous Huxley, the widely read and famous atheist of this century, once freely admitted that his rejection of Christianity stemmed from his desire to sin. He wrote, "I had motives for not wanting the world to have a meaning; consequently assumed that it had not; and was able without any difficulty to find satisfying reasons for this assumption. The philosopher who finds no meaning for this world is not concerned exclusively with the problem of pure metaphysics; he is also concerned to prove that there is no valid reason why he personally should not do as he wants to. . . . For myself . . . the philosophy of meaninglessness was essentially an instrument of liberation, sexual and political."[3]

Second, Peter explains God's delay in sending judgment. It is true that from our standpoint the judgment is slow in coming. But this is not because God is indifferent to sin or, worse yet, because he does not exist. It is because God's timing is not our timing and because He delays His judgment in order to give people opportunity to repent. Peter says, "But do not forget this one thing, dear friends: With the Lord a day is like a thousand years, and a thousand years are like a day. The Lord is not slow in keeping his promise, as some understand slowness. He is patient with you, not wanting anyone to perish, but everyone to come to repentance" (2 Peter 3:8, 9).

The second verse in this passage —"He is patient with you, not wanting anyone to perish"—has sometimes been used against people of the Reformed persuasion, as if it were a clear refutation of election. But it is precisely the opposite. What it teaches is that God takes the election of His own people so seriously that He delays even so great a matter as the final judgment until all who should be saved are born and subsequently come to personal faith in Jesus as their Lord and Savior. We notice that Peter's words are not directed to anyone indiscriminately, not to the world, but to "you," that is, to Christians. They are Peter's "dear friends." If a scoffer is among that number, the delay even of that which he is ridiculing is for his benefit. And the very situation he finds to be evidence against God or God's concern for humanity is precisely the opposite. God is delaying the judgment until this very one should come.

Peter's third point is that the judgment is inevitable. It may be delayed, but it is no less certain for that fact: "But the day of the Lord will come like a thief. The heavens will disappear with a roar; the elements will be destroyed by fire, and the earth and everything in it will be laid bare" (v. 10). How can Peter be so

---

[3]Aldous Huxley, *Ends and Means* (New York: Garland Publishers, 1938), pp. 270, 273.

certain? It is because God has said that this is what He will do and because He has already done it once in destroying the earth by flood in Noah's period.

AN APPLICATION

Peter's last point is an application: "Since everything will be destroyed in this way, what kind of people ought you to be? You ought to live holy and godly lives as you look forward to the day of God and speed its coming. That day will bring about the destruction of the heavens by fire, and the elements will melt in the heat. But in keeping with his promise we are looking forward to a new heaven and a new earth, the home of righteousness. So then, dear friends, since you are looking forward to this, make every effort to be found spotless, blameless and at peace with him" (vv. 11–14).

I do not know of anything in Genesis that teaches that Methuselah, Noah, and the other godly people of that generation grew in holiness as the day of God's judgment approached, but I am sure they did. Each sweep of the saw, each blow of the hammer, would remind them that the Flood was drawing closer and would encourage them to walk in a way that pleased God. I am sure that as the ark drew to completion they were more anxious to lead "spotless" and "blameless" lives than they were at the beginning. So should it be for us. We do not know when God's second and final judgment will come, but it is coming closer hour by hour, minute by minute. It could be at any time. So far as I know, there is no one living today who has the name Methuselah. But there could be one who should have that name—a person now living but who will die just before God's judgment.

"When he is dead, it shall come!" These are serious thoughts. Allow them to move you to faith in Jesus Christ, our ark of salvation, and to live a godly life for Him.

41

The Reign of Death

(Genesis 5:28–32)

When Lamech had lived 182 years, he had a son. He named him Noah and said, "He will comfort us in the labor and painful toil of our hands caused by the ground the LORD has cursed." After Noah was born, Lamech lived 595 years and had other sons and daughters. Altogether, Lamech lived 777 years, and then he died.

After Noah was 500 years old, he became the father of Shem, Ham and Japheth.

In the Middle Ages it was not unusual for scholars and other men of prominence to keep a skull on their desk to remind them that they, like the unfortunate victim, must die. The Latin name for such a skull was *memento mori,* that is, "a reminder of death," a reminder of the shortness of life and of the certainty that, however long or short it might be, everyone must eventually succumb to death and face God.

We have a *memento mori* in the fifth chapter of Genesis, in a sentence that occurs eight times in reference to the patriarchs: "and then he died." We find it first in verse 4, of Adam. It occurs thereafter in verses 7, 11, 14, 17, 20, 27, and 31, of Seth, Enosh, Kenan, Mahalalel, Jared, Methuselah, and Lamech—all of whom died, even though they were members of the godly line of Adam through Seth. The sentences must be read for their intended effect: "Altogether, Adam lived 930 years, *and then he died.* . . . Altogether, Seth lived 921 years, *and then he died.* . . . Altogether, Enosh lived 905 years, *and then he died.* . . . Altogether, Kenan lived 910 years, *and then he died.* . . . Altogether, Mahalalel lived 830 years, *and then he died.* . . . Altogether, Jared lived 962 years, *and then he died.* . . . Altogether, Methuselah lived 969 years, *and then he died.* . . . Al-together, Lamech lived 777 years, and then he died." These were long life spans, extending from 365 to 969 years, but each was cut off by death. Each patriarch died. Since we must also die, a study of these wrods can be a *memento mori* for us and our contemporaries.

ALL MUST DIE

The first point is the obvious one: all must die. It must not be passed over, for it is precisely here that we must feel the force of God's judgment. We have an expression used to justify hard work and other unpleasantries. We say, "We must live." But we would be far more accurate and wiser were we to change it and say, "We must die." For life is not certain. It is not established that we *must* live. Indeed, we may die at any time, and life even at its best is but a slow dying. Only death is certain. It is more certain even than taxes.

All must die! In the normal course of our lives we seldom give death a thought. We glance lightly over the obituaries. We read in the newspaper of someone important dying. We pass a funeral home or notice a hearse driving by. At best these things cause a momentary pause before we rush on to some pressing activity. But then death comes into *our immediate circle,* and it is at once quite different. A husband dies!

A wife dies! A child dies! Suddenly we are confronted with the fact that we are mortal. Is there anyone who has not felt the loss of some relative, close or distant? Hardly! Nearly all have lost someone, whether a parent or child or grandparent or friend. These are God's warnings to us. They are a reminder of our death and a warning to prepare for the moment in which we must meet God.

Charles Haddon Spurgeon, the great Baptist preacher, once wrote along these lines: "There be some of you who stand today like a man upon the shore when the tide is swelling towards his feet. There came one wave, and it took away the grandmother; another came, and a mother was swept away; another came, and the wife was taken; and now it dashes at your feet. How long shall it be ere it breaks over you—and you, too, are carried away by the yawning wave into the bosom of the deep of Death. . . . Children, husbands, wives, brothers, sisters, prepare to meet your God."[1]

It is possible that death has not touched you through your immediate family, particularly if you are young. But you cannot escape God's warning that easily. Death is staring at you from *every television or radio broadcast and every newspaper.*

In preparing this message I took time to glance through some recent newspapers and news magazines, and death was everywhere. The most startling was an accident involving the Sunshine Skyway Bridge over Tampa Bay just south of Saint Petersburg, Florida. At 7:30 in the morning in the middle of a thunderstorm, the Liberian freighter *Summit Venture* struck a bridge abutment and caused a 1,300-foot section of the roadway to tear loose and crash into the bay. Before traffic could be stopped, a Greyhound bus carrying twenty-three people, three cars and a pickup truck

had plunged off the end of the bridge into the water. All the passengers but one were drowned.

The same papers that carried news of this tragedy continued to report the grim aftermath of the United States' unsuccessful attempt to rescue fifty American hostages in Iran. Eight young men had died in that aborted mission, and now the papers carried photos and stories of the transfer of their bodies from Iran to the United States by way of Europe, and of the burial of some of them in Arlington Cemetery.

At the time this was happening a crack British commando unit stormed the occupied Iranian embassy in London, rescuing nineteen people who had been held hostage there for almost a week. But two of the hostages had been killed by the terrorists, one before and one during the raid. Five of the six terrorists were killed by the commandos.

In Liberia soldiers of the new government of Master Sergeant Samuel Kanyon executed thirteen members of the former civilian government, including the late president's older brother.

There were reports of death squads operating in Brazil, the Laotian attempt to wipe out the Hmong hill people of Thailand. In Cambodia one of the greatest tragedies of modern times continued as thousands upon thousands died of hunger and related diseases.

Warnings of death come closer and are more pressing even than these stories, for we have them in *ourselves.* We ourselves are dying. We reach our hand to our mouths and find missing or decayed teeth. We struggle with fine print and know that our eyesight is failing. We are losing our hair, or it is turning white. Our breath is short. We are easily exhausted. Some have heart conditions. Others suffer from equally serious ail-

---

[1]Charles Haddon Spurgeon, "Memento Mori," *The New Park Street Pulpit,* Vol. 6 (Pasadena, Texas: Pilgrim Publications, 1975), p. 145.

ments. Some have terminal diseases and do not even know about it. In time these diseases make themselves known and carry their victims away. The time is quickly coming when you and I must meet God.

The devil will say, "Don't worry about such things. Life is long. Enjoy yourself while you are young." But the devil has been a liar from the beginning, and life is not long. Life is short. The time is approaching when you and I and all people must stand before God our Judge. What will happen to you if you are not prepared to die? What will become of you?

THE WAGES OF SIN

This leads to the second obvious point of our *memento mori* from Genesis. Sin is the cause of our death, and consequently death is not natural. It is an intrusion into God's universe brought about by our own equally serious and sinful intrusion into God's prerogatives as Creator. How can we miss this in the context of the early chapters of Genesis? All we need to do is put Genesis 2:16, 17 over against Genesis 5:5. "And the LORD God commanded the man, 'You are free to eat from any tree in the garden; but you must not eat from the tree of the knowledge of good and evil, for when you eat of it you will surely die.'" Then, "Altogether, Adam lived 930 years, *and . . . he died.*"

To be sure, Adam had already died in spirit, that part of his being that had communion with God. He showed it by hiding when God came to him in the cool of the evening in the garden. His soul had begun to die. But here at last, even his body dies. God had said, "Dust you are and to dust you will return" (Gen. 3:19). Sin brought death to Adam, and by his sin death passed upon the race (Rom. 5:12).

There is a subtle attempt to escape the teaching of the Bible at this point by the argument, widely heard today, that death is quite natural. That is, there is no moral meaning to death. Death is just a necessary part of the whole mechanism of life. Life begins, develops, matures, and then fades away. It is the pattern of human existence.

Martyn Lloyd-Jones tells how a principal of a theological college in England once put the matter to him. They had been discussing the verse, "Unless a kernel of wheat falls to the ground and dies, it remains only a single seed. But if it dies, it produces many seeds" (John 12:24). The educator said, "That is quite simple. You people with your legalistic minds keep imposing your own ideas onto the beautiful, simple view of life which was taken by Jesus. Don't you see that he is just illustrating there this principle inherent in life? You put that seed into the ground; if it remains alive, it is of no further value, but if that seed dies and degenerates and decomposes, then a chemical process takes place that leads to the renewal of life, and out of that one seed you will have many blades of grass or corn. That is how it works. Nothing is lost. You say that when something dies that is the end of it. But such is not the case. When trees and flowers and animals die the decomposed matter to which they give rise is most valuable. It produces nitrogen, which is after all the basis of life, and many other essential constituents. Death leads to life by liberating the nitrogen that is needed to form the molecules of new life. Death is just part of the cycle of life."[2]

I am sure nearly everyone has heard that argument. But let me ask this question: If death is as natural and beneficial as all that, why do people fear death as they do? I do not mean, why do they prefer to go on living rather than die?

---

[2]D. M. Lloyd-Jones, *Romans: An Exposition of Chapter 5, Assurance* (Grand Rapids: Zondervan, 1971), p. 192.

Anyone who enjoys life would naturally prefer it to having life taken away. I do not even mean, why do people fear dying? Since death is often accompanied by pain it is understandable that people might fear the process of dying. I mean rather, why do people fear death itself? Why do they draw back from it with such loathing, if death is natural?

And they do fear it! Sometimes they put on a show of bravado and pretend they do not. But they do . . . and have, down through the centuries since the sin of Adam. In the age of Greece and Rome death was conceived as passage to the underworld, a dark and terrifying abode. It lay on the far side of the river Styx, and the dead were ferried there by Charon, the grim boatman of despair. Literature is filled with expressions of fear that grip the hearts of unbelievers as they face these terrors. Socrates said, "No one knows whether death . . . may not be the greatest of all good," but men "in their fear apprehend [it] to be the greatest evil."[3] Francis Bacon wrote, "Men fear death, as children fear to go in the dark."[4] Samuel Johnson, told of his horror at the death of a friend: "At the sight of this last conflict I felt a sensation never known to me before: a confusion of passions, an awful stillness of sorrow, a gloomy terror without a name."[5]

Why this fear, if death is so natural? The answer is that death is not natural. It is the grim wages of sin and is the prelude to judgment. Men fear death because they know it is the end of all delay and that after death they must stand face to face before the God they have offended. They may deny these truths. They may protest loudly against the thought of judgment. But in their inmost being they know that Hebrews 9:27 is not lying when it says, "Man is destined to die once, and after that to face judgment."

DEATH TRANSFORMED

What is to be done? How can we escape this dreadful end of life and the even more dreadful judgment of God that lies beyond? Left to ourselves we cannot. We can do nothing. But there was one, even the Lord Jesus Christ, who conquered death by dying and who by that death and the resurrection that followed forever transformed death for those who follow Him.

Horatius Bonar, one of Scotland's great divines and a father of the Scottish Free Church, wrote wisely of Christ's victory. "The first Adam dies, and we die in him; but the second Adam dies, and we live in him! The first Adam's grave proclaims only death; the second Adam's grave announces life—'I am the resurrection and the life.' We look into the grave of the one, and we see only darkness, corruption, and death; we look into the grave of the other, and we find there only light, incorruption, and life. We look into the grave of the one and find that he is still there, his dust still mingling with its fellow dust about it; we look into the grave of the other and find that he is not there. He is risen—risen as our forerunner into the heavenly paradise, the home of the risen and redeemed. We look into the grave of the first Adam and see in him the first-fruits of them that have died, the millions that have gone down to that prisonhouse whose gates he opened; we look into the tomb of the second Adam, and we see in him the first-fruits of them that are to rise, the first-fruits of that bright multitude, that glorified band, who are to

---

[3]Plato, "Apology," *The Works of Plato*, trans. by B. Jowett (New York: Tudor Publishing Company, n.d.), Vol. 3, p. 117.

[4]Francis Bacon, "Of Death," *Selected Writings of Francis Bacon* (New York: The Modern Library, 1955), p. 9.

[5]Samuel Johnson, "Death-bed the School of Wisdom," *The Rambler*, No. 54 (New York: E. P. Dutton & Co., 1953), p. 119.

come forth from that cell, triumphing over death and rising to the immortal life; not through the tree which grew in the earthly paradise, but through him whom that tree prefigured—through him who was dead and is alive, and who liveth for evermore, and who has the keys of hell and death."[6]

How has Jesus brought about this transformation? He has done it by bearing the punishment due to us for our sin. Consequently, though we still die physically, the fear of death is removed. The fear of death is fear of judgment, and Jesus has borne that judgment for us. He died in our place. He suffered the terrors of separation from God so that we might never be separated from Him. We sing about it in some of our great hymns.

> Jesus paid it all;
> All to him I owe:
> Sin had left a crimson stain;
> He washed it white as snow.

Or again,

> Jesus lives! Thy terrors now
> Can no longer, death, appall us;
> Jesus lives! By this we know
> Thou, O grave, canst not enthrall us.
>   Alleluia!

There are two great passages in the New Testament that speak of the Christian's transformed hope in death due to Christ's death on the cross and His resurrection. The first is in 2 Corinthians: "Now we know that if the earthly tent we live in is destroyed, we have a building from God, an eternal house in heaven, not built by human hands. Meanwhile we groan, longing to be clothed with our heavenly dwelling, because when we are clothed, we will not be found naked. For while we are in this tent, we groan and are burdened, because we do not wish to be unclothed but to be clothed with our heavenly dwelling, so that what is mortal may be swallowed up by life. Now it is God who has made us for this very purpose and has given us the Spirit as a deposit, guaranteeing what is to come. Therefore we are always confident and know that as long as we are at home in the body we are away from the Lord. We live by faith, not by sight. We are confident, I say, and would prefer to be away from the body and at home with the Lord" (2 Cor. 5:1–8).

The second passage is from Paul's letter to the Philippians. At the time of his writing this letter his trial before Nero was pending, and Paul was unsure of what the outcome would be. He might be acquitted. But again, he might be condemned. "No matter," says Paul. God was in charge, and Christ would be glorified in him whether by life or by death. He then expresses his own hope and firm anticipation: "For to me, to live is Christ and to die is gain. If I am to go on living in the body, this will mean fruitful labor for me. Yet what shall I choose? I do not know! I am torn between the two: I desire to depart and be with Christ, which is better by far; but it is more necessary for you that I remain in the body" (Phil. 1:21–24). In these verses Paul is saying that he is better off dead than alive, for death means entrance into the presence of the Lord Jesus Christ in heaven.

Two Deaths

This hope has transformed death for Christians in all ages. In the year 1899 two famous men died in America. One was an unbeliever who had made a career of attacking the Bible. The other was a Christian. The unbeliever was Colonel Ingersoll, after whom the well-known Ingersoll lectures on immortality at Harvard University are named. The believer was Dwight L. Moody.

---

[6]Horatius Bonar, *Thoughts on Genesis* (Grand Rapids: Kregel, n.d.), pp. 274, 275. Original edition 1875.

Ingersoll died suddenly, and his death was an unmitigated shock to his family. The body was kept at the Ingersoll home for several days because Ingersoll's wife could not bear to part with it, but it was finally removed because the health of the family required it. Ingersoll's remains were then cremated, and the display at the crematorium was so dismal that some of the scene was picked up by the newspapers and communicated to the nation at large. Ingersoll had used his great intellect to deny Christianity. But when death came there was no hope, and the departure was received by his friends as an uncompensated tragedy.

In the same year the great evangelist died. Moody had been declining for some time, and his family had taken turns being with him. On the morning of his death his son, who was standing by the bedside, heard him exclaim, "Earth is receding; heaven is opening; God is calling."

"You are dreaming, Father," the son said.

Moody answered, "No, Will, this is no dream. I have been within the gates. I have seen the children's faces." For a while it seemed as if Moody were reviving, but he began to slip away again. He said, "Is this death? This is not bad; there is no valley. This is bliss. This is glorious." By this time his daughter was present, and she began to pray for his recovery. He said, "No, no, Emma, don't pray for that. God is calling. This is my coronation day. I have been looking forward to it." Shortly after this Moody was received into heaven. At the funeral the family and friends joined in a joyful service. They spoke. They sang hymns. They heard the words proclaimed, "Where, O death, is your victory? Where, O death, is your sting? The sting of death is sin, and the power of sin is the law. But thanks be to God! He gives us the victory through our Lord Jesus Christ" (1 Cor. 15:55–57).

In Romans 5:14 Paul says that from Adam onward "death reigned." It reigned over Adam and has reigned over all his descendants. But death has been conquered and the power of death broken by the Lord Jesus Christ so that today all who believe in Him may live in hope.

42

Sons of God/Daughters of Men

(Genesis 6:1–4)

When men began to increase in number on the earth and daughters were born to them, the sons of God saw that the daughters of men were beautiful, and they married any of them they chose. Then the LORD said, "My Spirit will not contend with man forever, for he is mortal; his days will be a hundred and twenty years."

The Nephilim were on the earth in those days—and also afterward—when the sons of God went to the daughters of men and had children by them. They were the heroes of old, men of renown.

The first verses of Genesis 6 are transition verses. On the one hand, they wrap up the pre-Flood history of the earlier chapters, showing the state of degeneracy to which the race had fallen. On the other hand, they prepare for the story of Noah and the Flood that follows; it was because of this degeneracy that the Flood came. Unfortunately, the meaning of these verses is not self-evident. They have raised questions that have been discussed for years.

The passage tells us that "When men began to increase in number on the earth and daughters were born to them, the sons of God saw that the daughters of men were beautiful, and they married any of them they chose" (vv. 1, 2). This apparently straightforward statement is actually confusing because the subject of the sentence might refer to either of two things. "The sons of God" might mean descendants of the godly line of Seth, who according to this interpretation would be said to have married unbelieving women. Or it might refer to angels, as do the only other exact uses of the phrase in the Old Testament (Job. 1:6; 2:1; 38:7).

The thing that makes these verses so interesting is that three New Testament passages seem to refer to them: 1 Peter 3:18–22; 2 Peter 2:4, 5; and Jude 6, 7. These passages say in part: "Christ died for sins once for all, the righteous for the unrighteous, to bring you to God. He was put to death in the body but made alive by the Spirit, through whom also he went and preached to the spirits in prison who disobeyed long ago when God waited patiently in the days of Noah while the ark was being built" (1 Peter 3:18–20); "For if God did not spare angels when they sinned, but sent them to hell, putting them into gloomy dungeons to be held for judgment; if he did not spare the ancient world when he brought the flood on its ungodly people, but protected Noah, a preacher of righteousness, and seven others . . ." (2 Peter 2:4, 5); and "the angels who did not keep their positions of authority but abandoned their own home—these he has kept in darkness, bound with everlasting chains for judgment on the great Day" (Jude 6).

If these passages are related, as they seem to be, the incident of Genesis 6 has bearing on the doctrines of judgment, the afterlife, and even the work of Christ following His crucifixion but before His resurrection or ascension. The New Testament verses explain what Christ was doing when, as we say in the Apostles' Creed, "he descended into hell."

THE GODLY AND THE UNGODLY

The interpretation of Genesis 6 which takes "the sons of God" as referring to the godly line of Seth is most natural since it avoids the obvious problem of how spirit beings could copulate with humans. Moreover, it has weighty support in that it is the view of many theological giants of church history. It is not an early view—we will come back to that later—but it appears in such thinkers as Chrysostom and Augustine in the early church, and is adopted by reformers such as Luther, Calvin, and their followers.

Of the early views Augustine's is most important because he had a great influence on later interpreters. Moreover, he placed his interpretation within a broad theological context. Augustine's treatment occurs in *The City of God*, in which he is trying to trace the origin, nature and development of the two cities (the society of those who love God and the society of those who love self). This is significant, because it fits his objective to view Genesis 6 as continuing the story of the two cities which, according to Augustine, emerges in Genesis 4 and 5. He writes of the passage, "By these two names [sons of God and daughters of men] the two cities are sufficiently distinguished. For although the former were by nature children of men, they had come into possession of another name by grace. . . . When they [the godly race] were captivated by the daughters of men, they adopted the manners of the earthly to win them as their brides, and forsook the godly ways they had followed in their own holy society."[1]

This view fits into the pattern of Gene-sis 4 and 5. Moreover, it fits into the whole of Scripture in which, as Francis Schaeffer notes, "there is a constant prohibition . . . against the people of God marrying those who are not of the people of God."[2] If this is the proper interpretation of Genesis 6, the point is well taken.

THE SPIRITS IN PRISON

However, there are reasons for rejecting this interpretation in favor of the angelic or supernatural view, and it is to these we now come. The first reason is linguistic. That is, so far as the biblical use of the phrase "the sons of God" is concerned, there is every reason to take it as referring to angels.

This has been denied by the other side, of course. Keil and Delitzsch maintain that the angel view is "not warranted by the usages of the language" and is "altogether unscriptural."[3] But what is the evidence? The phrase "sons of God" *(bene elohim)* is used only three other times in the Old Testament, as indicated earlier—in Job 1:6; 2:1; and 38:7. In each case it clearly means spirit beings, twice those fallen spirits who accompanied Satan in his periodic appearances before the Lord in heaven. This is so clear that the translators of the New International Version drop the longer phrase entirely and simply substitute the word angels: "One day the *angels* came to present themselves before the Lord, and Satan also came with them" (Job 1:6; cf. also 2:1). A similar form of this phrase *(bar elohim)* is used in Daniel 3:25 of the fourth figure Nebuchadnezzar saw when he looked into the burning furnace into which Daniel's three friends had been thrown. In this case it probably refers to an unfallen angel or even a theophany, but the

[1]Augustine, *The City of God*, Book 15, p. 303.

[2]Schaeffer, *Genesis in Space and Time*, p. 126.

[3]C. F. Keil and F. Delitzsch, *Biblical Commentary on the Old Testament*, Vol. 1, *The Pentateuch*, trans. by James Martin (Grand Rapids: Eerdmans, n.d.), p. 128.

actual identity of the being involved is not given. Nebuchadnezzar merely says, "The fourth looks like a son of the gods."

An objection to this view says that the phrase "sons of God" is used in the New Testament of all believers, hence men and women, as opposed to angels or demons, and that it appears in Luke 3:38 specifically of Adam. But this actually proves the point. For what is it that distinguishes Adam (but not Eve), believers in the New Testament period (but not necessarily believers in the Old Testament period) and angels from all other beings in the universe? The answer is that each is directly created by God. Adam clearly was. So were the angels. Believers are termed "sons of God" because they are born of God directly by His Spirit (cf. John 3:3–8).

The second reason why the angel view of Genesis 6 should be preferred is that this was the view of the translators of the Septuagint, who rendered "sons of God" as "angels," and of other Jewish writers prior to the time of Christ. The key book is 1 Enoch. It is available to us through an Ethiopic text of which only three manuscripts survive. Yet in spite of this paucity of manuscripts it was probably "the most important pseudepigraph [a work written in the name of someone other than the actual author] of the first two centuries B.C."—the judgment of R. H. Charles.[4]

Enoch writes, "And it came to pass when the children of men had multiplied that in those days were born unto them beautiful and comely daughters. And the angels, the children of heaven, saw and lusted after them, and said to one another: 'Come, let us choose us wives from among the children of men and beget us children.' . . . They were in all two hundred. . . . [They] took unto themselves wives, and each chose for himself one, and they began to go in unto them and to defile themselves with them, and they taught them charms and enchantments. . . . And they became pregnant, and they bare great giants, whose height was three thousand ells. . . . And there arose much godlessness, and they committed fornication, and they were led astray, and became corrupt in all their ways" (chs. 6–8). The book continues by showing the judgment of God against the fallen angels, in which they are bound up in prison in "the uttermost depths" of the earth.

First Enoch is not a biblical book, of course. Its interpretation of Genesis 6 is not inspired. It could be wrong in many places and undoubtedly is. Nevertheless, it is significant for our interpretation of the text because it was apparently known by Peter and Jude who, in their oblique references to the same subject, seem to put their stamp of approval on it, at least in this matter.

Several studies ago, when we looked at Enoch and his preaching to the ungodly of his age, we quoted Jude 14, 15: "Enoch, the seventh from Adam, prophesied about these men: 'See, the Lord is coming with thousands upon thousands of his holy ones to judge everyone, and to convict all the ungodly of all the ungodly acts they have done in the ungodly way, and of all the harsh words ungodly sinners have spoken against him.'" We did not mention it at the time because it was not pertinent then, but these words are actually from 1 Enoch. The phrase "seventh from Adam" is found in 1 Enoch 60:8. The prophecy itself, containing the fourfold repetition of the word "ungodly," is found in 1:9. Since Jude clearly has Enoch in view in verses 14 and 15, how can he not also have Enoch in view in verse 6, just eight and nine verses earlier, when he says that "the angels who

---

[4]R. H. Charles, *The Apocrypha and Pseudepigrapha of the Old Testament in English*, Vol. 2, *Pseudepigrapha* (Oxford: The Clarendon Press, 1913), p. 163.

did not keep their positions of authority but abandoned their own home" have been judged and "kept in darkness, bound with everlasting chains for judgment on the great Day"?

When we carry our inquiry to 2 Peter we find the same situation. To begin with, 2 Peter and Jude are closely related in that most of 2 Peter 2 is paralleled in Jude, and there are parallels in the other two chapters. This causes us to think that Peter, like Jude, was probably also aware of the angel interpretation. Again, Peter uses language similar to Jude's in referring to the angels who sinned. He speaks of God's judging the angels by "putting them into gloomy dungeons to be held for [final] judgment" and of God's judging the people by flood.

We are moving in the same realm in 1 Peter, where Peter writes, "Christ died for sins once for all, the righteous for the unrighteous, to bring you to God. He was put to death in the body but made alive by the Spirit, through whom also he went and preached to the spirits in prison who disobeyed long ago when God waited patiently in the days of Noah while the ark was being built" (1 Peter 3:18–20). This text adds the idea of a special ministry of Christ to these fallen angels during His descent to hell between the times of His death and resurrection. It does not mean that He offered the gospel to them; that would suggest that after death there is a "second chance" for salvation—a doctrine repudiated elsewhere (Heb. 9:27; 2 Cor. 6:2). It is rather that Christ proclaimed His victory over sin and the devil to the demons. Peter refers to this event to encourage believers in their witness before this world's magistrates.[5]

STRANGE FLESH

The third reason for preferring the supernatural interpretation of Genesis 6 is the way in which both 2 Peter and Jude connect the judgment of God on the angels with the judgment of God on Sodom and Gomorrah, particularly the way in which Jude refers to the second incident. Apart from the language of Jude the connection could simply be that of two obvious examples of great judgment. But Jude seems to say more when, after having spoken of the judgment on the angels for their sin, he goes on to say, "In a similar way, Sodom and Gomorrah and the surrounding towns gave themselves up to sexual immorality and perversion" (v. 7). In this verse the comparison is not in the matter of judgment itself. Jude does not say, "In a similar way, Sodom and Gomorrah were judged." The comparison is rather in the area of the sin that occasioned the judgment, and this, as Jude shows, was a sexual sin of a particular kind. In some modern versions this is hidden by such translations as "sexual immorality and perversion" (NIV, PHILLIPS) or "unnatural lust/s" (RSV, NEB). But the Authorized Version is closer to the Greek text when it speaks of the Sodomites as "giving themselves over to fornication and going after *strange flesh* [*sarkos heteras*]." The men of Sodom did this in desiring sexual relations with the angels who had come to visit Abram and Lot (Gen. 18, 19). The implication would be that in doing so they recapitulated the sin of the angels of Genesis 6, who "in a similar way" had desired relationships with women.[6]

---

[5]Cf. Bo Reicke, *The Epistles of James, Peter and Jude* (Garden City, N.Y.: Doubleday, 1964), pp. 109–11.

[6]Paul's discussion of the nature of our resurrection bodies in 1 Corinthians has bearing on this interpretation, for he used the word *heteros*, meaning something that is entirely different, in comparing the glory of "heavenly bodies" and the glory of "earthly bodies" (1 Cor. 15:40). One verse earlier he spoke of the differences between the flesh of men, animals, and birds. But there he used the word *allos*, meaning different but nevertheless of the same kind.

The objection to this supposed union of angel flesh and human flesh is that the angels are supposed to be sexless, since Jesus said, "At the resurrection people will neither marry nor be given in marriage; they will be like the angels in heaven" (Matt. 22:30). But this is not the equivalent of saying that the angels are sexless or that they could not have had sexual relations with women if they had chosen to do so. In heaven human beings will not marry but will nevertheless retain their identity, which includes their being either male or female. In the same way, the angels could also have sexual identities. It is significant perhaps that when the angels are referred to in Scripture it is always with the masculine pronoun "he," and they are always described as men. So, as Henry M. Morris says, "When Jesus said that the angels *in heaven* do not marry, this does not necessarily mean that those who have been cast *out of heaven* were incapable of doing so."[7]

The final point of evidence for the angel view of Genesis 6 is the reference to the giants or Nephilim in verse 4: "The Nephilim were on the earth in those days—and also afterward—when the sons of God went to the daughters of men and had children by them. They were the heroes of old, men of renown."

Since we have no information about the results of an angel/human union, except what is found here, it is impossible to argue how such a union might produce giants. It is enough to say that it is conceivable that this could happen and that this is the probable meaning of verse 4. The New International Version has hedged its translation by refusing to translate, simply transliterating the Hebrew word Nephilim. But in Numbers 13:33 the word clearly means giants (though not necessarily those produced by an intermarriage of angels and human beings). What would be more

natural than that this union would produce the "mighty men" of antiquity? Since this verse specifically refers to the "heroes of old," what would be more probable than that this is the origin of those stories of half-human-half-divine figures present in virtually all ancient mythologies? The stories of Homer and other writers would be embellished, of course, but they probably reflect memories of these ancient outstanding figures of the pre-Flood period.

BACK AT THE RANCH

A study like this involves so many technical details that it is easy to find oneself wondering about the point of it all and asking whether the outcome really matters. In one sense, the natural interpretation is quite valid and its point well taken. But I am convinced that to view Genesis 6 in this way is actually to lose something important.

Earlier we pointed out that one thing in favor of the natural interpretation is that it seems to fit in well with the general theme of chapters 4 and 5, namely, the contrast between the godly and the ungodly lines. But this is not the only contrast we have seen in the opening section of Genesis. What of the serpent? What of Satan? What of his desire to subvert the race and draw men and women after himself against God? If Genesis 6 does not refer to demonic activity, Satan apparently fades out of the picture entirely after chapter 3. But if Genesis 6 refers to a further attempt by Satan to pervert the race, then we have a reminder of his continuing hostility not only to God but to ourselves as well.

Satan was in the garden when the promise of a deliverer was given. He heard God say, "I will put enmity between you and the woman, and between your offspring and hers; he will crush your head, and you will strike his heel" (Gen. 3:15). Like Eve, he too must have

---

[7]Morris, *The Genesis Record*, p. 166.

thought that Cain, the woman's off-spring, was the deliverer and must therefore have plotted to turn him into a murderer. He succeeded! He corrupted Cain by getting him to murder Abel, thereby eliminating one of Eve's children and rendering the other unfit to be the Savior. Yet Satan failed! For, as he was soon to learn, God simply continued on His unruffled way to develop the godly line through which the deliverer would eventually be born. What was Satan to do now? At this point he conceived the plan of corrupting the entire race by the intermarriage of demons and human beings. The Savior could not be born of a demon-possessed mother. So if Satan could succeed in infecting the entire race, the deliverer could not come. In narrating this incident, Genesis 6 is saying, in effect, "Meanwhile, back at the ranch the villain is still hatching his plots."

Satan is still doing it today. Because he is a being who learns by experience, he is a much wiser and more dangerous devil today than he was in the time before the Flood. A person who knows this and who knows that we struggle "not against flesh and blood, but against the rulers, against the authorities, against the powers of this dark world and against the spiritual forces of evil in the heavenly realms" (Eph. 6:12), will fear Satan and draw near to Jesus, who has defeated him.

Again, there is this practical application. Without detracting in the slightest from the fact that the Flood was a real judgment of God on the ungodliness of men and women and consequently a warning of an even greater judgment to come, we can also see that it was at the same time an act of the marvelous grace of God. For in preserving the race intact, uncontaminated by Satan's attempts at demonic perversion, God actually provided for our salvation through keeping open the way for the Redeemer to come. If Satan had succeeded, Jesus could not have been born and the race as a whole—including Adam and Seth and Enoch and all the rest—would have been lost. But by destroying the contaminated race and saving uncontaminated Noah and his immediate uncontaminated family and by binding the demons who participated in this great sin in Hades until the final judgment, God made the salvation to be achieved by Christ both sure and possible.

43

Only Evil All the Time

(Genesis 6:5–8)

The LORD saw how great man's wickedness on the earth had become, and that every inclination of the thoughts of his heart was only evil all the time. The LORD was grieved that he had made man on the earth, and his heart was filled with pain. So the LORD said, "I will wipe mankind, whom I have created, from the face of the earth—men and animals, and creatures that move along the ground, and birds of the air—for I am grieved that I have made them." But Noah found favor in the eyes of the LORD.

For anyone who has eyes to see, there is no doubt that the Reformed doctrine of total or radical depravity is found throughout Scripture. But of the many passages that teach it, hardly any are as clear or comprehensive as Genesis 6:5: "The LORD saw how great man's wickedness on the earth had become, and that every inclination of the thoughts of his heart was only evil all the time."

This verse had a profound effect on Martin Luther and was used by him with devastating force in his battles against Erasmus of Rotterdam. Erasmus had argued on behalf of free will, maintaining that, although men and women are sinners, there is nevertheless a certain amount of good within them through which they can turn from sin and believe on Christ unto salvation. Luther maintained that of themselves people can do nothing but sin and that, if any do turn to Christ, it is only because God was already there beforehand enabling and moving them to do it. Some years after this, in writing on Genesis, Luther referred to the earlier exchange and reiterated his position: "Without the Holy Spirit and without grace man can do nothing but sin and so goes on endlessly from sin to sin." But

"this knowledge of our sin is the beginning of our salvation" in that "we completely despair of ourselves and give to God alone the glory for our righteousness."[1] This despair should be the effect of our study also. Instead of congratulating ourselves on how good we are or how good we are becoming, we should turn from ourselves and lean on Christ alone for salvation.

A Lesser View

The prevailing opinion of sin in western Christianity is much less than this: namely, that, although man is indeed a sinner, there is nevertheless some good in him—at least some residual ability to choose God. Even some who hold to radical depravity teach it in ways that encourage this low view.

I remember how human sin and our consequent need of salvation was first taught to me. I was in Sunday school at the time, out in western Pennsylvania where I grew up, and I remember the Sunday school teacher illustrating our sin by a diagram borrowed from Donald Grey Barnhouse's book of children's lessons, entitled *Teaching the Word of Truth*. The diagram was built around the idea of a yardstick or ruler called "The

---

[1]Luther, *Luther's Works*, Vol. 2, pp. 40, 41.

Divine Measure," which occupied the left side of the figure. It represented God's standard of holiness: perfection. At the top of the yardstick a line was drawn across the paper bearing the caption, "Be ye, therefore, perfect" (Matt. 5:48 KJV). Has anybody ever lived up to this standard? Yes, the Lord Jesus Christ lived up to it. He was perfect in all ways. Therefore, a line representing Him was drawn beside the yardstick reaching from the bottom of the diagram entirely to the top. Everybody else has fallen short. This was shown by a series of lines of varying lengths, representing what were called "98% men," "90% men," "80% men," and "70% men." These had done well by human standards, but they had fallen short of God's standard. Two verses were used to characterize these people: Romans 3:23 ("All have sinned, and come short of the glory of God" KJV) and Romans 4:2 ("He hath something of which to glory; but not before God" KJV). The point was that although people appear to be quite good to us and may, in fact, actually be good by human standards, they nevertheless fail to please God and need a Savior.

I have no doubt that so far as it went this diagram was teaching something absolutely true. It was teaching that none of us is perfect and that we therefore need the grace of God in salvation. Because of this truth and the clarity with which it was presented, this diagram has been instrumental in leading many to an initial sense of their need, as a result of which they afterward came to faith in Christ. I have used it effectively myself. Nevertheless, the diagram has one great weakness. In putting lines representing 98%, 90%, 80% and 70% people in the same place and parallel to the line representing Jesus Christ, it inevitably suggests that human goodness is essentially the same as the goodness of Jesus and that all such people really need is that little bit of additional goodness

which, when added to their own, will make up 100%.

This is what is repudiated by Genesis 6:5. No doubt, from a human point of view, there is a "good" in man that allows us to regard some people as better than others. But this goodness must not be confused with God's goodness or this human standard compared with God's own. To put it graphically, men and women do not even appear on God's diagram. Or if they do, lines should be drawn, not upward toward perfection, but downward in varying degrees of opposition to God and His holiness. God does not say merely that people have failed to meet His standard. He says that the thoughts of their hearts are "evil all the time."

HOW BAD CAN IT BE?

Genesis 6:5 is meant to contrast with Genesis 1. When we are told in Genesis 6:5 that *"the LORD saw how great man's wickedness on the earth had become,"* we are to think of the many earlier statements that *"God saw"* what He had made, that it was good" (Gen. 1:4, 10, 12, 18, 21, 25, 31). How could the world not be good if God made it? Yet now, just five chapters later, the God who originally looked out on a good world is "grieved" that He made man and is determined to wipe all living creatures— "men and animals, and creatures that move along the ground, and birds of the air"—from the earth.

What is it that has changed God's outlook? It is sin! Moreover, it is sin viewed, not as mere imperfection, but as something thoroughly hostile to God's purposes and thoroughly infecting, like poison in drinking water.

The first thing these verses tell us is that sin is an *internal* matter. That is, it is not merely a question of such outward acts as adultery, stealing, murder, and other crimes, but of the thoughts of the heart. The verse says, "The LORD saw . . . that every inclination of *the thoughts of* [man's] *heart* was only evil all the time." It takes God to say this, of course, for you and I do not look on the thoughts of the heart. We look on the outward appearance ("The LORD does not look at the things man looks at. Man looks at the outward appearance, but the LORD looks at the heart," 1 Sam. 16:7). We see a man commit murder and say, "Well, that man is a murderer." Our observation of the outward act leads to a judgment of what the man is like inside. We are unable to do it in any other way. But God looks on the heart and tells us that the man is a murderer even though for one reason or another he may not actually have killed another person. We say, "He is a murderer because he murders." God says, "He murders because he is a murderer."

Our Lord said this too. In His day the religious leaders thought that a person became contaminated by eating "unclean" foods. Jesus taught that a person was contaminated not by what goes into him but by the state of his heart from which all truly evil things emerge: "Whatever enters the mouth goes into the stomach and then out of the body. But the things that come out of the mouth come from the heart, and these make a man 'unclean.' For out of the heart come evil thoughts, murder, adultery, sexual immorality, theft, false testimony, slander. These are what make a man 'unclean'" (Matt. 15:17–20).

Second, Genesis 6:5 tells us that sin is *pervasive*. That is, because it comes out of the heart, which controls what we think and do, sin necessarily affects every part of our being so that nothing we think, do, plan, or are is unaffected by it. This is the main thrust of the verse. It says that "*every* inclination of the thoughts of [man's] heart was *only* evil all the time."

We need to explain this carefully, of course. For when we say that men and women are "totally depraved" (a good theological term for "only evil all the

time"), we do not mean to say that they never do anything that we would call good or that they never have aspirations in the direction of real good. We mean rather that even their best is always spoiled by their essentially sinful nature. In one of his writings, Donald Grey Barnhouse imagines a thirsty person, who is in a doctor's office, picking up a glass and going over to a cooler containing sterilized water and filling the glass in order to take a drink. The glass begins to foam a bit, so he asks the doctor if something has been in the glass. "Yes," the doctor says, "diphtheria solution!" Our thirsty patient puts the glass back down in a hurry. Why? Wasn't the water pure? Yes, the water was pure, but the glass was dirty. Everything that came in contact with the glass was contaminated.

It is the same with the sin that comes out of the human heart. It contaminates everything.

This is why God, who sees things as they really are, describes the state of mankind severely. Jeremiah 17:9 says, "The heart is deceitful above all things and beyond cure. Who can understand it?" Psalm 5:9 declares, "Their heart is filled with destruction. Their throat is an open grave; with their tongue they speak deceit." Psalm 14:3 adds, "All have turned aside, they have together become corrupt." Paul, who quotes these and other Old Testament verses in Romans 3:10–18, declares comprehensively:

> There is no one righteous, not even one;
>   there is no one who understands,
>   no one who seeks God.
> All have turned away,
>   they have together become worthless;
> there is no one who does good,
>   not even one.
> Their throats are open graves;
>   their tongues practice deceit.
> The poison of vipers is on their lips.
>   Their mouths are full of cursing and
>   bitterness.

Their feet are swift to shed blood;
  ruin and misery mark their ways,
and the way of peace they do not know.
  There is no fear of God before their
    eyes.

But what of Jesus—the gentle, loving, compassionate "friend of sinners"? What did He think? I am reminded here of a section of an address by Roger R. Nicole for one of the Philadelphia Conferences on Reformed Theology. It was called "The Doctrines of Grace in Jesus' Teaching." It especially stressed Jesus' view of human evil. Nicole wrote, "Our Lord Jesus Christ, with all the concern, compassion and love which he showed to mankind made some very vivid portrayals of man's condition. He did not mince words about the gravity of human sin. He talked of man as salt that has lost its savor (Matt. 5:13). He talked of man as a corrupt tree which is bound to produce corrupt fruit (Matt. 7:17). He talked of man as being evil: 'You, being evil, know how to give good things to your children' (Luke 11:13). On one occasion he lifted up his eyes toward heaven and talked about an 'evil and adulterous generation' (Matt. 12:39), or again, 'this wicked generation' (v. 45). In a great passage dealing with what constitutes true impurity and true purity he made the startling statement that out of the heart proceed murders, adulteries, evil thoughts, and things of that kind (Mark 7:21–23). He spoke about Moses having to give special permissive commandments to men because of the hardness of their hearts (Matt. 19:8). When the rich young ruler approached him, saying, 'Good Master,' Jesus said, 'There is none good but God' (Mark 10:18). . . .

"Jesus compared men, even the leaders of his country, to wicked servants in a vineyard (Matt. 21:33–41). He exploded in condemnation of the scribes and the Pharisees, who were considered to be among the best men, men who were in the upper ranges of virtue and in the upper classes of society (Matt. 23:2–39).

"The Lord Jesus made a fundamental statement about man's depravity in John 3:6: 'That which is born of the flesh is flesh.' He saw in man an unwillingness to respond to grace—'You will not come' (John 5:40), 'You have not the love of God' (v. 42), 'You receive me not' (v. 43), 'You believe not' (v. 47). Such sayings occur repeatedly in the Gospel of John. 'The world's works are evil' (John 7:7); 'None of you keeps the law' (v. 19). 'You shall die in your sins,' he says (John 8:21). 'You are from beneath' (v. 23); 'Your father is the devil, who is a murderer and a liar' (vv. 38, 44); 'You are not of God' (v. 47); 'You are not of my sheep' (John 10:26); 'He that hates me hates my Father' (John 15:23–25). This is the way in which our Lord spoke to the leaders of the Jews. He brought to the fore their utter inability to please God.

"Following another line of approach he showed also the blindness of man, that is, his utter inability to know God and understand him. Here again we have a whole series of passages showing that no man knows the Father but him to whom the Son has revealed him (Matt. 11:27). He compared men to the blind leading the blind (Matt. 15:14). He mentioned that Jerusalem itself did not know or understand the purpose of God and, as a result, disregarded the things that concern salvation (Luke 19:42). The Gospel of John records him as saying that he that believed not was condemned already because he had not believed on the Son of God (John 3:18). 'This is the condemnation, that . . . men loved darkness rather than light, because their deeds were evil' (v. 19). He said that only the one who has been reached by grace can walk not in darkness but have the light of life (John 8:12). The Lord Jesus emphasized that it is essential for man to be saved by a mighty act of God if he is to be rescued from his condition of misery (John 3:3, 5, 7–16). Even in the Lord's Prayer the Lord teaches us to say, 'Forgive us our debts' (Matt. 6:12). And this is a prayer that we need to repeat again and again. He said, 'The sick are the people who need a physician' (Matt. 9:12). We are those sick people who need a physician to help us and redeem us. He said that we are people who are burdened and heavy-laden (Matt. 11:28). . . .

"The people who were most readily received by the Lord were those who had this sense of need and who therefore did not come to him with a sense of the sufficiency of their performance. The people he received were those who came broken-hearted and bruised with the sense of their inadequacy."[2]

After having reviewed such texts as these, one might think that everything that could possibly be said about man's sin has been said. But Genesis 6:5 adds still another, very important point. It is not only that sin is internal as well as external, nor that it is pervasive in that it affects everything we can possibly think or do. It is also *continuous,* for in God's judgment we all do "only evil *all the time.*" From our perspective a statement like that is almost beyond belief. We would not make it of other people, even the worst of people. We certainly would not make it of ourselves. But this is God speaking—God who sees all things and sees the heart—and God is truthful. One commentator writes of this portrait, "Had it been drawn by the pen of a prejudiced erring mortal it might have been supposed to exceed the truth. But this is not the testimony of man, but of God who sees things precisely as they are, and his infallible declaration is that the thoughts of man [are] evil without exception, without mixture, and without intermission."[3]

Noah Found Favor

Could a blacker picture of the utter depravity of man in his rebellion against God ever be painted? It is hard to think so. Yet just at this point, when the black thunderclouds of God's wrath against human sin are at their most threatening, a small crack appears. Grace shines through, and the promise of a new day dawns.

The older, Authorized Version says, "Noah found grace." But whether the word "grace" or the word "favor" is used to translate the Hebrew term *hēn,* the significant thing is that this is the first appearance of the idea in the Bible. It is true, of course, that Adam and Eve also found grace when they sinned; justice alone would have sent them into outer darkness forever. Seth and Enoch and all the others found grace. But here for the first time grace is explicitly mentioned. Since this is said of a time when the evil of a degenerate race was at its zenith, it indicates that so long as life lasts, regardless of the extent of the evil, there is always opportunity to find God's grace where alone it can be found, namely, in the work of Jesus Christ in dying for His people's salvation. Noah may not have known many details about that future work of Christ. But he looked forward to the deliverer and ordered his life accordingly.

Notice that Noah did not earn grace. Noah found grace. He was willing to accept God's judgment on his sinful and rebellious nature and place his hope in the Savior. It is the same today. We have no claim on God. We have not earned anything but His just wrath and our eventual destruction. But we can find God's grace in Christ.

---

[2]Roger R. Nicole, "The Doctrines of Grace in Jesus' Teaching" in *Our Sovereign God: Addresses Presented to the Philadelphia Conference on Reformed Theology 1974–1976,* James M. Boice, editor (Grand Rapids: Baker, 1977), pp. 38–41.

[3]George Bush, *Notes on Genesis* (Minneapolis: James Family Christian Publishers, 1979), Vol. 1, p. 120. Original edition 1860.

44

Noah

(Genesis 6:9, 10)

This is the account of Noah. Noah was a righteous man, blameless among the people of his time, and he walked with God. Noah had three sons: Shem, Ham and Japheth.

When Charles Haddon Spurgeon first began to preach in London in 1855, he was ridiculed perhaps more than any man in his generation. They said he was preaching an outmoded gospel, foolishness. Although many came to hear him, the sophisticated commentators of the day argued that his popularity with the rabble would be short-lived. "Up like a rocket, down like a stick," was their judgment. But Spurgeon hung on, saying that although he stood alone, he stood on the Word of God that cannot be shaken. He said that he was willing to be called a dog now, knowing that in fifty years he would be vindicated, while those who had reputations now would be discredited. Today we remember Spurgeon but cannot think even of the names of his detractors.

It is always that way for God's people. Athanasius stood alone. Luther stood alone. Knox stood alone. In their day they were ridiculed, threatened, sometimes even persecuted for their beliefs. But they triumphed because they believed God, whose word is never shaken.

A Solitary Saint

This was the case with Noah, the builder of the ark, whose story is recorded in the next major section of Genesis. We have already seen that Genesis is divided into sections marked off by the recurring phrase "This is the account (or generation) of. . . ." This phrase is found in eleven places (2:4; 5:1; 6:9; 10:1; 11:10, 27; 25:12, 19; 36:1, 9; 37:2); it occurs here at the beginning of Noah's story: "This is the account of Noah" (Gen. 6:9). His story runs through the sixth, seventh, eighth and ninth chapters of Genesis, thereby becoming the longest story of any individual in the book thus far. It is a story of faithful endurance in the midst of great wickedness, the story of a solitary saint.

Noah was the last descendant in the godly line of Adam through Seth. By the time of the Flood every one of these ancestors had died, but, like the righteous in all ages, their works lived after them—in this case in Noah, who had learned his lessons well. When Noah was born, six of these ancestors were still living: Enosh, Kenan, Mahalalel, Jared, Methuselah, and Noah's father, Lamech. We do not know a great deal about these men, but we can be sure that Enoch's preaching of a coming judgment would still be remembered and that the meaning and significance of Methuselah's name ("when he is gone it will come") would be in Noah's thoughts constantly. No doubt he would have been taught the ways of the Lord by Lamech, his father. This Lamech was a godly man (cf. the Lamech of chap. 4), for when he thought of the hardness of his labor and the pain of his toil, he recognized that this was the result of God's curse on the ground as partial judgment of the sin of Adam. Since

Noah means "comfort" or "rest," it may be that Lamech named his son "rest" in anticipation of that final rest from labor promised to the people of God.

Noah grew up in an environment of faith and by the grace of God became what he is said to have become. We are told, "Noah was a righteous man, blameless among the poeple of his time, and he walked with God" (Gen. 6:9). It was because of this that he was able to stand for God and with God against the ungodliness of the pre-Flood generation.

ALL OF GRACE

How did Noah get to be blameless before God? To answer this question we must go back to the preceding verse, verse 8, where we are told, "But Noah found favor (or grace) in the eyes of the LORD." Some people read these verses as if Noah found favor with God because he was righteous and lived a blameless life. But that is not the case and, in fact, to read it that way is to get it backward. Verse 9 does not come before verse 8, nor is there even a connecting or casual participle between them, as if to say, "Noah found grace *because* he was righteous." Actually, Noah's righteousness was the product of his having found favor and is therefore the proof of that favor, not its ground.

This is a great biblical principle, namely, that the grace of God always comes before anything. We imagine in our unsantified state that God loves us for what we are intrinsically or for what we have done or can become. But God does not love us because of that, nor is He gracious to us because of that. On the contrary, He loves us solely because He loves us. He is gracious to us only because He is.

Later on in the Bible we find this stated in classical language. God is speaking through Moses and is telling the people the cause of His loving them. He says, "The LORD did not set his affec-

tion on you and choose you because you were more numerous than other peoples, for you were the fewest of all peoples. But it was because the LORD loved you and kept the oath he swore to your forefathers" (Deut. 7:7, 8). Part of this statement makes immediate sense: the denial. That is clear enough. But at first glance the remainder of the sentence does not make sense. God did not love Israel because they were numerous, but, the sentence goes on to say, he loved them *because he loved them*. What kind of logic is that: I love you because I love you? Well, it may not be the logic of Aristotle, but it is the logic of grace. Grace is grace. If grace were based on anything in us, it would not be grace. In fact, it would not operate even as something less than grace, for there is nothing in us that can possibly draw forth God's favor. Yet grace does go forth to ourselves and others, who are undeserving.

But it is even more wonderful than that. For it is not merely that we are undeserving. We *are* deserving, but of precisely the opposite. We are sinners deserving God's wrath. Yet, as Paul says, "God demonstrates his own love for us in this: While we were still sinners, Christ died for us" (Rom. 5:8). Noah found this grace, and it changed his life accordingly.

WALKING WITH GOD

There are three areas in which God's grace is said to have changed the life of Noah. First, he is said to have become "a righteous (or just) man." Noah is the first man in the Bible of whom this is said, though he is not the first person who was so. It is important that this is said here in connection with the first mention in the Bible of God's grace, for it is the first fruit or expression of grace. Grace leads to righteousness. The Lord Jesus Christ said the same thing when He said to those who were professing to love Him, "If you love me, you will obey what I command" (John 14:15). So did the apostle John when he wrote to those of his day, "We know that we have come to know him if we obey his commands" (1 John 2:3).

We must not hurry over this truth. It applies not merely to Noah but to ourselves as well, and it is meant to check presumption in our lives. We have a tendency—we who know theology—to dismiss the force of a word such as this by applying it to our standing before God, rather than our actions. Since the word can rightly be translated "just" and since we know that we are justified through the work of Jesus Christ received by faith, we tend to think of this as justification and therefore dismiss its force. "After all," we say, "wasn't Noah a justified man? And aren't we also justified by the work of Christ? That's all there is to it." But that is not all there is to it. Noah was certainly justified by God through his faith in the coming Redeemer, who was the Lord Jesus Christ. We are justified in the same way. But that is not what these verses are talking about. What they are talking about is something we desperately need to know: namely, that if we are justified, we will begin to act justly. If we do not act justly, then our claim to be justified is mere presumption, and our faith, such as it is, is merely that dead faith of which James speaks, a faith that will justify no one (James 2:14–26). Do we act justly? Do we show the righteousness of God in areas of personal integrity, business, family life, and general morality?

We may notice here that Noah is not merely said to have been "a righteous man." He is also said to have been "a preacher of righteousness" (2 Peter 2:5). That is, he preached righteousness exactly as his great-grandfather Enoch had done before him. The reason he could do this is that he himself was righteous. We may draw the conclusion that the reason why we do not have more

preaching of righteousness in our day is that those who profess the name of Christ are often not living righteous lives.

What a need there is for us to live righteously and commend righteousness to our age! The world itself is crying out for it. Not long ago I read an article in the University of Pennsylvania *Gazette* about a professor in the sociology department of that school named Albert Hobbs. According to the article, he had been passed over for promotion many times because he had been unwilling to excuse lack of human morality by reference to genes or environment and has instead been calling for a return to the "old morality" of temperance, economy, individual responsibility, and hard work. Guy Tugwell, one of Franklin Delano Roosevelt's advisors, once said, "Forget man's character." Hobbs replied, "I say you can't forget individual character. . . . Born in man are potentials for evil as well as potentials for good, [and] until people learn to recognize the difference between right and wrong, good and bad, you'll have trouble."[1] What an opportunity for Christians to point to the morality of the Bible and to the Lord Jesus Christ, by whose power alone such morality is attainable.

The second area in which God's grace is said to have changed the life of Moses is in his relationship to others of his time. In this he is said to have been "blameless." This word is closely related to "righteousness," the idea that has gone before. Together they can cover, first, the outward performance of that which is right and, second, the inner state of uprightness out of which the righteous deeds come. In this context, however, the second word is probably related to how the people of Noah's time perceived him. The idea seems to be not only that Noah acted uprightly before the Lord but also that he acted in such a

---

[1]Christopher Davis, "The Old Morality" in the *Pennsylvania Gazette*, March, 1980, pp. 28–32.

way as to appear blameless in the eyes of the watching world.

Do we do that? Or do we compromise our profession by speech and conduct that cause the world to conclude that we are no different from it?

Finally, Noah is said to have "walked with God." This is the third area in which the grace of God affected his life, and it is closely related to the other two. We remember that in the case of Enoch, of whom it is also said that "he walked with God," three ideas went together: 1) his awareness of the coming judgment of God, 2) the ungodliness of his generation, which was the cause of the Flood, and 3) his walk with God. No doubt, each affected the others. The more Noah thought of the judgment of God, the more he was aware of the ungodliness of those around him. The more he was aware of their ungodliness, the closer he walked with God. The closer he walked with God, the more aware he was of judgment. Again, the closer he walked with God, the more aware he was of evil and unrighteousness. This is what happened to Noah. He walked with God, and this led him to live blamelessly and preach righteousness.

Maclaren said, "This communion is the foundation of all righteous conduct. Because Noah walked with God, he was 'just' and 'perfect.' If we live habitually in the holy of holies, our faces will shine when we come forth. If we desire to be good and pure, we must dwell with God, and his Spirit will pass into our hearts, and we shall bear the fragrance of his presence wherever we go. . . . We begin communion with him, indeed, not by holiness, but by faith. But it is not kept up without the cultivation of purity."[2]

I like that word "cultivation," because cultivation means work. It takes work to

be godly. Noah's name means "rest." He entered into rest in due course, as all who know God do. But he had years of hard labor, both physical and spiritual, before he did.

THE NAME OF NOAH

The final thing I want to note in this introductory study of Noah is not related to the text, but it is an interesting way of making a point that is biblical. It has to do with the appearance of Noah's name or variations of his name in the various languages of the world. We are assuming as we make this point that the Flood of Noah's day was a worldwide Flood, as the Bible declares it to be, and that knowledge of Noah therefore spread around the world with the post-Flood migrations. Indeed, we are going to see in time how flood stories are part of nearly every culture on the globe. What is of interest here, however, is the name of Noah itself. I draw at this point on a study of "Noah and Human Etymology" by the Swedish businessman Bengt Sage, who now lives in Australia.

To begin with, the name Noah passed into the ancient Sanskrit language where it became *Manu*. *Manu* was the Flood hero in the traditions of India, so it is highly probable that he and Noah are the same individual. *Ma* is the ancient word for "water." So *Manu* could mean "Noah of the waters." In the Hebrew Old Testament the word for "water" is *mayim*, the syllable *yim* being the standard Hebrew plural ending. The *ma* prefix is also the original form of the Spanish word *mar* and the French word *mer*, both of which mean "sea." The Latin word is *mare* from which we get such English words as "maritime," "mariner," and "marine."

In Sanskrit, *Manu* eventually came to mean "man" or "mankind." This is not surprising since, from the perspective of

---

[2]Alexander Maclaren, *Expositions of Holy Scripture*, Vol. 1 (Grand Rapids: Eerdmans, 1959), Part 1, p. 51.

ancient Indian civilization, Noah (or *Manu*) was the father of all the (post-Flood) peoples. *Manu* is related to the Germanic *Mannus*, the mythical founder of the West-Germanic peoples. *Mannus* is also the name of the Lithuanian Noah. The English word "man" is related to the Sanskrit *manu* through its German roots. Gothic, the oldest known Germanic language, used the form *manna* for "man."

In Egyptian mythology *Nu* was the god of waters, who sent an inundation to destroy mankind. *Nu* and his consort *Nut* were deities of the firmament and the rain.

In Europe the prefix *ma* seems often to have taken the form *da*, which is also an old word for "water" or "river." This led to the name "Don" in England, and to the European "Danube." The first Greeks, living in the coastal regions of Europe, were called *Danaoi* or "water people." Variants of the name Danube are: Donau, Dunaj, Duna, Dunau, and Dunay. The root of these names is *danu*, which means "flowing." The Latvian river Dvina was formerly called Duna, so it is also from the ancient root *danu*. The similarity of *danu* to *manu* is evident.

In Japan the word *maru* is used of large ships, the first really large Japanese ship (late sixteenth century) being called the *Nippon Maru*. In Japanese *maru* also means a rounded enclosure used for defense, therefore also a thing of good fortune. Noah's great ship was both.

On the American continent *manu* seems to have been modified in several ways. In the Sioux language it took the form of *minne*, meaning "water." Thus, we have the proper names Minneapolis, meaning "city of water," and Minnesota, meaning "sky blue water." The word is probably also preserved in the name of the Canadian province Mani-

toba (though this name may come from another source, meaning "the place of the Great Spirit"). In South America the name Managua, capital of Nicaragua, comes from a word meaning "surrounded by ponds."

Sage, from whom I am drawing this information, concludes, "Thus, Noah and the waters of the great Flood are not only recalled in the ancient traditions of all nations, but their names have also become incorporated in many and varied ways into the very languages of his descendants. The trails are tenuous and often almost obliterated, so that some of the inferred connections are speculative and possibly mistaken, but the correlations are too numerous to be only coincidental, thus adding yet one more evidence for the historicity of the worldwide flood."[3]

The point I draw is not that of Sage, though his is well taken. I note the extent to which this solitary righteous man of the pre-Flood generation, Noah, is remembered throughout the world when virtually all his unrighteous contemporaries are forgotten. A "dog now," but vindicated later! Forgotten now, but remembered later! That is what Noah was. It is what every true believer should be willing to be.

There is this point too. Even though others should forget and never remember, we can know that God remembers and that He has caused "a scroll of remembrance," containing the names of those who fear and honor the Lord, to be recorded (Mal. 3:16). Was Noah forgotten by God? Not at all! Jesus remembered Noah. He spoke of Noah's days, comparing them to the days just before His second coming: "As it was in the days of Noah, so it will be at the coming of the Son of Man. For in the days before the flood, people were eating and drinking, marrying and giving in mar-

---

[3]Bengt Sage, "Noah and Human Etymology" in *Impact*, May, 1980, a publication of the Institute for Creation Research.

riage, up to the day Noah entered the ark; and they knew nothing about what would happen until the flood came and took them all away. That is how it will be at the coming of the Son of Man" (Matt. 24:37–39; cf. Luke 17:26, 27). In the Book of Hebrews Noah's faith is commended: "By faith Noah, when warned about things not yet seen, in holy fear built an ark to save his family. By his faith he condemned the world and became heir of the righteousness that comes by faith" (Heb. 11:7).

Let us not fear to be forgotten by men and women if that is the price of being remembered by God. Even more, let us not fear to walk with God and live lives that are blameless before Him.

45

Noah's Ark

(Genesis 6:11–22)

Now the earth was corrupt in God's sight and was full of violence. God saw how corrupt the earth had become, for all the people on earth had corrupted their ways. So God said to Noah, "I am going to put an end to all people, for the earth is filled with violence because of them. I am surely going to destroy both them and the earth. So make yourself an ark of cypress wood; make rooms in it and coat it with pitch inside and out. This is how you are to build it: The ark is to be 450 feet long, 75 feet wide and 45 feet high. Make a roof for it and finish the ark to within 18 inches of the top. Put a door in the side of the ark and make lower, middle and upper decks. I am going to bring floodwaters on the earth to destroy all life under the heavens, every creature that has the breath of life in it. Everything on earth will perish. But I will establish my covenant with you, and you will enter the ark—you and your sons and your wife and your sons' wives with you. You are to bring into the ark two of all living creatures, male and female, to keep them alive with you. Two of every kind of bird, of every kind of animal and of every kind of creature that moves along the ground will come to you to be kept alive. You are to take every kind of food that is to be eaten and store it away as food for you and for them."
Noah did everything just as God commanded him.

In 1935 a story appeared in *Life Digest,* an Australian publication, in which a Russian aviator named Vladimir Roskovitsky claimed to have discovered Noah's ark. He had been stationed in a temporary military outpost in southern Russia just across the border from Turkey near Mount Ararat and had been told to test one of the Russian air force planes. In the course of these tests he and his co-pilot flew over Ararat and discovered on the edge of a retreating glacier what he later described as a boat comparable in size to many modern battleships. He wrote that "it was grounded on the shore of [a] lake with about one-fourth of the rear end still running out into the water, and its extreme rear was three-fourths under water. It had been partly dismantled on one side near the front, and on the other side there was a great door nearly twenty feet square, but with the door gone." Roskovitsky reported his find to his commanding officer, and an expedition was dispatched to Ararat which, according to the story, subsequently found the ark and photographed it. Accounts were forwarded to the Czar. Unfortunately, a short time after receiving this report the government of the Czar was overthrown and the photographs and reports perished.[1]

Is this story of the discovery of Noah's

[1]This account appears in many books dealing with the ark of Noah. See, for instance, Violet M. Cummings, *Noah's Ark: Fable or Fact?* (Old Tappan, N.J.: Fleming H. Revell, 1973), pp. 32–39; Tim F. LaHaye and John D. Morris, *The Ark on Ararat* (Nashville and New York: Thomas Nelson, 1976), pp. 73–85; and Alfred M. Rehwinkel, *The Flood in the Light of the Bible, Geology and Archeology* (St. Louis: Concordia, 1951), pp. 77–83.

ark true? It is hard to say. But one thing is certain: It was the launching point for many subsequent investigations and expeditions to Mount Ararat as a result of which much information (though no conclusive proof) came to light.

An Impossible Story?

Many would dismiss this and any other story, because they are convinced that the tale of Noah and his ark is mere mythology and, in fact, actually impossible. "Do you know how many species of animals there are?" they would say. "Millions and millions! There is no way these or even a small portion of them could be crammed into one ark, regardless of how big it is, and then be fed and cared for up to one year while the flood waters came and receded." But is it impossible? It is not, as a little investigation will show. Besides, regardless of how we might or might not imagine the details to work out, Christians for the most part are committed to the truthfulness of the story.

Let us look at the data. There is some disagreement among scholars on the exact value of a cubit, the unit of measurement by which the dimensions of the ark are given. The Babylonians had a cubit about twenty inches long. The Egyptians and the later Hebrews each had two different cubits, one of which was slightly longer and one of which was slightly shorter than the Babylonian measure. In all, the values run from about seventeen-and-a-half inches to twenty-four inches. Most Bible scholars believe the biblical cubit to have been about eighteen inches, and it is on the basis of this assumption that the translators of the New International Version give the dimensions of the ark as "450 feet long, 75 feet wide and 45 feet high" (v. 15).

Several things can be said about these measurements to begin with. First, if this was the size of the ark, it was of great proportions, greater than the size of any ancient sailing vessel. In fact, it was not until 1858 that a vessel of greater length was constructed: the *Great Eastern* (692 by 83 by 30 feet). Second, it can be shown through simulated tests in water that a box-like structure of the ark's dimensions is exceedingly stable, indeed, almost impossible to capsize. Whatever our judgment about the carrying capacity of the ark, therefore, there is an obvious presumption in favor of the design having come from God. For how would Noah or anyone else at that time know how to construct such a large seaworthy craft except by revelation?

What about the "millions and millions" of species? There is some difficulty in determining what is meant by the biblical word "kind," as in "two of every kind of bird, of every kind of animal and of every kind of creature that moves along the ground" (v. 20). If this corresponds to our modern classification of "family," the maximum number of families represented on the ark would be about seven hundred. But suppose the word actually corresponds to our word "species"? In that case, the number would be much higher—but not beyond the ark's capacity.

Tim LaHaye and John Morris in their book, *The Ark on Ararat*, cite the following table of the number of animal species put forward by Ernst Mayr, one of America's leading taxonomists.

Mammals	3,700
Birds	8,600
Reptiles	6,300
Amphibians	2,500
Fishes	20,600
Tunicates, etc.	1,325
Echinoderms	6,000
Arthropods	838,000
Mollusks	107,250
Worms, etc.	39,450
Coelenterates, etc.	5,380
Sponges	4,800
Protozoans	28,400
Total Animals	1,072,300

That is a large number, of course, but

not all these species had to be on the ark. Obviously the fish did not. Nor did the tunicates, echinoderms, mollusks, coelenterates, sponges, protozoans, most arthropods, and most worms. Simple subtraction brings the previously large number down to approximately 35,000 or 70,000 individual animals, one male and one female. Moreover, although we usually think of large animals when we think of the ark (elephants, hippopotamuses, giraffes), most land animals are in fact quite small. The average size is less than that of a sheep. Since 240 sheep fit comfortably in an average size two-deck railroad car and since the volume of the ark would have been equal to 569 such cars, calculations show that the animals to be saved would have fit into approximately 50 percent of the ark's carrying capacity, leaving room for people, food, water, and whatever other provisions may have been necessary.

As LaHaye and Morris note, "Such simple calculations are certainly not beyond the abilities of the scoffers. What does seem to be beyond them is the willingness to try to see if the biblical story is feasible."[2]

Is the Ark on Ararat?

In noting the shortcomings of the scoffers, evangelicals should not be blind to their own, however. One obvious blind spot is the hope of some to find evidence of the ark on Mount Ararat, the traditional place where it is said to have rested following the receding of the Flood. It is possible that it *may* be there—preserved for thousands of years by the eternal snows and visible only at times of unseasonably warm weather, as was the case when the Russian expedition is said to have discovered it. Roskovitsky may have seen it from the air.

But on the other hand (as LaHaye, Morris and others recognize), the Russian's story may be a complete or nearly complete fabrication. Our confidence in the story of Noah is to rest, not on this or any other discovery, but on the fact that the account of the Flood is related to us in the Word of God.

There are some interesting indications that the ark may be on Ararat, however—in addition to the Russian aviator's story. It is hard to know what credence to give them, but in a study such as this it is worth listing what the chief lines of evidence are.

1. First on the list is that Mount Ararat in Turkey has been the traditional site of the ark's resting place throughout known history (cf. Gen. 8:4) and that significant numbers of ancient travelers and writers claimed to have seen it. Berosus, the historian of Babylon, wrote in approximately 275 B.C., "But of this ship that grounded in Armenia some part still remains in the mountains of the Gordyaeans in Armenia, and some get pitch from the ship by scraping it off and use it for amulets." Josephus, the Jewish historian, wrote of the ark a generation after the time of Christ. He said that the Armenians show relics of the ark "to this day." He also claimed that the ark is mentioned by all who have written histories of the barbarians: Hieronymus the Egyptian, Nicolas of Damascus, and Berosus. In A.D. 180, Theophilus of Antioch wrote that "the remains [of the ark] are to this day to be seen in the Arabian mountains." Scores of church figures wrote along similar lines, including the great John Chrysostom.[3]

2. The second line of evidence is the monastery of Saint Jacob, several miles up the Ahora gorge on the higher reaches of Ararat. It was destroyed by an earthquake in 1840, but its existence

---

[2]*The Ark on Ararat,* p. 237. The discussion of the total number of species necessary to have been taken on board the ark is on pages 246, 247.

[3]The best collection of these historical references is in LaHaye and Morris, pp. 14–27.

goes back to the early centuries of the Christian era, when it was reportedly established to mark the site of and preserve relics from the ark. Some evidence of an even earlier occupation of the site remains in the form of ancient inscriptions and eight crosses carved into the stone. The crosses, whether from the earliest times or later, may stand for the eight who survived the Flood: Noah and his three sons, his wife and his sons' wives (Gen. 6:18).

3. An elderly Armenian named Haji Yearam, who later came to America, told of visiting the ark on Ararat in 1856 in the company of his father (who had himself gone there often as a boy) and three atheistic scientists. Their goal in visiting Ararat was to disprove the ark's existence. According to Yearam, the scientists were so enraged at discovering the ark that they tried to destroy it at first. But since they could not (it was too big and had petrified), they swore to keep silent about their find. This was the story Yearam told. The man to whom he told it adds the following corroborative detail. "One evening (I am pretty sure it was in 1918) I sat reading the daily paper in our apartment in Brockton. Suddenly I saw in very small print a short story of a dying man's confession. It was a news item one column wide and, as I remembered it, not more than two inches deep. It stated that an elderly scientist on his death bed in London was afraid to die before making a terrible confession. It gave briefly the very date and facts that Haji Yearam had related to us in his story." The Englishman was apparently one of the unbelieving scientists, and the story of his confession, if true, corroborates that of the Armenian.

4. In 1876 a distinguished British statesman and author, Viscount James Bryce, climbed Ararat and reported finding a four-foot-long piece of hand-tooled timber at a height of over 13,000 feet.

5. In 1883, after an earthquake that caused hugh quantities of rock and ice to be dislodged from the mountain, the British paper *Prophetic Messenger* carried the following story: "We have received from our correspondent in Trebizond news of the return of the commissioners appointed by the Turkish government to inquire into the reported destruction of Mosul, Ashak and Bayazid by avalanches. . . . The expedition was fortunate in making a discovery that cannot fail to be of interest to the whole civilized world, for among the vastness of one of the glens of Mount Ararat, they came upon a gigantic structure of very dark wood, imbedded at the foot of one of the glaciers, with one end protruding, and which they believe to be none other than the old ark in which Noah and his family navigated the waters of the deluge. The place where the discovery is made is about five days' journey from Trebizond, in the Department of Van, in Armenia, about four leagues from the Persian frontier." This report, only a portion of which is cited here, was picked up and commented upon by the *New York Herald* and *World*, the Chicago *Tribune* and *The Watchtower*.

6. Excluding those who lived on the mountain or authorities of the Turkish government, the first actual explorer to have visited Ararat was a youthful archdeacon of the church of Babylon named Prince Nouri. He claimed to have discovered the ark in 1887. He came from Malabar in South India and had a colorful career even apart from this discovery. He journeyed to Ararat, made at least three climbs, discovered the ark (according to his own testimony), and later presented his claim at the Chicago World's Fair in 1893, where the World Parliament of Religions was assembled. His story convinced a group of Belgians to launch an expedition to transport the ark to America, but the Turkish government refused the necessary permits.

7. Six Turkish soldiers claimed to

have climbed Ararat and to have spotted the ark in 1916.

8. In 1936 a young British archeologist named Hardwicke Knight was hiking across Ararat on a walking trip when he discovered interlocking hand-tooled timbers at a height of 14,000 feet.

9. During the second world war, American aviators often flew over Ararat en route from the U.S. air base in Tunisia to the Soviet air base in Erivan. According to a story in the U.S. Armed Forces newspaper *Stars and Stripes* in 1943, two pilots saw and photographed something they believed to be the ark. That issue of the *Stars and Stripes* has not been preserved, but many people claim to have seen it and the accompanying photograph. There are also reports of movies of the same object taken at this time.

10. In 1948 an Associated Press correspondent, Edwin Greenwald, announced from Istanbul that a Kurdish nomad named Resit had seen the ark. He wrote, "The petrified remains of an object which peasants insist resembles a ship has been found high up on Mt. Ararat, biblical landing place of Noah's Ark. Apparently hidden for centuries, it came to light last summer when unusually warm weather melted away an ancient mantle of ice and snow. While various persons from time to time have reported objects resembling a 'house' or a 'ship' on the mountain, Turks who have seen this new find profess it to be the only known object which could actually be taken as the remains of a ship." This report stimulated a number of organized attempts to relocate the ark, beginning with expeditions of the Oriental Archeological Research Expedition, founded by Dr. Aaron J. Smith, dean of the People's Bible College in Greensboro, North Carolina.

11. Between 1952 and 1955 (and again in 1969 as guide to an expedition sponsored by the SEARCH foundation) a wealthy French industrialist, Fernand Navarra, not only saw but also brought back pieces of hand-tooled timber said to have come from the ark. This wood has been examined, but the results are inconclusive. Navarra's claims have been disputed even by members of the SEARCH expedition.[4]

12. The last of these significant finds was by an oil and pipeline engineer and mining geologist named George Greene. He had a helicopter at his disposal and used it to find and photograph the ark in the summer of 1953. Greene enlarged the photos, returned to America and tried to interest various business associates in financing an expedition to study the craft from the ground. He was unsuccessful. Later his work took him to Utah, Nova Scotia, Texas, and finally British Guiana, where he was killed in 1962. His photos perished with him or at least have not been found.[5]

FAITH AND OBEDIENCE

It should be evident to a careful reader, even more so if the original accounts of these "discoveries" are studied, that *proof* of the existence of Noah's ark on Ararat has not been forthcoming, in spite of many expeditions and much work extending backward in time for more than a century. Evidence, yes! But proof, no! The best that can be said is that the ark may be on Ararat and that its discovery would undoubtedly delight many Christians and puzzle the world.

---

[4]Navarra published his claims, however, and his books have circulated widely. See, Fernand Navarra, *The Forbidden Mountain*, trans. by Michael Legat (London: MacDonald Press, 1956) and *Noah's Ark: I Touched It* (Plainfield: Logos Books, 1974).

[5]Most of this information, including quotes, is from LaHaye and Morris, but it is found in most other books on Noah's ark as well. In addition to those cited thus far, see John Warwick Montgomery, *The Quest for Noah's Ark* (Minneapolis: Bethany Fellowship, 1974).

But the present state of our knowledge is not without meaning. As we said earlier, faith in the story of Noah's flood is based, not on whatever physical evidence of the ark may or may not have been preserved, but on the Word of God, the Bible, which tells the story. This makes our faith essentially the same as Noah's. Noah did not have any physical evidence for the coming of the Flood when he began to build the ark. In fact, so far as the Flood was concerned, he had precisely the opposite. Up to this point in history it had never rained, but rather "streams [or mist] came up from the earth and watered the whole surface of the ground" (Gen. 2:6). Under such circumstances, what could have been more ridiculous from a human point of view than for Noah to have begun to build a gigantic ocean liner—on dry ground! Yet God told Noah to do it, and Noah based his faith not on what his reason or the taunts of his acquaintances may have told him but on his knowledge of God. And he obeyed God. The Book of Hebrews says, "By faith Noah, when warned about things not yet seen, in holy fear built an ark to save his family. By his faith he condemned the world and became heir of the righteousness that comes by faith" (Heb. 11:7).

These things are written for our instruction and example. We have not been told to build an ark, but we have been instructed to place our faith in Christ, who died for us. It is that we, like Noah, might be saved from the wrath to come.

46

God of the Covenant

(Genesis 6:18)

But I will establish my covenant with you, and you will enter the ark—you and your sons and your wife and your son's wives with you.

In the middle of the verses covered by our last study a term was introduced that is so important in biblical theology that we must pause to look at it. It is the term *covenant*. It occurs here for the first time in the Bible. After this it is used frequently. In all, it is found 253 times in the Old Testament and twenty times in the New Testament. Many of these references are to the ark of the covenant that stood at the heart of Israel's worship. Other texts speak of specific covenants established by God with such persons as Abraham, Moses, and David. Our text speaks of God's covenant with Noah: "But I will establish my covenant with you, and you will enter the ark—you and your sons and your wife and your sons' wives with you."

What is a covenant? A covenant is a promise. It has been defined more elaborately, of course—and rightly so. The great Princeton theologian Charles Hodge defines it as "a promise suspended upon a condition, and attached to disobedience a certain penalty."[1] O. Palmer Robertson calls it "a bond in blood sovereignly administered."[2] These definitions are right, but basically a covenant is a promise of God to people with whom He is dealing in a special way.

MANY COVENANTS

When we say that Genesis 6:18 is the first verse in the Bible to contain the word "covenant" we do not mean thereby that it is the first place in the Bible where the idea of a covenant occurs. Charles Hodge, whom we have just mentioned (like many Reformed theologians before and after him), finds the essential doctrines of salvation in a contrast between two main covenants, entitled the covenant of works and the covenant of grace. In this system the covenant of works is seen to have been established by God with Adam, the conditions being that if Adam obeyed God in the matter of the tree of the knowledge of good and evil and thus continued in holiness, he would continue to enjoy that life that flows from God's favor. But if he disobeyed by eating of the tree and thus lost that holiness, he would die. This covenant was established with Adam on behalf of all his descendants with the result that, when Adam exploited his option by sinning, the punishment of death passed not merely to him but to the entire human race.

In contrast to this covenant, Hodge and other Reformed theologians speak of a covenant of grace being established by God the Father with the Lord Jesus Christ according to which, on condition of Christ's perfect obedience both in life and unto death, God would save an innumerable company from among

[1]Hodge, *Systematic Theology*, Vol. 2, p. 117.
[2]O. Palmer Robertson, "The Christ of the Covenants," unpublished paper, copyright 1975, p. 2.

Adam's fallen family. Hodge distinguishes a covenant of redemption, established between the Father and the Son, and a covenant of grace, established between God and His people; but these are essentially part of one thing. The real contrast is between the covenant of works, through which no one will be saved and in accordance with which all are rather condemned, and the covenant of grace, through which those who are united to Christ are delivered.

In Robertson's treatment the matter is more carefully subdivided. He distinguishes between an initial covenant of creation and a subsequent covenant of redemption, the essential distinction Hodge makes in his discussion of the covenants of works and grace. But Robertson further subdivides the covenant of redemption into specific covenants with Adam, Noah, Abraham, Moses, David, and Christ. These are called covenants of commencement, preservation, promise, law, kingdom, and consummation respectively.

Whatever way we treat the covenants, the point is clear. God is not introducing a new way of dealing with people at this point of the Genesis account but is merely making explicit what has already been implicit in His dealings with Adam and the other antediluvian figures. In particular, God had already revealed the basic ingredient of the new covenant of redemption (or grace), for in His judgment on the serpent He had promised a deliverer to come: "I will put enmity between you and the woman, and between your offspring and hers; he will crush your head, and you will strike his heel" (Gen. 3:15). The patriarchs of this period, including Noah, lived by faith in that promise. So when God now establishes a further, explicit covenant with Noah, we are to understand it as an elaboration of principles that had already been revealed.

PROMISE TO PRESERVE

The promise of God to Noah is of quite broad extent and will be considered more fully when we get to the later passages that deal with it. This is the first; but there are four blocks of material in all (the latter three run together): Genesis 6:18; 8:20–22; 9:1–7 and 8–17. The later passages deal with God's promise never again to curse the ground for man's sin, the institution of capital punishment, and the specific reiteration of the covenant made with Noah and his family in which the sign of the covenant, the rainbow, is given. This last passage is really the fulfillment of the promise in our text: "Then God said to Noah and to his sons with him: 'I now establish my covenant with you and with your descendants after you and with every living creature that was with you—the birds, the livestock and all the wild animals, all those that came out of the ark with you—every living creature on earth. I establish my covenant with you: Never again will all life be cut off by the waters of a flood; never again will there be a flood to destroy the earth.'"

Since this is the first explicit mention of a covenant in Scripture we should expect to find the essential features of God's covenants made clear. This is exactly what we do find. There are several elements.

The first important feature of the covenants established by God is precisely that: they are established by God and not by man. This means—to use the technical word—that they are *unilateral*. Each of the covenants has the nature of an agreement; we must recognize this. But we must also recognize that they are not established in the way similar agreements might be reached between human beings. If people enter into an agreement to sell and buy a house, for example, the parties involved first have to sit down and agree to the terms. How much will be paid for the house? What will the payment cover—fixtures? appliances? carpeting? drapes? When will the house be available? When must the money be paid? Since both parties must agree to the answers to those and similar questions, in deciding these matters a certain amount of bargaining may take place. There can be trade-offs, compromises. Or the agreement can fall through. This is true of nearly any human agreement. But at this point the covenants established by God are quite different. God does not bargain. He does not compromise on terms. On the contrary, He merely announces what those terms are. This is what we mean when we say that the covenants of God are unilateral.

What were the terms of the covenant established with Noah? Essentially there were two. First, God established the means by which those who were to be saved from the Flood should be saved, namely, the ark. Second, God determined who should be saved by that means, namely, Noah and his sons, his wife and his sons' wives—eight persons. Noah did not debate these arrangements. He was not given the opportunity to do so.

The world does not like this kind of dealing, of course. The world is opposed to God's will, and the establishing of His will in this way seems to it to be arbitrary, autocratic, and insufferable. This is not the way God's people view the unilateral nature of God's promises. They rejoice, knowing that if God makes the terms, then the terms will be perfect. If we get into the action, we are certain to mess things up. Again, when God establishes a covenant, it is never to discourage us but to encourage us to do good works. In Noah's case, the promises of God were an incentive for him to keep working during the many long years the ark was being built.

Calvin, who undoubtedly sympathized with Noah in this respect due to his own long years of turmoil and service on behalf of the Reformation, wrote of the value of such promises: "Since the construction of the ark was very difficult, and innumerable obstacles might perpetually arise to break off the work when begun, God confirms his servant by a superadded promise. Thus was Noah encouraged to obey God. . . . Let us therefore know, that the promises of God alone, are they which quicken us, and inspire each of our members with vigor to yield obedience to God: but that without these promises, we not only lie torpid in indolence, but are almost lifeless, so that neither hands nor feet can do their duty. And hence, as often as we become languid, or more remiss than we ought to be, in good works, let the promises of God recur to us, to correct our tardiness."[3]

The second feature of God's covenants is that they are *eternal*. That is, God does not begin to do something in one way and then suddenly change His mind and begin to do something else or do it in a different way. He knows His plan from the beginning, announces it clearly and then does exactly what He has promised. This aspect of the covenant is particularly emphasized in Noah's case. It is emphasized in regard to God's promise never again to curse the ground and destroy its creatures: "As long as the earth endures, seedtime and harvest, cold and heat, summer and winter, day and night will never cease" (Gen. 8:22). It is emphasized by the giving of the rainbow as a sign: "This is the sign of the covenant I am making between me and you and every living creature with you, a covenant for all generations to come: I have set my rainbow in the clouds, and it will be the sign of the covenant between me and the earth. Whenever I bring clouds over the earth and the rainbow appears in the clouds, I will remember my covenant between me and you and all living creatures of every kind. Never again will the waters become a flood to destroy all

---

[3]Calvin, *Commentary on Genesis*, p. 258.

life. Whenever the rainbow appears in the clouds, I will see it and remember the everlasting covenant between God and all living creatures of every kind on the earth" (Gen. 9:12–16).

I am impressed at this point with how different God's promises are from human promises. We say, "An honest man's word is as good as his bond," but we know either that this is not true or that no one living is truly honest. People do break promises. When the Roman author Syrus Pubilius wrote, "Never promise more than you can perform," he was recognizing that people often do promise more than they perform and that their promises are therefore often quite worthless. George Chapman said, "Promise is most given when the least is said." Thomas Fuller observed, "A man apt to promise is apt to forget." William Hazlitt said cynically, "Some persons make promises for the pleasure of breaking them."[4]

How different is God! At the time of the dedication of the Jewish temple, King Solomon blessed the people, saying, "Praise be to the LORD, who has given rest to his people Israel just as he promised. Not one word has failed of all the good promises he gave through his servant Moses" (1 Kings 8:56). We say, "No matter how many promises God has made, they are 'Yes' in Christ. And so through him the 'Amen' is spoken by us to the glory of God" (2 Cor. 1:20).

This leads us to note that there are indeed many biblical promises, each of which is in a sense God's covenant with those who believe these promises and act on them. There are promises for every circumstance of life.

When I first went to France during my high school years I stayed in the home of a lovely French woman who told a story from her youth. She had been led to

Christ by Donald Grey Barnhouse during his early ministry in France and through her friendship with him was introduced to what the Barnhouse family called a promise box. It was a small box containing about two hundred tiny rolls of paper on which promises from the Bible had been written. The Barnhouses used to take one out whenever they needed a special word of comfort. This appealed to their young French friend. So she made a promise box herself, writing out all these same promises in French.

The time came when World War II swept over the European continent and France was particularly affected. The people struggled to live. At times, particularly toward the end of the war, food ran short, and the time came when this woman had no food for her family except a mass of potato peelings from a restaurant. Her children were emaciated. They were crying for food. She was desperate. In this tragic moment she remembered the promise box and turned to it, praying, "Lord, O Lord, I have such great need. Is there a promise here that is really for me? Show me, O Lord, what promise I can have in this time of famine, nakedness, peril and sword." She was crying by this time, and as she reached for the promise box, blinded by tears, she accidentally knocked it over and all the promises came showering down upon her, into her lap and tumbling to the floor. Not a promise was left in the box. She knew in a moment of great joy that the promises of God were beyond counting, that they were all for her and that they were indeed "Yes" and "Amen" in Christ Jesus.[5]

The final important feature of God's covenants is that they are established by *grace*. That is, there is nothing in us to merit them—nothing in Adam, nothing

---

[4]*Roget's International Thesaurus* (New York: Thomas Y. Crowell, 1953), p. 533.

[5]The story is also told by Donald Grey Barnhouse and appears, among other places, in *Let Me Illustrate*, pp. 253, 254.

in Noah or Abraham or Moses or David. The only merit anywhere is the merit of Christ, and it is on the basis of His work alone that the benefits of the covenants become ours. It is good that this is the case. If the covenant depended on our works or performance, we would be certain to fail and lose the benefits.

A NEW COVENANT

We must say at this point that there are covenants in the Old Testament, like that made by God with Adam, which are conditional and therefore depend on the obedience of men and women for their fulfillment. The great covenant of Deuteronomy is an example. It was given to the people for the experiencing of God's blessing in the Promised Land. If they obeyed the Lord and carefully followed all His commands, the result would be peace, prosperity, and blessing. If they disobeyed, there would be judgment (Deut. 27—29). The people did disobey, as we know, and the Syrian and Babylonian captivities were the result. These covenants showed that it was necessary for the promise of salvation to be on a different footing and prepared the way for the new covenant—the culmination of all the covenants—in Jesus Christ. Jeremiah expressed the need for the new covenant clearly.

> "The time is coming," declares the
>   LORD,
> "when I will make a new covenant
> with the house of Israel
>   and with the house of Judah.
> It will not be like the covenant
>   I made with their forefathers
> when I took them by the hand
>   to lead them out of Egypt,
> because they broke my covenant,
>   though I was a husband to them,"
>   declares the LORD.
> "This is the covenant I will make with
>   the house of Israel
>   after that time," declares the LORD.
> "I will put my law in their minds
>   and write it upon their hearts.
> I will be their God,
>   and they will be my people.

> No longer will a man teach his
>   neighbor,
>   or a man his brother, saying, 'Know
> the LORD,'
> because they will all know me,
>   from the least of them to the greatest,"
>   declares the LORD.
> "For I will forgive their wickedness
>   and will remember their sins no
>   more" (Jer. 31:31–34).

The author of Hebrews says that this covenant has been established with us through the work of Christ (Heb. 8:1–13; 10:1–18).

And so have all covenants! So has the covenant with Noah. That is why Peter can write as he does in his first letter, saying enigmatically, "Christ died for sins once for all, the righteous for the unrighteous, to bring you to God. He was put to death in the body but made alive by the Spirit, through whom also he went and preached to the spirits in prison who disobeyed long ago when God waited patiently in the days of Noah while the ark was being built. In it only a few people, eight in all, were saved through water, and this water symbolizes baptism that now saves you also—not the removal of dirt from the body but the pledge of a good conscience toward God. It saves you by the resurrection of Jesus Christ, who has gone into heaven and is at God's right hand—with angels, authorities and powers in submission to him" (1 Peter 3:18–22). Peter means that we are saved by our identification with Jesus Christ, just as Noah and his family were saved by being in the ark during the time of the great Flood.

This is the only way of salvation for anyone, and we must stand there or fail to stand. Edward Mote's great hymn puts it well.

> His oath, his covenant, his blood
> Support me in the whelming flood;
> When all around my soul gives way,
> He then is all my hope and stay.

> On Christ, the solid Rock, I stand;
> All other ground is sinking sand.

47

Jehovah Shut Him In

(Genesis 7:1–16)

The LORD then said to Noah, "Go into the ark, you and your whole family, because I have found you righteous in this generation. Take with you seven of every kind of clean animal, a male and its mate, and two of every kind of unclean animal, a male and its mate, and also seven of every kind of bird, male and female, to keep their various kinds alive throughout the earth. Seven days from now I will send rain on the earth for forty days and forty nights, and I will wipe from the face of the earth every living creature I have made."

And Noah did all that the LORD commanded him.

Noah was six hundred years old when the floodwaters came on the earth. And Noah and his sons and his wife and his son's wives entered the ark to escape the waters of the flood. Pairs of clean and unclean animals, of birds and of all creatures that move along the ground, male and female, came to Noah and entered the ark, as God had commanded Noah. And after the seven days the floodwaters came on the earth.

In the six hundredth year of Noah's life, on the seventeenth day of the second month—on that day all the springs of the great deep burst forth, and the floodgates of the heavens were opened. And rain fell on the earth forty days and forty nights.

On that very day Noah and his sons, Shem, Ham and Japheth, together with his wife and the wives of his three sons, entered the ark. They had with them every wild animal according to its kind, all livestock according to their kinds, every creature that moves along the ground according to its kind and every bird according to its kind, everything with wings. Pairs of all creatures that have the breath of life in them came to Noah and entered the ark. The animals going in were male and female of every living thing, as God had commanded Noah. Then the LORD shut him in.

It is hard to imagine a more thrilling section of Scripture than Genesis 7, for here at last, after God's warning of the earth's coming destruction and the instructions to Noah to prepare for it by building an ark, the climactic moment comes. God had told Noah of the pending Flood 120 years before. He had spent those years in active obedience, in the face of ridicule and possibly even the opposition of his contemporaries. We are not told that God said anything to him during all those long years, though He may have. But now the work is finished, and God speaks again: "Go into the ark, you and your whole family, because I have found you righteous in this generation. Take with you seven of every kind of clean animal, a male and its mate, and two of every kind of unclean animal, a male and its mate, and also seven of every kind of bird, male and female, to keep their various kinds alive throughout the earth. Seven days from now I will send rain on the earth for forty days and forty nights, and I will wipe from the face of the earth every living creature I have made" (Gen. 7:1–4).

Noah, who had obeyed for 120 years and had undoubtedly grown increasingly strong in his obedience during that time, did not fail to obey now. The story says: "And Noah did all that the

LORD commanded him" (v. 5).

I do not know whether it took Noah the entire seven days between the time of God's announcement and the beginning of the Flood to get moved into the ark. But I suppose, since he accomplished the move in that time, that there was a period of hours or days in which he and his family sat in the ark waiting for the rains to come. They must have looked very foolish, and may even have felt foolish themselves. The contemporary world, if it still payed any attention to Noah, must have considered this the absolute zenith of his folly. Perhaps the no-goods even came around to gawk and make foolish jokes. But the days passed: Sunday . . . Monday . . . Tuesday . . . Wednesday . . . Thursday . . . Friday . . . Saturday! Seven days! On the last day God shut the door, and the rains began.

SOURCE THEORY OF GENESIS

Few chapters of the Old Testament have received such hard treatment from the hands of the so-called higher critics. The chapter has been broken into parts, discredited as history and generally relegated to the realm of pious mythology—all in the name of scholarship.

The attempt to do this goes back to the year 1753, when a French scientist and physician named Jean Astruc published a work on the literary sources of Genesis. He observed that "in the Hebrew text of Genesis, God is designated by two different names. The first is Elohim, for, while this name has other meanings in Hebrew, it is especially applied to the Supreme Being. The other is Jehovah . . . the great name of God, expressing his essence. One might suppose that the two names were used indiscriminately as synonymous terms, merely to lend variety to the style. This, however, would be in error. The names are never

intermixed; there are whole chapters, or large parts of chapters, in which God is always called Elohim, and others, at least as numerous, in which he is always named Jehovah. If Moses were the author of Genesis, we should have to ascribe this strange and harsh variation to himself. But can we conceive such negligence in the composition of so short a book as Genesis? Shall we impute to Moses a fault such as no other writer has committed? Is it not more natural to explain this variation by supposing that Genesis was composed of two or three memoirs, the authors of which gave different names to God, one using Elohim, another that of Jehovah or Jehovah Elohim?"[1]

At first Astruc's work received little notice. Yet within a few years it was picked up mostly by German scholars and was expanded to include the whole of the Old Testament. Johann Eichhorn applied Astruc's approach to the Pentateuch, while Wilhelm De Wette and Edouard Reuss attempted to bring the results into line with Jewish history, Reuss concluding that in the correct historical sequence the prophets are earlier than the law, and the psalms later than both. The most popular and, in some sense, the culminating work in this field was the *Prolegomena* of Julius Wellhausen published in 1878. This work widely disseminated the four-stage documentary hypothesis known as JEPD (*J* for the Jehovah source, *E* for the Elohim source, *P* for the priestly documents and code, and *D* for the later editorial work of the Deuteronomist or Deuteronomic school). It dated the writing of the law after the Babylonian exile and placed only the Book of the Covenant and the most ancient editing of the *J* and *E* narratives prior to the eighth century B.C.

The profound change this involved is

---

[1]*Encyclopedia of Religion and Ethics*, Vol. 4, p. 315. See an earlier but shorter discussion of Astruc in chapter 14, "Are There Two Creations?" (Genesis 2:4–6), pp. 90–95.

clear in the words of E. C. Blackman, who hailed Wellhausen's achievement as making possible "the understanding of the Old Testament in terms of progressive revelation . . . a real liberation,"[2] and of Emil G. Kraeling, who noted that it also "marked the beginning of a completely secular and evolutionistic study of the Old Testament sources."[3]

These theories have been applied to the earlier chapters of Genesis too, of course. But the theory is particularly observable in regard to Genesis 7 because, as critic John Skinner points out, "The section on the Flood (6:5—9:17) is, as has often been observed, the first example in Genesis of a truly composite narrative," that is, one in which the supposed editor has carefully woven together the various strands of J and, in this case, P material to produce a narrative so brilliantly consistent that only an even more brilliant scholar can untangle it. This is what the scholars claim to have done. The scholar from whom I have just quoted pats himself as well as others on the back, saying, "The resolution of the compound narrative into its constituent elements in this case is justly reckoned amongst the most brilliant achievements of purely literary criticism."[4]

In Skinner's commentary the verses are not even considered in order. First, "The Flood according to J" is studied. It consists of verses 5–8 of chapter 6; verses 1–5, 7–20, 16b, 17b, 22 and 23 of chapter 7; and verses 2b, 3a, 6–12, 13b and 20–22 of chapter 8. Next the author considers "The Flood according to P." It consists of verses 9–22 of chapter 6; verses 6, 11, 13–17a (omitting 16b), 18–21 and 24 of chapter 7; verses 1, 2a,

3b–5, 13a and 14–19 of chapter 8; and verses 1–17 of chapter 9. In this breakdown the chief guideline is the use of the two names of God: Elohim and Jehovah. But other supporting features are alleged: 1) the distinctions between two of every kind of animal and seven of every kind, one of which is supposed to be in the J source and the other in P, 2) repetitive material, and 3) the fact that when the sources are sorted out each supposedly gives a more or less continuous narrative.

CREATOR AND REDEEMER

I want to answer this attack on the Flood story. But before I do I want to show how skeptical we should be of any scholar who thinks he can take a document written many thousands of years before his time in another language and in the categories of another culture and break it up so that part can be said to have come from one ancient source and part from another.

More than a generation ago in England, scholars of the JEPD school produced what was called the Polychrome Bible. Polychrome means "many colors," and it was called this because it was printed in colors corresponding to the sources that presumably lay behind the books we have. The J material was one color. The E material was another. So on with the P and D sections. Once, a man in England took writings of these men who produced the Polychrome Bible, writings from about twenty years before, and he blended them together, taking a paragraph here and a sentence there to produce one article. He sent it to them and said, "Tell me who wrote what." They could not even identify

[2]E. C. Blackman, *Biblical Interpretation* (Philadelphia: Westminster Press, 1957), p. 141.

[3]Emil G. Kraeling, *The Old Testament Since the Reformation* (New York: Harper and Brothers, 1955), p. 94. I discuss the Old Testament and New Testament higher criticism at greater length in *The Sovereign God*, pp. 97–109.

[4]John Skinner, *A Critical and Exegetical Commentary on Genesis*, 2nd edition, in "The International Critical Commentary" series (Edinburgh: T. & T. Clark, 1956), p. 147.

their own writings. So I say that apart from any answers that might be given, we should be extremely skeptical of any attempt to do what the higher critics claim to have done in accord with the JEPD theory.

But there are answers, of course. And the chief answer is that the names of God in the Old Testament deal with different aspects of God's person and are therefore used significantly—in ways that apparently escape the notice of unbelieving scholars. Elohim is the name of God as Creator. It is the most general name of God, because the most general relation God has to this world is that of Creator. It is through Him that all we see and know has come into being. Jehovah is the name of God as Redeemer. This is less general, but is characteristic of the Old Testament since it is a book dealing primarily with God's redeeming activities on behalf of His special people, Israel. This name does not occur in Genesis 1, where creation alone is in view. But it is prominent in Genesis 2, where the special relationship between God and the man and woman is developed fully.

In the Flood story the matter is more complex, as the higher critics recognize when speaking of the first "truly composite narrative." But the complexity is built into the very nature of the story as God deals with the animals as Creator but with Noah and his family in a uniquely redemptive way.

One of the great examples of the spiritual use of these names is a verse in our passage, verse 16. The critics break it into parts, attributing one part to E and the other to J or P, according to the use of the divine names. But in doing this they miss the point Moses is making. The verse says, "The animals going in were male and female of every living thing, as God [Elohim] had commanded Noah. . . ." (There God the Creator is

speaking. He is preserving the various animals of His creation.) "Then the LORD [Jehovah] shut him in." (In the second half of this verse, God is preserving His people.)

One commentator sees this clearly. "God, the awe-inspiring Ruler of all, *Elohim,* laid all these commandments upon Noah by virtue of his supreme authority. [But] in the same breath, with skillful use of the proper divine name, the author asserts that it was *Yahweh,* the always gracious and faithful, who 'closed the door after him.'"[5]

This is also the explanation of the apparent contradiction between those verses which say "take two of every animal" and those verses that speak of "seven of every *clean* animal." Chapter 6 speaks of animals in general, and God is speaking of preserving His creation. Two of every kind must be saved so that they can reproduce and so the species will not be exterminated by the Flood. Chapter 7 speaks of *clean* animals, that is, animals that were used for sacrifices and that, following the Flood, were also used for food. In this chapter Jehovah is adding to the earlier instruction that which would be necessary for the survival of Noah's family and for the practice of religion. Obviously, if Noah had come out of the ark after the Flood and had sacrificed a lamb—as he undoubtedly did, since Genesis says he sacrificed "some of all the clean animals and clean birds" (Gen. 8:20)—there would have been no more lambs. Or cows or doves or whatever!

That is not what happened. And the reason it did not happen is that God gave precise instructions as to what should be done and Noah obeyed God.

THREE LESSONS

We close with these lessons. First, when the Lord shut Noah and his family up in the ark, they were totally secure

---

[5]Leupold, *Exposition of Genesis*, Vol. 1, p. 299.

and thereby become an illustration for us of the believer's *perfect security* in Jesus Christ. The rains would come. The floods would rage. But nothing would touch these who had been sealed in the ark by Jehovah. It is interesting that God did not say, "Noah, it is time to shut the door. Get your sons to help you slide it closed and throw the lock." The Lord does not place the safety of His people in others' hands. He Himself throws the lock. It is said of Him, "What he opens no one can shut; and what he shuts, no one can open" (Rev. 3:7). The shutting in of Noah was the equivalent of our being sealed with the Holy Spirit (Eph. 4:30). Like him, we are not only saved; we are secure as well.

Second, there is a lesson of God's great *grace*. The last thing we are told in this story before the waters actually begin to come is that "the LORD shut him in." Presumably this was done at the last possible moment. Noah had been preaching God's righteousness, man's sin, and the coming of the great Flood for 120 years. He had experienced no success whatever. As he and his family went into the ark and waited there for the rains to begin falling, they would have been taunted by those who remained outside. These had not believed Noah. They were refusing to believe now. But still the door to the ark remained open, and any who wanted to could have gone inside. What great grace! What magnificent forbearance on the part of God! Since Noah had believed and had gone in, no one who stood without could say that the possibility of belief was closed to him. "Whoever willed" could come.

So also today. All who will may come. Many do not, but none of these can say that the possibility of repentance from sin and turning to Christ are beyond them.

Finally, there is a lesson in that there is an *end to grace*. Grace is great, but it is not unending. If it is spurned, the day of reckoning eventually comes. For one final week the door stood open. But the week ended, the door was closed and the Flood came. The same God who opens doors is Himself the door (John 10:7, 9). He also closes doors and refuses to open them—when the time for grace is gone.

Jesus taught this by a story. He told of ten virgins on their way to a wedding with their lamps. Five were wise and five were foolish. The five wise virgins had provided oil for their lamps. The foolish ones had failed to bring oil with them. While they waited for the bridegroom it grew dark and they all dozed off. Suddenly the bridegroom came. The wise virgins woke up and trimmed their lamps. The foolish virgins went off to get oil. While they were gone, those who were ready went in with the bridegroom to the wedding banquet. The story then says ominously, "And the door was shut." At this point the foolish virgins returned and called out to the bridegroom, "Sir! Sir! Open the door for us!"

He replied, "I tell you the truth, I don't know you." The door was not opened because the opportunity for entering was past (Matt. 25:1–13).

For you it is not yet past, whoever you may be. This is still the day of grace, and although it will end, it has not ended yet. Won't you come while there is still time? God said to Noah, "*Come* . . . into the ark" (Gen. 7:1, KJV). Isaiah said, "*Come*, all you who are thirsty, *come* to the waters; and you who have no money, *come*, buy and eat! *Come*, buy wine and milk without money and without cost" (Isa. 55:1). Jesus said, "*Come* to me, all you who are weary and burdened, and I will give you rest" (Matt. 11:28). At the end of the Bible we read, "The Spirit and the bride say, '*Come!*' And let him who hears say, '*Come!*' Whoever is thirsty, let him *come*; and whoever wishes, let him take the free gift of the water of life" (Rev. 22:17).

48

Was Noah's Flood a World Flood?

(Genesis 7:17–24)

For forty days the flood kept coming on the earth, and as the waters increased they lifted the ark high above the earth. The waters rose and increased greatly on the earth, and the ark floated on the surface of the water. They rose greatly on the earth, and all the high mountains under the entire heavens were covered. The waters rose and covered the mountains to a depth of more than twenty feet. Every living thing that moved on the earth perished—birds, livestock, wild animals, all the creatures that swarm over the earth, and all mankind. Everything on dry land that had the breath of life in its nostrils died. Every living thing on the face of the earth was wiped out; men and animals and the creatures that move along the ground and the birds of the air were wiped from the earth. Only Noah was left, and those with him in the ark.

The waters flooded the earth for a hundred and fifty days.

After the preparations had been made and Noah and his family had entered the ark, Jehovah shut the door and the flood and rains that were to destroy every living creature began (See Gen. 6:7).[1] According to the Bible, this was the most destructive event this world had experienced or will experience until the final judgment associated with the second coming of Christ.

A LOCAL FLOOD?

Until relatively recent times church people—scholars, pastors, laymen—accepted this account at face value and therefore believed in what is usually called a "universal" or worldwide flood as opposed to a merely "local" one. Today, however, many church scholars (including some evangelical ones) have argued that a universal flood cannot be meant by Scripture because of the innumerable difficulties this interpretation presents. Since the account speaks in universal terms, they believe it is to be interpreted phenomenally, that is, as a description of the Flood as it would

appear to Noah and the others who went through it. To them it would *seem* to be universal. They would describe it in this way, but the Flood would not necessarily have been a world flood.

Bernard Ramm holds to this interpretation.[1] Much of his discussion deals with the supposed weakness of the arguments of those who hold to a universal flood. But the real reason for his objections is the weight of problems he sees if the universal view is to be accepted. He thinks these require a series of stupendous miracles, greater even than the Flood itself.

Ramm begins with the assumption that the earth before the Flood was essentially the same as the earth we observe today and on that basis calculates the amount of water necessary to cover the highest mountains. If the earth were a perfect sphere, the ocean would cover the land to a depth of two-and-a-half to three miles. But the earth we know has mountains five to six miles high. To cover such mountains would require eight times more water than we now

[1]Ramm, *The Christian View*, pp. 229–49. See also William S. LaSor, "Was the Flood Universal?", *Eternity*, Dec. 1960, pp. 11–13.

have. God would have had to create that much new water, according to Ramm. Then he would have had to uncreate it after the Flood in order to get the world back to normal. Moreover, the creation of that much additional water would have altered the earth's weight and disturbed the earth's orbit around the sun and the moon's orbit around the earth. Needless to say, no past effects of this nature have been detected by astronomers.

Ramm believes that a mixing of salt and fresh water in such a flood would mean the destruction of many species of fresh-water and marine fish. Consequently, God would have had to provide "an entire marine creation" afterward. Ramm argues that the pressure of six additional miles of water on top of existing water would have crushed most marine species, strangely overlooking the thought that they might simply have moved upward through the water to their normal subsurface depth.

Again, how did the many species of animals from all over the world get to the ark to be transported by it? Ramm asks. How did land animals cross the oceans —from North and South America, from Australia? How did Noah manage to supply their need for unique and varying environments and provide their different foods?

These problems seem overwhelming to Ramm. So he concludes, "The flood was local to the Mesopotamian valley. The animals that came, prompted by divine instinct, were the animals of that region; they were preserved for the good of man after the flood. Man was destroyed within the boundaries of the flood; the record is mute about man in America or Africa or China. The types of vegetation destroyed quickly grew again over the wasted area, and other animals migrated back into the area, so that after a period of time the damaging

effects of the flood were obliterated. An examination of the references of the New Testament to the flood are not conclusive, one way or the other, but permit either a local or universal flood interpretation."[2]

THE LANGUAGE OF SCRIPTURE

How should we react to such arguments? We begin by noting that there are indeed problems with the idea of a universal flood (as there also are with a local flood) and that many of these problems may be unsolvable on the basis of our present knowledge. We may not be able to say, for example, how the various species of animals got to Noah's ark from distant continents. That is a problem. But not knowing *how* this happened is not the same kind of problem we would have if this were an utter impossibility. Animals do seem to get across vast bodies of water, and in most cases the water involved was not all that vast. Moreover, there was certainly time for migrations if Noah spent 120 years building the ark, as we suppose. It is not impossible that any animal could have reached Noah from anywhere on the earth in that period.

As to the creation of vast amounts of new water, so far as I know, no one currently holding to a universal flood would resort to this theory. Generally it is assumed that the surface of the earth was not as irregular as it is today and that the land was covered with existing amounts of water. It must have reached its present form afterward, perhaps even as a result of immense disruptions that the Flood caused.

The proper approach to whether the Flood was local or universal is not by these matters, however important they may be in their proper place. It is rather by the teaching of Scripture. And at this point it is hard to believe that the Bible does not in fact teach a Flood of

---

[2] *The Christian View*, p. 249.

worldwide dimensions. To be sure, as defenders of the local flood theory point out, the use of such words as "all" and "every" in Scripture does not always involve every single one of the items or individuals mentioned. When we are told in Matthew 2:3, that King Herod "was disturbed, and *all* Jerusalem with him," this does not necessarily mean every individual then living in Jerusalem, for there would presumably have been many who did not know of the Magi's visit. When David says prophetically, "I can count *all* my bones," he does not mean that every single bone in his body stood out prominently (Ps. 22:17). Still even the least experienced reader of Scripture can see the difference between expressions such as these and the deliberately strong, repetitive language of Genesis 7:17–24.

Verse 19 is important, for in that verse the Hebrew word for "all" *(kol)* occurs not once but twice, in what can only be called a near-Hebrew superlative. The text says that the flood waters rose greatly on the earth so that "*all* the high mountains under the *entire* heavens were covered." That means that the entire earth was covered. The word *kol* (or a variant of *kol*), occurs six more times in the passage, two of these in verse 22, in each case making the point that *all* birds, *all* livestock, *all* wild animals, and *all* people died. Moreover, it is not just this passage that must be dealt with. As Henry Morris points out, "Expressions involving universality of the Flood and its effects occur more than thirty times in Genesis 6–9." He says that "the wording of the entire record, both here and throughout Genesis 6–9, could not be improved on, if the intention of the writer was to describe a universal flood; as a description of a river overflow, it is completely misleading and exaggerated."[3]

Again, there is the nature of the Flood itself. If we are to take the language of the Bible seriously, as we must, the Flood of Noah's day was of long duration. The descent of rain and rise of the waters continued for forty days, by which time all the mountains of the then-existing earth were covered to a depth of more than twenty feet (Gen. 7:17–20). At that time the rains stopped and the waters began to go down. But they descended gradually so that it was 150 days after the rains had begun and 110 days after they had stopped before the bottom of the ark was able to touch Mount Ararat (Gen. 8:3, 4). Ten weeks after that the tops of the mountains became visible (Gen. 8:5). It was twenty-one more weeks before the waters had receded sufficiently for Noah and his family to disembark safely (Gen. 8:14, 15). In all, slightly over a year passed from the time the Flood commenced (Gen. 7:11) until the waters had dried up (Gen. 8:14), and even that time frame does not preclude the possibility that the waters may have continued to recede gradually for many more years with corresponding changes in the earth's topography.

A flood of that duration is not a local flood! No local flood could last that long! As John C. Whitcomb observes, "How a flood of such depth and duration could have covered only a limited portion of the earth's surface has never been satisfactorily explained."[4]

THE TOTAL PICTURE

To what has been said thus far in support of a world flood we should add additional biblical data. Morris lists twenty-six reasons why the Bible is describing a world flood, but let us take just four outstanding ones.

1. *The construction, outfitting, and*

---

[3]Morris, *The Genesis Record,* p. 199.

[4]John C. Whitcomb, Jr., *The World that Perished* (Grand Rapids: Baker, 1973), p. 46.

stocking of the ark would have been absurd if the Flood were local. We have already looked at the size and design of the ark. It was approximately 450 feet long, 75 feet wide, and 45 feet high—the dimensions of many modern ocean liners. A ship like that would have taken a great deal of time to build, and we are probably right in assuming that Noah began his work at the time of God's revealed intention to destroy the earth 120 years before the floods came. Moreover, the ark was admirably suited to its purpose, being of a size sufficient to accommodate the many thousands of individual animals that the Bible says were in it. What would have been the purpose of a ship like this if the Flood affected only the Mesopotamian river valley, as proponents of the local-flood theory maintain? It would have been far more sensible for God simply to have warned Noah to move out of the valley to higher ground, as he later warned Lot and his family to leave Sodom. The birds and animals could also have moved out of the area without having to be stored in the ark for an entire year.

2. After the Flood was over *God promised never again to destroy the earth by flood (Gen. 8:21, 22; 9:11, 15), and this is a false promise if the flood to which it refers was local.* There have been many local but terrible floods in earth's history. Many have perished in such floods. If God's promises refer to that kind of flood, they have been broken repeatedly. But this was not the nature of God's promises. They refer to the destruction of all creatures throughout the whole earth and the temporary cessation of the seasons which, God says, will never again occur: "Never again will I destroy all living creatures, as I have done. 'As long as the earth endures, seedtime and harvest, cold and heat, summer and winter, day and night will never cease'" (Gen. 8:21, 22). This makes sense only if the Flood of Noah's day was of worldwide dimensions.

3. In later chapters of Genesis *the Bible traces all the peoples of the earth to Noah and his three sons* (Gen. 9:18–10:32). It is true, as proponents of a local flood point out, that these verses do not mention peoples beyond the rather limited area of the Near East. In that sense the description is local. But neither do these verses preclude a further expansion to include other nations! They do not say that these are all the people who descended fron Noah. They do say that all the world's people came *from him!* "The sons of Noah who came out of the ark were Shem, Ham and Japheth. (Ham was the father of Canaan.) These were the three sons of Noah, and from them came the people who were scattered over the earth" (Gen. 9:18, 19). "From these the nations spread out over the earth after the flood" (Gen. 10:32).

4. *Other biblical references to the Flood presuppose its universality or at least do not oppose this interpretation.* There are quite a few such texts: Job 22:15, 16; Psalm 104:5–9; Isaiah 54:9; Hebrews 11:7; 1 Peter 3:20; 2 Peter 2:5; 3:5, 6. Some are quite explicit, as Psalm 104:5–9.

> He [God] set the earth on its
>   foundations;
>   it can never be moved.
> You covered it with the deep as with
>   a garment;
>   the waters stood above the
>   mountains.
> But at your rebuke the waters fled,
>   at the sound of your thunder they
>   took to flight;
> they flowed over the mountains,
>   they went down into the valleys,
>   to the place you assigned for them.
> You set a boundary they cannot cross;
>   never again will they cover the earth.

The most significant text is 2 Peter 3:5, 6, because in this passage Peter is arguing against a constant natural behavior of the elements (the doctrine of uniformitarianism) that a local flood theory would imply. Peter is looking forward to a day when people will no longer take the promise of Christ's future coming seriously, and he is countering the reason they will give for their skepticism. They will say, "Where is this 'coming' he promised? Ever since our fathers died, everything goes on as it has since the beginning of creation" (v. 4). That is, they will argue that God does not intervene in history to overturn the observable workings of nature. What we see now was also characteristic of the past and will be of the future. We have nothing out of the ordinary to fear. Peter replies that there are two past events that cannot be explained on the basis of this uniformitarian viewpoint. The first is the creation itself when "by God's word the heavens existed and the earth was formed out of water and with water" (v. 5). The second is the Flood when "the world of that time was deluged and destroyed" (v. 6). Peter goes on: "By the same word the present heavens and earth are reserved for fire, being kept for the day of judgment and destruction of ungodly men" (v. 7).

In this passage the one event since the creation of the world to which Peter appeals to show that the theory of those who think all things will continue on as they have is the Flood. This is meaningless if Peter was thinking of a local flood such as had obviously occurred from time to time even in his day and has occurred many times since. "It was the flood to which Peter appealed as his final and incontrovertible answer to those who chose to remain in willful ignorance of the fact that God had *at one time* in the past demonstrated his holy wrath and omnipotence by subjecting 'all things' to an overwhelming, cosmic catastrophe that was on an absolute par with the final day of judgment, in which God will yet consume the earth with fire and cause the very elements to dissolve with fervent heat" (v. 10).[5]

JESUS AND THE ARK

This same connection with His coming future judgment characterized our Lord's reference to Noah in Matthew 24:37–41 (cf. Luke 17:26, 27): "As it was in the days of Noah, so it will be at the coming of the Son of Man. For in the days before the flood, people were eating and drinking, marrying and giving in marriage, up to the day Noah entered the ark; and they knew nothing about what would happen until the flood came and took them all away. That is how it will be at the coming of the Son of Man. Two men will be in the field; one will be taken and the other left. Two women will be grinding with a hand mill; one will be taken and the other left."

The Flood's universality is important because it is the teaching of the Bible, but within that context it is especially important because it is the one great historical demonstration by God that in the day of wrath none shall escape His justice. The universal Flood is important because it is proof of a final, universal judgment.

That judgment came once, and it will come again. But we note that even as Christ speaks of judgment, he speaks also of those who will belong to Him in that day and will be spared (Matt. 24:40, 41) Like those in the ark—Noah and his wife, his three sons and their wives—those who are united to Christ by saving faith shall be borne up above the waters of that final judgment and shall be kept safe. As in Noah's day, the judgment that sweeps down on the world will bring eternal loss to those who have rejected the way of salvation but eternal bliss and security to those who are in Christ. In the ark Noah was surrounded by the evidence of judgment, but he was safe. So may you be, if you are in Christ. If you are not, now is the time to renounce your sinful way of life and come to Him.

---

[5] *The World That Perished,* p. 58.

49

The Evidence of Flood Traditions

(Genesis 7:17–24)

For forty days the flood kept coming on the earth, and as the waters increased they lifted the ark high above the earth. The waters rose and increased greatly on the earth, and the ark floated on the surface of the water. They rose greatly on the earth, and all the high mountains under the entire heavens were covered. The waters rose and covered the mountains to a depth of more than twenty feet. Every living thing that moved on the earth perished—birds, livestock, wild animals, all the creatures that swarm over the earth, and all mankind. Everything on dry land that had the breath of life in its nostrils died. Every living thing on the face of the earth was wiped out; men and animals and the creatures that move along the ground and the birds of the air were wiped from the earth. Only Noah was left, and those with him in the ark.

The waters flooded the earth for a hundred and fifty days.

During the mid-nineteenth century (c. 1845) British orientalists began excavations of the ancient city of Nineveh, the capital of Assyria, and brought its treasures back to England, including 20,000 clay tablets and fragments of tablets covered with cuneiform inscriptions. The work of sorting out these tablets was difficult, but it was entrusted to a twenty-two-year-old assistant in the Department of Antiquities of the British Museum named George Smith. Smith was a genius at this kind of work. He sorted the tablets, acquired an expert knowledge of cuneiform script and began translations.

In 1872, while he was translating, Smith came across a small fragment of a tablet on which he read the words, "The mountain of Nisir stopped the ship. I sent forth a dove, and it left. The dove went and turned, and a resting place it did not find, and it returned." Smith recognized that these words resembled part of the biblical account of the Flood and immediately began to search for other fragments of the story. In time he found other parts of this account and

other copies. He put these together (still with many gaps) and presented them to a meeting of the Society of Biblical Archaeology in December of that year. The text was strikingly similar to Genesis. In both, a worldwide flood is brought on by the wickedness of men and women. In both, a selection of animals and people is saved by being taken onto a large ship, though the Babylonian account gives the dimensions of the ark as those of a perfect cube. In the Babylonian account the Flood lasts seven days; in the Bible the embarkation lasts seven days. In both cases a raven and a dove are sent out of the ark; the Babylonian account adds a swallow. After the Flood a thanksgiving offering is made and is accepted favorably by God (the Bible) or the gods (the Babylonian epic). Each ends with a covenant guaranteeing that the earth will never again be destroyed in this way.

Smith's discovery created a major stir among scholars, as might be imagined. Before this it was assumed that the Babylonian traditions of the Flood, preserved by the ancient historian Berosus, had been borrowed from Genesis during the Babylonian captivity of the Jewish people. These stories dated from before the captivity, however. So they provided independent verification of the Bible's story. (It is conceivable that the Genesis account could have been borrowed from the Babylonian, but that is not the case since the difference of detail and outlook show that neither is dependent on the other.)

A stir was also created among the British people. The *London Daily Telegraph* asked Mr. Smith to go to Assyria at its expense to search for further Flood tablets. Smith did and was remarkably successful. He discovered further fragments of the very tablet he had worked on at the British Museum as well as others. In all, he returned to Nineveh three times and died there on his third expedition.

World Traditions

The importance of the Babylonian flood account, part of what is now known as the Gilgamesh Epic, is not merely that it is an independent testimony to the fact of an ancient flood, though it is that. It is also one of many similar accounts to be found in the historical legends of literally hundreds of people scattered across the globe. This fact is not usually fully appreciated. Hundreds of flood stories abound throughout the world in various cultures and are therefore evidence not merely of the historicity of the Flood but of its universal extent, since the people having these stories presumably have them because of their descent from the Flood's survivors.

Let me give some examples. Dan Shaw, a linguist working with Wycliffe Bible Translators among the *Samo-Kubo* tribe of Papua, New Guinea, reports a flood story of these isolated people. Back at the dawn of time certain people were tormenting the lizards with which this area of New Guinea abounds. At last the lizards could stand it no longer. They complained to the Lizard Man, and he sent a rain that caused flood waters to rise until everyone but two brothers was drowned. These escaped by sailing off on a raft that was just big enough for the two of them. In the Samo-Kubo tribe the most meaningful relationship a man can have is with his brother, hence the part of the story about two brothers being saved. Apparently, it did not occur to the Samo-Kubo tribe that the repopulation of the earth by two brothers would be biologically impossible.[1]

Thus a hitherto unknown tribe with almost no contact with the outside world has as part of its legendary past a story of a destruction by flood similar in many ways to the biblical story. There are differences, of course, but the essence of the story remains.

It comes as a surprise to many Americans to learn that stories of a destructive flood and the deliverance of select human beings abound among the American Indians. The *Athapascan* tribe on the West Coast has a story in which one human being, Nagaitche, is saved from the Flood by riding on the head of a mythological figure named Earth. The *Papago* Indians of Arizona tell of the deliverance of a man named Montezuma and a friendly coyote. They survive in a boat that Montezuma had prepared and kept hidden on a mountain top. After the Flood the coyote is sent out to see how much land is visible. The *Arapaho* Indians tell of the deliverance of the first Arapaho, who escaped the Flood by sitting on a high mountain. The *Algonquins*, who lived in the northeastern section of the United States, relate how a great evil snake brought a flood on human beings and how some were saved by a daughter of one of the spirits who helped them into a boat.

---

[1]The story is reported in *The Ark on Ararat*, p. 231, by LaHaye and Morris.

In the rest of the Americas the same thing is true. *Brazilian* tribes have some knowledge of the Deluge. In *Peru* Indians report that many years before there were any Incas in the world, all people were drowned by a great flood, except six who became the progenitors of the now-existing races. They were saved on a large raft. The original inhabitants of *Cuba* believe that "an old man, knowing the Deluge was to come, built a great ship and went into it with his family and an abundance of animals; and that, wearying during the continuance of the Flood, he sent out a crow, which as first did not return, staying to feed on the dead bodies, but afterwards returned bearing a green branch."

In a *Mexican flood tradition*, Coxcox, who is also called Tezpi by other tribes, saved himself, his family, and some animals by embarking in a boat or raft. As the Flood began to subside he sent out a vulture, which did not return, and a hummingbird, which did, bearing a branch with green leaves.

The natives of *Alaska* believe that the father of their ancestors had been warned in a dream that a flood would destroy the earth. He built a raft, on which he saved himself, his family, and animals. The animals, who could then talk, complained about their many months on the boat. So after the waters had gone down and they had all alighted from the boat, the animals lost their powers of speech as a punishment.

The *Hottentots* call the progenitor of their race Noh. The natives of *Greenland* have a tradition in which ten generations of men lived on the earth before the Flood and only one man was spared. The *Hawaiians* say that in the old days there was great wickedness on earth and that only one man was righteous. His name was Nu-u. He made a great canoe with a house on it, filled it with plants and animals, and escaped on it when the Flood came. After the Flood had ended and he saw the moon for the first time,

he thought it was Cane, the great god. He worshiped it, which displeased Cane, and Cane came down on a rainbow to reprove him. After he had returned to heaven the rainbow remained as a token of Cane's forgiveness.

The people of *Wales* have a legend in which the lake of Llion is said to have burst and overflowed the land. Everyone was drowned except Dwyfan and Dwyfach and pairs of every kind of animal, which they preserved. Every living thing has descended from these survivors.

The *Lithuanians* tell how the supreme god Pramzimas decided to destroy everyone by a great flood. After twenty days only a remnant of people remained on a great mountain, and they would have been drowned too if Pramzimas had not accidentally dropped the shell of a nut he was eating. The people used this as a boat and were saved.

The traditions of *India* and *China* tell the same stories, with even more significant details. In India the Hindus regard Manu as the progenitor of the race. He had been warned of the pending flood by a fish, who told him to build a ship and put into it all kinds of seeds, together with seven Rishis or holy beings. The Flood came. People drowned. But Manu's ship was drawn to safety by the fish who finally caused it to ground on the highest summits of the Himalaya mountains. In this story eight people were saved, and Manu is called "righteous among his generation." Even more remarkable, the Hindus preserve a story in which Manu later became drunk and lay uncovered until cared for by two of his sons, a close retelling of the story found in Genesis 9:20–27.

In the *Chinese traditions* Fah-he escapes the deluge with his wife, his three sons and his three daughters, and from these the earth was repopulated.

Manetho, who lived about 250 B.C., tells of a flood story present in the ancient myths of *Egypt*. In this a man named Toth is saved. In Manetho's day the Deluge tradition was connected with a festival of commemoration for the dead in which a priest placed an image of Osiris in a sacred ark and sent it off into the sea. This was observed on the seventeenth day of Athyr, which corresponds to the date given in Genesis 7:11 for the Flood's beginning.

The *Greeks* had a flood tradition. The Roman poet Ovid tells it at length in his *Metamorphoses*. [2]

FLOOD TRADITIONS TABLE

Two people who have done much work in collecting these worldwide Flood traditions are Tim LaHaye and John Morris, who present a full listing in *The Ark on Ararat*. Their list is grouped by areas of global distribution, and it is worth reproducing.

These flood traditions vary, as has already been evident. But there is much agreement too. In 88 percent of them

Middle East and Africa

Africa (Central)
Babylon
Bapedi Tribe (South Africa)
Chaldea
Egypt (Pharaoic)
Egypt (Priestly)
Hottentots
Jumala Tribe
Lower Congo
Masai Tribe
Otshi Tribe (Kabinda)
Persia (Ahriman)
Persia (Bundehesch)
Persia (Testrya)
Persia (Yima)
Persia (Zala-Cupha)
Syria

Pacific Islands

Alamblack Tribe (New Guinea)
Alfoors of Ceram
Ami
Andaman Islands
Australia
Bunya
Dutch New Guinea (Mombrano River)
East Indian Island
Engano
Falwol Tribe (New Guinea)
Fiji
Fiji (Rohora)
Flores Island
Formosa Tribesmen
Hawaii (Mauna-Ka) Tribesmen
Hawaii (Nu-U)
Kabidi Tribe (New Guinea)
Kurnai Tribe (Australia)
Leeward Islands
Maoris (New Zealand)
Melanesia
Micronesia
Nais
New Britain
Otheite Island
Ot-Danoms
Polynesia
Queensland
Rotti Tribe
Samoa
Samo-Kubo Tribe (New Guinea)
Sea Dyaks (Borneo)
Sea Dyaks (Trout)
Sea Dyaks (Sarawak)
Sumatra
Tahiti
Toradias
Valman Tribe (New Guinea)

---

[2]These stories are related with varying amounts of detail by several writers. I have drawn largely on the accounts by Rehwinkel in *The Flood in the Light of the Bible, Geology and Archeology*, pp. 127–52. Other important works are James G. Frazer, *Folklore in the Old Testament* (London: Macmillan and Co., 1919) and Hugh Miller, *The Testimony of the Rocks: Geology in Its Bearings on the Two Theologies, Natural and Revealed* (Edinburgh: Thomas Constable and Co., 1857).

Far East

Anals (Assam)
Bahnara (China)
Bengal Kolhs
Benua-Jakun (Malasia)
Bhagavata-Purana
China (Fo-hi)
China (Joa)
China (Tao-tse)
Cingpaws (Upper Burma)
India (Rama)
Kamars (Central India)

Kamchadales (India)
Karens (Burma)
Lolos (South China)
Mahabharata
Matsya-Puranta
Menangkabans (Sumatra)
Satapatha Brahmana
Singphos (Burma)
Sudan
Tartary Mongols

Europe and Asia

Celts
Druids
Finland
Iceland
Kelts
Lapland
Lithuania

Norway
Rumania
Russia
Siberia
Transylvania
Wales

Hellenic Cultures and Authors

Apamea (Cibotos)
Apollodorus
Aristotle
Athenian
Cos (Merops)
Crete
Diodorus
Hellenucus
Lucian
Megaros
Ogyges (Boeotia)

Ovid
Perirrhoos
Pindar
Plato
Plutarch
Rhodes
Samothrace
Sithnide Nymphs
Stephanus
Thessalonica

North America

Acagchemens
Aleutian Island Indians
Algonquins (Manabozho)
Appalachian Indians
Araphos
Arctic Eskimos
Athapascans
Blackfoot Indians
Caddoques
Central Eskimos
Cherokees
Chippewas
Crees
Delaware Algonquins
Dogribs
Eleuts
Eskimos (Alaska)
Eskimos (Norton Sound)

Kolosh
Koloshes
Lake Tahoe Indians
Lenni-Lanape Indians
Luisenos
Mandans
Mantagnais Algonquins
Menominees
Montagnais
Natchez Indians
New California Indians
Nez Perces
Ojibway
Pacullies
Papagos
Pimas
Potawatomi Indians
Rio Erevato Indians

Esquimax	Salteaux Algonquins
Flatheads	Sarcees
Greenland	Smith River Indians
Great Lakes Indians	Spokanas
Haidas	Thlinkuts
Hareskins	Thlinkuts (Yehl)
Huron Indians	Thompsan Indians
Innuit Eskimos	Tinneh Indians
Iroquois	Twangs
Kathlamets	Virginia Indians
Knistineaus	Yakimas

Central America

Achagnas	Mayas
Antilles	Mexico (Coxcox)
Aztecs	Mexico (Mexitli)
Aztecs (Coxcoxtli)	Michoacans
Canaris	Muratos
Cholulans	Nicaragua Indians
Cholulas	Rio-Crevato Indians
Coras (Highland)	St. Domingo Indians
Coras (Lowland)	Tlascalans
Cuban Indians	Toltecs
Huichals	

South America

Abederys	Macusis
Ackawois	Maypures
Araucanians	Orinoco Indians
Arawaks	Pamarys
Brazilian Mountain Indians	Peru (Bomara)
Brazilian Sea Coast Indians	Peru (Guancas)
Caingans	Peruvian Indians
Carayas	Peru (Manco Capak)
Chiriguanos	Rio de Janeiro Indians
Colombian Indians	Tamanacs
Incas	Terra-Firma Indians
Kataushys	Tierra del Fuego Indians

there is a favored family. In 70 percent survival is due to a boat. In 95 percent the sole cause of the catastrophe is a flood. In 66 percent the disaster is due to man's wickedness. In 67 percent animals are also saved. In 57 percent the survivors end up on a mountain. In smaller percentages birds are sent out, a rainbow is mentioned, and eight persons specifically are saved.

Moreover, there is a predictable pattern to these variations if we assume that the story of the Flood is true and that the descendants of Noah spread out over the earth after the Flood bearing the memory of the Flood with them. In the Middle East the stories are very similar. But the farther one goes from the place where the story originated the more incidental circumstances, local color, and cultural elements creep in. LaHaye and Morris conclude, "The universal Flood traditions can only have come from a common source, embellished with local color and culture, but retaining enough pertinent data to convey both historical and moral concepts."[3]

Hugh Miller, a careful investigator of these stories in the 1800s, wrote, "The destruction of well nigh the whole human race in an early age of the world's history by a great deluge appears to have so impressed the minds of the few survivors and seems to have been handed down to their children, in consequence, with such terror-struck impressiveness, that their remote descendants of the present day have not even yet forgotten it. It appears in almost every mythology, and lives in the most distant countries and among the most barbarous tribes."[4]

WILLFUL IGNORANCE

Yet strangely, in spite of widespread knowledge of the Bible and the persistence of flood traditions in virtually every culture and nation on the globe, modern man seems to have forgotten the Flood of God's judgment and argues as those whose views Peter anticipated: "Where is this 'coming' he promised? Ever since our fathers died, everything goes on as it has since the beginning of creation" (2 Peter 3:4). Why is this? There is only one explanation. It is not that the evidence for the intervening judgment of God in history is lacking. The evidence abounds. It is rather, as Peter says, that our contemporaries "deliberately forget" (v. 5) these things so they can continue in their own sinful way unbothered by such disturbing concepts as accountability, sin, judgment, and the destruction of the ungodly.

It is better to be disturbed now, in the day of God's grace, than later in the day of His wrath. Disturbance such as this should lead to repentance, faith in the Lord Jesus Christ, and salvation. Indeed, God is patient with us so this may happen. As Peter says, "He is patient with you, not wanting anyone to perish, but everyone to come to repentance" (v. 9). Will you? Will you allow the fact of God's past destruction of the world by water to warn you of the pending destruction of the world by fire in the day of Christ's future judgment on the sins of mankind? Today is your day of opportunity, and all who will turn from sin may come to Christ and be saved. He said, "Whoever comes to me I will never drive away" (John 6:37).

---

[3]*The Ark on Ararat*, p. 329. The table of global flood traditions and a discussion of their significance occurs on pages 233–39.
[4]*The Ark on Ararat*, p. 268.

50

Geological Evidence for the Flood

(Genesis 7:17–24)

For forty days the flood kept coming on the earth, and as the waters increased they lifted the ark high above the earth. The waters rose and increased greatly on the earth, and the ark floated on the surface of the water. They rose greatly on the earth, and all the high mountains under the entire heavens were covered. The waters rose and covered the mountains to a depth of more than twenty feet. Every living thing that moved on the earth perished—birds, livestock, wild animals, all the creatures that swarm over the earth, and all mankind. Everything on dry land that had the breath of life in its nostrils died. Every living thing on the face of the earth was wiped out; men and animals and the creatures that move along the ground and the birds of the air were wiped from the earth. Only Noah was left, and those with him in the ark.

The waters flooded the earth for a hundred and fifty days.

Anyone who has been attentive to the movement of the last two chapters and is alert to the title of this one should expect that discussion of the "Geological Evidence for the Flood" will wrap up the main thesis: there was a flood, just as the Bible says, and the flood was of world-wide dimensions. The first study considered the Bible's own teaching. According to it, "the waters rose and increased greatly on the earth, and the ark floated on the surface of the water. They rose greatly on the earth, and all the high mountains under the entire heavens were covered. The waters rose and covered the mountains to a depth of more than twenty feet" (Gen. 7:18–20). This teaching is supported by the material reviewed in study two. That is, the Bible's teaching about a world-wide flood seems to be corroborated by flood traditions found among hundreds of widely scattered peoples and cultures of the globe. The culminating evidence should be geological.

Unfortunately, the situation is not as neat as that, and we must admit that the existing geological evidence for a world-wide flood is just not overpowering. Some would say that it is even nonexistent.

There have been claims that geology proves the Flood, of course. In an archeological campaign to Ur in 1928–29, Sir Leonard Woolley, a distinguished British archeologist, found an eight-foot stratum of clean clay beneath the Sumerian city and beneath that the remains of an entirely different city and culture. He claimed that this was incontrovertible evidence of the Genesis Flood. When just a few months later another archeologist, Stephen Langdon, announced that he had found a similar clay deposit at Kish, several hundred miles to the north, many concluded that this was indeed confirmation of the biblical account and that the Flood was at least of local distribution. Unfortunately, it was later announced that the flood deposits of the two cities were not contemporaneous and that the flood at Ur did not even inundate the entire city. Francis R. Steele, who at that time was Assistant Professor of Assyriology at the University of Pennsylvania, denounced

Woolley's conclusions, insisting that "the presumed 'evidence' had nothing whatever to do with the Flood recorded in the Bible."[1]

The Mesopotamian River valley was inundated by floods many times in ancient history, but all were apparently local floods. None has any particular claim to being the Flood associated with the name of Noah.

Flood Geology

The most ambitious of all efforts to cite geological evidence for Noah's Flood is the relatively recent attempt by the Creation Research Society of Ann Arbor, Michigan, and the Institute for Creation Research Society of San Diego, California, to view great portions and perhaps even most of the existing geological features of this earth as having been produced during the Flood year. This theory was discussed at some length in an earlier chapter.[2]

According to John C. Whitcomb and Henry M. Morris, the best-known exponents of this view, nearly all the existing fossils and hence the various levels of sedimentary rock in which they are found were produced by the Flood during the year the waters were on the earth. According to traditional geology, each level of sedimentary rock is evidence of a lengthy era in which water covered the area, later receded, and then advanced once more to create a new layer. Hundreds of such layers exist in some places. So according to traditional and widely accepted geology, water advanced and receded in these places for millions of years. Not so, say Whitcomb and Morris. If the Flood was as extensive and destructive as the Bible says, most of the earth's soil, plants, and animals must have been swept away before it

and would have settled in the oceans as layer upon layer of debris. According to their theory, the simplest marine organisms must have been buried first, after that other forms of marine life, eventually plants and animals. This hydrodynamic selectivity process would account for the gradation of forms in such rock, which biologists and others use as evidence for an evolution of species.

Creationists think their views are reinforced by the fact that conditions in our day are forming very few potential fossil deposits, and those that do exist are unusual. They think it obvious that the existing fossils must have been produced, not by slow natural processes, but by some past catastrophe of sufficient magnitude and scope to account for them.

If the creationist view is correct, then virtually all geological phenomena—rock strata, fossils, coal beds, oil deposits, and other things—are proof of the Flood, and there is no need to hunt further. The matter is settled. Unfortunately, not everyone is convinced that the evidence can be accounted for in this way. One person who is not is Davis A. Young, a Christian geologist now teaching at Calvin College in Grand Rapids. He inclines in the direction of a world-wide flood, though he is not certain that a proper interpretation of the Bible requires it. His difficulty at the point of the Whitcomb and Morris theory is not with the Bible's teaching so much as with their geology. He finds four major objections.

1. *Heat Flow from Solidifying Lava.* The first of Young's objections is a complex one and should be read in its entirety by anyone seriously investigating this problem. In brief, the objection is

---

[1]Francis R. Steele, "Science and the Bible," *Eternity*, March 1952, p. 44. For a comprehensive list of those both accepting and rejecting Woolley's views see Whitcomb and Morris, *The Genesis Flood*, pp. 109–111, especially footnote 2 on p. 111.

[2]See "Views of Creation: Six-day Creationism" (Gen. 1:1, 2), pp. 56–61.

this. Throughout the world there are places where molten lava, called magma, has pushed itself up between various layers of fossil-bearing rock and has then been covered over by more fossil-bearing rock. It has disturbed the first rock, which was obviously there before it. But it has not disturbed the second rock which was therefore clearly laid down after it. An example, which Young discusses at length, is the Palisades sill in northern New Jersey opposite New York. According to Flood geology, the first fossil-bearing rock would have had to have been laid down during the early stages of the Flood, after which the lava would have disturbed the layers and then hardened and eventually been covered over with more fossil-bearing material—all during the Flood year. The difficulty, however, is that lava does not cool as quickly as this particular sequence of events would require. The Palisades material, which is about 1,000 feet thick, would have taken several hundred years to cool so that it would not disturb the upper layers of fossil-bearing rock, and the Palisades sill is relatively thin so far as intruded magma formations are concerned. Estimates for the cooling of the Muskox intrusion in western Canada is 7,000 years, for the Stillwater intrusion in Montana 50,000 years, and for the Bushveld complex in South Africa 200,000 years.

2. *Radiometric Dating.* Various means of dating rock by the decay of radioactive substances lead to ages of hundreds of millions of years for certain kinds of intruding lava, such as the Palisades sill. Since it disrupts fossil-bearing rock, the fossil rock must have been laid down prior to it, that is, millions of years ago—too early for the Flood geology theory.

3. *Metamorphism.* Certain chemical changes in rocks require high tempera-tures and considerable pressure before they occur. The only known way of accounting for these temperatures and pressures is for the rocks to have been buried under miles of other rock. Since these rocks are sedimentary and contain some fossils, they must have originated during the Flood year, according to Whitcomb and Morris. Since they are covered over with other fossil-bearing but non-metamorphised rock, they must have been buried under miles of rock and then returned to the suface during the Flood year. But there is no known means of explaining how this could happen.

4. *Plate Techtonics.* Certain kinds of fossil-bearing rocks go back to the time when the continents were joined to-gether. According to the Flood geolo-gists, the continents would have had to have moved from that original position to their present position at an extremely rapid rate and in relatively recent times. No one can explain how that could have happened and, in fact, it does not seem to have been the case.[3]

TYPES OF EVIDENCE

Does this mean that there is then no possible geological evidence that might be due to the Flood's activity? No. It only means that we must be careful how we treat it and that we must be conscious of the fact that the final word has undoubt-edly not been heard yet. Without at-tempting to place all these elements into one great theory, we can point to the following things as perhaps being due to the Flood in some manner and as at least hard to explain without it.

1. Scattered throughout the world in various places are *large caches of animal bones* in what geologists call "rubble drift in ossiferous fissures." Ossiferous fissures are great rents in the earth, such as occur during earthquakes or other

---

[3]Young, *Creation and the Flood,* pp. 171–213. Each of his four points should be read as Young presents them, since only the simplest restatement is presented here.

violent disruptions of the earth's surface. Rubble drift is a kind of deposit in such fissures apparently placed there by water during the disruption in which the rents occurred. Such fissures have been found in England, France, southern Spain, Germany, Russia, and other countries. The interesting thing about them is that many are filled with bones of such animals as elephants, rhinoceroses, hippopotamuses, reindeer, horses, pigs, and oxen. The skeletons are not intact. They have been ripped apart. But the bones are not scattered. They are thrown together in almost unbelievable profusion. It is a final interesting feature of such deposits that they usually occur on isolated hills of considerable height.

A classic example is an isolated hill in the area of Burgundy, France, in the Saar valley. The hill rises 1,030 feet above the surrounding plain and has near its top a fissure crowded with animal bones. In this fissure the bones of animals not usually found together are intermixed. On the island of Cerigo, near Corfu, there is a mountain called the mountain of bones. The area involved is a mile in circumference at the base, and from base to summit it is literally covered with skeletons. The Rock of Gibraltar has bone-filled fissures that are 300 feet deep. In a cavern near Palermo, Sicily, more than twenty tons of bones have been discovered. In the northwest corner of Nebraska there is a hill on which a bone bed was discovered in 1876. It is estimated that the bones of about 9,000 complete animals are buried on this one hill. There are similar examples from the Russian steppes near Odessa, from Brunswick and Stuttgart, Germany, from Malta, and from other places.

What can account for the collection of so many bones of so many mutually hostile animals in such unlikely environments—if not the worldwide Flood of Genesis 6–9? One commentator writes, "A great flood of water is the only reasonable explanation for this strange phenomenon. For what else could have driven these animals together on hilltops and caused them to perish in such numbers but the waters of an all engulfing flood?"[4]

2. The existence of *large inland bodies of water* and the remains of such bodies, called fossil lakes, is best explained by the Deluge. Today much of this water is gone, as we might expect, due to evaporation and drainage in the millennia since the Flood. But at one time there were vast inland seas on literally every continent. The area of China now known as the great Gobi desert was once an inland lake of a size comparable to the present Mediterranean. It is referred to as the great Han Hai or interior sea by the Chinese. Lake Baikal in Siberia is a presently existing sea, which was at one time much bigger than it is today. It stands at 1,500 feet above sea level. Areas of India, Mongolia, Turkestan, Africa, and Central Asia were once inundated. It is well known that large areas of North America were once covered by seas or inland lakes. Geologists call these: Lake Algonquin, which filled the Great Lakes region to a height about twenty-six feet above the present level of the lakes; Lake Iroquois, which covered much of New York state; Lake Agassiz, which covered parts of Minnesota, North Dakota, and the Canadian provinces of Saskatchewan, Manitoba and Ontario; and Lake Bonneville, which filled the valley of Utah's Salt Lake and was about the size of Lake Michigan.

Geologists ascribe different origins to these inland and fossil lakes, and it may well be that there have been different

---

[4]Rehwinkel, *The Flood in the Light of the Bible, Geology and Archeology*, p. 186. For a full discussion of these bone deposits see pp. 179–87.

origins for them. The land may have fallen and then been raised again, even to heights of 1,000 or more feet. But it must be admitted that a deluge of a magnitude such as that described in the Bible would be a satisfactory explanation for these lakes since it would provide sufficient water to fill the basins.

3. *Coal beds and oil fields* could have been produced by the Deluge. The creation of coal and oil in the immense quantities known to us is an amazing thing, usually ascribed to the action of natural forces over millions if not billions of years. But it is conceivable that much or even all of this could have been created at nearly one time through the burial of large quantities of vegetable and animal matter by Flood activity.

4. The last of these strange facts is the astonishing preservation of thousands upon thousands of *mammoth bodies in Siberia*. The mammoth was a member of the elephant family and looks like an elephant in reconstructed pictures. But it was larger, standing twelve to thirteen feet high at the shoulder, and was covered with a thick coat of long, coarse, black hair. Its tusks could be nine or ten feet long and measure two-and-a-half feet around the base. Each one weighed on the order of 180 to 200 pounds, as compared with the 40-pound tusks of an average elephant today. The mammoth roamed over most of North America and nearly the whole of Europe. He was particularly abundant in northern Asia.

It is almost impossible to exaggerate the number and distribution of the mammoth remains in northern Asia, particularly Siberia. This area of Russia stretches more than 2,000 miles along the Arctic Ocean. It is level, much like our midwest, and is so thoroughly frozen due to the continual cold at this northern latitude that only a few feet of the topmost soil ever thaws out and that only for a few weeks in mid-summer. It

is here in this vast, forbidding waste that these creatures are found. Whole areas are filled with fossil bones. One island, Lachov, is said to be composed almost entirely of bones. In other areas, not merely bones but whole animals—bones, skin, tusks, hair and all—are preserved so thoroughly that the creatures seem lifelike even today. Moreover, a surprising number of mammoth carcasses and skeletons have been discovered in an upright, standing position, just as they lived. Clearly they were frozen suddenly and thus preserved nearly intact until now.

How many mammoths were there? It is impossible to calculate. But people have been in the business of collecting the ivory tusks of these creatures from the year A.D. 900 at least, and in one twenty-year period in which records were kept tusks of at least 20,000 mammoths were taken from just one Siberian deposit. Experts estimate that as many as five million of these creatures may have perished all at one time. What known geologic or atmospheric cause could have overwhelmed them, young and old alike, buried them and then preserved them until today? The best possible explanation is a world-wide Flood followed by a change in climate so drastic that these northern areas, which had been temperate before, now became arctic and thus preserved these magnificent creatures frozen in the ground.[5]

THE RISING SEA

There is one last point. In a general way, it is possible to graph the level of the oceans of the world as they existed thousands of years into the past. This graphing might not show a brief unusual variation—not even a flood that covered everything—but it does give an average height century by century over quite a few millennia. Twenty thousand years ago the water was 240 to 300 feet

[5]*The Flood,* pp. 238–54.

lower than we know it now. From that point it rose gradually to approximately present levels. For the past 4,000 or 5,000 years it has been almost constant. But here is the interesting thing: about 6,000 years ago it rose ten to twelve feet above the present level which, so far as we know, was the highest the seas have ever been.[6]

A rise of ten feet could not have produced the destruction of every living thing, which the Bible says the Flood of Noah's day did. But it could be the aftermath of that Flood, the peak of which, because of its short duration, might

have left few if any other tell-tale marks on the earth.

At present geology does not prove the Flood, but it does not disprove it either. And it actually discloses quite a few items that might best be explained by a flood of world-wide dimensions. There is no reason for the Christian to reject the simple meaning of the Genesis story— nor for anyone else to reject it either. On the contrary, there is every reason to take it as simple truth and move on from that point to ponder the grave warning of God's ultimate judgment of sin embodied in it.

---

[6]Statistics from Rhodes W. Fairbridge, "The Changing Level of the Sea," in the *Scientific American*, May 1960, as cited in Paul A. Zimmerman, editor, *Rock Strata and the Bible Record* (St. Louis: Concordia, 1970), pp. 197–200.

51

The God Who Remembers

(Genesis 8:1–19)

But God remembered Noah and all the wild animals and the livestock that were with him in the ark, and he sent a wind over the earth and the waters receded. Now the springs of the deep and the floodgates of the heavens had been closed, and the rain had stopped falling from the sky. The water receded steadily from the earth. At the end of the hundred and fifty days the water had gone down, and on the seventeenth day of the seventh month the ark came to rest on the mountains of Ararat. The waters continued to recede until the tenth month, and on the first day of the tenth month the tops of the mountains became visible.

After forty days Noah opened the window he had made in the ark and sent out a raven, and it kept flying back and forth until the water had dried up from the earth. Then he sent out a dove to see if the water had receded from the surface of the ground. But the dove could find no place to set its feet because there was water over all the surface of the earth; so it returned to Noah in the ark. He reached out his hand and took the dove and brought it back to himself in the ark. He waited seven more days and again sent out the dove from the ark. When the dove returned to him in the evening, there in its beak was a freshly plucked olive leaf! Then Noah knew that the water had receded from the earth. He waited seven more days and sent the dove out again, but this time it did not return to him.

By the first day of the first month of Noah's six hundred and first year, the water had dried up from the earth. Noah then removed the covering from the ark and saw that the surface of the ground was dry. By the twenty-seventh day of the second month the earth was completely dry.

Then God said to Noah, "Come out of the ark, you and your wife and your sons and their wives. Bring out every kind of living creature that is with you—the birds, the animals, and all the creatures that move along the ground—so they can multiply on the earth and be fruitful and increase in number upon it."

So Noah came out, together with his sons and his wife and his sons' wives. All the animals and all the creatures that move along the ground and all the birds—everything that moves on the earth—came out of the ark, one kind after another.

In the closing days of the second world war I was seven years old, and my father was stationed with the Air Force at Barksdale Field, Louisiana—with the family. We knew that the war was ending. Many servicemen had been sent home. We were looking forward to a discharge too and had even begun to pack so we could leave quickly if the papers came through. I remember my father explaining that when we were discharged we would have to leave quickly or run the risk that other orders might come through canceling the discharge.

When our discharge did come, school was in session, so I was told that we would leave as soon as I got home that afternoon. I was so excited! I could hardly wait to get on the school bus, get back to the base, and then get off at our corner. When the bus stopped I ran up the sidewalk and the steps to our front door. It was locked. Surprised and a bit subdued, I went around to the back door and found that it was locked too. At last I found a window I knew could not be locked and after prying it up with a nail I crawled over the sill into a room adjoining the kitchen. It was empty. So was the entire house. I will never forget making my way slowly from room to room with the sinking sensation that in the rush of packing and the need to "leave quickly lest our orders be canceled" I had somehow been left behind. Actually, my parents had only gone off briefly for a last-minute errand. While I was wandering through the empty house they had returned and were waiting outside in the car for the school bus, which they thought had not yet dropped me off. But it was a sad little boy they saw backing out of the window of the room next to the kitchen after my tour of the empty house had been completed.

ALONE ON THE DEEP

Reflecting on that experience, I have some appreciation for Noah's feelings after he had been drifting on the endless world-sea for almost a year, following the onslaught of the Flood. He had been a man of faith, "blameless among the people of his time" (Gen. 6:9). But he was human too, and the sea is a very lonely place. Imagine drifting in a large ship—not merely overnight, but night after night, month after month, for a year—with nothing in sight. During those months, faith or no faith, Noah must have wondered whether God had not forgotten him, his family, and the animals as they floated like insignificant bits of refuse on the great tide.

There would be spiritual considerations too, and Noah, being spiritual, would have been sure to think of them.

Robert S. Candlish, a nineteenth-century expositor of Genesis, puts Noah's possible train of thought like this: "Far down in the unfathomable depths below lies a dead and buried world. Noah, shut up in his narrow prison, seems to be abandoned to his fate. He cannot help himself. And in this universal visitation of sin—this terrible reckoning with sinners—why should he obtain mercy? What is he, that when all else are taken, he should be left? May he not be righteously suffered to perish after all? Is he not a sinner, like the rest? Does he not feel himself to be 'the chief of sinners'?"[1] Noah's very spirituality would have opened him up to such feelings. And when he thought like this, he would have felt himself to be abandoned by his heavenly Father much more keenly than I (or anyone else) ever felt abandoned by an earthly father.

Are you in that state even as you read these words? Do you feel abandoned? Does God seem to have forgotten you? If that is the case, the eighth chapter of Genesis is for you particularly, for its theme is that God has not forgotten. God remembers. The chapter begins, "But God remembered Noah and all the wild animals and the livestock that were with him in the ark."

GOD REMEMBERS

We have to see this from Noah's point of view, of course. But it is just here that the verse is so valuable. If we were to look at it from God's point of view, we would have to argue, as many commentators have done, that, of course, this is an anthropomorphism, God merely speaking as if he were a man. We would have to assert that, of course, God had never actually forgotten Noah, for God never forgets anything. This would be true. The only difficulties are that it is all so abstract and that it misses the impor-

---

[1]Robert S. Candlish, *Studies in Genesis* (Grand Rapids: Kregel, 1979), pp. 135, 136. Original edition 1868.

tant connection between God's remembrance of Noah and his showing in tangible ways that he remembered. When we look at this from Noah's point of view, this is wonderful. Although Noah felt himself to be abandoned by God and was abandoned so far as any direct intervention of God or a word from Him during the Flood year was concerned, those days were now overcome. God acted again! God spoke again! And Noah's depression must have fled away like storm clouds after the sun had again begun to shine.

That is the point at which this story communicates hope—if you think yourself to be abandoned by God. The hope is not in abstract reasoning to the effect that God is aware of all things and is therefore aware of you. That is true, but it is not always helpful. The hope is in knowing that although God has not acted in your life for what is perhaps a long time, nevertheless He will act again. And in the meantime, your job is to go on in faithful obedience to what He has already shown you—however long ago that was.

God remembered Noah in three ways. First, he began to *remove the water*, the aftermath of His great judgment on the world. The story says, "He [that is, God] sent a wind over the earth and the waters receded. . . . The water receded steadily from the earth. At the end of the hundred and fifty days the water had gone down, and on the seventeenth day of the seventh month the ark came to rest on the mountains of Ararat" (vv. 1, 3, 4).

I do not know whether this is what Moses had in mind, but I suspect that as he wrote these words he was thinking of the creation story of Genesis 1 and was picturing this later work of God as a new creation. At the beginning of Genesis we are told that "the *Spirit* [the Hebrew word is *ruach*] of God was hovering over the waters" (Gen. 1:2). This is the word used in Genesis 8:1 (though it is translated "wind" rather than "Spirit"), and

this plus the obvious similarity of scene inevitably takes our minds back to the beginning. As a result of the Flood, the earth had returned to a form much like that described in Genesis 1. It was dark, due to the storm clouds that brought the rain. It was covered with water. There was no life, except (in this case) for the tiny cargo encompassed in the ark. But then the Spirit of God, the divine wind, began to blow across the surface of the waters. The waters were separated from the dry land. The clouds began to dissipate. The sun appeared. Eventually, the grass, plants, and trees began to renew themselves, and the animals and people aboard the ark were sent forth into the brave new world before them.

As I say, I am not sure that this is what Moses had in mind. But if it is, it is a way of saying that when God remembers, He often does it with a new burst of power. During the darkness you may have felt quite dead. But suddenly the life of God is there again, and you suddenly begin to move forward. We have to trust God during the bad times, like Habakkuk, who said,

Though the fig tree does not bud
 and there are no grapes on the vines,
though the olive crop fails
 and the fields produce no food,
though there are no sheep in the pen
 and no cattle in the stalls,
yet I will rejoice in the LORD,
 I will be joyful in God my Savior
 (Hab. 3:17, 18).

Yet we are also to look ahead to the days of restoration, like Amos.

"The days are coming," declares the LORD,
 "when the reaper will be overtaken
 by the plowman
 and the planter by the one treading grapes.
New wine will drip from the mountains
 and flow from all the hills. . . .
They will plant vineyards and drink
 their wine;
 they will make gardens and eat their
 fruit"
 (Amos 9:13, 14).

The second way God remembered Noah was by giving him *a sign* through the sending out and return of the dove. Noah wanted to see if the ground had become dry enough for the animals and people to disembark, so he sent out birds to test the environment. A raven was dispatched, but it just kept flying around. Next Noah sent out a dove. The first time it flew out and returned, but the second time it returned with a freshly plucked olive leaf in its beak. When Noah saw this he knew that the waters had receded, that the earth was renewing itself, and that the judgment was past. The sign of a dove carrying an olive branch was so moving that the symbol is used as a token of peace even today.

In a manner similar to this, God also gives signs to His people today. This is an area that is often so personal that few talk about it. But in my repeated opportunities to talk with those who have lost a husband or wife, a son or daughter, a job, their health—people who are going through a great flood and sometimes are tempted to feel abandoned—I have found that again and again they tell me of some small but meaningful thing God has done to assure them that what they are enduring is not mere chance but rather part of the wise and loving plan of God.

Because the family has itself told these things in writing, I can share the account of the death of their son David by the well-known pediatric surgeon, now Surgeon General, Dr. C. Everett Koop and his wife Elizabeth. In *Sometimes Mountains Move*, their account of David's death in a mountain-climbing accident, they tell of a sequence of events God sent to reassure them. Their son had decided to go to the far west for graduate school, away from his home in Philadelphia. So they were gradually

getting accustomed to seeing him less. Each of the family members had in recent days spent special and unusual times with David. Dr. Koop had received hundreds of letters from bereaved parents or parents whose children were dying, as the result of an article he had published in *Reader's Digest*. Responding to those letters was an important preparation for what was to come. On the Sunday morning following their son's death the responsive reading in church was Psalm 18, in which they read, "As for God, his way is perfect" (v. 30), "He maketh my feet like hinds' feet, and setteth me upon my high places" (v. 33) and "Thou hast enlarged my steps under me, that my feet did not slip" (v. 36). In the aftermath of David's death several people became Christians and David's brother Norman entered the Christian ministry.[2]

This is what I mean by signs. God does not always spare us the distress, because He has a purpose in such things both for ourselves and others. But He has a way of reassuring us that He has not forgotten, that He remembers our distress and that He is still working all things for good to those who love Him.

The third way God remembered Noah was by *words*. He spoke to him again, saying, "Come out of the ark, you and your wife and your sons and their wives. Bring out every kind of living creature that is with you—the birds, the animals, and all the creatures that move along the ground—so they can multiply on the earth and be fruitful and increase in number upon it" (vv. 16, 17). As I read the account, I sense that God had not spoken to Noah in a direct way for over a year, for the last time we are told God spoke was in chapter 7: "Go into the ark, you and your whole family" (v. 1). Noah was in the ark a year and ten days. So for all that time he apparently received no

---

[2]C. Everett Koop and Elizabeth Koop, *Sometimes Mountains Move* (Wheaton, Ill.: Tyndale House, 1979).

new word from God. This must have added greatly to his sense of loneliness. "Why doesn't God speak to me?" he must have asked. But at last God did speak, and Noah knew he had been remembered.

You may be going through a period in which God seems to be silent. You pray, but the heavens seem to be made of iron. You wonder if God has heard you. What should you do in such circumstances? You should do as Noah did: go on as you have been going and wait for God to speak again. Notice that in Noah's case, when God finally did speak, Noah obeyed by doing exactly what God told him to do (vv. 18, 19). Noah obeyed then because he had been obeying previously. You will also obey God best if you have been practicing obedience during the dark hours.

NOAH REMEMBERED

There is one last point, the true marvel of the story. We have focused on the truth that God remembers, but there is no real surprise in that. It is God's nature to remember. He is faithful. To be sure, this is the first time in the Bible where we are told that God remembered something: "But God remembered Noah and all the wild animals and the livestock that were with him in the ark" (Gen. 8:1). But this is not the last time. Several chapters farther on we are told that God "remembered Abraham" (Gen. 19:29). Later we are told that "God remembered Rachel," Isaac's wife (Gen. 30:22). Psalm 9 tells us that God "remembers . . . the afflicted" (v. 12). Many times God is said to remember His covenant or His promises. The psalmist writes that he "remembered us in our low estate" (Ps. 136:23).

What is the marvel, then, if it is not that God remembers? *It is that Noah remembered.* He remembered God. He showed it by coming out of the ark, building an altar, and then sacrificing some of all the clean animals and clean birds as sin offerings—thus coming to God once again as a sinner and in the way appointed.

Why is this surprising? It is surprising because it is not our nature to remember God or God's goodness. We forget and at no time more readily than immediately after we have been delivered from some distressing situation. A classic example is the Lord's healing of the lepers He encountered on the way to Jerusalem as He walked along the border between Samaria and Galilee. There were ten of them. As Jesus walked along they stood at a distance and cried out, "Jesus, Master, have pity on us." Jesus did have pity. He healed them. Then He told them to go and show themselves to the priests, which the law required. The priests would certify that they were clean so that they could return to society. A little later one leper came back and thanked Jesus profusely. He was a Samaritan. Jesus asked, "Were not all ten cleansed? Where are the other nine? Was no one found to return and give praise to God except this foreigner?" (Luke 17:11–19).

Noah was not like this. Instead of merely bursting from the ark and kicking up his heels with happiness to at last be free again, which we could well understand, he built an altar, offered sacrifices, and gathered his family to thank the God who had delivered them from the great Flood.

Let me challenge you thus to remember God. The Bible says, "Remember your Creator in the days of your youth" (Eccl. 12:1). We have a tendency to forget God in our youth, thinking that obedience to God and worship of God can be put off. That is great folly. The Bible says, "Remember God now."

The Bible also says, "Remember the LORD in a distant land" (Jer. 51:50). Jeremiah writes this, thinking about the deportation of his people to Babylon after the conquest of Jerusalem. His point is that while they were there, cut off from their roots, surrounded by a pagan culture and enticed by others' sins, the people would tend to forget God. They must not do so! And neither must we. Many Christians are in a distant land. Their school or work has separated them from their roots. They are in a new place. They have new friends. There are temptations to sin, and the devil is always present to remind them that no one, least of all anyone back home, will know. But that is precisely what we must not do. We must remember the Lord in a distant land as well as at home.

Finally, we may think of Jonah who declared while in the belly of the great fish, "When my life was ebbing away, I remembered you, Lord, and my prayer rose to you, to your holy temple" (Jonah 2:7). For all of us life is ebbing away in some sense. For many it is almost gone. Now is the time to remember, to hang on, to worship God to the end. From youth to old age, in sickness and in health, at home or away from home—remember God. And the God who remembers will be your joy and comfort both now and in the life to come.

52

Never Again! Never Again!

(Genesis 8:20–22)

Then Noah built an altar to the LORD and, taking some of all the clean animals and clean birds, he sacrificed burnt offerings on it. The LORD smelled the pleasing aroma and said in his heart: "Never again will I curse the ground because of man, even though every inclination of his heart is evil from childhood. And never again will I destroy all living creatures, as I have done.

> *"As long as the earth endures,*
> *seedtime and harvest,*
> *cold and heat,*
> *summer and winter,*
> *day and night*
> *will never cease."*

The greatest wonder of Genesis 8 is not that God remembered Noah but that Noah remembered God. It is not our nature to remember, least of all things that are spiritual. But Noah did remember. We are told that as soon as he left the ark "Noah built an altar to the LORD and, taking some of all the clean animals and clean birds, he sacrificed burnt offerings on it" (Gen. 8:20). This offering was both a thank offering for the deliverance Noah and his family had received, and a sin offering by which Noah confessed need of atonement for his and his family's transgressions. If life was to begin anew, it was to begin with a proper and thankful approach to God—at least so far as Noah had anything to do with it.

Noah's actions on leaving the ark did not mean that he approached this new life without anxiety. In the ark he would have wondered if God had abandoned him. Now, upon exiting, he would have been struck afresh with the terrors of God's judgment and would have wondered if a great destruction might not be poured forth again. After all, he was a

sinner—and so were his children. The same tendencies to evil that had led to the wickedness of the antedeluvian world were in them all. Would it not inevitably happen that they would sin greatly and that a fresh judgment of God would be called forth? Look at the world: a world beginning to renew itself but showing every indication of the horrible judgment that had just ended—bare hills, uprooted trees, vast bodies of slowly receding water. What was to prevent that water from rising once more and thus reinundating the land? What was to prevent him and his family from justly perishing at last because of sin?

It is against this background that God's covenant with Noah was given. God knew Noah and reassured him that in spite of the sin they both knew lay in the human heart, the creatures of the earth would not be destroyed again. God said, "Never again will I curse the ground because of man, even though every inclination of his heart is evil from childhood. And never again will I destroy all living creatures, as I have done" (v. 21).

GOD'S COVENANT

These verses from Genesis 8 and 9, plus a verse from chapter 6, constitute one of the fullest discussions of a divine covenant in the entire Bible. It is not the only covenant.[1] There was a previous covenant with Adam, though the word itself was not used, and there are subsequent covenants with Abraham, Moses, David, and the Lord Jesus Christ. Yet this is an important covenant and deserves careful attention, if for no other reason than that it is the first explicit discussion of the theme in Scripture. It was introduced in Genesis 6:18. In chapters 8 and 9 it is discussed in three parts: 1) God's promise never again to destroy the earth by flood (Gen. 8:20–22), 2) the institution of capital punishment as a central feature of it (Gen. 9:1–7), and 3) a specific reiteration of the covenant in which the rainbow sign is given (Gen. 9:8–17).

We noticed in our earlier discussion that in this and most of the other covenants there are three features. The covenants are unilateral, which means that they are established by God and not by man. They are eternal, as God is eternal. They are always of grace, for nothing in man (not even his obedience to the terms of the covenant) merits them. These features are very visible in Genesis 8:20–22.

First, everything said is *by God* and according to His pleasure. We have speculated on what Noah may have said or may have been thinking during these days, but so far as Genesis is concerned he is not recorded as having said anything. All is of God. Thus we have: "The LORD smelled the pleasing aroma and said in his heart: 'Never again will I curse the ground because of man. . . . And never again will I destroy all living creatures, as I have done'" (8:21); "Then God blessed Noah and his sons, saying . . ." (9:1); "Then God said to Noah

and to his sons with him: 'I now establish my covenant with you and with your descendants after you and with every living creature that was with you'" (9:8–10); "I establish my covenant with you" (9:11); "And God said, 'This is the sign of the covenant I am making between me and you and every living creature with you'" (9:12); "I will remember my covenant between me and you" (9:15); "So God said to Noah, 'This is the sign of the covenant I have established between me and all life on earth'" (9:17).

This feature of the narrative reflects a high view of God and immediately sets Genesis off from other ancient writings. In fact, it is a powerful evidence that this book is what it claims to be, a supernatural revelation of God to men and women and not a record of human thoughts about and aspirations after God. The idea of God establishing terms with us, which we are therefore merely to receive with gratitude, is foreign to our natural way of thinking. Indeed, it is entirely absent from other ancient religions. In the religions of the pagan world the relationship of a person to God (or one of the gods) is conceived as a bargain. The person does something for God as a result of which God is placed in his debt and is supposed to do something for the person. It may be sacrifice. In wartime great sacrifices were made to ensure the success of expeditions. It may be some other form of devotion. Whatever the case, the man and God meet on equal terms and agree to do things of mutual benefit to one another. The earliest chapters of Genesis present an entirely different concept. In them man does not bargain, for man has nothing to bargain with. God establishes the covenant according to His own good pleasure.

Second, the covenant is *eternal*. I do not mean that it is eternally eternal in the

---

[1]See "God of the Covenant" (Gen. 7:18), pp. 267–71.

sense that it will endure as long as God endures, for the conditions to which it applies will themselves not endure. It is eternal in the sense that so long as the conditions endure the covenant will be unalterable. This is the essential point of the verses that end Genesis 8. "Never again will I curse the ground because of man, even though every inclination of his heart is evil from childhood. And never again will I destroy all living creatures, as I have done. As long as the earth endures, seedtime and harvest, cold and heat, summer and winter, day and night will never cease" (vv. 21, 22). These verses could hardly make the point more emphatically. Three times they use the word "never"—"*Never* again will I curse the ground. . . . *Never* again will I destroy all living creatures. . . . Day and night will *never* cease." The repetition of phrases regarding the days and seasons have a similar effect.

It is good to have God say "never," because use of the word by human beings is often ludicrous. Haven't you done something so foolish that you said, "Well, I've learned my lesson; I'll never do that again"? But then you did it again. Haven't you ever looked at someone else's sin and said, "I'll never do that"? But you did. That is the way with human beings. We promise beyond what we can guarantee. Like Peter we say to Jesus, "Even if I have to die with you, I will never disown you" (Mark 14:31). But we do deny Him. Only God can say "never" and stick by it without fail.

God's promises never to do something or never to let something happen are among the most precious in His Word. In Judges 2:1, God is reported as saying to the Israelites, "I will never break my covenant with you." Psalm 15 lists a number of items that involve an upright way of life and concludes: "He who does these things will never be shaken" (v. 5). Psalm 55:22 says, "Cast

your cares on the LORD and he will sustain you; he will never let the righteous fall." Proverbs 10:30 declares, "The righteous will never be uprooted." Jesus used the word "never" on many occasions, more than any other personality in Scripture. He said, "Whoever drinks the water I give him will never thirst" (John 4:14); "He who comes to me will never go hungry, and he who believes in me will never be thirsty" (John 6:35); "If a man keeps my word, he will never see death" (John 8:51); "My sheep listen to my voice; I know them, and they follow me. I give them eternal life, and they shall never perish; no one can snatch them out of my hand" (John 10:27, 28); "Whoever lives and believes in me will never die" (John 11:26). In Hebrews God is quoted as saying, "Never will I leave you; never will I forsake you" (Heb. 13:5; cf. Deut. 31:6). These promises cover the whole spiritual life of the believer, from initial faith in Christ to eternal security and victory over death. In the case of Genesis 8:20–22 they cover a regular sequence of days and seasons as long as earth lasts.

The third feature of the covenant is *grace*, which is also clear in these verses. God establishes His covenant with Noah and his descendants, "even though every inclination of [man's] heart is evil from childhood" (v. 21). This part of God's promise must have been particularly comforting to Noah, knowing that he was a sinner and that sin might well erupt in terrible fashion again. In spite of his sin God would save him and would never again destroy humanity.

ORIGINAL SIN

In Martin Luther's lengthy exposition of Genesis (8 volumes) this phrase is treated at length, for he rightly recognized it as a highly important passage on original sin. In Luther's day, as in ours, people disliked this teaching and exerted much effort to explain it away.

They said that it is not that the heart *is* evil but only that it *inclines* to sin. They would not have used this term, but what they had in mind was the "blank slate" idea that became so popular in the nineteenth-century philosophy of human development. According to this view, the child is born morally neutral and sins later only because of the unhealthy moral environment to which this "innocent" inclines. That is comforting philosophy since it makes sin someone else's fault, but it is not what this verse teaches. It teaches that the heart *is* evil and that this is true from the individual's earliest days.

Luther writes, "He who says that the sensations and thoughts of the human heart are inclined toward evil from youth on is not making an insignificant statement, particularly since Moses declared previously, in chapter six (v. 5), that every thought of the heart is bent on evil at all times, that is, that it strives after evil and in its bent, impulse and effort is under the influence of evil. For instance, when the adulterer is inflamed with desire, even though opportunity, place, person and time are lacking, he is still plagued by lustful emotions and cannot concentrate on anything else in his thoughts. . . .

"Moses adds 'from his youth' because this evil lies hidden in early age and is dormant, as it were. The period of our infancy is spent in such a manner that reason and will seem dormant, and we are borne along by animal drives only, which pass away like a dream. We have hardly passed our fifth year when we look for idleness, play, wantonness and pleasures, but shun discipline, shake off obedience and hate all virtues, but especially the higher ones of truth and justice. Reason at that time awakes as from a deep sleep and becomes aware of some pleasures, but not yet the true ones, and of some evil things, but not yet the worst, by which it is possessed.

"But when reason has matured, then, after the other vices have somehow become established, there are added lust and the hideous passion of the flesh, revelry, gambling, quarreling, fighting, murder, theft and what not. Just as parents have need of the rod, so now the magistrate needs a prison and bonds to keep the evil nature under control.

"Who is not aware of the vices of the more advanced years? It is then that greed, ambition, pride, treachery, envy, etc., come rushing and crowding in. Moreover, these vices are all the more harmful since this age is more adroit at covering them up and adorning them. Here the sword of the magistrate is not adequate; the fire of hell is needed to punish such great and numerous crimes. Hence it is correctly stated above, in the sixth chapter (v. 5): 'The heart of man, or the imagination of his heart, is only evil every day, or at all times,' and in this passage: 'It is evil from its youth.'"[2]

The only quarrel I have with this excellent exposition of Luther's is that he has not stated the sins of youth forcefully enough. In Luther's treatment sin almost seems passive before the age of five. It is not so. It is active even then. Donald Grey Barnhouse told how one of his children exhibited her sinful nature before she could talk. The family was living in France at the time and had a French nanny who had taught the baby motions to a little French song. The song was about marionettes. As the words were sung the child's hands were made to go around in a circle to immitate the dancing and then they were placed behind the back to show how the dancers went backstage at the end of the act. The song went:

> Ainsi font, font, font
> Les petite marionettes.
> Ainsi font, font, font—

---

[2]Luther, *Luther's Works*, Vol. 2, pp. 122, 126, 127.

Tois petits tours
et puis sont vont.

The child was not allowed to suck her thumb and her parents usually smacked the baby's hand lightly to get her to stop. One day Dr. Barnhouse came into the nursery and there was no doubt as to what the baby had been doing. There was the mouth and the thumb, and there was a long string of saliva between them. As soon as the daughter saw him, she immediately began to make her little hands go through the motions of the marionette song as if to say, "No, dear father, you are mistaken. It may look as if I was sucking my thumb, but actually I was doing the little marionette song that seems to please you so much."

David was right when he said, "Surely I have been a sinner from birth, sinful from the time my mother conceived me" (Ps. 51:5).

From Fear to Favor

This passage provides a pattern for what sinful human beings must do to find God's favor. In a sense, we can do nothing; God has done everything. But we can at least come to God in the way God Himself has appointed and be assured as we come that He will receive us and will remain faithful to us within the covenant of salvation.

As sinners we appear before God as Noah did emerging from the ark. We have been recipients of His common grace. If God had not been favorable to us, we would have perished long before now. Yet we are sinners. We merit God's judgment, just as others do. Left to ourselves the sin within will undoubtedly bring us to perdition. We will perish utterly. What are we to do? We know not what to do. But God has set a way before us: the way of sacrifice. He has shown from the earliest days of the race, going back to Eden, that although sinners merit death for their transgressions it is nevertheless possible for a substitute to take the sinner's place. An innocent may die. God Himself showed this when He killed the animals and then clothed Adam and Eve in the animals' skins. This is the way Noah came to God after he exited from the ark. It is the way you and I must come today, though we do not actually offer sacrifices but rather look back in faith to the perfect sacrifice of the Lord Jesus Christ offered in our place. He is the lamb "slain . . . from the creation of the world" (Rev. 13:8). He is "the Lamb of God, who takes away the sin of the world" (John 1:29).

What happens as we come to God through faith in the perfect and finished work of Jesus? We find that God is pleased, and we hear Him promise that we are now His and that we shall never perish—not for this life, not for eternity. Our relationship with Him "will never cease."

53

The Test of Human Government

(Genesis 9:1–7)

Then God blessed Noah and his sons, saying to them, "Be fruitful and increase in number and fill the earth. The fear and dread of you will fall upon all the beasts of the earth and all the birds of the air, upon every creature that moves along the ground, and upon all the fish of the sea; they are given into your hands. Everything that lives and moves will be food for you. Just as I gave you the green plants, I now give you everything.

But you must not eat meat that has its lifeblood still in it. And for your lifeblood I will surely demand an accounting. I will demand an accounting from every animal. And from each man, too, I will demand an accounting for the life of his fellow man.

> *"Whoever sheds the blood of man,*
> *by man shall his blood be shed;*
> *for in the image of God*
> *has God made man.*

As for you, be fruitful and increase in number; multiply on the earth and increase upon it."

The second part of God's covenant with Noah is found in Genesis 9:1–7. It deals with human government, among other things, and it does not take a careful reading of the passage to see that a new set of conditions for man's life on earth is introduced in it. Previously, when Cain killed Abel, God did not kill Cain. He pronounced a curse on him and condemned him to be a wanderer on the earth. But when Cain complained that whoever would find him would kill him, God said, "Not so; if anyone kills Cain, he will suffer vengeance seven times over" (Gen. 4:15); He put a mark on him for protection. At the end of chapter 4, there is no suggestion that Lamech, who killed a young man, was even judged by God or even had to defend himself before an earthly tribunal. Now, however, God introduces the death penalty and thus indirectly establishes the human

governments that are to wield it.

Why did God do this? Like his giving of the law somewhat later, it was undoubtedly to restrain man's passions. Luther said, "God establishes government and gives it the sword to hold wantonness in check, lest violence and other sins proceed without limit."[1] But recognizing this, I wonder if there is not also something more. Let me explain.

One of sin's unpleasant consequences is the never-ending desire of the sinner to excuse himself, regardless of how guilty he and everyone else knows he is. This is true now and must have been true in these early ages of the race too. When Adam sinned he blamed Eve and indirectly God Himself ("The woman you put here with me—she gave me some fruit from the tree, and I ate it," Gen. 3:12). The woman blamed the serpent ("The serpent deceived me," Gen.

---

[1]Luther, *Luther's Works*, Vol. 2, p. 141.

3:13). I can imagine, though the Bible does not explicitly say so, that after the murder of Abel by Cain and the increased violence in the days leading up to the Flood, someone must have come along with the excuse that the reason so much crime existed is that God had not given men and women the right to punish the offender. "Look at what happened when Cain killed Abel," this person might have said. "Did Cain get what he deserved? Not at all! God actually protected him. Why, if we had been allowed to make an example of Cain, if we had been allowed to put him to death, we could have nipped behavior like his in the bud. People would have been afraid to murder, and we would have been spared this misery. The violence on earth is God's fault." In view of that argument, which I am sure must have been made, it is possible that the establishment of the death penalty in Genesis 9 is actually "a test of man by human government," a test of this theory.

Is the wickedness of man due to the lack of proper threats and penalties? Can the death penalty (and other lesser penalties) end crime? God puts it to the test. He grants the power. As we know, the argument of the objector proves wrong and the problem is seen to reside, not in the lack of proper penalties, but in the incorrigible wickedness of man's heart.

SUBMIT TO THE AUTHORITIES

The many failures of human government, which are the failures of human beings themselves, must not blind us to the truth that government is nevertheless directly and divinely established. That is, the authority of the state is from God and must be obeyed, save in those areas where from time to time it opposes itself to the greater authority which is God's. It is as Paul said: "Everyone must submit himself to the governing authorities, for there is no authority except that which God has established. The authorities that exist have been established by God. Consequently, he who rebels against the authority is rebelling against what God has instituted, and those who do so will bring judgment on themselves. For rulers hold no terror for those who do right, but for those who do wrong. Do you want to be free from fear of the one in authority? Then do what is right and he will commend you. For he is God's servant to do you good. But if you do wrong, be afraid, for he does not bear the sword for nothing. He is God's servant, an agent of wrath to bring punishment on the wrongdoer. Therefore, it is necessary to submit to the authorities, not only because of possible punishment but also because of conscience" (Rom. 13:1–5).

There are two errors that people tend to make in regard to human government. One is disregard for the state. It is a refusal to recognize its authority, expressed in a scorn of public leaders and a flaunting of perfectly valid laws. This is what Paul is primarily dealing with in Romans. The other error is to regard the state more highly than we ought, believing that the government will solve our problems. This is the characteristic error of American democracy, particularly at the present time.

A sound view of the state involves the following propositions:

1. *The essential element of government is force.* This is not something that we like to think about carefully, because "force" is not supposed to be good in our culture. We think it bad to force children to do something, for instance. We prefer to give them "options," present the good as being "in their best interests," offer "rewards" rather than punishments. Again, we have an almost inbred reaction against being forced to do anything. When we think about government, particularly one we favor, we do not like to think of it as existing by force and operating through force. We

like to think of it giving moral guidance, appealing to the best in its people and providing an environment for growth and self-fulfillment. It is true that government does do some of these things. Nevertheless, we must not be blind to the fact that its essential operating element is force.

Let me give an example. We have a system of so-called voluntary self-assessment of income tax in this country. When you fill out your form each April you can read on the front of the tax booklet that we are a country unique in the world in that each year millions of Americans voluntarily assess their own tax and voluntarily pay those billions of dollars that keep the government running. But income tax is not really voluntary. If you do not believe it, try refusing to pay your tax some year. Or refuse to pay even part of it. Say you object to the part that is used for nuclear weapons or aid to the cities or head-start programs for minorities. What will happen? Will the government say, "Well, our tax system is voluntary; if this person doesn't want to pay, there's just nothing we can do about it." You know perfectly well that won't happen. You will be billed and fined, and if you still refuse to pay, a constable will eventually arrive at the door and you will be arrested. Besides, your assets will be seized to pay the delinquent taxes. The matter is not at all voluntary. It is mandatory, and the proof of it is the government's final use of force to accomplish its objectives.

Let me give another example. Suppose you are a businessman who is becoming bogged down under the increasing mounds of government red tape. You have so many forms to fill out that you decide you just will not fill them out this year. What will happen? You know what will happen. The government will close down your business and arrest you for violating its laws.

2. *Government cannot develop morality*. When I say this I am sure you under-

stand that the key word is "develop." It is not that the government is unconcerned with morality. Indeed, morality is the only valid basis for law. If the government passes a law against stealing and enforces it with the sword, the only valid basis for that act is that stealing is wrong. If it is not wrong, then the act of government is tyranny—an unjust and intolerable restriction of freedom. If it is wrong, then the government is acting properly. It is the same with all laws. The only valid basis for any law is a previously existing morality. We see this in the institution of capital punishment in Genesis 9:6. Here government is given the right to take the murderer's life on the basis that the one killed was "in the image of God" and that the act was therefore an offense to God.

To recognize the connection between law and morality is not to say that the government can develop morality in its citizens, however, for it cannot. It can proscribe penalties. It can enforce them. But it cannot develop the morality those penalties and their enforcement express. If you doubt this, think back to the prohibition era. Government outlawed liquor, but the traffic in alcoholic beverages flourished. Similarly, prior to the Supreme Court act of January 22, 1973, legalizing abortion, abortions in the United States were illegal. But they were still performed! Their illegality did not ensure the regard for human life we desire.

Someone will argue that the act of the court legalizing abortion opened a floodgate for abuse, and that is true. Far more infants are murdered before birth today than previously, now nearly one and a half million per year in this country. But that is only to say that the law was a restraint on desires that were already present, not that it created contrary desires, which it did not do.

At best, government will express in laws and enforce by its inherent power the sense of morality already present (or absent) in its citizenry. But the morality itself must come from another source. What can that be? If it is not the morality of mere pragmatism (what works) or the morality of consensus (what most of us want, and the others do not count), it must be the morality of revealed religion working its way into national life through those citizens who know and sincerely desire to please God. In other words, to go back to my previous examples, the only thing that will restrict the use and abuse of alcohol in a society is the conviction of a majority of its citizens that this is wrong. Or again, the only thing that will reduce or eliminate abortion (which may, of course, eventually be expressed in a constitutional amendment or other law, outlawing it) is the deep conviction on the part of many that abortion of babies is murder and that murder, even of the unborn, is intolerable. This means that your convictions in these and other areas and your forthright expression of them are more important in the ultimate analysis than the laws that may be forthcoming.

If the morality is not there to support the laws, then even the laws themselves may be used immorally. The law can be used to get out of paying one's debts, escape a just prison sentence, cheat the innocent, oppress the poor, and commit similar atrocities.

3. This leads to the third proposition: *a healthy government needs a healthy citizenry*. If government cannot produce morality, it must be provided with morality from a religious source. If it does not have this element among its people, then government itself becomes corrupt and tyrannous.

This, too, has a conclusion in regard to Christian people. In a declining cultural and moral environment, such as our own, the greatest need is not for more laws or even for a greater spiritual sensitivity on the part of unbelievers, but rather for confession of sin and a deep moving of the Spirit of God among God's people. This is the burden of one of the most important texts of the Bible relating to national renewal. It occurs in 2 Chronicles 7, the same chapter in which Solomon's dedication of the temple is described. That night, after the festivities, the Lord appeared to the king and gave him these words, "If my people, who are called by my name, will humble themselves and pray and seek my face and turn from their wicked ways, then will I hear from heaven and will forgive their sin and will heal their land" (2 Chron. 7:14). Notice that the cure for healing is not the replacement of the ruler or the election of a better ruler (even a "born-again" one). It is the repentance and renewal of God's people. Why? Because this is the only way renewal can come. Government cannot provide it, as we have seen. Even a "born-again" president cannot provide it. Government can only deal in force, and what is needed is a forceful new apprehension of what is right and wrong.

Jacques Ellul uses this insight to demythologize the state in his book, *The Political Illusion*.[2] He shows that current Western faith in the state to solve our most basic problems is the height of folly. He calls on the individual to resist its ever-expanding encroachment on our lives. In times of moral decline the state will inevitably expand or else be overthrown, because the need for order demands it. But in times of high morality, which is synonymous with times of great faith and spiritual awakening, the government need function only in a minimal way. That is better! The best situation is as few laws as possible.

NO KING BUT CAESAR?

My fourth point deserves separate treatment, for it is one we especially

---

[2]Jacques Ellul, *The Political Illusion*, trans. by Konrad Kellen (New York: Vintage Books, 1967).

need to hear: *since the state has been established by God it is responsible to God.* This is true whether or not the state exists in an age of spiritual depth and morality. To go back to our text, we note that it is God who established the state in His covenant with Noah—not Noah, not the church. We notice in Romans 13 that it is God who has ordained the existing powers (v. 1). This means, on the one hand, that the state has certain divinely ordained authority over us. But it also means, on the other hand, that the state for its part is under God's authority and cannot justly or safely disregard His law or its divinely given function.

At the trial of Christ, which was actually a trial of the Roman government, the chief priests are said to have told Pilate, "We have no king but Caesar" (John 19:15). It is hard to believe they said this, for they hated Caesar and his appointees in Palestine. But they did say it and thus betrayed how far they were from God and into what danger they had fallen. By appealing to Caesar alone and by rejecting Christ they were eliminating the only ultimate check on godless rulers. If God is in the picture, even under the worst of tyrants He may at least be appealed to and He may actually correct the injustice. But if God is gone, if His authority is not recognized, then there is nothing left but the whims or cruelty of corrupt but powerful men.

We may be more specific. Without God in the picture, there is no rein on Caesar. And Caesar needs a rein! In America we recognize this secularly, for we have developed a system of checks and balances according to which one branch of government limits another. Congress makes laws that govern all citizens; but the judicial branch can declare them unconstitutional. The President appoints Supreme Court justices; but Congress has authority to impeach the President. The President may initiate programs; but Congress must fund them. We recognize the need for checks and balances on the secular level because we know by experience that men in power are untrustworthy. But if this is true on the merely human level, how much truer it is on the cosmic level. God is ultimate. If we forsake God, we are at the mercy of our governors.[3]

Christians must remind the state of this ultimate responsibility. We speak in America of government deriving its powers from the consent of the governed, but there is more to it than that. Government derives its authority from God and is responsible to God. Our role is to remind the state of that fact and challenge it to operate accordingly.

Can we? Will we? Not as we are presently living—for self and substance! We can do it only as we are first possessed by the Lord Jesus Christ and determine to follow Him at whatever cost. In another writing I speak of three necessities. First, we must fix in our minds that God is truly sovereign in human affairs, including affairs of state. Second, we must know the Bible and its teachings. The reason for this is that one may be willing to do the right thing and yet not know what the right thing is, since the issues are not always black and white but gray. We can respond to such situations properly only when we know what Scripture teaches. Third, we must be willing to surrender everything, even life itself, if that is necessary. Nothing is achieved by those who refuse to sacrifice. Our self-indulgent age desperately needs to learn that. But it will not learn it from the state, which sacrifices nothing. As a moral force the state is destitute. The world can learn sacrifice only from Christians, who have learned it from their Lord.

---

[3]I discuss these issues at greater length in chapter 16 of *God and History* (Downers Grove, Ill.: InterVarsity Press, 1981).

54

Sign of the Covenant

(Genesis 9:8–17)

Then God said to Noah and to his sons with him: "I now establish my covenant with you and with your descendants after you and with every living creature that was with you—the birds, the livestock and all the wild animals, all those that came out of the ark with you—every living creature on earth. I establish my covenant with you: Never again will all life be cut off by the waters of a flood; never again will there be a flood to destroy the earth."

And God said, "This is the sign of the covenant I am making between me and you and every living creature with you, a covenant for all generations to come: I have set my rainbow in the clouds, and it will be the sign of the covenant between me and the earth. Whenever I bring clouds over the earth and the rainbow appears in the clouds, I will remember my covenant between me and you and all living creatures of every kind. Never again will the waters become a flood to destroy all life. Whenever the rainbow appears in the clouds, I will see it and remember the everlasting covenant between God and all living creatures of every kind on the earth."

So God said to Noah, "This is the sign of the covenant I have established between me and all life on the earth."

A preacher can talk about God as the Ancient of Days and many other things—this seems entirely appropriate. But a sign-maker? I almost did not do it, until I began to remember that the Lord Jesus was a carpenter and began to think about the signs God makes.

There are two different kinds of signs in the Bible. Some are miraculous, what the Bible speaks of as "signs and wonders." There are whole clusters of these signs. Moses gave a series of such signs to Pharaoh. The miracles of Exodus, the plagues, were proof that God is truly God. In the New Testament we find the same thing during the earthly ministry of Jesus. The miracles were to show that Jesus was, as Nicodemus confessed, "a teacher who has come from God" (John 3:2). The other kind of biblical sign is not miraculous, at least not necessarily so. It is a symbol of spiritual truth. (Of course, these sometimes overlap. When the Lord Jesus Christ did certain miracles, such as the multiplying of the loaves and fish in Galilee and then spoke of Himself as the bread of life, He was doing what was miraculous but at the same time was a symbol of the truth that He satisfies the needs of the human soul.) Genesis 9:8–17 introduces us to the second kind of sign, the sign that is a symbol.

HEALING FOR THE SCARRED

The rainbow was given to Noah following the Flood, and the essential nature of this sign is that it is a thing of beauty. This is a case of the grace of God ministering to Noah after what must have been a most traumatic experience.

We speak of people being wounded by things that have come into their lives. Noah and those who were with him must have been wounded by the Flood. They had not endured personal physical loss, but the civilization they had known was wiped out. The Flood was a holocaust of major and unique proportions. It is difficult to see how they could have come through an experience like that without the wounds of the past on them. These wounds are the probable reason for the noticeable repetition as God gives the covenant. In the early chapters of Genesis the events more or less fly by. If we have any complaints about the early chapters of Genesis, humanly speaking, it is that God did not take time to tell us more. We have all kinds of questions. By contrast, in the story of the Flood we have great repetition. This one incident is expanded into several chapters, and when God gives the covenant He reiterates it again and again. In chapter 6 God says, "I'm going to establish a covenant." In chapter 8 we get the covenant in detail. Then, at the beginning of chapter 9 God expands on it even more fully saying, "I am never again going to destroy the earth by flood." In the verses we are looking at now, God enacts the covenant and gives the sign of the rainbow.

Why this reiteration? It is not for the sake of God, who does not need to repeat things, but for the sake of Noah who needed to hear them. He needed to be reassured. He was wounded in soul. So God said again and again, "I am never again going to destroy the world by flood. You have seen the ugliness of sin and its effects, the horror of my judgment. I want to reassure you that I will not send a flood again, and in order to do that I am making a beautiful rainbow in the sky as the pledge of my promise." As Noah looked at the rainbow he must have said, "Yes, that ministers to me. Because the God who is giving me this beautiful sign is not going to put us through such a judgment again."

I do not know where you fall in that picture. But I know there are many people who carry the scars of the past within them. There is a book by William Styron entitled *Sophie's Choice*. It tells the story of a young Jewish woman who survived one of the German death camps. She was confronted with a choice as she entered the camp. This choice is not talked about in the early pages of the book. It comes out only in the end. But when you get to it you know that it alone explains the agony of the earlier pages. As Sophie entered the death camp she had two children with her. One of the guards, apparently on a whim, told her she could keep one child but would have to let the other go off to the furnaces to die. This marred the mother irredeemably, and in the end she committed suicide because she was not able to cope with the past. There are people who have wounds like that—people who have suffered loss and tragedy.

To you I say, God is the God of beauty. God makes signs of beauty to say, "I know that life is filled with tragedy. Sin is ugly. But I am the God of beauty. I am the God who is able to overcome these things, and I call you away from them to Myself." At the end of the Bible, in Revelation, we have a picture of God sitting on His throne around which is a rainbow. Look forward to that and let God's beautiful sign minister to your soul.

Sign for the Lonely

Farther on in Genesis we come to Abraham. Abraham was a pioneer, and the problem Abraham labored with was loneliness. He had left his family, nation, and culture, going from Ur of the Chaldees on the far side of the Arabian desert across the fertile crescent into Palestine. God had directed him in this, and he had gone obediently and trustingly. Yet all that he had known was behind. The picture we have of Abraham in these early days is of a lonely man, accompanied only by his immediate family, in a land that was not his own.

What does God do for Abraham? God

takes him outside his tent on one of those crystal clear desert nights and directs him to look upward. Then, as Abraham looks up into the great expanse of the night sky, God points out the myriads of stars and promises him that this is what his posterity will be like. Abraham might feel alone, but he is to know that those who descend from him, not merely his physical children—though that is involved too—but his spiritual children, are going to be as numerous as those stars of heaven.

Are you lonely? Many people in our culture are lonely. Families have broken up. Relatives have died. Some are living by themselves in our great impersonal cities. I speak to many who feel alone. God says, "I want you to see things as I see them. I want you to see the great host of those who are My children, among whom you have your place. You are a part of that company." Again we turn to Revelation, the last book of the Bible, and we see God's description of those who are gathered around the throne of God, worshiping. What are we told? We are told that there are thousands upon thousands of God's people. You may feel lonely now, but one day you will experience the fullness of that great fellowship.

BRIDGE TO THE FUGITIVE

Abraham had a grandson whose name was Jacob. We have interesting stories about Jacob, and one of these contains a sign God made for him. Jacob was not a likable character. He was what we would call a "momma's boy." Besides that, he was not averse to cheating people to get what he wanted. The tragedy of a life like this is that the person inevitably alienates his friends and family. This is what Jacob did. He treated his brother Esau so badly that eventually Esau said he was going to kill him. Jacob had to get away from the danger. So we have the story of Jacob fleeing, all by himself, perhaps as a rela-

tively young man, out into the world, with no friends, having left behind his father, mother, brother, and whatever other immediate family he had.

The first night out he is sleeping in the mountains, his head on a rock for a pillow. He is feeling alienated. For if Abraham was alone, Jacob was not only alone but also isolated. It is here that God steps in. God makes a sign for Jacob. The sign is a great stairway from earth to heaven, with angels ascending and descending on that stairway. It is a bridge. That is the essence of the sign. God is saying to Jacob, "Even though you have alienated yourself from your family and friends, nevertheless, I choose not to be alienated from you. I establish this bridge. I want you to know that communication is there. I come to you. You can come to Me. I am with you wherever you go."

Jacob, the outcast, replies, "Surely the Lord is here. The others may be gone. I may have separated myself from them, but the Lord is in this place and I didn't know it." Jacob called the place Bethel, the "house of God," and he carried the memory of that sign with him during the years of his exile (Gen. 28:10–22).

There are many alienated people in our day. They are alienated because of their own acts. They do not like to face that, but if they will face it, then the barriers they have set up can be torn down. In the meantime God says, "I want you to know that the starting place is this: although you have alienated yourself from others I choose not to be alienated from you. I am the God who builds stairways. The greatest of these is the stairway on which the Lord Jesus Christ descended when He came to earth to be your Savior." God points you to that stairway and says, "If sin has produced alienation in your life, I want you to look to this stairway and come to Me."

COURAGE FOR THE DEFEATED

I think of another sign God made, a

sign for Moses. At this period in his life Moses had been forced to flee from Egypt. Some of the experiences that had been lived before by Abraham and Jacob were his as well but, in addition to the loneliness and alienation, Moses must also have had a sense of defeat. He had understood early in his life that he was to be the deliverer of God's people. He had been educated in the courts of Pharaoh and was taught, as Stephen said, "in all the wisdom of the Egyptians." But being raised as an Egyptian did not turn his head. He still recognized that he was a member of this outcast group of people who were being treated as slaves, and he identified with them (Heb. 11:25). He determined to lead them out of Egypt.

At last the day came. He saw an Egyptian beating a Hebrew slave, and he turned on the Egyptian and killed him. He thought, "Now the revolution will begin. I've taken the first step. God has chosen me. They're going to rally around. . . ." But this was not God's way. Instead of a revolution, word spread that Moses had killed an Egyptian and Moses had to flee. He ran to the far side of the desert where he would be safe, and he lived there for forty years. He was forty when he killed the Egyptian. He lived forty more years in the desert. Now he was eighty, and he was defeated for good.

Some people feel defeated at thirty or forty or at sixty-five when they retire. This man was *eighty*. What is God doing? All the gifts, training, and opportunities he had! He has been wasting these for eighty years. His life is over, and if ever there is a story of defeat it is the story of Moses.

But God gave Moses a sign. It was a burning bush. As Moses described it, it was a bush that was remarkable for the fact that it did not burn up! It was burning, but it did not burn up. Why? Because it was a symbol of the presence of the eternal and everlasting God. Thus it

was that Moses, who felt defeated, who felt that life was running out and his opportunities were gone, was brought face to face with the nature of the God he served. His life might be running out, but God's was not running out. He might be defeated, but God was not defeated. God would do what God would do—in the life of Moses or anyone else! God called him and said, "Moses, now is the time when I am going to send you to Egypt. And this is the message: Tell Pharaoh, 'Let my people go.'"

Do you feel defeated? Have you had opportunities and then wasted them? Do you feel that you will never get them back again? God is the eternal God. God can take you right where you are and can bring victory out of defeat. He can do that which is spiritually lasting, not only for this life (for you die, and the things you do live on only for a few years anyway) but for all eternity. That is the great thing about things spiritual. Everything material will pass away. The Lord himself said, "Heaven and earth will pass away" (Matt. 24:35). But that which is spiritual abides forever. What is done for Jesus Christ now—the stand that is taken, the word that is given, the moral victory that is won—no matter how insignificant it may appear in the world's eyes, is something that is going to last into the farthest reaches of eternity. Even the angels are going to inquire into it and say, "Look at the grace and power of our God who is able to do that in the life of a sinner." That is our privilege. God makes this sign to encourage us to go on.

Rest for the Weary

In Exodus 31 God gives another sign: the sabbath. God says to Israel, "You must observe my Sabbaths. This will be a sign between me and you for the generations to come" (Exod. 31:13). What is the essence of the sabbath? The essence of the rainbow is its beauty; the essence of the stars is their number; the essence of the stairway is its bridging a gap; the essence of the burning bush is God's presence. The essence of the sabbath is that it is a time of rest for weary people. Moses had led the people out of Egypt, and they had wandered in the desert for many years. At last they had come to their land, and God gave them the sabbath as a symbol of the rest they were to find in Him.

The application is to those who are weary in the Lord's work. Are you weary in the Lord's work? I am sure you are, because the apostle Paul said to people in his day, "Let us not become weary in doing good" (Gal. 6:9). He would not have said that if we did not become weary. This is one of my favorite Bible verses because it goes on to say, "Let us not become weary in doing good, for *at the proper time we will reap a harvest* if we do not give up." Are you weary? If so, God holds the symbol of his rest before you. There is a rest that "remains . . . for the people of God" (Heb. 4:9). If you have to look ahead to a future of unvarying continuation of the things you are doing, with all the trials, toils, and problems, it can be most defeating. How can you keep going day after day, year after year, knowing that as you grow older your strength is weakening and time is running out? How can you do it? You can if you know that there is a rest from your labors.

I started some long-distance running recently, and I found that it is a great help if the course is marked off in segments. After three, four, or five miles I'm tired and ready to stop. But then I come to a little marker, and the marker says "three and a half miles" or "four and a half miles." I say, "Well, it's only another half mile [or mile]; I can hang on that long." And I do! It is the same spiritually. Work is tiring. There is weariness in work, especially Christian work. It is worse than any other work. I do not know of any work that is harder than Christian work. It requires more effort

and more perseverance over a longer period of time. Like the title of a recent book, it is *A Long Obedience in the Same Direction.* But knowing that there is a rest at the end (and even some along the way) we keep going.

SALVATION FOR THOSE LEFT OUT

One evening out in the fields surrounding the town of Bethlehem a group of shepherds were taking care of their sheep. No one had a good opinion of shepherds. They were not even allowed to testify in a court of law, because everyone assumed that people like that would lie. So they were a left-out people, and there they were on this particular night. Suddenly an angel appeared in the sky and an announcement was given that the Messiah had been born in Bethlehem. The angel said to the shepherds: "This will be a sign to you: You will find a baby wrapped in strips of cloth and lying in a manger" (Luke 2:12).

The essence of this is the glorious condescension of our God. What had God done? He had come down, not merely as far as the peaks of Olympus, but beyond; not merely as far as the palaces of the Roman Caesars, but beyond; not merely as far as the courts of Herod or the great hall of the Sanhedrin, but beyond. He had come down, down, down to a manger, being born of a poor family who did not even have a place to lay their heads. He had come to the stable of Bethlehem.

If you feel left out—there are many who do—learn that God is here to take you in. He does not say, "Well, here's My house. Come on over. I'll open up a room for you somewhere." He reaches out to you. He has become like you. In fact, He has become even more lowly than you in order that there might be no barrier. All He asks is that you recognize that He has done it.

I think the Lord is grieved that so few receive His signs. On one occasion people came to Jesus and said, "What miraculous sign then will you give that we may see it and believe you?" This must have made a real impression, because the gospel writers repeat these words many times over in their Gospels (Matt. 12:38; 16:1; Mark 8:11; Luke 11:16; John 2:18; 6:30). Whenever the people asked that, the Lord must have thought over all the signs He had given. These were ample to lead people to faith. But what He said to these unbelievers most often was: "A wicked and adulterous generation asks for a miraculous sign! But none will be given it except the sign of the prophet Jonah. For as Jonah was three days and three nights in the belly of a huge fish, so the Son of Man will be three days and three nights in the heart of the earth" (Matt. 12:39, 40, etc.). That is the sign above all other signs. Jesus "died for our sins according to the Scriptures, . . . was buried, . . . was raised on the third day according to the Scriptures" (1 Cor. 15:3, 4) that you and I might know that we can have forgiveness of sins and everlasting life.

All these signs could be meaningful to you. But even if the others are not, at least allow this one to touch your heart: Jesus Christ was crucified in your place. He is risen. He is coming again. Allow Him to draw you to Himself for salvation.

55

The Fall of Noah

(Genesis 9:18–29)

The sons of Noah who came out of the ark were Shem, Ham and Japheth. (Ham was the father of Canaan.) These were the three sons of Noah, and from them came the people who were scattered over the earth.

Noah, a man of the soil, proceeded to plant a vineyard. When he drank some of its wine, he became drunk and lay uncovered inside his tent. Ham, the father of Canaan, saw his father's nakedness and told his two brothers outside. But Shem and Japheth took a garment and laid it across their shoulders; then they walked in backward and covered their father's nakedness. Their faces were turned the other way so that they would not see their father's nakedness.

When Noah awoke from his wine and found out what his youngest son had done to him, he said,

> *"Cursed be Canaan!*
> *The lowest of slaves*
> *will he be to his brothers."*

He also said,

> *"Blessed be the LORD, the God of Shem!*
> *May Canaan be the slave of Shem.*
> *May God extend the territory of Japheth;*
> *may Japheth live in the tents of Shem,*
> *and may Canaan be his slave."*

After the flood Noah lived 350 years. Altogether, Noah lived 950 years, and then he died.

The title of Thomas Huxley's futuristic novel *Brave New World* comes from a line of William Shakespeare in which a savage (repeated in Huxley's novel) exclaims of those from a higher civilization, "O what a brave new world to have such people in it." We might be inclined to speak those words over Noah and his family as they emerged into a world from which the ungodly had been removed by God's terrible and all-encompassing judgment. What a brave new world to have such people in it! Alas, the citizens of this new world were also sinners, as those who had gone before. The evil that was in the world, which had called forth God's wrath

against the human race, was also in the ark in the hearts of Noah and his family. It was now to break forth. Like Adam before him, Noah now also falls into sin, and his sin likewise effects his descendants.

We might suppose that having lived through such a terrible demonstration of God's wrath and now beginning again with God's covenant promises never again to destroy the earth by flood, the human race from this point on would have adhered to the path of righteousness. But this is not the case. We read that Noah "proceeded to plant a vineyard" and that "when he drank some of its wine, he became drunk and lay un-

317

covered inside his tent" (Gen. 9:20, 21). This led to a greater sin on the part of Noah's son Ham and to a curse on Ham's descendant Canaan.

Should we not exclaim with Jeremiah, truly "the heart is deceitful above all things and beyond cure. Who can understand it?" (Jer. 17:9)?

ALL FALL SHORT

The verses that end Genesis 9 fall into three parts: the fall of Noah, the sin of Ham, and the prophecy that the entire episode occasions. The fall of Noah is the place to start, for it is the basis of the other incidents and the source of many practical lessons about sin's consequences.

The first thing the fall of Noah teaches us is that *anyone can sin*. No one is above or beyond temptation. We remember that back at the beginning of the Flood story, when Noah and his family were introduced for the first time, it was said of Noah: "Noah was a righteous man, blameless among the people of his time, and he walked with God" (Gen. 6:9). In the New Testament Noah is called "a preacher of righteousness" (2 Peter 2:5). This is a character judgment matched by very few biblical characters. We would not expect God to make that assessment of us but would gladly look to Noah for how we should conduct ourselves. We want to be righteous and blameless, and walk with God. Yet here is Noah, our example, falling into sin. If he can sin, anyone can, ourselves included.

This story is another small proof of the divine inspiration of the Scriptures. As Arthur W. Pink says, "It is human to err, but it is also human to conceal the blemishes of those we admire. Had the Bible been a human production, had it been written by uninspired historians, the defects of its leading characters would have been ignored, or, if recorded at all, an attempt at extenuation

would have been made. Had some human admirer chronicled the history of Noah, his awful fall would have been omitted. The fact that it is recorded and that no effort is made to excuse his sin, is evidence that the characters of the Bible are painted in the colors of truth and nature, that such characters were not sketched by human pens, that Moses and the other historians must have written by divine inspiration."[1]

Since this story is told by God and not by a mere human author, it follows that it is true—that Noah did fall. Therefore, anyone can fall. If Noah sinned, we are surely not exempt from it.

This judgment needs to be strengthened, however, for the point of the story is not merely that anyone *can* fall but that *everyone does*. If this story existed by itself apart from the rest of the Book of Genesis, it would make the first point but not necessarily the second. It would say that anyone can fall but not that all do. However, the story is not isolated. It occurs in the context of a book in which the deterioration of character is traced in personage after personage and the message of the book as a whole seems to be: "There is no one righteous, not even one; there is no one who understands, no one who seeks God. All have turned away, they have together become worthless; there is no one who does good, not even one" (Rom. 3:10–12).

Genesis begins with man (Adam) in Eden under the blessing of God. But sin enters and the book ends with a man (Joseph) in a coffin in Egypt, a place of bondage. The first child, Cain, is named in expectation of the coming Deliverer ("Here he is"). But Cain becomes a murderer. Noah likewise falls, for all sin and "fall short of the glory of God" (Rom. 3:23).

There is this lesson too. Noah was 600 years old when the Flood came, so he had lived righteously before God for a

---

[1]Pink, *Gleanings in Genesis*, p. 121.

long time. In his youth and for most of his life he was "blameless among the people of his time." But now, in his latter years, he mars that earlier record. Is this a unique incident? Not at all. It is merely one good example of the fact that many in the Bible were strong in living for God when they were young but departed from the will of God when they were older. Moses sinned late in life by striking the rock and taking some of God's glory to himself, as a result of which he was not permitted to enter the Promised Land. David sinned with Bathsheba when he was in his fifties. Solomon departed from the will of God when he was old. It has been thus for many. Past success does not provide power for future victory. So although we cry "Remember your Creator in the days of your youth" (Eccl. 12:1), we have to cry "Remember him in middle age and in old age as well." None of us is ever past temptation or the need of God's sustaining grace.

The third lesson is precisely this last point: given our sure drift toward sin, *only* the power and grace of God can help. We think of Jesus' words to Peter before Peter's fall. Peter had walked with Jesus for three years and no doubt thought that he was able to stand against Satan's wiles in his own strength. You would not catch Peter doing anything Noah did! Above all, he would never deny his Lord! But Peter did deny Him. He brought shame on Christ's name and would have become a castaway, a spiritual derelict, were it not for something Christ did for him. He told Peter about it: "Simon, Simon, Satan has asked to sift you as wheat. But I have prayed for you, Simon, that your faith may not fail. And when you have turned back, strengthen your brothers" (Luke 22:31, 32).

John H. Gerstner has pointed out that Peter was the first to sing the words of that hymn, so popular among certain Christians: "Lord, we are able." But after his fall he learned to sing it correctly: "Lord, we are *not* able." Peter learned that it was necessary to draw near to Christ and stand in His power. And he learned to encourage his brothers and sisters to do so as well. Gerstner writes, "Even in our best condition we cannot meet Satan; but in our weakened and debilitated state, sinning far more than we live virtuously, we are able to conquer him because Christ has given us the victory."[2]

The Curse of Canaan

Our troubles begin with the second part of this story. The first part is sad, but it is not difficult to understand. We can easily see ourselves in Noah's shoes and can try to learn the lessons he undoubtedly learned. This is not true of the second part. What we are told is straightforward enough: "Ham, the father of Canaan, saw his father's nakedness and told his two brothers outside. But Shem and Japheth took a garment and laid it across their shoulders; then they walked in backward and covered their father's nakedness. Their faces were turned the other way so that they would not see their father's nakedness" (vv. 22, 23). As a result of Ham's sin, his son Canaan is cursed. But when we read this we are puzzled. What was so bad about Ham's seeing his father's nakedness? Why should this merit Noah's curse? And why, even if the curse is merited, is it pronounced on Canaan, Ham's son, rather than on Ham himself? Is this not a case of the innocent being punished for the guilty? Just what is it all supposed to mean?

We are not the only ones to be puzzled by this part of the story. Many have been, and the result has been a great variety of explanations of what Ham did or may have done to Noah. One answer,

---

[2]John H. Gerstner, "The Language of the Battlefield" in Boice, editor, *Our Savior God*, p. 162.

favored by certain liberal scholars, is that Ham did nothing—that two separate stories have been pieced together by a redactor and that Canaan was the true violator of his father's father.[3] This is hardly acceptable for those who take the text seriously.

In a recent issue of *Bibliotheca Sacra*, published by Dallas Theological Seminary, Allen P. Ross examines some of these theories and concludes (I believe rightly) that there is no need to read anything more into Genesis than the text actually says. It is worth quoting part of his argument. "Many theories have been put forward concerning this violation of Ham. Several writers have felt that the expression 'he saw his nakedness' is a euphemism for a gross violation. Cassuto speculates that the pre-Torah account may have been uglier but was reduced to minimal proportions. Greek and Semitic stories occasionally tell how castration was used to prevent procreation in order to seize the power to populate the earth. The Talmud records that this view was considered by the Rabbis: 'Rab and Samuel [differ], one maintaining that he castrated him, and the other that he abused him sexually.' The only possible textual evidence to support such a crime would come from Genesis 9:24, which says that Noah 'found out what his youngest son *had done* to him.' But the remedy for Ham's 'deed' is the covering of Noah's nakedness. How would throwing the garment over him without looking undo such a deed and merit the blessing?

"Bassett presents a view based on the idiomatic use of the words 'uncover the nakedness.' He suggests that Ham engaged in sexual intercourse with Noah's wife, and that Canaan was cursed because he was the fruit of that union. He attempts to show that to 'see another's

nakedness' is the same as sexual intercourse, and that a later redactor who missed the idiomatic meaning added the words in 9:23.

"But the evidence for this interpretation is minimal. The expression *rā āh 'erwāh* is used in Scripture for shameful exposure, mostly of a woman or as a figure of a city in shameful punishment, exposed and defenseless. This is quite different from the idiom used for sexual violation, *gālāh 'erwāh*, 'he uncovered the nakedness.' It is this construction that is used throughout Leviticus 18 and 20 to describe the evil sexual conduct of the Canaanites. Leviticus 20:17 is the only occurrence where *rā āh* is used, but even that is in a parallel construction with *gālāh*, explaining the incident. This one usage cannot be made to support . . . an idiomatic force meaning sexual intercourse.

"According to Genesis 9 Noah uncovered himself (the stem is reflexive). If there had been any occurrence of sexual violation, one would expect the idiom to say, 'Ham uncovered his father's nakedness.' Moreover, . . . if Ham had committed incest with his mother, he would not likely have told his two brothers, nor would the Torah pass over such an inauspicious beginning for the detested Canaanites (see Gen. 19:30–38).

"So there is no clear evidence that Ham actually did anything other than see the nakedness of his uncovered father."[4]

This does not mean that Ham merely stumbled in an accidental way into the tent where his father was lying and thus saw his nakedness, however. There would be no blame in that. Most likely, the sin was in the way he reacted to his discovery. He could have covered his father as his two brothers did, but in-

---

[3]Gene Rice, "The Curse that Never Was (Genesis 9:18–27)," *Journal of Religious Thought*, 29 (1972), pp. 5, 6; and Thomas O. Figart, *A Biblical Perspective on the Race Problem* (Grand Rapids: Baker, 1973), pp. 55–58.

[4]Allen P. Ross, "The Curse of Canaan," *Bibliotheca Sacra*, July-September 1980, pp. 229, 230.

stead he went and told them, apparently making fun of his father's drunken and uncovered state. It was an attack on his father's honor.

Moreover, it may have been a repudiation of his father's religion. Robert Candlish makes this point well: "He [Ham] not merely dishonoured him as a parent—he disliked him as a preacher of righteousness. Hence his satisfaction, his irrepressible joy, when he caught the patriarch in such a state of degradation. Ah! he has found that the godly man is no better than his neighbours; he has got behind the scenes; he has made a notable discovery; and now he cannot contain himself. Forth he rushes, all hot and impatient, to publish the news, so welcome to himself! And if he can meet with any of his brethren who have more sympathy with this excessive sanctity than he has, what a relief—what a satisfaction—to cast this choice specimen in their teeth; and so make good his right to triumph over them and their faith ever after."[5]

The only thing that is worse than committing a specific sin is the devilish delight of finding out and reveling in that sin in others. This Ham did! His brothers, by contrast, grieved for their father and did what they could to remove the indignity.

CURSE AND BLESSING

According to some theology, Noah would have lost his salvation when he became drunk and lay uncovered in his tent. But Noah had been sealed into one of the eternal covenants of God, and although he was uncovered physically, he was nevertheless covered over by the righteousness of Christ. He was still God's child, and God was about to use him again. He is to prophesy. "Just as Jonah was given a great task to do after his flight and his folly, so Noah is given

a new opportunity to be the mouthpiece of God. The circumstances of his sin are made the framework of the prophecy which God speaks through him. The man who was drunk with wine is now filled with the Spirit (Eph. 5:18). He is now covered with the garment of prophecy and speaks forth the will and the Word of God."[6]

Noah's prophecy contains an outline sketch of history, focused in a general way on the descendants of Noah's three sons. As such it has three parts: 1) a curse on Canaan, the son of Ham, and blessings upon 2) Shem and 3) Japheth.

The curse on Canaan is the most difficult to understand because, as we suggested in an earlier question, it is hard to see why he should be cursed rather than his father, who actually did the wrong. But we note the following. First, it is a biblical principle (whether liked by us or not) that the sins of the fathers *are* visited on the children even to the third and fourth generations (Exod. 20:5). Second, the punishment, though inflicted on Canaan, was appropriate to Ham since he reaped exactly as he had sown. He sinned as a son and was punished in his son. Third, the assigning of the punishment to Canaan may have been (as is so often the case in God's judgments) a function of the mercy of God, who could have cursed Ham and all his descendants but instead restricted the punishment to only this fourth part, Canaan being only one of Ham's four sons. Whatever the reasoning may be, the judgment is nevertheless pronounced: "Cursed be Canaan! The lowest of slaves will he be to his brothers" (v. 25).

We are going to see in the next chapter that this curse was pronounced on the ancient peoples of the Near East, most of whom were later conquered by the Jews under Joshua. But notice this: they were

---

[5]Candlish, *Studies in Genesis*, pp. 158, 159.
[6]Barnhouse, *Genesis*, pp. 65, 66.

not the Negro races. In an earlier generation prejudiced minds used this text to justify their enslaving of Africa's black populations, but this is without any biblical basis and is a proof rather of the expositors' sin. Not until the middle of the nineteenth century, when the slave trade was at its height, did anyone ever imagine that Ham was the father of the black races or that there was a curse on them.

The second part of Noah's oracle is a blessing on Shem or, as Noah actually puts it, on Shem's God. "Blessed be the LORD, the God of Shem! May Canaan be the slave of Shem" (v. 26). This is a great blessing because it is a new step in the Old Testament's unfolding messianic prophecies. The first messianic prophecy was in Genesis 3:15, in which a Deliverer was promised who should crush the serpent's head. It is evident as the story of Genesis unfolds that he will appear in the godly line of Seth rather than the ungodly line of Cain. Now, in a prophecy made following the Flood, the line of descent is narrowed to the Semitic peoples, who descended from Shem and whose story is particularly unfolded

in the remainder of Genesis. In time the promise is narrowed still further to the house of David and to his descendants: Joseph (in the line of David's son Solomon) and Mary (in the line of David's son Nathan). The prophecy of blessing in Genesis is fulfilled in Jesus Christ.

Finally, there is a prophecy for Japheth and his family. Two things are said of Japheth: first, God will extend his territory (the name Japheth means "enlarge" so this is a play on words), and second, he will live in the tents of Shem (v. 27). This latter promise is to be taken spiritually, meaning, not that the descendants of Japheth shall take over Shem's territory, but that they shall enter into his spiritual blessings through association with the Semite peoples. The descendants of Japheth have established the great nations of this world. America is in this line of descent. But our blessing does not come from our extensive territory or wealth but from our acquaintance with the God of Israel and our faith in Him who will yet sit upon the throne of His father David and reign forever.

56

The First Table of Nations

(Genesis 10:1–5)

This is the account of Shem, Ham and Japheth, Noah's sons, who themselves had sons after the flood.
The sons of Japheth:
Gomer, Magog, Madai, Javan, Tubal, Meshech and Tiras.
The sons of Gomer:
Ashkenaz, Riphath and Togarmah.
The sons of Javan:
Elishah, Tarshish, the Kittim and the Rodanim. (From these the maritime peoples spread out into their territories by their clans within their nations, each with its own language.)

The tenth chapter of Genesis, although often passed over by Bible readers as a mere list of names, is actually a remarkable historical document. A generation ago it was common for highly critical scholars to decry its worth. S. R. Driver, best known for his contribution along with Francis Brown and C. A. Briggs to the *Hebrew and English Lexicon of the Old Testament*, said, "The Table of Nations contains no scientific classification of the races of mankind [and] no historically true account of the origin of the races."[1] Yet today, even the most hostile critics are inclined to acknowledge this Table's extraordinary importance and accuracy. William Foxwell Albright wrote rather early in his career, when he was far from being as conservative as he later became, "The tenth chapter of Genesis . . . stands absolutely alone in ancient literature, without a remote parallel, even among the Greeks, where we find the

closest approach to a distribution of peoples in genealogical framework. . . . The Table of Nations remains an astonishingly accurate document."[2]

It is obvious, even from a cursory examination, that the chapter is attempting to show the general outline of the expansion of the peoples and nations of the world from Noah's three sons, after the Flood. In this it becomes a bridge between what we would call "pre-history" (history for which we have no other historical documents or monuments) and the historical times of Abraham and his descendants, with which the next section of Genesis deals.

Genesis 11 is a genealogy. It gives the descendants of Seth through Terah to Abraham, listing (as Gen. 5 also does) the ages of the fathers at which their chief sons were born and the total years of their lives. But Genesis 10 is not like that. It lists names—the sons of Noah

---

[1]S. R. Driver, *The Book of Genesis*, 3rd edition (London: Methuen and Company, 1904), p. 114.
[2]William F. Albright, "Recent Discoveries in Bible Lands," an appended article in Robert Young, *Analytical Concordance to the Bible* (Grand Rapids: Eerdmans, reprint, n.d.), p. 30.

and their sons—but these sometimes become names, not merely of the ancestors of people, but also of the peoples or nations involved. An example is "the Kittim and the Rodanim" of verse 5. These are groups of people descended presumably from two sons of Javan named Kit and Rodan respectively. But they are not listed as individuals. They are listed as peoples, along with two other names which, by contrast, are not peoples but individuals: Elishah and Tarshish. Again, although the text does not explicitly say so, there are obviously whole families of nations that are left out. The table lists seven sons of Japheth (v. 2); but in the ensuing verses only the descendants of two of those sons are listed: three sons of Gomer and four sons (or peoples) of Javan. The same selectivity is evident throughout the chapter.

Does this suggest that the Table of Nations is inaccurate after all? There are some who have said so, but actually the opposite is the case. The fact that whole ranks of descendants are left out really points to the writer's veracity, for he has included no more than he in fact actually knew to be the case. Thus, while we will undoubtedly find the descent of major blocks of the world's peoples unexplained, we will nevertheless find the lines of descent listed here to be accurate.

Indo-Europeans

The basic division of this chapter is among the three sons of Noah, and the first of these (the most briefly treated) is Japheth. The author of this document tells least about Japheth, presumably because he knew least about those who descended from him. Still, what he tells is very important and of great interest, if for no other reason than that Japheth is our ancestor, the father of what are called the Indo-European peoples.

Let us stop right there and think of the importance of that designation: Indo-European. Indo has to do with India or the countries to be found in that general direction when moving eastward from the Middle East. European has to do with the peoples of the European continent. We do not generally think of these two areas of the world as having a common history or even a common origin. We say, "East is east and west is west." Nothing seems more remote or farther from us or our way of thinking than some of the eastern nations—the mentality of Iran, for example. Why then do we speak of anything being Indo-European? The answer, not really suspected in Western thought until the nineteenth century, is that the languages of the east and the languages of the west are related, requiring a common-language ancestor. That is why, for example, serious linguistic students will often go to India to study Sanskrit as the closest known language of the original of this entire block of languages.

Webster's New Collegiate Dictionary states that the Indo-European languages are "the most important linguistic family of the globe, comprising the chief languages of Europe together with the Indo-Iranian and other Asiatic tongues. In the nineteenth century, comparative and historical study of these languages, called also *Indo-Germanic* or *Aryan*, established their descent from a common ancestor, spoken in the late Stone Age, probably in eastern Europe, by a people or group of peoples of unknown, perhaps mixed, race. This unrecorded language and, in some degree, the civilization and religion of those who spoke it, have been largely hypothetically reconstructed by scientific philological method. The prehistoric dialects of the primitive Indo-Europeans accompanied their migrations into India, Persia, Greece, Rome, and the western borders of Europe, where they are found at the beginning of history. The parent speech was highly inflected, but historically the general tendency of the Indo-European languages has been toward the analytic type, as in French or English."

In a table accompanying this rather extended definition, this family of languages is divided into two types: the eastern or *satem* division (involving the languages of India, Afghanistan, Iran, Armenia, the Balkans, Bulgaria, Yugoslavia, Russia, Czechoslovakia, Poland, parts of Germany, east Prussia, Lithuania and Latvia) and the western or *centrum* division (involving the languages of Greece, Italy, France, Spain, Portugal, Switzerland, Romania, Cornwall, Wales, Brittany, Ireland, Scotland, Scandinavia, parts of Germany, the Netherlands, Belgium and England).

As I said earlier, this relationship of east and west, established by their common language origin, was largely unknown and unsuspected until the technical linguistic work of the nineteenth century. Yet this is precisely what we find in Genesis in regard to Japheth's descendants. Even more, we find it in regard to Japheth himself, for his name has been preserved in both branches of the Indo-European family. The Greeks traced themselves back to Japetos (a variant form of Japheth); there is a reference in Aristophanes' *The Clouds*. The eastern peoples have him in the Flood account where he is known as Iyapeti; Noah gave him the land north of the Himalayan mountains.

THE SONS OF JAPHETH

1. The first of Japheth's sons is *Gomer*, in which we recognize the name Germany, though the derivation is long and circuitous. We are told that he had three sons: Ashkenaz, Riphath, and Togarmah.

To judge from such ancient historians as Herodotus, Strabo, and Plutarch, Gomer's family settled to the north of the Black Sea, giving their name to the ancient district known as the Cimmeria (the Crimea). Later they expanded westward into Europe. They settled in France as the Gauls, in Spain as the Galacia, and in Briton as the Celts—all of which names are related, being variations on the original three-consonant name G-M-R. (Linguists will see the connection.) Further developments have given us Gomerland, which becomes Cumber-land, Umbria, Ireland, and the ancient ancestors of the Welsh, the Cymri. "Thus," as one commentator writes, "Gomer's children and his children's children went far up into Europe, where, despite their separation both in time and distance, the name of their ancient forebear was preserved among them."[3]

The names of Gomer's sons are interesting. Numerous identifications of those descended from *Ashkenaz* have been made, but nearly all commentators agree that they are people who settled to the north of Palestine above what is called the Fertile Crescent. The name Ashkenaz is preserved in the name of Lake Ascanius and in the people of the region, the Askaeni, mentioned by Homer. A part of these people may have become the Trojans of the Trojan War, for a prince of the royal family of Troy was called Ascenius. Some of these people later moved into Germany, as a result of which the Jews identify Ashkenaz with the Germans to this day. Some are called Ashkenazi Jews.

Little can be said about *Riphath,* though Josephus identifies him as the ancestor of the Paphalagonians. Europe may be derived from this name.

Togarmah is almost certainly the ancestor of the ancient Armenians. They are mentioned twice by Ezekiel (Ezek. 27:14; 38:6). This word has given us the names Turkey and Turkestan. By an inversion of letters, Armenians came to be

---

[3]Arthur C. Custance, *Noah's Three Sons: Human History in Three Dimensions* (Grand Rapids: Zondervan, 1975), p. 85.

called the House of Targom. Again, it is possible that the name Germany is derived from Togarmah; but if this is the case, it probably did not derive from Gomer, as suggested earlier.

2. Three of Japheth's sons (Magog, Tubal, and Meshech) should be taken together, for in one way or another these have given us the extremely northern people, the Russians. It is hard to trace the word *Magog*, though Josephus says that the people of Gog (Magog could mean "the place [or territory] of Gog") were the Scythians, who later became a large part of the Russian stock. On the other hand, it is not at all hard to trace *Meshech* and *Tubal*. These names often occur together, obviously showing a close relationship between the peoples bearing these names. Ezekiel does this: "Son of man, set your face against Gog, of the land of Magog, the chief prince of Meshech and Tubal; prophesy against him and say: 'This is what the Sovereign LORD says: I am against you, O Gog, chief prince of Meshech and Tubal'" (Ezek. 38:2, 3). The early history of the tribes of Meshech and Tubal is found in Herodotus, who writes that in his day these lived in the province of Pontus in northern Turkey.[4] Josephus gives them the same location but says that by his time the ancient names of Meshech and Tubal had become Meschen and Theobelian.[5] Later, these tribes pushed on north and east of the Black Sea into what is now Russia.

It is hard to miss the preservation of these names in the two most important centers of the eastern and western halves of the modern state of Russia: Moscow and Tobolsk. Moscow is on the Moskva River. Tobolsk is on the Tobol. In the valley of the Tobol there are five to ten other cities whose names are obvious variations on the ancient tribal words.

Here the same names are given to ancient peoples who occupied parts of northern Turkey and Russia, to two major cities and to two great rivers in Russia, as well as to many lesser places. It is part of this same picture that the word translated "chief prince" in Ezekiel is *rosh* or *rus*, from which the name Russia comes.[6]

3. Thus far, the peoples considered have been of the European half of the Indo-European family. The next name gives us the other half, although little is said about this descendant. The name is *Madai*, the ancestor of the Medes (as in "Medes and Persians"). The Medes settled into what is now Persia and were probably ancestors in part of these people. The Aryans, who later migrated into India, came from this branch of Japheth's family.

4. Of the seven sons of Japheth, more is said about the fourth, *Javan*, than any other. This is no surprise, since Javan fathered the various Greek peoples, and these, because of their geographical location along the edges of the Mediterranean Sea, were better known to the Jews of the Middle East than others. The Table of Nations says that the sons of Javan were "Elishah, Tarshish, the Kittim and the Rodanim," adding, "From these the maritime peoples spread out into their territories by their clans within their nations, each with its own language" (vv. 4, 5).

We think of the Greeks as belonging to various families—the Hellenes, Ionians, Achaeans, and Dorians. But to the ancient people of the east they were known by only one name: Yavan or Ionian. This term comes from Javan. Our most inclusive term (with the exception of the word "Greek") is Hellas, from which we have the words Hellenist and Hellespont. It is a derivative of *Elishah*. Elishah

---

[4]Herodotus, *Histories*, III, 94; VII, 78.
[5]Flavius Josephus, *Jewish Antiquities*, I, 124, 125.
[6]I have discussed these three names in *The Last and Future World* (Grand Rapids: Zondervan, 1974), pp. 105, 106.

has also given us Eilesians, a name known to and popular with Homer. *Tarshish* is a city, the one to which Jonah tried to escape when running away from God (Jonah 1:3). Its location is uncertain, but it is generally identified with Tartessos in Spain. *Kittim* is Cyprus. *Rodanim* is Rhodes. The Rhone River is probably named from the Rodanim, some of whom probably settled at its mouth.

5. The last of Japheth's sons is *Tiras* who, according to Josephus, became the ancestor of the Thracians and perhaps eventually the Etruscans. They were from Italy. In time these became a part of the Roman Empire along with other peoples.

Four Great Truths

The interesting thing about this expansion of the Indo-European peoples, in addition to the accuracy of the names given in Genesis, is that it is a precise fulfillment of the prophecy made concerning Japheth in the preceding chapter. There Noah is cited as saying, "May God extend the territory of Japheth; may Japheth live in the tents of Shem, and may Canaan be his slave" (Gen. 9:27). This is what happened. God enlarged the territory of Japheth to include the whole of Europe and even parts of Asia. Moreover, if the expansion of the races proceeded as anthropologists and others today believe—from northeastern Russia across the Bering Strait into Alaska and from there down into the North American and South American continents—this family of nations eventually possessed most of this world's territory.

But at what cost! Apart from those Indo-Europeans who remembered their roots and delighted to take refuge in the descendant of Shem, the Messiah, this block of peoples has gained the whole world at the loss of its soul. It will not find its soul save in Him who created it originally.

The sons of Japheth should have mastered four great truths: that there is one God to which their roots bear record, that all the peoples of the earth are one people, that truth is one, and that there is only one salvation. But we have not remembered this. Abandoning the true God, we have made other gods "like mortal man and birds and animals and reptiles," as Paul says in Romans (1:22). Having lost our knowledge of the one God, we have also lost our awareness that the peoples of the earth are one people. Therefore, we have exalted ourselves and have tried to exploit those we consider to be inferior. We have abandoned belief in one truth and so seek truth in a plurality of forms. Most tragic of all, we have lost sight of God's promise of a deliverer, which goes all the way back to God's words to our first parents in Eden on the occasion of the Fall.

In his commentary Calvin bemoans those who "voluntarily become forgetful of the grace and salvation of God," pushing "memory of the deluge" far into the past and little remembering "by what means or for what end they had been preserved."[7] Many of these are with us today. If you are one, learn from this Table of Nations. Turn from your rebellion against the true God and come to Him in Jesus where alone He may be found.

---

[7]Calvin, *Commentary on Genesis*, p. 313.

57

The Warrior States

(Genesis 10:6–20)

The sons of Ham:
   Cush, Mizraim, Put and Canaan.
The sons of Cush:
   Seba, Havilah, Sabtah, Raamah and Sabtecah.
The sons of Raamah:
   Sheba and Dedan.
Cush was the father of Nimrod, who grew to be a mighty warrior on the earth. He was a mighty hunter before the LORD; that is why it is said, "Like Nimrod, a mighty hunter before the LORD." The first centers of his kingdom were Babylon, Erech, Akkad and Calneh, in Shinar. From that land he went to Assyria, where he built Nineveh, Rehoboth Ir, Calah and Resen, which is between Nineveh and Calah; that is the great city.
Mizraim was the father of
   the Ludites, Anamites, Lehabites, Naphtuhites, Pathrusites, Casluhites (from whom the Philistines came) and Caphtorites.
Canaan was the father of
   Sidon his firstborn, and of the Hittites, Jebusites, Amorites, Girgashites, Hivites, Arkites, Sinites, Arvadites, Zemarites and Hamathites.
Later the Canaanite clans scattered and the borders of Canaan reached from Sidon toward Gerar as far as Gaza, and then toward Sodom, Gomorrah, Admah and Zeboiim, as far as Lasha.
These are the descendants of Ham by their clans and languages, in their territories and nations.

Not many students today learn Latin, but a generation ago nearly everyone did, so there are still people who can recognize and even translate a Latin phrase. How about *E pluribus unum* ("one from many"), a phrase appearing on the great seal of the United States? Or *Hoc est corpus meus* ("This is my body"), the Latin translation of 1 Corinthians 11:24, which meant so much to Luther and his understanding of the Lord's Supper? *In vino veritas? Et cetera?* Of all these phrases that stick with us today there is probably none that so takes us back to those early Latin classes as the first line of Julius Caesar's classic account of his military campaigns in Gaul,

which established his reputation not only as a general but as a writer: *Gallia est omnis divisa in partes tres* ("On the whole Gaul is divided into three parts").

With one change, this sentence might be pronounced over the division of the peoples of the world described in chapter 10 of Genesis. Substitute "earth" (*terra*) or "peoples" (*gentes*) for Gaul, and you could say that, according to this chapter, the inhabited world is divided into three parts—corresponding to those people descended from Noah's three sons. We have looked at one of these lines, the line of Japheth, which produced the Indo-European peoples. The second part of that human family,

Ham's descendants, is our subject now.

SOUTH AND EAST

The distribution of the Indo-European people was eastward into certain parts of Persia and India, and westward and northward into Europe and points beyond. The descendants of Shem, as we are yet to see, tended to stay in the area of the Middle East. This leaves, by a simple process of elimination, the south (Africa) and the far east (all oriental countries) to have been settled by Ham and his descendants. This is actually the case, although it is far more difficult to trace these peoples than it is to trace those in the other family trees.

According to Genesis 10, Ham had four sons: Cush, Mizraim, Put, and Canaan. The third, Put, is not mentioned again. The others—Cush, Mizraim, and Canaan—are mentioned in order to list those who descended from them. There are five sons of Cush (Seba, Havilah, Sabtah, Raamah, and Sabtecah), plus two grandsons who descended from Raamah (Sheba and Dedan). Seven names are attached to Mizraim, though these are not individuals as listed but rather peoples: the Ludites, Anamites, Lehabites, Naphtuhites, Pathrusites, Casluhites and Caphtorites. Of Canaan it is said, "Canaan was the father of Sidon his firstborn, and of the Hittites, Jebusites, Amorites, Girgashites, Hivites, Arkites, Sinites, Arvadites, Zemarites and Hamathites" (vv. 15–18). In this list there is a combination of a genuine name (Sidon), plus the names of peoples, which may, of course, go back to specific descendants of Canaan though the ancestor is not mentioned.

It is difficult to trace these peoples, as I said. Still something can be noted. *Cush* is the Bible's name for Ethiopia in Africa, although there was also a Cush in Arabia and although (in vv. 8–12) Cush is linked to Nimrod who established the first world empire at Babylon in the valley of the Euphrates. Apparently this branch of Ham's family divided into two parts, one migrating southward into Africa, and the other going east. Seba, Havilah, Sabtah, Raamah, and Sabtecah have been identified with sites in Arabia.

In the Bible *Mizraim* is the customary name for Egypt. Therefore, although we do not know how to place or identify the offspring attributed to him (the Ludites, etc.), we may suppose that these pushed on into Africa and so settled that great continent.

Put (or Phut) is Libya, applied to the region of North Africa west of Egypt. Josephus uses the term this way.

Canaan is the ancestor of the various tribal groupings that settled the land given to Israel and were later conquered by them under Joshua. They are mentioned many times throughout the Old Testament. The only exceptions are Sidon, the presumed founder of the city of Sidon, somewhat to the north, and the Hittites, who (although some settled in the Holy Land) were actually founders of an extensive empire that flourished in what is today modern Turkey. The Hittites were in Canaan in the time of Abraham (Gen. 15:19–21; 23:10) and were still a great power in the days of Solomon, one thousand years later (2 Chron. 1:17).

Thus far the distribution of peoples over the world's territory is fairly comprehensive. But there is one obvious omission: the Orientals. Where do they fit in? It is possible that we cannot know, since the lists of Genesis 10 are not necessarily complete. But there are two possibilities, both of which may be right. First, although the Hittite empire endured for more than 800 years, it nevertheless fell suddenly, and there are indications that the survivors fled eastward into China. This is not unreasonable, for the ancient trade route between Europe and China went through the area to the east of Turkey, the great trading city being Samarkand (now in southern

Russia). This was the route Marco Polo took when he opened a new era of commerce many centuries later. It is a part of this picture that in the ancient cuneiform monuments the Hittites are called "Khittae," which may have given us the eastern name Cathay. Again, archeologists note a number of similarities between the Hittites and the Mongols: shoes whose toes turn up, the custom of doing up hair in a pigtail, pioneer work in the smelting and casting of iron, and the domestication of horses.

The other possibility concerns the Sinites, who descended from Canaan. These people receive scant mention in Genesis, but the patriarch of the clan, Sin, may have been very important. His name became that of an important near-eastern deity, appearing in such names as Sennacherib (meaning "May the god Sin prosper the brothers") and Sinai. We do not know where these people settled other than the Holy Land, but the name Sin is found widely in the east. It is found in the Chinese names Siang and Sianfu, for instance. Thinai was a trading city in western China. Tsin became a dynasty, the word itself coming to mean "purebred." Manchu emperors used this word as a title. It is believed that Tsin was used by the Malays in the form Tchina and was then brought back to Europe by the Portuguese as China. Even today we use the word "Sin" of the east, speaking of Sinology (a study of China) or Sino-American relations.[1]

The First World Empire

There is an interesting feature of Moses' treatments of these descendants of Ham that is at once recognizable to anyone who reads this chapter. It is the parenthesis that fills verses 8–12. It comes in the middle of the table of nations and, in a sense, interrupts it. These verses deal, not with the general movements of peoples and nations, but with one particular descendant of Cush, Nimrod, who is said to have been the founder of the first world empire. Here is the first place in the Bible where the word "kingdom" occurs. Significantly, it is used, not of God's kingdom (as it is later), but of this first rival kingdom of Nimrod. This matter was obviously of great importance to Moses, for a related parenthesis occurs in the first nine verses of chapter 11, in the story of the tower of Babel.

What is so significant about Nimrod? The fact that he established cities and built a kingdom is important, of course. But there is much more that can be said.

Nimrod was the first person to become a "mighty" man. Our text calls attention to this by using the adjective "mighty" three times in describing him: "Nimrod . . . grew to be a *mighty* warrior on the earth. He was a *mighty* hunter before the LORD; that is why it is said, 'Like Nimrod, a *mighty* hunter before the LORD'" (vv. 8, 9). The adjective also occurs in a similar way in 1 Chronicles 1:10. Why is this emphasized? Is it good or bad? A little thought will show that it is bad. The empire of Babylon under Nimrod was an affront both to God and man, an affront to God in that it sought to do without God (Gen. 11:1–9) and an affront to man in that it sought to rule over other people tyrannously. Martin Luther was on the right track when he suggested that this is the way the word "hunter" should be interpreted. This is not talking about Nimrod's ability to hunt wild game. He was not a hunter of animals. He was a hunter of men—a warrior. It was through his ability to fight and kill and rule ruthlessly that his kingdom of Euphrates valley city states was consolidated.

One commentator renders this para-

---

[1]For a fuller study of these names and their possible derivations see Custance, *Noah's Three Sons*, pp. 101–12; and Morris, *The Genesis Record*, pp. 249–57.

graph: "Cush begat Nimrod; he began to be a mighty despot in the land. He was an arrogant tyrant, defiant before the face of the Lord; wherefore it is said, Even as Nimrod, the mighty despot, haughty before the face of the Lord. And the homeland of his empire was Babel, then Erech, and Accad, and Calneh, in the land of Shinar. From this base he invaded the kingdom of Asshur, and built Nineveh, and Rehoboth-Ir, and Calah, and Resin between Nineveh and Calah. These make up one great city."[2]

Here we have a great city. But it is great, not as Jerusalem is great (as God's city), but great in its defiance of God. This is man's city, the secular city. It is *of* man, *by* man, and *for* man's glory.

The later Babylon of Nebuchadnezzar is the clearest biblical illustration of these elements. It is about Nebuchadnezzar, who embodies the secular city, and God, who operates through Daniel and his friends. The key to the Book of Daniel is in the opening verses which say that after Nebuchadnezzar had besieged and conquered Jerusalem (though it was "the Lord [who] gave Jehoaikim king of Judah into his hand"), he took some of the sacred vessels of the temple treasury, brought them to Babylon and there "put the vessels [in the treasury] house of his god" (Dan. 1:2). This was Nebuchadnezzar's way of saying that his gods were stronger than Jehovah. And so it seemed! God had certainly permitted Nebuchadnezzar to triumph over his own people in punishment for their sins.

One evening Nebuchadnezzar had a dream that involved a great image. It was of gold, silver, brass, and iron. The head was of gold. This represented the kingdom of Nebuchadnezzar and was God's way of acknowledging that Babylon was indeed magnificent. But, as God went on to point out, Babylon would be succeeded by another king-

dom represented by the silver arms and chest of the figure, that kingdom by another represented by the figure's brass middle portions, and then that by a kingdom represented by the legs of iron. It was only at the end of this period that the eternal kingdom of God in Christ would come and overthrow all others, grow and fill the earth. In this vision God was telling Nebuchadnezzar that he was not as important as he thought he was and that it was God Himself who rules history.

In the next chapter Nebuchadnezzar sets up a gold statue on the plain of Dura. On the surface this seems to be only the foolish gesture of a vain monarch who insists that the statue be worshiped as a symbol of the unity of the empire. However, when the story is read with the vision of the statue of chapter 2 in view, one realizes that the later episode actually shows Nebuchadnezzar rebelling against God's decree. God had said, "Your kingdom will be succeeded by other kingdoms, kingdoms of silver, brass and iron." Nebuchadnezzar replied, "No, my kingdom will endure; it will always be glorious. I will create a statue of which not only the head will be of gold, but the shoulders, thighs and legs also. It will all be of gold, for it will represent me and my descendants forever." This personal involvement with the statue explains the king's violent reaction when the three Jewish men refused to bow down to it.

It also explains the violent reaction of the secular mind to Christian claims today. It is not just a question of the Christian God versus other gods, each one presumably thinking that his or her god is the true one. It is the rebellion of man against God, *period*. God is He to whom we are responsible. But fallen men and women do not want to be responsible to anyone. They want to rule themselves. They want to exclude God

---

[2]Barnhouse, *The Invisible War,* p. 192.

even from His own universe.

That the secular city is also by man and for man comes out in the remainder of Nebuchadnezzar's story. One day, a year or more after the earlier incident, Nebuchadnezzar was walking on the roof of his palace in Babylon and he looked out over the city. He was impressed with its magnificence. Judging himself to be responsible for this, he took to himself the glory that should have been given to God, saying, "Is not this the great Babylon I have built as the royal residence, by my mighty power and for the glory of my majesty?" (Dan. 4:30). It was a claim that the earthly city had been constructed *by* man and *for* man's glory.

In one sense this was true. Nebuchadnezzar had constructed the city, and his conquests had brought it to great architectural splendor. Again, he had undoubtedly constructed it for his glory, as Nimrod had constructed the first Babylon for his glory. What both had forgotten is that ultimately it is God who rules in the affairs of men and that the achievements of a secular ruler are made possible only through the common gifts of God to humanity.

So God promises to bring the secular city down. Nebuchadnezzar had judged himself superior to those around him because of his political achievements, so superior that he had no need of God. Now God speaks to show how mistaken Nebuchadnezzar was. God says, "This is what is decreed for you, King Nebuchadnezzar: Your royal authority has been taken from you. You will be driven away from people and will live with the wild animals; you will eat grass like cattle. Seven times will pass by for you until you acknowledge that the Most High is sovereign over the kingdoms of men and gives them to anyone he wishes" (Dan. 4:31, 32). The judgment is put into effect immediately. Nebuchadnezzar's mind goes from him, and he is driven from the city. The text says, "He

was driven away from people and ate grass like cattle. His body was drenched with the dew of heaven until his hair grew like the feathers of an eagle and his nails like the claws of a bird" (v. 33). Eventually Babylon itself fell, never to rise again.

FACING THE CURSE

It is interesting that in this particular branch of Ham's family we have a reversal (probably deliberate) of God's judgment on Canaan for Ham's sin in ridiculing Noah. God had pronounced a curse on Canaan through Noah, saying, "Cursed be Canaan! The lowest of slaves will he be to his brothers" (Gen. 9:25). But so far as we know, in these early days God did not put this prophecy into effect by subjecting Canaan, his descendants, his brothers, or any of their descendants to Shem or Japheth. This happened later through Israel's invasion of the Promised Land, but it did not happen in these early days. Instead, it is the brother of Canaan, Cush, and his descendants who determine to enslave the others.

I say this may be deliberate, for I can imagine Nimrod to have thought in this manner. He may have said, "I don't know about the others, but I regard this matter of the curse of God on Canaan as a major disgrace on my family, one that needs to be erased. Did God say that my uncle Canaan would be a slave? I'll fight that judgment. I'll never be a slave! What's more, I'll be the exact opposite. I'll be so strong that others will become slaves to me. Instead of 'slave,' I'll make them say, 'Here comes Nimrod, the mightiest man on earth.'"

This is the normal reaction of the human spirit when faced with God's curse. It says, "I'll defy it. I'll take care of my own problems." So it creates the arts, raises an army, builds its cities, and marches out to make a name for itself in defiance of God's decrees.

But God's decrees are not overturned

this way. God's curse is not successfully defied. There is only one way we can escape God's curse, and that is at the point where God takes the curse on Himself. There is no reason why He should do this. But He does. He comes in the person of Jesus Christ "taking the very nature of a servant [a *slave*], being made in human likeness" and thus "being found in appearance as a man, he humbled himself and became obedient to death—even death on a cross!" (Phil. 2:7, 8). Thus "Christ redeemed us from the *curse* of the law by becoming a curse for us" (Gal. 3:13). And what happens? Having thus subjected Himself, He is given a name that is "above every name" (Phil. 2:9) and declared to be the ruler of heaven and earth. That is our pattern: to come to Christ where the curse of God against sin is poured out, to be clothed in His righteousness, and then to learn that path of humble service to others within the human family which is the true and only road to real greatness.

58

Noah's Second Son

(Genesis 10:21–32)

Sons were also born to Shem, whose older brother was Japheth; Shem was the ances-
tor of all the sons of Eber.
The sons of Shem:
  Elam, Asshur, Arphaxad, Lud and Aram.
The sons of Aram:
  Uz, Hul, Gether and Meshech.
Arphaxad was the father of Shelah,
  and Shelah the father of Eber.
Two sons were born to Eber:
  One was named Peleg, because in his time the earth was divided; his brother was
  named Joktan.
Joktan was the father of
  Almodad, Sheleph, Hazarmaveth, Jerah, Hadoram, Uzal, Diklah, Obal, Abimael,
  Sheba, Ophir, Havilah and Jobab. All these were sons of Joktan.
  The region where they lived stretched from Mesha toward Sephar, in the eastern hill
country.
These are the sons of Shem by their clans and languages, in their territories and
nations.
These are the clans of Noah's sons, according to their lines of descent, within their
nations. From these the nations spread out over the earth after the flood.

Up to this point we would think that Shem was the oldest son of Noah. This is because, whenever the sons are mentioned, the order is always: Shem, Ham, and Japheth. We would think that Shem was first, Ham second, and Japheth third. Now we learn that Japheth was actually the oldest (though some translators render verse 21: "Shem, the older brother of Japheth"), and that the order should be: Japheth, Shem, and Ham. That is, Shem was Noah's second son, even though his descendants have not been listed until now.

It is not hard to see why Moses placed the account of the descendants of the three sons in this order. Japheth has given us the Indo-European peoples. Ham was the progenitor of those who settled Africa, Mesopotamia, and the east. But Shem produces the Semites from which Israel came. Since the rest of Genesis is to be concerned with these latter peoples and the way God led and blessed them, it is obvious that Moses has simply withheld this part of his account for emphasis. It is his pattern to get less important matters out of the way first so that he might then concentrate on what is of primary importance. We read in verse 21 that "Shem was the ancestor of all the sons of Eber." Eber was actually Shem's great-grandson, as the table shows, but he is mentioned here to show the importance of this line. Eber has given us the name Hebrew. So Moses is saying that this is the line from which the Jewish people came.

We see this in another way. The line of Japheth is traced to the second generation, Ham's to the third. But the line of Seth is traced through five generations —just in this table. Then, after the parenthesis that deals with the tower of Babel, the line is pursued through Arphaxad (generation by generation) to Abraham, with whom the next section of the book especially deals.

THE SONS OF SHEM

In spite of the obvious importance of this line, there is less to say about it than has been said about the lines of Japheth and Ham. We begin with Shem's five sons.

The first son is *Elam,* the ancestor of the Elamites who are widely known both from the Old Testament and from ancient monuments. In the time of Abraham, a king of Elam, Chedorlaomer, led an invasion into Canaan (cf. Gen. 14:1–16), and Abraham was forced to attack him and his allies in order to rescue Lot. These people originally lived to the east of Mesopotamia, had their capital at Susa (or Shushan), and eventually merged with the Medes to form the Persian empire. It is interesting that at one time scholars were declaring the Bible to be in error at this point since, as they believed, the people who settled the area of Elam, southeast of Mesopotamia, were not Shemites. Subsequent excavations have shown the Bible to be right. Apparently the descendants of Shem did settle the region but were later driven out by the Babylonians as a result of the expansion under Nimrod.[1]

Asshur was apparently the founder of the Assyrians, though nothing is known about him personally. On the other hand, Assyria has already been mentioned in this chapter, in verse 11. We were told that Nimrod invaded Assyria, as part of his expansionary plans, and there built Nineveh, Rehoboth Ir, Calah, and Resen. As a result, the Assyrians became a racially mixed people, combining the cultures, languages, and religions of their joint Shemitic and Hamitic stock.

Nothing is known about *Arphaxad* except that he was in the line that eventually led to Abraham. Because of this, his name is repeated in verse 24, where his descendants are given ("Arphaxad was the father of Shelah, and Shelah the father of Eber"), and in the full genealogy in chapter 11 ("When Arphaxad had lived 35 years, he became the father of Shelah. And after he became the father of Shelah, Arphaxad lived 403 years and had other sons and daughters," vv. 12, 13).

Lud was probably the ancestor of the Lydians who lived, at least at one period, in Asia Minor. They are mentioned by Josephus.

Aram is the father of the Aramaeans, who are the Syrians. The language of these people became important to the later history of Israel. Henry Morris writes, "These people also became a great nation, even finally seeing their Aramaic language adopted as almost a *lingua franca* for the leading nations of the ancient world, including Assyria and Babylonia. Some of the Old Testament (portions of Daniel and Ezra) was apparently originally written in Aramaic, and it was a common spoken language among the Jews at the time of Christ."[2]

Of Shem's five sons, three are not mentioned again: Elam, Asshur, and Lud. Moses mentions Aram, saying that he had four sons (*Uz, Hul, Gether,* and

---

[1]See S. R. Driver, *The Book of Genesis,* 3rd edition (London: Methuen and Company, 1904), p. 128; *Annual of the American Schools of Oriental Research,* 9 (1929), p. 22ff.; and V. G. Childe, *New Light on the Most Ancient East* (London: Kegan Paul, 1935), pp. 133–46.

[2]Morris, *The Genesis Record,* p. 259.

Meshech), and *Arphaxad*, as we indicated earlier. We know nothing of Aram's sons except that Uz eventually became the name of a region of Arabia. It was the homeland of Job, according to Job 1:1 (cf. Jer. 25:20).

THE EARTH DIVIDED

The descendants of Shem through Arphaxad *(Shelah, Eber, Peleg)* are mentioned again in chapter 11. But Peleg deserves special notice because of a detail given about him. It is said that "in his time the earth was divided" (v. 25). Whatever this sentence refers to, it is at least clearly connected with the name Peleg, because Peleg means "divided." If he was named to mark the event, the event was important—as, indeed, even the special mention of it here would indicate. But there is no explanation, and determining what this refers to is difficult. There are three main theories.

1. *That it refers to a divine revelation to Eber of how the earth was to be divided among the peoples of the world.* Robert Candlish takes this view. "At the very time when the swarm, if we may so speak, is about to hive, and is on the wing—when, led by Nimrod, and inspired by him with a new spirit of enterprise, men are bursting the bounds of their former habitation—Eber receives a commission from God to divide the earth among them—to announce to the several tribes and families their appointed homes, and to lay down, as on a map, their different routes and destinations. This charge he executes, and in memory of so remarkable a transaction, he gives the name of Peleg, signifying 'division,' to his son, born about the time when it took place. In some such way the earth is allocated, by the command of God, as by a solemn act or deed,

to which reference is more than once made in other parts of Scripture. It is of this transaction that Moses speaks in his memorial song, when, expressly appealing to 'the days of old,' he describes 'the Most High as dividing to the nations their inheritance, separating the sons of Adam, and setting the bounds of the people' with an eye, especially, 'to the number of the children of Israel' (Deut. 32:8). And Paul, also, preaching at Athens, testifies of God, not merely as having 'made of one blood, all nations of men for to dwell on the face of the earth'—but also as having 'determined the times before appointed, and the bounds of their habitation' (Acts 17:26)."[3]

The ancient Jewish Book of Jasher, quoted favorably by Joshua in 10:13, has the same kind of interpretation but on a naturalistic note: "It was Peleg who first invented the hedge and the ditch, the wall and bulwark; and who by lot divided the lands among his brethren."[4]

2. *That it refers to a catastrophic geological event in which the earth was split up violently into its present continental masses.* This interpretation was suggested in the last century, long before scientists were advancing the theory of continental drift. It was a far-out idea then. It is less so today. It would have to be shown that some sudden event started the continental drift process, that the continents moved apart fairly rapidly early in human history and that they have slowed to their present, nearly indetectable motion today for this interpretation to be plausible.

3. *That it refers to the division of the peoples of the earth as a result of the confusion of languages at Babel.* This is less exciting than the former interpretation, but it is most obvious in view of chapter

---

[3]Candlish, *Studies in Genesis*, pp. 172, 173. R. Jamieson has a similar suggestion in *Commentary Critical, Experimental and Practical on the Old and New Testament*, Vol. 1, *Genesis–Deuteronomy* (Glasgow: Collins, 1871), p. 118.

[4]Cf. Custance, *Noah's Three Sons*, p. 116.

11 and in view of several references to the division of peoples in chapter 10. For example, in verse 5 it is said of the Greeks, the sons of Javan, "From these the maritime peoples spread out into their territories by their clans within their nations, each with its own language." Verse 32 says, "These are the clans of Noah's sons, according to their lines of descent, within their nations. From these the nations spread out over the earth after the flood." Again, in chapter 11 there are references to a scattering of the peoples following the confusion of languages (vv. 4, 8, 9). It is true that in each of these three places the words are different: in 10:5 and 32 the word is *parad* ("separate"), in 10:25 *palag* ("divide"), and in 11:4, 8 and 9 *napas* ("disperse"). This weakens the point slightly. Still, the words are nearly synonyms, and in any case it is reasonable to interpret one division by another. Since the divisions of 10:5 and 32 and 11:4, 8 and 9 are national and geographic, based on a difference in languages, it is wise to infer that this is the meaning of the division in 10:25 too.

Besides, there is this detail. Although we are not told who Nimrod's father was, only that he was a descendant of Cush (whose literal sons are mentioned), Nimrod must have been in at least the fifth generation, counting Noah as the first. And if this was the case (and he was not farther down the line), Nimrod was a contemporary of Eber, who was also in the fifth generation from Noah through Shem. We may think, therefore that the development of Babel and the building of its tower went on in Eber's lifetime and that he named his son "division" when he witnessed what God did at Babylon.[5]

THE SONS OF JOKTAN
The last descendants of Noah in the table of nations are the sons of Joktan, Peleg's brother. Thirteen of these are mentioned, and every one of them appears to have settled in Arabia, particularly in the south. "*Almodad* is perhaps traceable to Al Mudad; *Sheleph*, in Yemen represented by Es Sulaf, and perhaps being the Salapeni of Ptolemy; *Hazarmaveth*, today Hadramaut; *Jerah*, adjoining the latter, being possibly found in the name of a fortress, Jerakh; *Hadoram*, represented by the Adramitae in southern Arabia, mentioned by Pliny and Ptolemy; *Uzal*, which is probably the old name of the capital of Yemen; *Diklah*, a place of some importance in Yemen, known as Dakalah; *Obal*, preserved perhaps in several localities in south Arabia, under the name Abil; *Abimael* is completely unidentified; *Sheba* might suggest the Sabeans; *Ophir*, perhaps represented by Aphar, the Sabaean capital of which Ptolemy speaks under the name Sapphara (Georg. 6, 7) and which is possibly modern Zaphar; *Havilah*, the district in Arabia Felix, known as Khawlan; and *Jobab*, usually identified with the Jobarites mentioned by Ptolemy among the Arabian tribes of the south, and which it is suggested was misread by him as *Iōbabitai*, instead of an original *Iōharitani*."[6]

The last verses of the chapter summarize what has been said. We have been told of twenty-six nations coming from Shem, thirty from Ham (not including the Philistines, who are mentioned only as a footnote), and fourteen from Japheth—seventy in all.

"OUR WRETCHED STATE"

This brings us to the end of Genesis 10, a chapter that is surely one of the most interesting and important in the entire Word of God. It has taught us several important things: 1) the unity of

---

[5]This is Morris' view, *The Genesis Record*, pp. 260, 261.
[6]Custance, *Noah's Three Sons*, p. 117.

the human race, the point at which the chapter ends, and 2) the reliability of the Bible, which this chapter (amply supported by recent findings in linguistics, anthropology and archeology) demonstrates. These points have been made before. They do not need restating.

What I would like to do, as I close my studies of this chapter, is to present the thoughts of the great Martin Luther as he finished his studies. He did not have the abundance of historical detail of the peoples of Genesis 10 that we have today, though he traced out much of it very well. But he did think deeply about the importance of this passage being in the Word of God and of how ignorant we would be, even of our origins, apart from it. He wrote: "Whenever I read these names, I think of the wretched state of the human race. Even though we have the most excellent gift of reason, we are nevertheless so overwhelmed by misfortunes that we are ignorant not only of our own origin and the lineal descent of our ancestors but even of God Himself, our Creator. Look into the historical accounts of all nations. If it were not for Moses alone, what would you know about the origin of man? . . .

"Of this wretched state, that is, of our awful blindness, we are reminded by the passage before us, which gives us instruction about things that are unknown to the whole world. What do we have about the very best part of the second world besides words, not to mention the first one, which antedated the Flood? The Greeks wanted to have the account of their activities preserved, the Romans likewise; but how insignificant this is in comparison with the earlier times, concerning which Moses has drawn up a list of names in this passage, not of deeds!

"Hence one must consider this chapter of Genesis a mirror in which to discern what we human beings are, namely, creatures so marred by sin that we have no knowledge of our own origin, not even of God Himself, our Creator, unless the Word of God reveals these sparks of divine light to us from afar. Then what is more futile than boasting of one's wisdom, riches, power, and other things that pass away completely?

"Therefore we have reason to regard the Holy Bible highly and to consider it a most precious treasure. This very chapter, even though it is considered full of dead words, has in it the thread that is drawn from the first world to the middle and to the end of all things. From Adam the promise concerning Christ is passed on to Seth; from Seth to Noah; from Noah to Shem; and from Shem to this Eber, from whom the Hebrew nation received its name as the heir for whom the promise about the Christ was intended in preference to all other peoples of the whole world. This knowledge the Holy Scriptures reveal to us. Those who are without them live in error, uncertainty, and boundless ungodliness; for they have no knowledge about who they are and whence they came."[7]

Thanks to the Word of God, we have that knowledge in order that we might know not only who we are and from where we have come, but also how far we have fallen and who alone is able to lift us up from our sin and bring us back to Paradise.

---

[7]Luther, *Luther's Works*, Vol. 2, pp. 207–209.

59

The Tower of Babel

(Genesis 11:1–9)

Now the whole world had one language and a common speech. As men moved eastward, they found a plain in Shinar and settled there.

They said to each other, "Come, let's make bricks and bake them thoroughly." They used brick instead of stone, and tar instead of mortar. Then they said, "Come, let us build ourselves a city, with a tower that reaches to the heavens, so that we may make a name for ourselves and not be scattered over the face of the whole earth."

But the LORD came down to see the city and the tower that the men were building. The LORD said, "If as one people speaking the same language they have begun to do this, then nothing they plan to do will be impossible for them. Come, let us go down and confuse their language so they will not understand each other."

So the LORD scattered them from there over all the earth, and they stopped building the city. That is why it was called Babel—because there the LORD confused the language of the whole world. From there the LORD scattered them over the face of the whole earth.

The tenth and eleventh chapters of Genesis are composed of genealogies of nations and peoples designed to link the story of Noah and the Flood, which fills chapters 6 through 9, with the story of Abraham and his descendants, which fills the remainder of the book. The genealogies begin with Noah's three sons—Shem, Ham, and Japheth—and move eventually to Terah from whom Abraham is born. At two points there are parentheses dealing with the founding of the first world empire under Nimrod. The first parenthesis is 10:8–12. The second is 11:1–9.

These two go together. The first tells of Nimrod's exploits. The second does not mention Nimrod but speaks rather of an attempt to build the city of Babylon, a central feature of which was to be a great tower. On the surface these seem to be accounts of two quite separate incidents. But this is not the case. The second does indeed tell of the founding of Babylon, but we learn from the first that Babylon was the initial city of Nimrod's city-building empire. Moreover, as we study them we see that the founding of Babylon and the building of the tower of Babel in chapter 11 are an elaboration of the earlier narrative. In the first we have an emphasis on Nimrod—what he was like, what he did, what his goals were. In the second we have a treatment of the same theme but from the perspective of the people who worked with him. In each case there is a desire to build a civilization without God.

THE FIRST "COME"

The account of the building of Babylon begins by saying that the world had one common language (as would be expected due to the people's common descent from Noah) and since part of the world's people moved eastward, some settled on the plain of Shinar or Babylonia. So far, so good. God had told the descendants of Noah to "increase in number and fill the earth" (Gen. 9:1), a reiteration of the command originally given to Adam and Eve in Paradise

339

(Gen. 1:28). The settlement of Shinar could be construed as a partial fulfillment of that command. Yet as we read on we find that the goal of this particular settlement was not to fulfill God's command but to defy it. From the beginning Babylon's goal was to resist any further scattering of the peoples over the earth and instead to create a city where the achievements of a united and integrated people would be centralized.

The Bible reports this desire as an invitation to "come" together to work on this great project. It is the first important "come" of the story. "They said to each other, 'Come, let's make bricks and bake them thoroughly.' They used brick instead of stone, and tar instead of mortar. Then they said, 'Come, let us build ourselves a city, with a tower that reaches to the heavens, so that we may make a name for ourselves and not be scattered over the face of the whole earth'" (Gen. 11:3, 4).

Three things are involved in this invitation: 1) a vision for the city, 2) a desire for a name or reputation, and 3) a plan for a new religion. The plan for a city does not need to be examined at length; we have already discussed it in our study of Nimrod.[1] The important point is that it was not God's city, as Jerusalem was. It was man's city, the secular city. As such it was constructed by man for man's glory. The last of these desires—to construct a place for man's glory—is involved in the word "name": "Come, let us . . . make a *name* for ourselves and not be scattered over the face of the whole earth." It was the desire for a reputation but, more than that, also a desire for independence from God. This reputation was to be earned by man apart from God. It was to be his alone.

We cannot forget that one characteristic of the God of the Bible is that He

names people. He gives them names symbolic of what He is going to do with them or make of them. God named Adam (Gen. 5:2), Abraham (Gen. 17:5), Israel (Gen. 32:8), even Jesus (Matt. 1:21). In each case, the names point to what God has done or will yet do. The people of Babylon wanted none of this. They wanted to establish their own reputation and eliminate God entirely.

Reaching for the Stars

Thus far in our study of Babylon the one element that has been missing is religion. But that is where the famed tower of Babel comes in, in my judgment. I say "in my judgment," but I must add that most commentators sense this truth, even though they interpret the tower in different ways. Luther says that the words "reaches to the heavens" should not be applied to the height alone but rather should be seen as denoting "that this was to be a place of worship."[2] Candlish says, "The building of the tower 'unto heaven' had undoubtedly a religions meaning."[3] Morris writes that in his desire to build a great empire Nimrod realized that the people needed a religious motivation strong enough to overcome their knowledge that God had commanded them to scatter abroad on the earth. He feels that the tower satisfied that need and was therefore "dedicated to heaven and its angelic host."[4] Let me tell you what I think the tower means.

First, it should be regarded as having a religious end because the Bible traces all false religions to Babylon and this is the only element in the description of early Babylon that can have this meaning. We would expect something like this from the nature of Babylon and its culture and from what is told us of all cultures that turn away from God. Ro-

[1]See chapter 57, "The Warrior States" (Gen. 10:6–20), pp. 328–33.

[2]Luther, *Luther's Works*, Vol. 2, p. 213.

[3]Candlish, *Studies in Genesis*, p. 174.

[4]Morris, *The Genesis Record*, p. 270.

mans says that when people reject the knowledge of God they inevitably turn to false gods, making them like "mortal man and birds and animals and reptiles" (Rom. 1:23). The citizens of Babylon had rejected the knowledge of the true God. Therefore, we should expect the creation of a false religion as part of their dubious cultural achievements. Again, the Bible speaks of "mystery Babylon," that is, of the reality symbolized by the earthly city, saying that it is "the mother of prostitutes and of the abominations of the earth" (Rev. 17:5). This refers, as do the ideas of prostitution and abomination throughout the Bible, to false religion.

There is evidence that this was the case historically. Morris notes, "The essential identity of the various gods and goddesses of Rome, Greece, India, Egypt, and other nations with the original pantheon of the Babylonians is well established. [In fact], Nimrod himself was apparently later deified as the chief god ('Merodach' or 'Marduk') of Babylon."[5]

Second, there is the description of the tower. Most of our translations speak of a tower that should "reach" to the heavens, but it is hard to think that even these people could have been foolish enough to suppose that they could do this literally. Or even if they did, it is hard to think of them as being foolish enough to build their tower on the plain of Shinar, that is, almost at sea level, when they could equally well have built it on the top of a nearby mountain and thus have begun with a few thousand feet head start. Actually, this is probably not at all what was involved. In the Hebrew text the words "to reach" do not occur. The text speaks of the top of the tower as "in," "on," "with," or "by" the heavens (all four being possible translations of the one Hebrew preposition). This could mean that the top was dedi-

cated *to* the heavens as a place of worship (the view of Morris) or even that it had a representation *of* the heavens (a zodiac) upon it.

I think this last possibility is the real meaning, for the reason that astrology, which focuses on a study of the zodiac, originated in Babylon. Turn to any book on astrology and you will find that it was the Chaldeans (another name for the inhabitants of Babylon) who first developed the zodiac by dividing the sky into sections and giving meanings to each on the basis of the stars that are found there. A person's destiny is said to be determined by whatever section or "sign" he is born under. From Babylon, astrology passed to the empire of ancient Egypt where it mingled with the native animism and polytheism of the Nile. The pyramids were constructed with certain mathematical relationships to the stars. The Sphinx has astrological significance. It has the head of a woman, symbolizing Virgo, the virgin, and the body of a lion, symbolizing Leo. Virgo is the first sign of the zodiac, Leo the last. So the Sphinx (which incidentally means "joining" in Greek) is the meeting point of the zodiac, indicating that the Egyptian priests believed the starting point of the earth in relation to the zodiac lay in Egypt, on the banks of the Nile.

By the time the Jews left Egypt for Canaan, astrology had infected the population there. Hence, some of the strictest warnings in the Bible against astrology date from this period (Lev. 19:31; Deut. 18). Still later, astrology entered the religious life of Rome.

The interesting thing about these biblical denunciations of astrology is that astrology is identified with demonism or Satanism in the sense that Satan and his hosts were actually being worshiped in the guise of the signs or planets. This is the reason for the Bible's

---

[5]*The Genesis Record*, p. 264.

stern denunciation of these practices. Are we to think, then, that Satan was entirely absent from the original attempt to build a civilization without God? Was he absent from the formation of this first non-biblical religion? I don't think so. If he was, then the religion of the tower was actually a satanic attempt to direct the worship of the human race to himself and those former angels who, having rebelled against God, were now already demons. No doubt, as Morris suggests, "This project was originally presented to the people in the guise of true spirituality. The tower in its lofty grandeur would symbolize the might and majesty of the true God of heaven. A great temple at its apex would provide a center and an altar where men could offer their sacrifices and worship God. The signs of the zodiac would be emblazoned on the ornate ceiling and walls of the temple, signifying the great story of creation and redemption, as told by the antediluvian patriarchs." But God was not in this worship. Satan was. Thus, the forms of religion became increasingly debased, and the worship of the devil and his hosts became more noticeable. "From some such beginning soon emerged the entire complex of human 'religion'—an evolutionary pantheism, promulgated via a system of astrology and idolatrous polytheism, empowered by occultic spiritism and demonism."[6]

Satan is a great corrupter, so it is even possible that this system of religion was a perversion of an earlier, true revelation in the heavens of God's plan of redemption. It has been suggested seriously and with considerable evidence that the formations of stars were originally named by God (or the godly patriarchs) as a reminder of godly things, perhaps even to the point of forecasting the coming of the great Deliverer who should crush the head of Satan.[7]

THE SECOND "COME"

The time when the Lord Jesus Christ was to crush Satan's head was still far off, but in the meantime God was going to crush this first attempt at Satanism. He was not going to do it with flood or fire or some other fierce manifestation of His invincible wrath. He was going to do it in an entirely unlooked-for manner. Instead of destruction, God performed a miracle in the minds and vocal cords of the builders. He confused their language so that now, instead of speaking together and working together, their words brought confusion and an inevitable (because it was divinely appointed) scattering of these people over the earth.

There are several interesting features of this part of the story. The first is a second use of the word "come." Earlier the builders had used this word for the calling of their council: "*Come*, let's make bricks. . . . *Come*, let us build ourselves a city" (vv. 3, 4). But now God uses the word as He assembles His heavenly council and moves to confuse their language: "*Come*, let us go down and confuse their language so they will not understand each other" (v. 7). It is a way of saying that God always has the last word. Like Jonah, we can say "but" to God (Jonah 1:3), although God always has the last "but" (Jonah 1:4, KJV). We can assemble our councils; but God will assemble His council, and the decree of God's council will prevail. It follows that those who choose to go their own way will always end up frustrated. The prize so earnestly sought after becomes a bubble that bursts at the first touch. The fruit of desire becomes like ashes in the mouth. We may chafe against this, but it will always be this way because we live in God's world, not our own, and because God has determined to make bitter anything that is prized above Himself.

---

[6]*The Genesis Record*, pp. 270, 272.

[7]See, for example, Duane Edward Spencer, *The Gospel in the Stars: An Analysis of the Doctrine of Biblical Astrology* (San Antonio: Word of Grace, 1972).

The second interesting feature of this part of the story is that God *came* down to see the tower the men of Babylon were building. This is an anthropomorphism, that is, God being described as if He were a man. (We are not to think that God actually had to get off the throne of the universe and come down to earth to determine what the builders were doing. All things are known to God always.) But it is not a "crude anthropomorphism," as some have chosen to call it. It is used with effect. Here were men attempting to build a great tower. The top was to reach to the heavens. It was to be so great that it and the religion and defiance of God it represented would make a reputation for these citizens of Shinar. There it stood, lofty in its unequalled grandeur. But when God wants to look at it He comes down. He has to stoop low to see this puny extravagance.

It is always thus. When you stand on the ground and look up at the great pyramids of Egypt they seem immense. But when you fly over them in an airplane, even at a low altitude, they seem like pimples on the surface of the earth. The twin towers of the World Trade Center in New York City look great. But from the air they look like miniature dominoes. The Eiffel Tower is a mere protuberance. So also with our intellectual or spiritual achievements. The greatest is nothing compared to the immensity of the universe, not to mention the universe's Creator. The only truly significant accomplishments are God's (sometimes in and through us), for only these partake of the nature of God and endure forever, as God does.

INVITATIONS TO "COME"

We have seen two different uses of the word "come" in this story. The first was spoken *by man to man against God*. The second was spoken *by God to God* (another early intimation of the Trinity) *against man*. It would not be right to end without noting that the Bible also knows a third use of the word "come" in which an invitation is extended *by God to man for man's benefit*. God says, "Come now, let us reason together. . . . Though your sins are like scarlet, they shall be as white as snow; though they are red as crimson, they shall be as wool" (Isa. 1:18). Jesus says, "Come to me, all you who are weary and burdened, and I will give you rest" (Matt. 11:28). "The Spirit and the bride say, 'Come!' And let him who hears say, 'Come!' Whoever is thirsty, let him come; and whoever wishes, let him take the free gift of the water of life" (Rev. 22:17).

What is the result when we who hear God's invitation come to Him? It is just as He says! Our sins are washed away. Our burdens are lifted. Our spiritual thirst is quenched. Moreover, the effects of the curse are overturned and the proper desires of the human heart are provided for, not by man in rebellion against God, to be sure, but by the gracious and forgiving God Himself from whom all truly good gifts come. The curse was the confusion of languages, but God brings blessing from the curse. He gives understanding in spite of the language barrier and even promises (Pentecost is an earnest of the fulfillment) that the nations will worship together, presumably in one voice and with full understanding of each other. The Babylonians wanted a city. Their city could not stand. But God provides His people with a city with foundations that will endure forever. Nimrod's people wanted a name. But to those who stand with God and who overcome, God promsies: "Him who overcomes I will make a pillar in the temple of my God. Never again will he leave it. I will write on him the name of my God and the name of the city of my God, the new Jerusalem, which is coming down out of heaven from my God; and I will also write on him my new name. He who has an ear, let him hear what the Spirit says to the churches" (Rev. 3:12, 13).

60

An End and a Beginning

(Genesis 11:10–32)

This is the account of Shem.

Two years after the flood, when Shem was 100 years old, he became the father of Arphaxad. And after he became the father of Arphaxad, Shem lived 500 years and had other sons and daughters.

When Arphaxad had lived 35 years, he became the father of Shelah. And after he became the father of Shelah, Arphaxad lived 403 years and had other sons and daughters.

When Shelah had lived 30 years, he became the father of Eber. And after he became the father of Eber, Shelah lived 403 years and had other sons and daughters.

When Eber had lived 34 years, he became the father of Peleg. And after he became the father of Peleg, Eber lived 430 years and had other sons and daughters.

When Peleg had lived 30 years, he became the father of Reu. And after he became the father of Reu, Peleg lived 209 years and had other sons and daughters.

When Reu had lived 32 years, he became the father of Serug. And after he became the father of Serug, Reu lived 207 years and had other sons and daughters.

When Serug had lived 30 years, he became the father of Nahor. And after he became the father of Nahor, Serug lived 200 years and had other sons and daughters.

When Nahor had lived 29 years, he became the father of Terah. And after he became the father of Terah, Nahor lived 119 years and had other sons and daughters.

After Terah had lived 70 years, he became the father of Abram, Nahor and Haran.

This is the account of Terah.

Terah became the father of Abram, Nahor and Haran. And Haran became the father of Lot. While his father Terah was still alive, Haran died in Ur of the Chaldeans, in the land of his birth. Abram and Nahor both married. The name of Abram's wife was Sarai, and the name of Nahor's wife was Milcah; she was the daughter of Haran, the father of both Milcah and Iscah. Now Sarai was barren; she had no children.

Terah took his son Abram, his grandson Lot son of Haran, and his daughter-in-law Sarai, the wife of his son Abram, and together they set out from Ur of the Chaldeans to go to Canaan. But when they came to Haran, they settled there.

Terah lived 205 years, and he died in Haran.

Sacred history has periods called "silent years," years in which no special revelation from God or no special acts of God are recorded. One example is the 400-year break between the death of the last of the Old Testament prophets and the appearance of an angel to Zecharias to announce the birth of John the Baptist. An earlier example is the gap between the dispersion of the peoples of the earth after their attempt to build the great tower at Babel and God's calling of Abram.

These are years with which the second half of Genesis 11 is concerned. The first half has recounted the incident at Babel, in which Nimrod and his followers attempted to create a civilization without

God, the tower being its focal point. But this is the last incident until the call of Abram. The second half of the chapter, even though it fills twenty-three verses, gives no historical information. Instead, it merely presents the line from which Abram (and eventually the Lord Jesus Christ) came. The verses begin with Shem, one of Noah's three sons, and trace the line of descent through ten generations: Shem, Arphaxad, Shelah, Eber, Peleg, Reu, Serug, Nahor, Terah, and Abram. This was an age of rapid spiritual decline. The departure from the knowledge of the true God begun at Babel continued until by the time of Abram virtually the entire race, including even Abram's immediate ancestors, had become idolaters. It was nevertheless an age in which God continued to preserve a remnant of faithful men and women through whom the true history of the world was passed on and the true worship of the God of heaven was perpetuated.

This last truth was a great encouragement to Martin Luther, who doubtless felt himself to be living in a similar dark age. He wrote, "Lest we suppose that Satan had been allowed to remove the sunlight of the Word utterly from the world and to suppress the church, the generation of the holy fathers is set before us, to show us that by the mercy of God the remnants were preserved and the church was not completely wiped out."[1]

The Account of Shem

It is a literary device of Genesis, which we have spoken of earlier, that it marks the significant narrative sections by use of the Hebrew word *toledoth*, meaning "account" or "generations." The term is used eleven times in all, always as a title for what follows. It occurs first at Genesis 2:4 in the sentence "This is the account of the heavens and the earth when they were first created." What follows is an account of the first years of earth's history, including the creation of Adam and Eve, their fall into sin, and the emergence of the two humanities that sprang from them. After that it occurs of "the written account of Adam's line" (Gen. 5:1), "the account of Noah" (Gen. 6:9) and "the account of Shem, Ham and Japheth, Noah's sons" (Gen. 10:1). In the passage being studied in this chapter this word occurs twice more, once of "the account of Shem" (v. 10) and once of "the account of Terah" (v. 27). Since the word will not occur again for fourteen more chapters (in chap. 25 of "the account of Abram's son Ishmael," v. 12, and "the account of Abram's son Isaac," v. 19), it is evident that "the account of Terah" introduces a new and lengthy section of the book. In the second half of chapter 11 we therefore have a clear end to the old world—Adam through Nahor—and the beginning of a new spiritual world in Abram.

The genealogies present problems, however, and it is necessary to deal with at least a few of them. First, it is well known that in Luke 3:36, in a genealogy of Jesus covering in part the same material as in Genesis 11, there is an extra name. Luke inserts the name of Cainan between Arphaxad and Shelah (cf. Luke 3:36 with Gen. 11:12). Normally one might explain the additional name as a copyist's error, supposing that the eye of the copyist accidentally dropped down to verse 37 of the manuscript he was duplicating, where Cainan (Cain, the son of Enos) occurs, and that he then mistakenly added it to the previous verse. Such errors do occur in ancient manuscripts. In this case, however, the explanation probably will not work, because the additional name also appears in the Septuagint (Greek translation) of the Old Testament at Genesis 11:12 and thus predates Luke's gospel. Since the

---

[1]Luther, *Luther's Works*, Vol. 2, p. 228.

Septuagint was written about one hundred years before Christ, it is reasonable to think that Luke got his extra name from it.

Was Luke in error in picking up the name this way? Not necessarily, for it is not necessary to conclude that either the Hebrew text of Genesis, on the one hand, or the Greek text of the Septuagint and Luke, on the other, is wrong. It may simply be a case of a deliberately omitted generation in the earlier genealogy, a practice we know was also followed elsewhere.[2] If that is the case, we have a warning not to take the years in Genesis 11 as necessarily giving an all-inclusive coverage of this period. That is, the period may have been longer than a mere adding up of the ages of the fathers at the birth of their first son would indicate. The formula "Patriarch *A* became the father of Patriarch *B*" might mean only "Patriarch *A* became the father of one from whom Patriarch *B* descended."

The solution to one other important problem tends in this direction. It concerns Abram. According to Genesis 11:32, Terah, Abram's father, lived 205 years and died in Haran. According to Genesis 12:4, Abram left Haran when he was seventy-five. According to Acts 7:4, where Stephen is recounting these events, Abram left Haran after his father Terah died. Putting these facts together, Abram would have been born in the 130th year of Terah's life, because 205 minus 75 equals 130. But Genesis 11:26 says, "After Terah had lived 70 years, he became the father of Abram, Nahor and Haran." Which is right? Was Abram born when Terah was 70 or when he was 130?

The best answer is that Abram was probably born when Terah was 130 and that Genesis 11:26 is misconstrued when it is supposed to teach that Terah was 70 when he had Abram. Abram is listed first because he is the most important, the one through whom the line of descent is traced. But this does not necessarily mean that Abram was the oldest. He may well have been born later. We have a similar case in the listing of Noah's three sons—Shem, Ham, and Japheth—where the order of birth was actually Japheth, Shem, and Ham.

This means (as in the case of Cainan) that room must be left in Genesis 11 for more than a strict totaling of the years of the fathers at the time of their firstborn sons. In the case of Abram's birth the addition would be sixty years. In the earlier case there are no figures to go on, but a number of years would have intervened. There may be other omissions that we do not know about. According to a *strict* chronological interpretation, the time spans and dates would be as they appear on the chart. Many patriarchs would have lived into the lifetime of Abram, who would have died in the year 2123 at the age of 175 (Gen. 25:7), and three of them (Shem, Shelah, and Eber) would have outlived him. If Abram was born when Terah was 130 (dying in the year 2183), he would still have been outlived by Eber. Of course, this overlapping of generations may itself indicate that the overall time span is longer than the strict chronological interpretation indicates.[3]

END OF WORLD HISTORY

We go back to the matter of the silent years, mentioned in the introduction. Up to this point the Genesis narrative has been concerned with the race as a whole, charting peoples and nations as these spread out over the world follow-

---

[2]See "The Oldest Man Alive" (Gen. 5:25–27), pp. 232–37.

[3]For a more detailed discussion of the problems of this chronology see: Whitcomb and Morris, *The Genesis Flood*, Appendix II, pp. 474–89; Warfield, "On the Antiquity and Unity of the Human Race" in *Biblical and Theological Studies*, pp. 238–61; Schaeffer, *Genesis in Space and Time*, pp. 154–56; and the various commentaries.

THE GENESIS 11 CHRONOLOGY

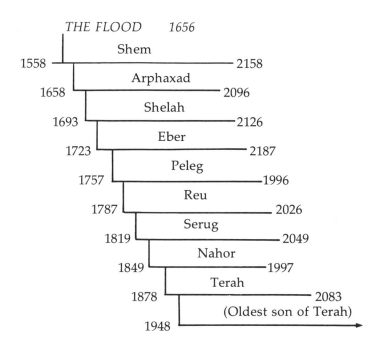

THE FLOOD   1656

Shem
1558 ——————————————— 2158

Arphaxad
  1658 ——————————————— 2096

Shelah
    1693 ——————————————— 2126

Eber
      1723 ——————————————— 2187

Peleg
        1757 ——————————————— 1996

Reu
          1787 ——————————————— 2026

Serug
            1819 ——————————————— 2049

Nahor
              1849 ——————————————— 1997

Terah
                1878 ——————————————— 2083
                    (Oldest son of Terah)
                  1948 ———————————————→

ing the Flood. But this overview ends with the account of the attempt to build Babylon. From this point the story deals with special people (Abram and his descendants) and a special nation (Israel). The fact is ominous. It is as though God is writing an end, so far as He is concerned, to world history.

Is this not an Old Testament way of saying, as Paul does of the human race at large in Romans, that "God gave them over . . ." (Rom. 1:24, 26, 28)? They would not have God, so God would not have them; they gave God up, so God gave them up. This is Paul's meaning in the New Testament book, and it is the implied meaning of the abandonment of the history of the nations at this point by the author of Genesis. They are dispersed at Babel, and that is the end of it. Hereafter they will only be incidental to the story as they interact with God's people. It is not until much later—in fact, until after the coming of Jesus Christ—that we begin to see the nations

regathered and brought to obedience again.

When God gives the nations over (or "up" as the KJV has it), we are not to suppose that He gives them over to nothing—as if they just float away on their own and do perfectly well without Him. On the contrary, when God gives nations or individuals up, He gives them up to the laws of His own spiritual universe, and this means that apart from a grounding in Him and the truths of revealed religion their course will always be downhill.

In Romans Paul plots this decline in moral values. First, God gave them up to "sexual impurity" (v. 24). Next He gave them up to "shameful lusts" (v. 26). Finally, He gave them up to "a depraved mind" (v. 28), in which they not only sinned but approved of those who sinned as they did, thus maintaining that sin is not sin and that wrong is right (v. 32). This would have been true of the decline of the nations in the post-Babel period too. But in addition, the original true religion of these nations would have given way to superstition, idolatry, polytheism, and eventually to that debased animism known today among the most primitive tribes.

This is not the way we have been taught to think, of course. We have been taught the opposite, that is, that the primitive stages of the race were marked by animism and that this progressed upward to polytheism which in turn produced monotheism. But this is not the way it happened. Genesis teaches the reverse, and it is even the case that evidence gathered from the so-called primitive tribes increasingly points to the accuracy of the Genesis account.

I point here to a book published by Robert Brow, entitled *Religion: Origins and Ideas*. Brow is a student of comparative religions, and his complaint is that an evolutionary theory of development of religion does not fit the facts. He points to the work of anthropologists who suggest that monotheism may be the most "primitive" of religious forms. "Their research suggests that tribes are not animistic because they have continued unchanged since the dawn of history. Rather, the evidence indicates degeneration from a true knowledge of God." In his reconstruction this early knowledge of the true God came first, accompanied by animal sacrifices that were a way of acknowledging that the worshiper had offended against God and needed to make atonement for his or her offenses. In time polytheism entered, providing a pantheon of gods and goddesses who were worshiped not because they were imagined to be higher or greater than the original true God but because they were lesser and therefore less to be feared. At this point priests emerged to take over the functions of sacrifice, and the religions degenerated

ever further. According to Brow the so-called "primitive" tribesman is actually closer to the truth of religion than his civilized and sophisticated counterpart.[4]

If the opening chapters of Genesis have taught us anything, it is surely that nations and people do not move upward when they abandon God. They move downward. And they continue on their downward track until God, by grace, intervenes to save them and start them moving upward again.

God began such an upward path with Abram.

FLOW OF HISTORY

At the beginning of this volume, when discussing the significance of our origins, we showed how people chafe against a world view that seemingly imprisons them within fixed moral laws in history. They construe this as bondage and attempt to shake free of such laws. The chief way they attempt to do this is by denying God. The modern quest for autonomy is essentially the same as Adam's in his sin or the builders of the tower of Babel's in theirs. Unfortunately, just as they imagine that they have been successful in shaking free of God, these great rebels discover that they have achieved their autonomy at the price of personal worth and meaning. If there is no God, it is true that there are no restraints. But there is no meaning either—not to one's origin, not to one's present existence, not to one's end. Life is all one big, colossal accident.

But these rebels are wrong, and this is where the "bad joke" of modern secular life turns into the "good news" of Christianity. This good news starts with *God*. It tells us that there is a God. It says that He, not chance, is the origin of all things, and that for this reason alone the things that are have meaning.

---

[4]Robert Brow, *Religion: Origins and Ideas* (Chicago: InterVarsity Press, 1966). The quotation is from p. 11.

Christianity's good news also extends to *man* as part of God's creation. It says that we are not chance beings either, rather that we have been made by God in His image and that we have value to Him. We were made to be companions of God and partners with Him in ruling the universe. True, we have fallen from that high calling. We have sinned in Adam and subsequently by our own personal choices. Sin has alienated us from God and made us slaves of what we were destined to rule. But we still have value in God's sight, even in our fallen state. People today need to hear this good news. They do not know who they are, where they have come from, or where they are going, and without this knowledge they cannot make sense of their existence.

The good news also includes the diagnosis of our ills. They are traceable to *sin.* On the surface this seems to be bad news, for sin is bad. However, the diagnosis is good, since it is only as we have a correct diagnosis that we can begin to face and (by the grace of God) actually begin to solve our problems. Francis Schaeffer writes, "If a man attributes a wrong cause to the dilemma and divisions of men, he will never come up with the right answer no matter how good a will he has. Man as he stands since the Fall is not normal, and consequently the solution must be appropriate to what we know to be the cause of his problems and his dilemma. A mere physical solution is inadequate, because man's dilemma is not physical. Nor can it be metaphysical, because the problem of man, as we know it in Genesis 1–11, is not primarily metaphysical. The problem of man is moral, for by choice he stands in rebellion against God. And any appropriate solution must fill this moral need."[5]

The Bible's good news also tells of that *solution.* It is not unfolded at great length in Genesis, for we are still at the beginning in this book. But it is suggested. It concerns the Deliverer who should be born of the woman and who should one day crush the head of Satan though His own heel would be wounded in the process. Today we know Him as the Lord Jesus Christ.

Finally, the good news of the message of God to man in Genesis is that because God is active in history, *history* and not just the mere existence of man has meaning. We have a beginning and an end, but history also has a beginning and an end. It is going some place along the path and according to the laws predetermined for it by God. For this reason, what I do (and not merely what I am) has meaning. If I sin—if I turn from God, seeking to deify myself, and if I oppress my neighbors, treating them as things rather than as people in whom the image of God is still reflected—I bring destruction on myself and harm those others also. I will be judged for it. On the other hand, if I seek God and His righteousness—if I attempt to serve God and others faithfully, as God gives me light—then I enhance the good and become a vehicle of His blessing.

In the next section of this book (and in the next volume of these studies) we will see how one man, Abram, did precisely that and how God literally changed the course of history through him.

---

[5]*Genesis in Time and Space,* p. 160.

Subject Index

Scripture Index